To Don Weldon

And so begins the startling adventures of the most sensational strip character of all time: *Superman!* A physical marvel, a mental wonder, *Superman* is destined to reshape the destiny of the world!

—*Action Comics* #1, June 1938

As I have pointed out to you many times, our company has very little to gain in the monetary sense from the syndication of this material.

–Letter to Jerry Siegel from DC Comics publisher
Jack Liebowitz, 1938

CONTENTS

INTRODUCTION

When you think about it, Lex Luthor's got a point: everything comes easy to Superman. That, in fact, is pretty much his whole shtick: entitled superiority.

We plod along the ground, he soars overheard. To ward off the ravages of age, we grunt with weights and sweat on treadmills; he tosses SUVs around like cardboard and will never lose his perfect eight-pack. We are plain, soft, unkempt things; he is impossibly handsome and lantern-jawed, with only a single S-shaped spit curl descending from his hairline like the tail of a lemur. (To readers of his very first adventures, back in the heyday of Brylcreem, an out-of-place lock of hair on a character's head must have signaled derring-do: "Here, then, is a man of action! Look! See how his coif-fure cannot be contained by puny Earth pomade!")

And it's not like the guy invented himself, as Batman did, or came by his powers in a freak accident, as Spider-Man did. No, his amazing abilities are simply his birthright, coded into his genes like that weird blue-black hair of his.

Superman is every handsome, athletic, trust-fund kid who roars his convertible into the high school parking lot as the sweater around his neck flutters in the breeze. Why has a schmuck like *that* endured for seventy-five years?

This book sets out to find the answer to that question. Or rather, the answers. Because, of course, there are many, some more inherently worthy of exploration than others. Superman's status as a corporate-owned, heavily licensed nugget of intellectual property into which millions of marketing dollars have been sunk, for example, may be the most important reason he's still around, but it's the least interesting. Because after seventy-five years, Superman has become more than a function of cross-platform synergy and optimized revenue streams.

He endures because he long ago transcended the various media that deliver him to us; he has entered our planet's collective consciousness. This means that each of us holds, in our minds and hearts, our own unique idea of Superman. The precise idiomatic fuel mixture varies: to many, he's simply George Reeves; to others, he's Christopher Reeve or Bud Collyer or that humorless stiff who used to lecture Wendy and Marvin about our precious natural resources on old episodes of *Super Friends.* To someone like me, who grew up devouring Superman comics and posing all of my action figures in classic Superman flying pose (even, heretically, nonflyers like Batman and Spider-Man), Superman is pretty much how Curt Swan (his definitive artist in comics of the sixties and seventies) used to draw him: kind, caring, and wondrously, endearingly square.

As this book details, Superman's perceived status as a static fixture of popular culture, an unchanging icon of spandex-clad heroism, is an illusion. Examining the Man of Steel during the course of his seventy-five years reveals that everything about him exists in a state of perpetual flux. The particulars of his origin and his power-set have vacillated wildly. So, too, has his persona continually evolved: in his first few years of life, he was our hot-headed, protective big brother; he spent the forties and fifties assuming the role of our coolly distant father; he morphed in the sixties and seventies into our bemused, out-of-touch uncle; and he even became—mercifully briefly, in the benighted nineties—our mulleted, hillbilly cousin.

His rogues' gallery changed, as well. For the first few years of his life, Superman was the ballistic missile brought to the knife fight, as writer Jerry Siegel simply let his grinning Man of Steel hopelessly outmatch petty thugs, goons and yeggs. When that inevitably began to pall, Superman started facing off with pesky tricksters and mad scientists armed with deadly gadgets. Later, when the radio show introduced a mysterious substance that could actually kill the Man of Steel, the stakes rose considerably. Since then, the threats to his existence—and to the world and, in point of fact, to the cosmos itself—have only escalated exponentially.

Even the thing that is most immediately recognizable about the guy—his costume—isn't immune to change. Hell, in 2011, he even lost the red underpants, if you can imagine.

Yet to nonfans, Superman exists primarily as a memory of childhood, and we tend to think of the things we loved at a young age as frozen in amber, preserved exactly as they were when we last spared them a thought. This is one reason that his publisher's decision to temporarily kill off the Man of Steel in 1992—conceived as little more than a publicity stunt—touched off a surprising wave of collective nostalgia and reflexive outrage: it felt, to the many who actually thought DC would keep him dead, like a curiously personal attack on something good, innocent, and fondly (if dimly) remembered.

Superman changes as our culture changes. The only thing about him, in fact, that has remained untouched, inviolate, since *Action Comics* #1 hit the stands in April 1938 is his motivation. That motivation is at once the simplest of them all and the hardest to unpack: he is a hero. Specifically:

1. He puts the needs of others over those of himself.
2. He never gives up.

These are his two most essential attributes, the elements that make a Superman story a Superman story. As we will see, even when all of the other, more recognizable pieces of Super-iconography are in place—the costume, the powers, the spit curl, and so on—if one or both of those two bedrock elements are missing, our mind rebels; we instinctively reject it. It's just not *Superman*.

The Man of Steel remains the most recognizable figure of the superhero genre, and the superhero genre continues to dominate the comics marketplace (and, lately, the box office as well). Yet this is an uncertain time. As more and more artists and writers look to tell a wider variety of stories, the comics medium is incrementally diversifying. This, combined with the rise of digital distribution, when comics fly through the ether to alight on iPads and smartphones, means that the monthly superhero comic book as we know it today is not long for this world. Meanwhile, film critics and audiences are showing increasingly advanced symptoms of spandex fatigue.

As we will see, though, Superman is bigger than the comics that birthed him, bigger even than the films and the television series that have infused him throughout our culture. He will endure in some form for another seventy-five years and another, because, unlike Spider-Man and Batman, he is not the hero with whom we identify; he is the hero in whom we believe. He is the first, the purest, the ideal. As long as character traits such as selflessness and perseverance manage to retain any cultural currency whatsoever, we will need a Superman to show us what they look like.

Before we begin, however, indulge me in some quick bits of housekeeping: it is impossible to tell the story of Superman without acknowledging the legal, financial, and emotional struggles of Jerry Siegel and Joe Shuster and their respective estates to claim the recognition and remuneration they are owed. That, however, is not the subject of this book, which is concerned with Superman as a cultural phenomenon. I encourage those interested in the story of Siegel and Shuster to read Gerard Jones's excellent *Men of Tomorrow* (Basic Books, 2004) and to consider, while they're at it, making a donation to the Hero Initiative (www.heroinitiative.org), a nonprofit organization that provides a safety net for aging comic book creators in need of emergency medical aid and financial support.

I am also deeply indebted to the many comics and popular culture historians before me who have grappled with the impact of the Man of Steel. Where that impact can be meaningfully informed by commentary from the writers, the editors, and the artists who bring him to life, I have included it.

To avoid confusion, please note that the publication date on the cover of a given comic book is generally two months ahead of the time that issue actually appeared on newsstands. The June 1938 issue *Action Comics* #1, for example, went on sale in mid-April. Unless specifically mentioned—as is the case when it is necessary to cite real-world events concurrent with an issue's appearance on the stands—I have used the cover dates throughout.

DC Comics was founded in 1934 as National Allied Publications and later became both National Comics and National Periodical Publications. The name of the corporation has been DC Comics since 1977; to simplify matters, the publisher is referred to as DC Comics throughout.

1

"AND SO BEGINS . . ."

It's the spring of 1938. Late April. You're ten years old, and you've just shelled out ten cents for a comic book.

With that hard-won dime, you could have spent the afternoon at the movies or the ball park or over at Woolworth's soda fountain, but you settled on a comic. That's not unusual, of course; everyone you know reads comics. For as long as you can remember, though, the stuff on the stands has mostly consisted of newspaper comic strips, simply reprinted and repackaged: *Tarzan* and *Popeye*, *Flash Gordon* and *Buck Rogers*, *Terry and the Pirates*. You much prefer reading them collected like this. They're easier to carry—you can fold them up and jam them in your back pocket—and they're easier to follow, when you can plow through several weeks' worth of Little Orphan Annie's adventures in one go.

This comic is different—and thus a bit of a gamble. Like the other comics on the stands, it's an anthology, containing eleven different features. You don't recognize any of these characters from the funnies, however. No, these are new stories, starring jut-jawed guys with chewy names like Sticky-Mitt Stimson, Chuck Dawson, Pep Morgan, and Scoop Scanlon. There's a story about a magician named Zatara that looks promising, but some of the rest of it leaves you cold—a page called "Stardust" features Hollywood gossip about Fred Astaire and Constance Bennett (yawn), and there's a take-your-medicine historical yarn about Marco Polo.

The thing that really grabs you, though, is the cover. It features a circus strongman lifting a green automobile over his head and smashing it against a large rock. Several men scatter from the vehicular carnage, in fear for their lives. *That's* more like it.

When you settle in to read, you find that the first feature opens with a brief intro to the guy on the cover, who turns out not to be from the circus—or even from planet Earth. This one-page preface is an odd thing, slapping together science fiction ("As a distant planet was destroyed by old age, a scientist placed his infant son within a hastily devised space-ship, launching it toward earth!"), slapstick (a pince-nez flies from the nose of an orphanage staffer goggling at the sight of a diapered infant lifting an armchair above his head), and science fact (a panel titled "A Scientific Explanation of Clark Kent's Amazing Strength" provides just that, by way of comparing the alien being to an ant and a grasshopper).

In a Single Bound

In the first panel of the story that begins on the next page, a dark figure vaults through the night air. His powerful pose is that of a hurdler at the height of his jump: head thrust out before him, body bent at the waist, folded in on itself like a switchblade. His torso lunges forward at such an extreme angle, in fact, that it meets the top of his left leg, which is parallel to the ground. His right leg, having provided the force that launched him into the air, stretches behind him like the tail of a plane.

Below the figure—far below, impossibly far—lies a countryside shrouded in darkness. In the foreground, a lonely road curves in and out of shadows thrown by moonlight streaming through the trees. At the bottom of the panel sits a stately white house. We are high enough up to note the color of its roof (red) and to see that it sits on a large parcel of land. Beyond the house lies a thick copse of trees and, far in the distance, another house.

There is wealth here. It's something you can't help but notice. You're too young to remember what things were like before the Crash of '29, when money was easier to come by. It's hard for you to imagine that world, but it probably looked a lot like this verdant, well-tended neighborhood, which lies as far from the crowded tenements of the city as it does from the dust storms still raging through the American prairie.

Your attention returns to the figure captured midleap. The expression on his face is impassive, unreadable, two quick horizontal strokes of ink to denote eye and nose, a thicker swipe to suggest a mouth slightly open in exertion. He's garbed in a form-fitting costume that, combined with the splay of his forceful legs, lends him an air of dramatic, even balletic, grace. You cannot make out details of the outfit, but you can see enough of it to be reminded of the colorful leotards worn by midway strongmen and acrobats. And that's not the only thing about this strange figure that evokes the Big Top.

He's wearing a cape, a bright, scarlet, patently ridiculous-looking thing, frankly: the kind of gaudy touch of spectacle favored by trapeze artists as they ascend to the platform, but that they always have the sense to throw off with a flourish before actually taking to the air.

But it's that cape—or, more specifically, the way it billows out behind him—that conveys something else about this man, something the accompanying caption imparts in breathless, urgent prose: "A tireless figure races thru the night. Seconds count. Delay means forfeit of an innocent life."

Speed. That's what the cape says. The man's pose conveys power and purpose, but it's that silly, melodramatic fabric remnant that, more than anything, *shows* you that this man is *racing against time*. You can almost hear it flutter and snap as he slices through the wind.

There's something else about the image, something mysterious and thrilling, even lurid, and it has to do with what this leaping figure carries in his arms: a woman, bound and gagged. He grips her roughly around the waist as if she is a battering ram or a lance he's tilting at some unseen foe. In what seems a cruel touch, he holds her head so that she faces the ground as it hurtles up to meet them. The hem of the flimsy gown she wears catches the wind; we see that her bare arms are tied behind her back.

Over the next few pages, you will learn more about the blonde in the vampy dress. She is a murderess who has framed an innocent woman for her crime. That innocent woman is due to be electrocuted at midnight, hence our hero's urgent mission: delivering the real killer to the governor's expansive estate and convincing him to issue a pardon in the nick of time.

That action—including a set piece in which the man in the leotard breaks into the governor's mansion, forces himself past a gun-wielding butler, and rips the steel door of the governor's bedroom from its hinges—takes up only the first three story pages. In the nine that follow, he will stop a wife beater, go on a date with a beautiful reporter, see that reporter kidnapped by a gang of thugs, smash the thugs' car against the side of a mountain, rescue the girl, receive an assignment to cover a South American war, head to Washington, D.C., to expose a crooked U.S. senator, and brutally threaten a shifty weapons magnate.

But all of that comes later. First there is that panel—the muscular, garishly garbed figure; the vast estates stretching below; the helpless woman. Power. Money. Sex.

It's a dark species of wish-fulfillment, stripped down to the nerve, the kind that exists in the confused moment when idle childhood daydreams first deepen into teenage longings.

You've never seen, or felt, anything like it. You want more.

Jerry and Joe

The two young men who first prepared that potent mixture knew from teenage longings.

When they met in 1931, Jerry Siegel and Joe Shuster were a pair of quiet, intense Jewish high school kids in Cleveland who shared a passion for a just-emerging genre of storytelling called science fiction.

Siegel was a shy kid, a bespectacled loner who didn't go in for sports and who pined after exactly the kind of girls who ignored guys like him. He directed that passion into writing for Glenville High's weekly newspaper, where he pounded out book reviews, as well as elaborate, purple-prosed, self-mocking parodies of the pulp magazines he adored: noir spoofs, Doc Savage pastiches, jungle-adventure satires. His most popular creation, "Goober the Mighty," lampooned both his beloved Tarzan and the "physical culture" movement, with its regimens of wheat germ and weight lifting promoted by Bernarr Macfadden's Charles Atlas.

Siegel's friend Shuster was a short, nearsighted boy whose chief outlet, aside from his own devotion to those very same bodybuilding regimens Siegel delighted in skewering, was cartooning. He and Siegel collaborated on ideas for newspaper comic strips, sending packet after packet to various newspaper syndicates—stories about

gadget-wielding detectives, cavemen, Hollywood starlets, and futuristic adventurers—only to have them firmly rejected.

While waiting for the wider world to take note of their talents, Siegel self-published a magazine with the suitably stentorian
title *Science Fiction: The Advance Guard of Future Civilization*. Within
the mimeographed pages of what was one of the very first "fan-
zines," Siegel wrote editorials, reviews, and stories under various
pen names, accompanied by illustrations from Shuster and another
schoolmate; he charged fifteen cents per issue.

That simple act placed Siegel at the vanguard of a wholly new
movement, one embodied by men and women whose approach to
specific elements of popular culture was deeper, more obsessive, more
completist than their fellows. To them, the "junk culture" that others
found dismissible could engender profound discussions and deep dis-
agreements, all of which took place in an argot that those same others
would find impenetrable. This movement had no name, then, but in the
decades that followed, many would accrue to it: Nerd. Geek. Fanboy.

In the second issue of *Science Fiction*, published in 1932, Siegel
reviewed a then-two-year-old novel titled *Gladiator* by Philip Wylie,
a gleefully pulpy, ham-fisted piece of work with pretensions of social
commentary. The plot: a scientist injects his pregnant wife with an
"alkaline free-radical serum," causing her to give birth to a son of
superior strength and intellect. ("I'm like a man made out of iron
instead of meat," the youth muses.) Bullets bounce off his chest. He
can lift tremendous weights. His parents admonish him to hide his
abilities from the outside world as he grows to manhood. When he
reaches adulthood, the boy attempts to use his gifts to lift up his
fellow man, only to be feared and loathed. When, at novel's end, he
dares to confront God, he is struck and killed by a bolt of lightning
in a passage of mock-biblical prose ("Madness was upon him and
the bitter irony with which his blood ran black was within him.").

Siegel, ur-nerd that he was, ate it up.

And spat it out: The very next issue of *Science Fiction* (dated
January 1933) featured a story called "The Reign of the Super-
Man," written by Siegel under a pseudonym and illustrated by
Shuster. Professor Ernest Smalley plucks a "starving vagrant" from
a bread line and injects him with an element he's isolated from a
meteor. The subject of the experiment (referred to, throughout,
as "the Superman") promptly gains the power of ESP, murders his

creator, and begins to enslave others with his mind. His plan: to generate thoughts of hate that would turn mankind upon itself.

Like Wylie before him, Siegel concluded his *machina* by invoking a *Deus*: When the Superman is confronted by a reporter who offers a prayer of salvation to "the Omnipotent One," the serum immediately wears off, leaving a "drooping, disillusioned man," deeply chastened by his actions.

Secret Origin

Months later—exactly how many is disputed—Siegel had a brainstorm. Make the Superman a good guy, not a villain. He got Shuster to draw up the idea; during the next few years, they played with the concept, until it took on its now-familiar shape.

What survives of their very first pass at what would become the Superman we know is a hasty concept sketch for a proposed newspaper strip. He's not yet a costumed crime fighter, just a muscular man in a tight tank top and dress pants who hoists a criminal over his head. Behind him, a pair of thugs fruitlessly empty a machine gun at his Herculean form. At his feet lies the trunk of a tree (which, we are led to believe, our hero ripped from its stump with his own hands). Above his head is emblazoned the word *Superman* (here, at least, the definite article has been dispensed with).

Emblazoned is the right term—the letters of the name take on a shape that's more crudely and simply formed than the logo now recognized around the world. Yet its roots are clearly seen. The letter S assumes a greater size than those that follow, which are arranged in a slight but perceptible convex curve, an Art Deco arc. Here, too, is the signature three-dimensional illusion; Shuster employs vanishing-point perspective to make the letters appear to rise from the page.

Next to the muscular figure, a simple quatrain floats in the air:

> A genius in intellect—
> A hercules in strength—
> A nemesis to wrong-doers—
> The Superman!

The earlier name remains, but the motivation has changed—and with it, inevitably, the power-set. Siegel and Shuster saw this new character as a heroic man of action, and heroes don't bend others to their will via mind control. That's the province of villains.

So, what *do* heroes do? They inspire others through bold, dynamic action. They demonstrate their powers in dramatic (read: fun for Shuster to draw) ways.

Building the Hero: Superstrength

Even then, there was ample precedent for characters who performed astounding feats of muscular might: at the time when Siegel drew up that first concept sketch, the supertough, über-muscled Doc Savage had just debuted in the pulps. Like Wylie's Gladiator before him, Doc was a "Superman" (a word his publishers used in advertising his adventures) who'd been shaped into the height of mental and physical perfection by "a team of scientists."

Science—specifically physics—also played a hand in the astounding deeds of two pulp heroes whom the boys knew well. Edgar Rice Burroughs's *John Carter of Mars* was an Earthman whose normal human strength was greatly enhanced whenever he found himself transported to the red planet, due to its weaker gravity. John Carter had been around for decades by the time Siegel and Shuster began to hatch their hero, and when it came time to explain Superman's amazing strength, they would ultimately decide to simply invert Burroughs's formula.

They weren't the only ones. In the pages of a spring 1935 issue of *Astounding Stories* magazine, the hugely influential science fiction writer John W. Campbell's story "The Mightiest Machine" featured a character named Aarn Munro. Born on Jupiter, Munro gained tremendous strength when he traveled to Earth, due to its much weaker gravity.

And, of course, there was Popeye.

The character first appeared in 1929, but in 1933 the first Fleischer Studios animated shorts debuted, full of wild, er, eye-popping depictions of superstrength and muscular mayhem that Siegel and Shuster adored. "I thought, [*Popeye*] is really great," Siegel told interviewer Tom Andrae years later, "but . . . what if it featured a straight adventure character?"

Evidence of the next stage of Siegel and Shuster's creation comes via a single surviving sheaf of Shuster's drawing paper filled with hastily scribbled language—dashed snippets of promotional copy the boys brainstormed to help sell their creation to newspaper syndicates. Today, these few lines read, in roughly equal measure, as turgid ad-copy bombast and eerily prescient mission statement:

> The greatest single event since the birth of comic-strips!
> A strip we sincerely believe will *sweep the nation*!
> The Super-Strip of Them All!
> The greatest super-hero strip of all time!

Note how Siegel breathlessly slapped the prefix *super-* onto the word *hero* almost as an afterthought—and in so doing, summoned into being an entirely new, uniquely American genre.

They also created, in the very same moment, the superhero genre's most enduring cottage industry: merchandising. On this same page, Shuster doodled Superman's face on boxes of crackers, model kits, and undershirts. The boys were savvy enough, in a world of Buck Rogers toy ray guns and Little Orphan Annie secret decoder pins, to know that licensing their creation's likeness was a way to net them more money—and help ensure that "the Superman" would catch on.

Persona

Although a few adventure strips, such as *Buck Rogers*, had begun to appear, most newspaper comics of the time remained truer to the medium's roots as "funnies"—gag strips full of high slapstick, broad characters, and groan-inducing puns. Thus, Siegel and Shuster took pains to ensure that their "straight-adventure" character would keep one foot in the funnies. Their solution was one that played to Siegel's love of gag writing; they would make Superman a hero who cracked jokes.

The version of Superman that Shuster drew on that strip of paper looks a lot like the one that would be introduced to the public two years later. He stands with his hands on his hips, grinning a smile so broad that it narrows his eyes to slits. It is the smile of the swashbuckling adventurer reveling in his own exploits, the one worn by Douglas Fairbanks Sr. in films Shuster and Siegel loved as young boys: *The Mark of Zorro* and *Robin Hood*.

It is a smile that says: Here is a hero who literally laughs at danger.

Costume

At this early stage, the hero's signature outfit is still taking shape. The undershirt and the dress pants of the 1933 sketch are gone, replaced by a trapeze-artist's leotard: tights, shorts, belt—and that striking, idiosyncratic cape. The "bright red boots" that would become so associated with the character are still years away.

To audiences of the time, a character in a leotard would evoke the circus, which, though the country was struggling under the Great Depression, loomed larger than ever in the American psyche. It was the heyday of the Flying Wallendas and lion-tamer Clyde Beatty; 1934's *The Mighty Barnum* brought Wallace Beery's gleeful Big Top huckster to movie houses across the country. Readers were used to seeing strongmen and aerialists squeezing themselves into brightly colored, body-hugging fabrics to make their exploits more visible to the back rows.

But the primary-colored union suit Superman wore had a more direct antecedent as well: in their newspaper strips, both Buck Rogers and Alex Raymond's Flash Gordon alternated between military uniforms and flight suits that were essentially colorful, form-fitting leotards—some of Flash's outfits even featured a starburst chest insignia. With their bold colors and outlandishly immodest muscle-hugging lines, those flight suits must have jumped off the pages of Sunday newspapers filled with square-jawed detectives in rumpled brown jackets and ties.

To the shorts-over-tights look, Siegel and Shuster added a cape to catch the wind and help convey Superman's tremendous speed and power. (Siegel had first hit on the combination of tights/shorts/cape/chest emblem in a 1936 story starring Dr. Occult, Ghost Detective, one of the first of several characters the boys sold to DC Comics while the Superman rejection slips piled up.)

In the years to come, the length and design of Superman's cape would continue to change, but it would become as much a part of the character's iconic appeal as the chest insignia. Which, at this stage, remains a simple, inverted yellow triangle—still no hint of the five-sided "S-shield" emblem that would take years to evolve and would become one of the most widely recognized symbols of the twentieth century.

Secret Identity

The addition of an outlandish costume helped bring another concept into sharper relief, one that had been part of the character's
creative DNA from the very beginning. "When all the thoughts
were coming to me, the concept came . . . that Superman could have
a dual identity, and that in one of his identities he would be meek
and mild, as I was, and wear glasses, as I did," Siegel said.

This bifurcated existence would set Superman apart from the
Tarzans, Buck Rogerses, and Flash Gordons of the world. Even
the Phantom (who debuted in 1936) had mostly mothballed
his civilian identity once he devoted himself to fighting evil in
purple tights.

No, the adoption of a secret identity cast Superman squarely
in the mold of characters such as the Shadow (a character from the
pulps who made his first appearance on the radio in 1930). Yet in
the books, at least, the Shadow used several identities (Kent Allard,
Lamont Cranston, Henry Arnaud) in his war on crime. More similar
antecedents to the meek Clark Kent identity can be found in the
Scarlet Pimpernel (who first appeared in a 1903 play by Baroness
Emmuska Orczy) and Zorro (who debuted in 1919).

Both characters committed themselves to political causes with
zeal. The Pimpernel staged daring rescues of French aristocrats
sentenced to death by guillotine during the Reign of Terror. Zorro
dedicated himself "to avenge the helpless, to punish cruel politicians," and "to aid the oppressed" in Southern California during the
Spanish Colonial era. Both men strategically concealed their heroic
identities by adopting public personas diametrically opposed to
their dashing true selves—that of effete fops with no interest in the
social crusades that enmeshed their alter egos.

The Pimpernel and Zorro were each the subject of popular films
during the time Siegel and Shuster were coming up with Superman,
so the notion of a hero throwing off suspicion by adopting the guise
of a milksop was ready-at-hand. Enter: Clark Kent.

Shuster based Clark's look on that of another ur-nerd, the film
comedian Harold Lloyd, and Siegel gave him a comically timid persona that—as many have pointed out over the years—could easily be
read as a less-than-flattering caricature of our weaknesses, a glimpse
of just how spineless we humans must seem to a Man of Steel.

And yet, by so perfectly embodying the element of wish ful-fillment at the heart of the character, that Clark/Superman dual-ity neatly provided us small, grasping humans with the "in" we needed—a stake in his larger-than-life adventures. In his cantanker-ous essay "The Great Comic Book Heroes," cartoonist Jules Feiffer sums it up: "[Superman's] fake identity was our real one. That's why we loved him so."

The influence of the Pimpernel and Zorro doesn't stop with a secret identity. Both the 1934 film *The Scarlet Pimpernel* and 1936's Zorro feature, *The Bold Caballero*, include something else that would become central to the Superman mythos, namely, a love triangle with a distinctly masochistic kink. In both films, the heroine disdains the hero's milquetoast public pose yet is powerfully attracted to his grinning, swashbuckling true self.

Disguises and misdirections, of course, are elements of classic farce, but both Zorro and the Pimpernel added that extra twist of the knife, cruelly lampooning the Fickleness of Woman's Passions (to say nothing of Her Powers of Observation). To two hormonal teens who unrealistically idealized—and bitterly resented—the beautiful, unattainable girls who ignored them to swoon over the football team, it was a very appealing worldview.

Both the Pimpernel's and Zorro's secret identities were wealthy landowners, but that wasn't Siegel and Shuster's style. The Depression had hit their families hard. So instead of a wealthy man about town, the alter ego Siegel and Shuster had in mind was an honest working stiff—a reporter.

The 1931 film *The Front Page* had made the newsroom of a great metropolitan newspaper look like a place where tough men and brassy broads traded barbs before rolling up their sleeves to chase down hot scoops and expose corruption. And from a straightforward plot perspective, a reporter could monitor the police band radio to keep alert to crimes in progress and other emergencies, giving their hero a convenient means to find himself in the thick of the action.

A Strange Visitor from Another Planet

By 1937, Siegel and Shuster had sold several characters to DC Comics, mostly two-fisted tough guys in strips such as *Spy* and *Slam Bradley*. But their love of science fiction pulp adventure continued (their strip *Federal Men* allowed them to indulge their love for rocket ships and giant robots), which is likely why they weren't deterred by the rejection letters that deemed the idea of a superpowered alien too crude, juvenile, and outlandish for readers to accept. (Actually, Siegel did briefly grow frustrated enough—or, at least, impatient with repeated rejection—to collaborate with two other artists on a slightly altered Superman treatment. In these versions, it wasn't an alien scientist, but the last man on the Earth of the far distant future, who sent his infant son back in time to the present age, when his advanced physiology lent him tremendous strength. These treatments were no more successful, and Siegel soon reunited with Shuster on their original conception.)

As mentioned, the formula for Superman's otherworldly origin and ensuing powers was a simple inversion of Edgar Rice Burroughs's John Carter stories. Instead of an Earthman gaining fabulous powers on another world, an alien from a more advanced planet arrived on Earth and developed astounding strength. Instead of transporting a mundane human to a fantastic setting, they'd bring a fantastic superhuman to our world and have him go about performing amazing feats in the streets and alleys of the city. For the first few years of Superman's existence, Siegel and Shuster were careful to tell grounded, recognizable stories of earthly crime and corruption, in which the Man of Steel's existence was the only element of science fiction or fantasy to be found. That disconnect, they decided, would provide the excitement and much of the humor.

The decision to make their hero both an orphan and an immigrant lent the character an emotional resonance that action heroes such as Flash Gordon lacked. The character's tragic backstory would be pushed to the background, however, until the 1950s, when writers (including Siegel) would turn their attention to exploring the doomed planet Krypton. That move would supply a huge cast of characters and introduce somber, ennobling overtones that would become a part of Superman forever.

Yet here at the beginning, Siegel and Shuster didn't bother much with all of that sob-story stuff. At the very outset, the "distant planet" from which their hero hailed didn't even rate a name; it's as if, for all of their passion for science fiction, Siegel and Shuster initially regarded Superman's intergalactic origin as little more than a story point to tick off, something to be dutifully invoked to explain why their Man of Tomorrow could perform such amazing feats.

The Superman they envisioned was too upbeat—and far too busy—to waste time on survivor's guilt and introspection. He had things to do. He was also, quite simply, the ultimate American: a Gatsby who'd arrived on a bright new shore, having propelled himself there by burning his own past as fuel. The Old World could no longer touch him, and now it was left to him to forge his own path.

Introducing: Superman

The story of how Siegel and Shuster finally sold all rights to Superman (for $130—ten dollars per page) to DC Comics, and the decades of outrage, anguish, and legal maneuvering that followed, has been told elsewhere in great detail. Readers seeking a comprehensive and elegantly written account of this history are advised to start with Gerard Jones's *Men of Tomorrow* (Basic Books, 2004).

Siegel and Shuster had hoped to sell a newspaper strip, which would provide a steady stream of royalties, but were asked by DC to rework their pitch treatment into a thirteen-page comic book story that would be the lead feature of the new book called *Action Comics*. The result appeared on newsstands on or about April 18, 1938, with a June cover date.

Siegel and Shuster decided to devote the entire first page to their hero's origin story. This is bare-bones, just-the-facts storytelling, with no room for proper nouns—names such as Krypton, Smallville, Metropolis, Jor-El, Lara, Ma and Pa Kent—all of that would come later.

Panel one: As a city crumbles to dust, a red rocket ship bursts skyward through the roof of a lurching skyscraper. Caption: "As a distant planet was destroyed by old age, a scientist placed his infant son within a hastily devised space-ship, launching it toward Earth!"

Panel two: From overhead, we see car headlights strike the rocket, where it has come to rest. "When the vehicle landed on earth, a passing motorist, discovering the sleeping babe within, turned the child over to an orphanage." With Siegel's use of the phrase "sleeping babe," a biblical subtext forever becomes part of Superman's creative DNA; the reader may think of Moses among the reeds or Jesus in the manger. It's not something Siegel and Shuster would pursue themselves, but it's an element of the character that would inspire comics writers and filmmakers in years to come.

Panel three: A diapered infant stands erect, holding a large red sedan chair over his head with one hand, while a bearded man and a nurse look on, agog. "Attendants, unaware the child's physical structure was millions of years advanced of their own, were astounded at his feats of strength."

Panel four is split into three images showing the adult (still-unnamed) man in action ("When maturity was reached, he discovered he could easily"). In the first image, a man in a blue business suit is seen striding through the air ("Leap 1/8th of a mile and hurdle a twenty-story building") above two skyscrapers. Flying would come later; for now, he merely leaped from place to place, and for the first three years of his life, that "1/8th of a mile" statistic would feature prominently in any mention of his power-set in the comics, on the radio, and elsewhere.

In the next image, the man is dressed in red overalls at a construction site, where he effortlessly hoists a steel girder over his head ("Raise tremendous weights"), while his fellow workmen gawp.

Next, the man is seen back in the blue suit, racing a locomotive ("Run faster than an express train")—and winning. It wasn't enough, to Siegel and Shuster, that Superman was stronger and faster than other men; they wanted to show that he was better than the machines men built, as well. In just a few issues, he would outrace an airplane for good measure.

As years passed, and those machines got even stronger and faster, so did Superman. Yet the image of Superman racing a train became one that future writers and artists would return to again and again.

The panel of super-feats concludes with the caption "and nothing less than a bursting shell could penetrate his skin!"

The next panel contains no image, only the first-ever mention of this character's name and an explanation of his motivation, flatly stated: "Early, Clark decided he must turn his titanic strength into channels that would benefit mankind. And so was created . . ."

And there, in the next panel, we see him for the first time: "*Superman!* Champion of the oppressed, the physical marvel who had sworn to devote his existence to helping those in need!" He stands there in all his glory, a figure in a bright blue, scoop-neck leotard and red trunks, a vermilion cape billowing in the wind behind him. We can't make out the details of the bright yellow emblem in the center of his chest. His pose is, frankly, odd—he stands with his knees slightly bent, holding his arms away from his sides. His forearms angle toward the ground; the pose is meant to lend him the air of a man about to spring into action, but the effect is that of a marionette or a particularly beefy scarecrow.

It seems odd that Shuster should draw such a stiff and uncomfortable-looking Superman, because his style was more kinetic. He worked fast, and it showed in his drawing: his line work was thin and—as demand increased and his already poor eyesight worsened—even scratchy. He'd never become the exacting drafts-man that his contemporaries Milton Cainiff and Alex Raymond were, but his rough execution (he'd often concentrate on fore-ground action and merely indicate a background) lent his panels a distinct sense of urgency.

The final panel of the introduction is devoted to "A Scientific Explanation of Clark Kent's Amazing Strength":

> Kent had come from a planet whose inhabitants' physical structure was millions of years advanced of our own. Upon reaching maturity, the people of his race became gifted with titanic strength. Incredible? *No!* For even today on our world exist creatures with *super-strength!* The lowly ant can support weights hundreds of times its own. The grasshopper leaps what to a man would be the space of several city blocks.

Again, this explanation—that Superman shared his physical gifts with all other members of his Kryptonian "super-race"—wouldn't last. By the early fifties, writers were attributing Superman's pow-ers to atmospheric and gravitational differences between Earth and Krypton.

But for now, it would serve.

First Outing

In this first adventure, Superman didn't have much in common with the "Big Blue Boy Scout" who has become enshrined in the collective cultural memory by television and film. He was a tough-talking, two-fisted bruiser who was quick with a smirk and a sarcastic quip.

He was impatient, given to anger, and prone to violence. He was a bully to bullies and a reckless one. He was, in point of fact, kind of a jerk. And he'd stay that way for a while.

His very first act: bounding across the well-manicured lawns of the wealthy on his way to the governor's estate in the middle of the night, carrying a bound and gagged young woman like a sack of potatoes. He lands, roughly depositing the still-bound woman against a tree. "Make yourself comfortable!" he snaps, racing toward the governor's house. "I haven't time to attend to it!"

He bangs on the door, waking the butler. "I must see the governor!" he shouts. "It's a matter of life and death!"

Rebuffed, Superman crashes through the door. When the butler produces a gun, Superman shouts, "Put that toy away!"

"I warn you," says the butler, "take another step and I shoot!"

Superman takes that step, and the butler is true to his word. And then, for the very first time, "The bullet ricochets off Superman's tough skin!" In years to come, this act will become synonymous with the Man of Steel; every episode of the 1950s *Adventures of Superman* television show will feature a scene in which thugs fire on George Reeves's Superman, while he rolls his eyes and looks chagrined, as if embarrassed by his attackers' gauche display.

But here, at least, we don't see the bullet hit; Siegel positions the viewer behind the action, watching over Superman's shoulder. The focus of the panel is the butler in his bathrobe, smiling grimly as he shoots.

Superman swiftly disarms the butler, convinces the governor to issue a pardon, and promptly disappears.

Next, we get our first glimpse of Clark Kent, walking down the front steps of his townhouse: blue suit, brown fedora, glasses. He scans the front page of the *Daily Star* ("Curry Released" is the banner headline) and whispers to himself, "Good! I'm not mentioned!"

Here, Siegel and Shuster introduce into the mix two wildly improbable notions: one, that a man who dresses up in a leotard and a cape and performs inhumanly strong stunts hopes not to call attention to himself, and two, that people who saw a man dressed up in a leotard and a cape and performing inhumanly strong stunts would not tell everyone they knew about it.

At the offices of the *Daily Star* (it would take two years [*Action* #22] for the name to unceremoniously, and without explanation, switch to the *Daily Planet*), Kent is called into his as yet unnamed editor's office and asked whether he's ever heard about Superman. In what will swiftly become a fixture of all portrayals of the Man of Steel, Clark's dialogue is not-so-slyly pitched past the other characters in the scene to offer the reader a sidelong wink: "Listen, Chief, if I can't find out anything about this Superman, no one can!"

A colleague informs Kent of "A phoned tip—wife-beating at 211 Court Ave!" and he speeds out of the office.

Arriving at the scene of the domestic disturbance, Superman interrupts a man beating his wife with a blackjack, easily lifts him over his head with one arm (already his signature move), shouts, "This is putting mildly the treatment you're gonna get!" (note the vaguely Yiddish sentence structure), and hurls the man so hard against the distant wall that plaster goes flying.

"Hearing police sirens, Superman hurriedly dons street clothes over his uniform." And in the process, grimly muses to himself that "It would just be too bad if they searched me."

And so begins another central conceit of the character: that Kent simply wears his Superman uniform (elsewhere referred to as his "super-suit" and "action-costume") under his street clothes. Without this notion, one of the most iconic, oft-iterated images of the Man of Steel, that of Clark Kent ripping open his shirt to reveal the S-shield, would never exist.

In the 1930s and 1940s, an era of loose-fitting pants and thick wool suits, readers never questioned the concept. But later writers and artists would play with this notion to add tension to the stories (what if someone or something came along and ripped Clark's shirt open?) and develop ingenious exegeses to account for fanboy questions, such as, Where does Superman put Clark's street clothes? Does he just stuff the cape down his pants or what?

Thus far in the story, Clark hasn't seemed particularly meek or mild-mannered. In fact, we've seen him boasting of his journalistic prowess to his editor, dashing off to cover a potentially dangerous story, and grimly joking with a policeman as he stands over the unconscious wife beater. But now Lois Lane enters the story and, in so doing, delineates a key element of Clark Kent's character forever. Or until 1986, anyway.

We see Clark stepping up to Lois's desk. Shuster draws him differently than he has up to this point: stoop-shouldered, chin lowered in supplication. "W-what do you say to a—er—date tonight, Lois?" he stammers.

Lois, a pretty, pin-curled slip of a thing, looks up from her typewriter impassively. "I suppose I'll give you a break . . . for a change."

That night, the two dance together at a nightclub, Clark in his blue suit, Lois in a slinky red number. When he asks why Lois avoids him at the office, she casts her gaze far away. "Please Clark!" she sighs, "I've been scribbling 'sob stories' all day long. Don't ask me to dish out another."

Which is to say: When she was first introduced, Lois Lane wasn't a tough, fast-talking girl reporter, à la Rosalind Russell's Hildy Johnson. She was a "sob sister"—a dismissive term given to female reporters who wrote human interest stories, often with heart-tugging, sentimental hooks. It would take until the first Superman radio adventures—and, not coincidentally, for *His Girl Friday* to hit theaters—for Lois to slowly assume a harder, more fiercely competitive edge.

A thug named Butch, sitting at a nearby table with his cronies, notices the comely Lois and decides to do something about it. "I said run along, I'm cuttin' in!" he snarls at Clark.

At this, Clark offers a rejoinder that sounds puzzling to modern ears: "But this is not a robber's dance!"

A robber's dance is a Slovak folk dance performed around a fire—by men only. Clark is joking here, pretending that he thinks Butch is asking to dance with *him*. (Not the act of a milksop, it must be noted.)

Butch expresses his outrage in Dead-End-Kid speak ("Tryin' t'get flip? Move quick if y'know what's good for ya!") and Lois gets affronted—at Clark ("Are you going to stand for this?").

But here, the meek, mild-mannered Clark truly manifests for the first time. Or, as the caption puts it matter-of-factly, "Reluctantly, Kent adheres to his role of a weakling." He dissembles, and Lois seethes. "You can stay and dance with him if you wish," she says to Clark, hands on her hips, "but I'm leaving *now*!"

When Butch attempts to force her onto the dance floor, she slaps him, to Clark's inner delight ("Good for you, Lois!" he thinks) and outward horror ("Lois, don't!" he shouts).

Butch turns on Clark. "Fight, you weak-livered pole-cat!" he says, pushing his hand into Clark's face.

"Really," says Clark, "I have no desire to do so!"

Meanwhile, Lois has already gotten her hat and coat and climbed into a cab. "You asked me earlier in the evening why I avoid you," she tells Clark through the taxi window. "I'll tell you why now: Because you're a spineless, unbearable *coward*!"

She'll say much harsher things to Clark in the coming months and years. Gradually, their relationship will become significantly more nuanced and adult, but here at the outset Lois's attitude toward Clark is pure icy contempt. It's not a particularly enlightened depiction of the female psyche, but Siegel and Shuster were perpetuating a view of women that the culture—particularly, film comedies of the time—was serving up regularly. And it was one that likely resonated with those very first, very young male readers: girls as aloof, disdainful creatures who were prone to outbursts and insults.

Back in the nightclub, Butch leaves with his hoods in tow, determined to follow Lois and teach her a lesson. Little do they realize, as they speed off after Lois's taxi in their green sedan, that they are being followed themselves by a mysterious figure. . . .

Butch's car drives Lois's taxi into a ditch. Butch manhandles her into his car and takes off. Superman overtakes the car, and what follows are three wordless, dynamic panels containing the issue's set piece—a scene so emblematic Shuster adapted it for the cover.

Superman hoists the sedan over his head and shakes it violently with one arm so that its occupants spill out (while he uses the other arm to gently lower Lois to the ground). He smashes the car against the mountainside, pulverizing it, while the three goons run screaming into the night.

Superman grabs Butch and hangs him by his suit jacket from the top of a nearby telephone pole and lands next to Lois, who recoils. He looms over her, a cruel smirk on his chiseled face: "You needn't be afraid of me. I won't harm you." The reader notices that one of her dress straps slides tantalizingly off her shoulder, down her arm.

Superman deposits Lois at the city limits, advising her "not to print this little episode."

He needn't have worried; the next day, Lois's editor scoffs at her story: "Are you sure it wasn't pink elephants you saw?" Lois returns to her desk, chastened. When Clark approaches her, apologizing for his spineless behavior, she ignores him, her face once again a mask of icy patrician reserve.

Clark's editor calls him into his office to complain that "the front page is getting so dull I've even got to headline card-games" (which, given the lack of Superman content, seems likely). Clark is given a new assignment to head to the small South American republic of San Monte to "stir up news. . . . Take along a camera and try to send some good shots back with your articles."

That night, inexplicably, Kent grabs a train to Washington, D.C., instead. There, in the Capitol building, he sneakily photographs a rushed hallway meeting between a Senator Barrows and a shady-looking man (Shuster gives him cadaverous cheekbones and a pencil mustache for good measure) and overhears their plans to meet later, at the senator's home.

The man, Clark learns, is "the slickest lobbyist in Washington," though no one knows for whom he works. Later that night, Superman hangs from the window ledge of the senator's apartment, high above the busy D.C. streets below (Shuster's Washington, a place of teeming skyscrapers, bears no resemblance to the real District of Columbia). There, he eavesdrops as senator and lobbyist confer.

Superman confronts the oily man as he leaves the senator's building, demanding to know for whom he works. The lobbyist feigns ignorance. Already, the reader can predict that our hero will extort the information he wants through physical violence—all in the name of justice, of course.

Indeed, Superman grabs the man by the leg and leaps into the air, alighting on a telephone wire. The lobbyist screams, terrified that they will be electrocuted. Superman races along the wire, carrying the flailing man like a football, calmly imparting a science lecture all the while: "Birds sit on telephone wires, and *they* aren't electrocuted, not unless they touch a telephone pole and are grounded." At which point, of course, the Man of Steel hops over the top of a telephone pole with inches to spare, inciting a fresh round of screams.

Superman leaps from the telephone wire to the dome of the Capitol building. "What a magnificent view!" he taunts, looking over the city. "I wonder if we could jump all the way to that building?"

In the final panel of his first story, we return yet again to a depiction of Superman vaulting through the air with a frail human in tow—this time, however, it's different. "Missed," says the Man of Steel, vainly reaching out toward the building beyond his grasp. "Doggone it!"

And that's where *Action* #1 leaves our hero and his hapless charge—plummeting toward the city street far below. "And so begins the startling adventure of the most sensational strip character of all time: Superman!" blares an ad at the bottom of the page. "A physical marvel, a mental wonder, Superman is destined to reshape the destiny of the world! Only in *Action Comics* can you thrill at the daring deeds of this superb creation! Don't miss an issue!"

And then it's over. On the next page, a black-and-white cowboy strip starring "Chuck" Dawson, fastest gun in the West, begins.

Our Story So Far

Here, then, is what young readers in that April of 1938 were faced with: A visitor from an unnamed planet with the strength of Popeye, who dressed up like Flash Gordon. A tough guy in an unnamed city who beat up bullies gleefully, with no compunction about roughing up criminals if it meant getting his way.

That much, at least, he had in common with many a two-fisted crime-buster who populated the pulps. Yet for some reason—and utterly unlike those rough-and-tumble cops and private dicks—this guy regularly disguised himself as a weakling. And when he did so, he even let a dishy dame walk all over him.

But, of course, there was the action—leaping through the night, tossing cars around as if they were made of papier-mâché, exposing corruption in Washington, and—wait, what? *Why* had he gone to Washington, exactly?

No explanation had been offered. What did it have to do with his South American assignment? And what would happen when he and that lobbyist collided with the pavement?

Whatever the reason—the costume, the super-deeds, the humor, the dual identity, the comely lasses, or some combination of it all—a nerve was struck.

Within weeks, most of *Action Comics* #1's two-hundred-thousand-copy print run had been sold.

2

TRUTH, JUSTICE . . . (1938–1941)

Milestones

1938: *Action Comics* debuts

1939: *Superman* comic, daily newspaper strip debut

1940: *Superman* radio serial begins

1941: First Fleischer Studios' Superman cartoons released

First appearance of Superman/Clark, Lois Lane, Krypton, the *Daily Star/ Daily Planet*, Metropolis, Lex Luthor, Jimmy Olsen (in the radio serial)

It would take DC Comics several months before its executives realized what they had on their hands. The next few issues of *Action Comics* sported more conventional comic-book covers—men parachuting from biplanes, jungle adventurers, and so on. In fact, Superman wouldn't even appear on the cover again until issue #7— about as long as it took retailers to let his publisher know that kids were coming into their stores in droves, clamoring for *Action Comics*. Not that they asked for it by name.

To kids of the spring and summer of 1938, *Action* was better known as "the comic with Superman in it."

Why? What was it that they responded to so strongly? To answer that question, let's examine the handful of stories that made up the Man of Steel's first year of existence.

Superman, Bully for Peace

Action Comics #2 features a decidedly antimilitaristic Superman who's far removed from the über-patriot he would become in just a few years' time. Having survived his fall to the pavement without a scratch, Superman learns that a powerful munitions magnate named Norvell has been bankrolling a crooked lobbyist, who has been attempting to create a market for Norvell's goods. Superman confronts the weapons maker (after surviving a machine-gun barrage and sending his guards scurrying with their barrels wrapped around their necks). "You see how effortlessly I crush this bar of iron in my hand?" he snarls to Norvell. "That bar could just as easily be your neck!"

He coerces Norvell to take a steamer to the war-torn South American republic of San Monte, or he'll "tear out your cruel heart with my bare hands!" The next day, Norvell dutifully boards the boat, as does Clark—and Lois, who's being sent to the war zone to "send back dispatches colored with my distinctive feminine touch!"

That night, as Superman, in full costume(!), stands at the railing, gazing moonily out at the ocean(!), two of Norvell's goons sneak up behind him and push him into the sea. Undaunted, the Man of Steel simply swims to San Monte ahead of the ship and meets a shaken Norvell at the dock. Once again, he threatens the weapons manufacturer with violence—unless he joins the San Monte army. Superman joins, too, to ensure that Norvell doesn't desert.

Here, for the first time, Superman eagerly ditches his "action uniform" to pose as someone besides Clark Kent. As we'll see over the next few months, he's frequently given to disguising himself in the pursuit of justice—so frequently that in these early stages, it's practically an ancillary superpower.

That night, Superman leaps into the enemy camp, snaps a picture of generals conferring in their tents, and mails the photos to "the *Evening News* . . . Cleveland, Ohio." (*Action* #1 had established that Clark works for the *Daily Star*, so this was either an error or, more likely, a deliberate wink to Siegel and Shuster's hometown newspaper.)

Meanwhile, a vampy "woman of mystery" plants a stolen document in Lois's hotel room, causing her to be brought up on charges, put on trial, and sentenced to death within the span of a single panel.

Superman arrives in the nick of time, throws his body in front of the firing squad, and leaps into the air, carrying a grateful Lois to safety.

Their second-ever interaction, in its entirety:

> Lois: Superman!
> Superman: Yes! And still playing the role of gallant rescuer!
> Lois: What manner of being are you?
> Superman: Save the questions!

On the way to drop Lois back on the ship, Superman interrupts a soldier torturing a prisoner. This scene is notable because it underscores both Superman's basic sense of fairness and his ruthlessness, two things that at this early stage are inextricably linked. The Man of Steel picks up the torturer, promising to "give you the fate you deserve, you torturing devil!" and hurls him through the air, to his apparent death. ("The torturer vanishes from view behind a grove of distant trees with a pitiful wail.")

As his last act before finishing his mission, Superman kidnaps the commanders of both armies. "I've decided to end this war by having the two of you fight it out between yourselves," he says. When the two men cannot recall what their armies are fighting about, Superman takes charge: "Gentlemen, it's obvious you've only been fighting to promote the sale of munitions! Why not shake hands and make up?"

Why not, indeed? The two men do, as a proud Superman looks on, and Clark heads back to his editor with the story.

Out of Costume

Issues 3 and 4 of *Action Comics* contain what to modern eyes seem like wildly incongruous Superman tales.

In *Action* #3, the reader glimpses Superman in costume in precisely one panel—out of ninety five. The story concerns a greedy industrialist who skimps on safety measures in his mines. Superman disguises himself as a miner and rescues several workers trapped in a cave-in. Later, Clark Kent confronts the owner about the conditions in the mine, only to get laughed out of the man's office.

That night, Superman again dons miner's garb and allows himself to get caught attempting to crash a fancy ball held at the owner's estate. Conveniently, if implausibly, the owner decides to move the party to the unsafe mine. As the drunken guests enjoy their revels, Superman causes a cave-in, exposing the hazardous conditions. The mine owner repents his selfish ways.

The story features little of what we come to associate with Superman—no leaping through the air, no Lois, only a few notable feats of strength, and no costume. What the story does feature, however, is Superman's basic sense of fairness, and his pitched resentment at the thoughtlessness of the greedy who lord their position over that of the honest working man.

In *Action* #4, it's back to basics, although Lois is still missing in action. Once again, we see Superman leaping over skyscrapers, racing yet another locomotive, but the story dispenses with a thread about a hit-and-run driver to focus on defending—fair play on the local university's gridiron? Superman again turns to the art of disguise, donning "some make-up grease-paint" to impersonate a lowly football benchwarmer—whom Superman proceeds to drug and kidnap, to keep him out of the way until the Man of Tomorrow's plan can come to fruition. The plan in question: use his tremendous powers to win games, expose the crooked coach—and win the benchwarmer back the girl who dumped him because she was ashamed to be seen with a lowly football scrub. (The girl, it should be noted, bears a striking physical and attitudinal resemblance to Lois Lane.)

All the Elements in Place—Down to the Boots

It's in *Action* #5 that we get our first real glimpse of the formula that will endure:

1. A crisis that will send Superman racing against time (in this case, a dam is cracking, threatening thousands of lives).
2. Clark's job as framing device (the *Daily Star* editor assigns Clark to cover it).
3. A scheming, resourceful Lois (she sends Clark chasing a wild goose story about septuplets before dashing off to cover the story herself).
4. Daring deeds (Superman chases *yet another* locomotive, uses his strength to prevent a bridge from collapsing under it, and keeps the dam from breaking as long as he can).
5. Rescuing Lois (whose car has been swept up by the flood).

As he leaps homeward with her, she kisses him deeply and sighs, "The first time you carried me like this I was frightened—just as I was frightened of you. But now I love it—just as I love you." Superman is nonchalant, but Clark eagerly forgives Lois for tricking him.

Lois, for her part, is unimpressed, providing the sixth classic element: Lois's rejection. Which, at this early stage, is remarkably harsh (she thinks Clark a "spineless worm").

This issue also represents the first appearance of the complete Superman outfit as we know it today, as bright red boots replace the blue-stockinged feet of the previous issues for the first time.

"You're a Superman"

Action #6 offers plenty of playful winks to the reader as it widens the perspective, giving us the first real glimpse of the world around the Man of Steel—and how eager that world is to embrace him.

Long before they'd sold the character, Siegel and Shuster had envisioned Superman's face on cereal boxes and model kits. In this issue, they took that idea further, unwittingly intimating the cottage industry that would quickly arise around merchandising Superman's image.

A con man pretending to be Superman's manager shows up to meet Clark Kent, "meek ace reporter of the *Daily Star*." He boasts that he has licensed the Man of Steel's image for a radio show, a brand of gasoline, an automobile, bathing suits, costumes, "physical development exercises," and movie rights. "Why I've even made a provision for him to appear in the comics!"

To Clark's bemusement, the con man arranges a time for the reporter to meet and interview Superman. This offer is overheard by a bow-tied office boy listening at the door (our first glimpse of the character who will become Jimmy Olsen), who promptly reports it to Lois Lane. She manipulates Clark into a date on the condition that he take her along to the Superman interview. Outwardly, Clark is thrilled; inwardly, he chuckles.

They begin the evening at a nightclub, where a singer belts out a torch song called "You're a Superman." (When Siegel and Shuster created this scene sometime in the summer of 1938, the notion that their creation could saturate popular culture enough to figure in a song lyric—even a fictional one of Siegel's devising—was a throw-away gag. This would change.)

Determined to scoop Clark, Lois slips a drug into his drink. When he pretends to pass out, she goes to meet the con man. Clark takes Lois's behavior in stride and dashes to catch up. Together, Lois and Superman foil the grifter—and the Superman impersonator he's hired.

Superman vs. Urban Decay

In *Action Comics* #7, Superman appears on the cover for the first time since issue 1; a banner declaring "Superman appearing in this issue and every issue" suggests that publishers were beginning to clue in to the phenomenon on their hands. In this issue, Superman—wearing bright yellow boots, due to a coloring error—saves a failing circus by joining it.

Superman doesn't appear on the cover of *Action Comics* #8, nor is there any mention of him. Yet this issue includes several notable developments, including the first mention of a superpower that has now become an established part of the character: superhearing.

It will not be called that name for a while yet, and it is not nearly as powerful as it will become in a few decades' time, when Superman is somehow able to hear through the soundless vacuum of space and detect events occurring many light-years away.

At this stage, it's just strong enough to allow him to eavesdrop on the mutterings of some of his fellow courtroom spectators, young men caught up in a crime ring. He rounds up the delinquents (freeing some from police custody in the process, which makes him a wanted man) and returns them to the shoddy tenements they call home. When lecturing them doesn't work, he scoops them in his arms and proceeds to scare them straight with his tried-and-true "leaping onto telephone wires" trick. He then pauses for a moment of super-reflection: "It's not entirely your fault that you're delinquent—it's these slums—your poor living conditions—if there was only some way I could remedy it!"

Soon, he figures out a way. "So the government rebuilds destroyed areas with modern cheap-rental apartments, eh?" he says, demolishing a building with his hands. "Then here's a job for it! When I finish, this town will be rid of its filthy, crime-festering slums!"

The authorities call in the National Guard to stop his path of destruction, and Superman departs. The razed slums are replaced by "splendid housing conditions," and the police publicly declare war on the Man of Steel—while the police chief confides in Clark Kent off the record—"I think he did a splendid thing and I'd like to shake his hand!"

The Clark/Lois/Superman Triangle

The cover of *Action Comics* #9 features a runaway roadster crashing through a fence toward the reader—and, tellingly, the words "In this issue: Another thrilling adventure of Superman!" In the tale's opening image, Superman smashes a military tank into the ground, just as he did to the green sedan on the cover of *Action* #1. The war in Europe was never far from the minds of Superman's creators—or his readers.

Meanwhile, Lois's contempt for Clark grows positively venomous ("Clark Kent, I *despise you*. . . . I absolutely *loathe* you! You contemptible weakling! Don't you dare even to talk to me anymore!"). A wounded Clark asks if there's someone else, and for the first time, the comic's bizarre love triangle settles firmly into shape ("Yes! There is someone else! He's grand! He's glorious! He's terrific! He's everything you're not! Brave, bold, handsome—superb! . . . Superman!").

Clark excuses himself and finds an empty office. "But once the door is shut behind him, an amazing thing occurs—his woeful expression disappears! He clutches his sides and doubles! Then shrieks with . . . *laughter*!"

This is the dynamic that would stay in place for decades: Lois throwing herself at Superman, while spurning Clark; Clark making a show of pursuing Lois, while remaining aloof to her as Superman. As Siegel and Shuster conceived it, the triangle existed for one reason: to cast Lois as a fool, a figure for Superman—and the reader—to mock.

Future writers would posit that Superman spurns Lois's advances because he simply wants Lois to accept him for who he "really" is—Clark. The abiding flaw in that reasoning, of course, is that, in Siegel and Shuster's imagination, Clark isn't the "real" Superman—he's a caricature, a goof, a broad imitation of a species he evidently regards as weak and ineffectual.

Superman vs. Torture, Stockbrokers, and . . . Reckless Driving?

Action Comics #10 features Superman on the cover again, battling a warplane of unknown origin. The villain of the story is a cruel prison warden who brutalizes his inmates. Once again, Superman goes undercover, this time as a member of a chain gang, to expose the deplorable prison conditions.

In *Action Comics* #11, the Man of Tomorrow investigates a suicide and uncovers a crooked brokerage firm selling stocks in a nonexistent oil well. The normally two-fisted, thug-tossing Superman initiates a remarkably circuitous chain of events, which includes disguising himself as "Homer Ramsey" (who, in his cocked fedora, bears a striking resemblance to Dick Tracy) to buy up shares of the worthless stock, racing another locomotive, building a well and striking oil, selling the now valuable shares back to the stockbrokers, and kidnapping them in their pajamas. He carries the swindlers to their oil field and proceeds to destroy the well.

In the process, Superman avails himself of a heretofore-unmentioned superpower for the first time: "Superman's *X-ray eyesight* and super-acute hearing permit him to see and hear all in the shabby room."

Action Comics #12 sees the Man of Tomorrow waging a one-man war against reckless driving. He forces his way into a radio station to issue a dire warning. He visits an impound lot to destroy the cars of traffic violators, smashes up secondhand car lots selling unsafe autos, and destroys an automobile manufacturing plant, "because you use inferior metals and parts so as to make higher profits at the cost of human lives!"

Finally, he grabs the mayor and hangs from the city morgue's window ledge with him, forcing the man to peer in at the bodies of those killed in auto accidents. "You can see to it that traffic laws are strictly obeyed and that driving permits are issued only to responsible drivers!" Superman intones.

The final panel of the story is an ad for a "new thrilling adventure strip" launching in the May issue of Detective Comics: *The Batman*!

The Deluge

One year after his first appearance, Superman was a phenomenon. *Time* magazine declared "Superman is fast becoming the no. 1 juvenile vogue in the U.S."

Monthly sales of *Action Comics* had more than doubled; print runs now exceeded 1 million.

Superman paper dolls, wooden action figures, paint sets, puzzles, coloring books, and games began to flood the nation's five and dimes. (In a particularly savvy marketing move, Daisy Manufacturing released the Official Superman Krypto-Raygun in the run-up to Christmas 1940—a gun-shaped light that "flashes a thrilling scene from a 28-picture Superman Adventure Story on the wall each time you pull the trigger!" In a less-than-astonishing coincidence, the issue of *Action Comics* that appeared on newsstands at the time showed Clark repairing to his never-again-mentioned laboratory and emerging with "The Krypto-Raygun—a startling invention with which I can snap pictures—they are developed right in the gun—and can be flashed upon a wall!") Soon parents could buy their children Superman moccasins, underwear, playsuits, and swim trunks.

And in April 1939, *Superman* #1 appeared on the stands.

A Book of His Own

Superman was something that had never existed before: a comic book devoted exclusively to a single character. It weighed in at sixty-four pages, and the cover of the quarterly comic (demand was so great it quickly went bimonthly) promised, "The complete story of the daring exploits of the one and only Superman!" and delivered on that promise by restoring the original beginning of the tale Siegel and Shuster had prepared for *Action Comics* #1 but had been forced to trim to fit *Action*'s thirteen-page format.

In place of *Action*'s rushed, cramped one-page treatment, *Superman* #1 devotes two pages to relating the Super-origin. The extra space allows Shuster's art to breathe: we can see the rivets on the "experimental rocket-ship" that hurtles through space, leaving the doomed planet behind.

Though they barely rated a mention in *Action* #1, here, for the first time, we meet the elderly couple who adopt him. They warn him to hide his strength from others to avoid scaring them but to use it to help mankind "when the proper time comes."

Next, the young boy discovers his powers (one panel finds young Clark in knee-pants hurtling over skyscrapers), which include the now inevitable racing of a locomotive.

We see a mournful Clark standing over the graves of his foster parents—the first time this now-crucial aspect of the character's history is mentioned.

The opening story reveals how Clark gets his job at the *Daily Star*: he overhears the editor sending reporters to cover a mob at the county jail, races to the scene in his Superman outfit, and violently stops a crowd from lynching a prisoner.

"Who are you?" asks the sheriff.

"A reporter," says the man in blue tights and a scarlet cape.

The grateful inmate informs Superman that a nightclub singer framed him for murder, along with a woman scheduled to be electrocuted that very night. Clark calls the editor with the story and gets hired immediately.

Clark goes to see the singer, who pulls a gun on him. He crushes the barrel like paper and has her sign a confession. He ties her up, hoists her in his arms, and leaps through her window, just as a radio bulletin announces that the woman she framed is about to be electrocuted.

From that point on, the story is exactly that of *Action Comics* #1—the governor's estate, the wife beater, Clark's date with Lois at the roadhouse, and his trip to Washington, D.C. The rest of *Superman* #1 simply reprints *Action Comics* #2–4, plus gives a full-page treatment explaining Clark's powers (which features an image of a futuristic Kryptonian city, with inhabitants leaping through the air in a very familiar pose).

Those first issues of *Superman* also included two-page prose stories of Superman's adventures, written by Siegel. This was a gambit that allowed the issues to ship using the lower postage rate reserved for magazines that could attest to possessing "literary merit."

For a dime, a kid could join the Supermen of America Fan Club and receive a Superman pin, a membership card emblazoned with the motto "Strength—Courage—Justice," and a code book for deciphering messages found in the comics.

Superman #1 went through three print runs and sold 900,000 copies. Less than a year later, it was selling 1,300,000 copies per issue.

See You in the Funny Papers

Yet of all of the dizzying achievements of that first year, the development that most thrilled Siegel and Shuster was the sale of a daily *Superman* strip to the McClure newspaper syndicate, which debuted on January 6, 1939 (a Sunday strip would follow in November). By the end of the year, the *Superman* strip appeared in sixty newspapers across the country, and that number would keep growing.

It was Siegel and Shuster's long-delayed dream come true—and as they'd always predicted, newspaper syndication was much more lucrative than comics—but that meant more work. Shuster was already turning out comics pages at a breakneck pace: In addition to *Superman*, he and Siegel were now producing *Slam Bradley*, *Spy*, *Federal Men*, and *Radio Squad*, and the grind strained his already poor eyesight even further. To keep up with explosive demand, Shuster created an art studio in Cleveland and hired Paul Cassidy and Wayne Boring (and eventually Leo Novak, John Sikela, Ed Dobrotka, and others) to "ghost" the comics for sixty-four dollars a week. In interviews over the years, Siegel has insisted that Shuster was intimately involved with the ghosted art—often reworking the ghost-artist sketches completely. Even as his eyesight continued to fail, he would generally ink all of the main character's faces, to imbue his spirit into the product.

A First Look at Krypton

The first two weeks of the *Superman* newspaper strip allowed Siegel and Shuster room to explore Superman's origin in a way that deepened the character's backstory by providing the first real glimpses of his lost homeworld and introducing his Kryptonian parents to the chronicles.

"Krypton, a distant planet so far advanced in evolution that it bears a civilization of Supermen—beings which represent the human race at its ultimate peak of perfect development!" booms the stentorian caption, as we glimpse a giant world floating in space. What follows is pure space opera of a sort that *Action* and *Superman* comics assiduously avoided, preferring to ground Superman's exploits in the everyday.

Yet on this first version of Krypton, every citizen is capable of amazing feats—indeed, we initially glimpse Jor-L (the name would change to Jor-El in the 1942 novelization), the planet's "foremost scientist," racing and leaping hundreds of yards up to the balcony of his bedroom, where his wife, Lora (later Lara), waits with their newborn son, Kal-L.

As the happy couple coos over their baby, an earthquake tears their home apart. Jor-L saves his wife and child from the wreckage and sets off for his "other residence." (The Ls were apparently well-to-do.) The drawing of Jor-L leaping into the air with Lora and Kal-L in tow (he grabs her by the wrist) suggests that either Kryptonian females do not share the astonishing abilities of Kryptonian males, or simply that Lora is content to let Jor-L drive.

Jor-L resolves to uncover the cause of the recent quakes that have plagued the planet and disappears into his laboratory. As befits a man recounting a creation myth, Siegel indulges his fondness for biblical phrasing: "And then, on the fifth day, Jor-L learns the terrible truth . . ."

He informs Lora that their homeworld is doomed. A distressed Lora looks to the "free and aloof" stars. This inspires Jor-L, who decides to build a great space ark to take all of Krypton's population to safety. The final panel of the first week's strips finds Jor-L and his wife standing in profile as Jor-L gestures skyward, a tableau that could have been lifted from a socio-realist mural.

Jor-L takes his conclusion to "the Council," who judge his fears unfounded and refuse to help him build his ship. Undaunted, Jor-L constructs a model rocket ship and prepares to send it on a trial journey to the planet Earth. Yet just as he makes ready to fire the empty rocket, a final, cataclysmic earthquake rocks the planet. The model ship is too tiny to save them all. The rocket streaks into the sky carrying young Kal-L; we get a final glimpse of Jor-L and Lora embracing as they perish.

The ship speeds through space, narrowly avoiding meteors and the "molten death" at the heart of a giant sun, only to land safely on Earth. The last strip of the two-week origin reiterates the *Action Comics* version—here again, a passing motorist rescues the babe, orphanage attendants marvel at the diapered infant's tremendous strength, the boy grows to maturity and decides to help humanity. No mention is made of the Kents or their role in shaping the young man's identity.

During its twenty-year run, the *Superman* newspaper strip liberally borrowed characters, storylines, and, in many cases, entire panels from previously published comics adventures but reiterated them in ingenious ways to tell self-contained stories that unspooled during the course of three weeks to four months.

Funny Page Firsts

It was in the *Superman* newspaper strip published on November 13, 1939, that the *Daily Star* unceremoniously became the *Daily Planet*. (The name change wouldn't go into effect in *Action* and *Superman* until the following spring.)

On June 7, 1939, Clark Kent, while on assignment in "Boravia," sends his editor a telegram addressed to "Metropolis, NY." Meanwhile, in the September 1939 issue of *Action Comics* (which would have been on newsstands in June), Clark Kent poses the question "How come gambling is permitted to flourish in the city of Metropolis?" These concurrent instances represent the first times that the Man of Steel's home city is given a name.

It was in the newspaper strip, on November 16, 1940, that Superman's arch-villain Luthor (who had by then squared off with Superman several times in the comics) first attained his signature look.

Up to that point, whenever he'd faced the Man of Steel in the comics, the mad scientist Luthor was a gaunt figure with a shock of bright red hair and a thin-lipped sneer—but in Luthor's first appearance in the daily strip, he was depicted as a scowling, heavyset bald man in a lab coat. Some believe this was a mistake, that the artist had hastily referenced Luthor's first appearance in the comics but in so doing mistook a different character—a bald, heavyset henchman in a lab coat—for the villain himself. Months later, when the character next appeared in the comics, he was drawn as he'd appeared in the daily strip and would remain that way for decades. Two decades later, after a series of protracted legal battles with DC, Jerry Siegel would find himself writing Superman stories once again. In one of the oddest of these, he would transform Luthor's baldness into the central motivating principle behind the villain's abiding hatred of Superman. (More on this later.)

The *Superman* newspaper strip also saw the first appearance, in the early spring of 1944, of the mischievous, magical other-dimensional pest Mr. Mxyztplk—he first appeared in the comics (*Superman* #30) several months later.

Beginning in 1949, the newspaper strip also featured a long-running storyline in which Clark Kent married Lois Lane—without telling her his secret. In the comics, Superman, Lois, and Clark remained locked in their love triangle, but in the newspaper strip, the super-marriage lasted for two and a half years—until the writers decided it had all been a dream.

Up, Up, and Away: The Radio Adventures Begin

DC Comics hired former pulp fiction writer Robert Maxwell (real name: Robert Joffe) to run "Superman, Inc."—a division tasked with channeling the Man of Steel's comics adventures into radio and other media. In 1939, Maxwell partnered with press agent Allen Ducovny to write and record demos of four 15-minute radio episodes that might drum up potential sponsors. These episodes departed from the comics in small but significant ways: the newspaper was the *Daily Flash*, not the *Daily Star*, its blustering editor was named Paris White, not George Taylor; a character known only as "Miss Lane" was a switchboard operator, not a girl reporter; and Superman arrived on Earth not as an infant but as a fully grown man—complete with outfit.

Maxwell and Ducovny resolved to write an introduction that would orient young listeners and draw them into the story, so they mixed together passages Siegel had used in his monthly comic book introductions and added some breathless prose of their own. This introduction would be reworked continually over the years; its rhythms and cadences would quickly filter through every medium the character touched, becoming a signature element of cartoons, movie serials, comics, and television shows, but even here, in its first incarnation, it contains phrases that would still be associated with the character seventy-five years later.

> Narrator: Boys and girls, your attention please! The "Blank Corporation" presents a brand-new adventure program, featuring the thrilling adventures of an amazing and incredible personality! Faster than an airplane! More powerful than a locomotive! Impervious to bullets!
> Male: Up in the sky—look!
> Female: It's a giant bird!
> Male: It's an airplane!
> Male: It's Superman!
> Narrator: Superman! A being no larger than an ordinary man, but possessed of powers and abilities never before

realized on Earth. Able to leap into the air an eighth of
a mile in a single bound, hurdle a twenty-story building
with ease, race a high-powered bullet to its target, lift tremendous weights, and rend solid steel in his bare hands
as though it were paper. Superman! Strange visitor from a
distant planet. Champion of the oppressed! Physical marvel extraordinaire, who has sworn to devote his existence
on Earth to helping those in need.

Actors were hired, many of whom were already working on the
Terry and the Pirates radio show, including Agnes Moorehead, a member of Orson Welles's Mercury Theatre, who played Superman's
mother, Lara.

Maxwell considered using two different actors for the parts of
Clark Kent and Superman but was impressed by the audition
of Clayton "Bud" Collyer—one of radio's most in-demand actors,
who was already a regular on NBC's *Terry and the Pirates* and *Road
of Life*, as well as ABC's *Listening Post*. Collyer gamely auditioned
for the dual role—but then read the scripts and balked, worried
that they seemed too juvenile. "The whole idea embarrassed me,"
he said.

Yet there was no question in Maxwell's mind or Ducovny's. "No
one else's audition even came close. Collyer's reading perfectly created the essence of Superman's dual identity," Ducovny told writer
Anthony Tollin years later.

Collyer accomplished this via a simple but ingenious vocal
inflection that has since been embraced and iterated by every actor
who has donned the blue tights. He employed a distinctly boyish,
gee-whiz tenor for Clark and a rich basso profundo for the Man of
Steel. Several actors who tried out could pull off that simple trick,
of course. What set Collyer apart was the adroitness with which
he conveyed the Clark-to-Superman transition so that the listener
could picture it clearly, by crossing the distance between milksop
and he-man in just two deft hops down the vocal staircase: "This
looks like a job/*for*/SUPERMAN."

It is something the comics couldn't capture: the sound of a sudden transformation—weakness into strength, timidity into courage, uncertainty into resolve. It crystallized within a span of mere
seconds why the character appealed to so many boys who found

themselves on the cusp of adolescence. Here was a promise that manhood would finally come—and when it did, *look out*.

Collyer was worried about his reputation and continued to resist; Maxwell continued to press. Eventually, Collyer relented, becoming the first actor to portray Superman, and the four demo episodes were recorded. The sound of Superman leaping through the air was produced with a crude wind machine.

The first two demo episodes, which recount the Man of Steel's origin, contain long passages that would get reused often during the course of the radio series. "The Baby from Krypton" finds Jor-L warning Krypton's Governing Council that "Krypton is doomed!" only to find his prediction vehemently rejected. The episode ends with baby Kal-L's rocket escaping and the planet exploding into dust.

In the next episode, an adult Superman arrives on Earth and promptly stops a runaway trolley, saving the lives of a father and son. On their advice, he gets a job at a "great metropolitan" newspaper. In the final two demo episodes, Superman squares off against the Shark, a wily saboteur targeting an advanced submarine.

Maxwell and Ducovny shopped the show around to all four radio networks, Mutual, CBS, NBC Red, and NBC Blue. The networks didn't bite, pointing to Krypton's horrible fate (and Superman's orphaned state) as too scary for young children. And with the United States still officially neutral in the burgeoning war, the notion of someone sabotaging U.S. ships might ruffle feathers the networks were keen on keeping smooth.

Then Hecker's Oat Cereal expressed interest. The sabotage episodes were retooled to focus on a missing locomotive instead; staff writers were hired to churn out additional scripts. One of these writers, George Lowther, would soon serve as narrator and would author the first novelization of Superman's adventures.

In the new radio scripts, the *Daily Flash* became the *Daily Planet*, Paris White became Perry White. (Such was the power of the radio program that it altered the comics' continuity forever in several ways. In less than a year's time, the *Daily Star* and its editor George Taylor would be unceremoniously and permanently replaced on the comics page by the *Daily Planet* and Perry White, respectively.) The sound of Superman's gravity-defying "single bounds" was retooled as well—mixed with archival recordings of a windstorm and a bomb whistling through the air. (Almost immediately, the show dispensed with the comics' references to leaps and jumps and began to describe Superman as "flying through the air." The Fleischer cartoons followed a similar progression—initially depicting a leaping Superman but quickly switching over to depict him soaring through air. It looked less silly. The comics, however, wouldn't make up their minds on that leap/flying score for years—at times showing him seemingly hovering in the air, at times showing him scaling buildings to reach the upper floors. It wouldn't be until 1943 that he was depicted unequivocally flying on the comics page.)

Finally, at 5:15 in the evening of Monday, February 12, 1940, on ten radio stations along the East Coast and one in Los Angeles, *Superman* debuted. The show aired three times a week and quickly became a sensation—though the reviews were mixed.

> *Billboard*: "An utterly, completely, totally and absolutely incredible affair . . . tremendous."
> *Variety*: "Defies all measurements of realism, sanity or sense . . . chock-full of inconsistencies and absurdities."

In two months' time, *Superman* was the highest-rated kids program airing three times a week, and its numbers kept growing. A sponsor in Philadelphia created Superman Bread, boasting "additional vitamins, plus minerals, and roughage."

Superman the Secret Weapon

Less than a week after *Superman* debuted, the February 17, 1940, issue of *Look* magazine hit newsstands. On the cover, a luscious Rita Hayworth beams out at the reader, shaking a pair of red maracas, while the titles of articles float in the darkness above her head: "What it Means to be Neutral, by Dorothy Thompson"; "I Love Jitterbugs . . ."; "Tommy Dorsey Answers Artie Shaw." And finally, just above the red garland of flowers in Hayworth's hair, the words "'Superman' Captures Hitler and Stalin."

The editors of *Look* commissioned Siegel and Shuster to write a two-page story outlining "How Superman Would End the War." In the pages of *Action* and *Superman*, references to the escalating conflict in Europe and elsewhere were kept deliberately oblique. Even in a two-issue storyline that sends Lois and Clark to Europe as war correspondents, the comics refused to engage the increasingly grim realities of the European war: the warring nations were fictionalized (Galonia and Toran), and the cause of their hostilities was revealed to be a madman named Luthor, who, armed with a mysterious green ray and a militarized dirigible, plots to engulf humanity in a global war that will leave it weakened, allowing him to seize control of the world. (In another issue, Luthor is revealed to be behind the Great Depression itself. The man got around.)

In the pages of *Look*, however, Siegel and Shuster got to use their favorite tactic, something that had inspired them in the first place: they could drop their fantastically powerful creation into a real-world situation and let the ensuing disconnect fuel the action and the humor.

Thus, we see Superman braving barrages of bullets as he descends on the Siegfried Line of forts and bunkers along Germany's western border ("The Nazis claim the Westwall is invulnerable. Well here's where I found out!"), ties the gun barrels into knots, and rips the cement structures apart with his bare hands. "Come and get 'em!" he shouts to the waiting French forces, before heading deeper into Germany. Warplanes engage him, but he makes short work of them and crashes through the ceiling of Hitler's mountain retreat.

"Kill the swine!" Der Fuhrer shrieks. "Don't let him touch me!"

Yet touch Hitler Superman does, grabbing him by the neck and lifting him into the air. "I'd like to land a strictly non-Aryan sock on your jaw, but there's no time for that!" And then, as he has done with so many petty crooks before, Superman leaps into the sky, carrying a screaming Adolf Hitler behind him like a bag of garbage.

He interrupts Joseph Stalin as he's reviewing his troops, grabs him, and takes off ("Next stop—Geneva, Switzerland!") and delivers them to the League of Nations. "Gentlemen, I've brought before you the two power-mad scoundrels responsible for Europe's present ills." The two dictators are summarily charged with unprovoked aggression against defenseless countries, as the Man of Steel looks on.

It was not the kind of thing the Nazis, who knew a thing or two about the power of propaganda, were prepared to overlook.

"Superman Is a Jew!" screamed the headline of an editorial in the weekly newspaper of Hitler's SS two months later. "Jerry Siegel, an intellectually and physically circumcised man who lives in New York, is the inventor of a colorful figure. . . . The inventive Israelite named this pleasant guy with an overdeveloped body and underdeveloped mind 'Superman.' He advertised widely Superman's sense of justice, well-suited for imitation by the American youth. As you can see, there is nothing the Sadducees won't do for money!"

War with Germany was looking increasingly inevitable, and the radio show—but not the comics—began to take on a stronger anti-Nazi stance. Sinister German agents became common adversaries.

The First Public Appearance

On April 30, 1939—the 150th anniversary of George Washington's inauguration—the 1939–1940 New York World's Fair opened for business. Franklin Delano Roosevelt and Albert Einstein gave speeches. More than 200,000 people attended.

To coincide with the event, DC Comics published a ninety-six-page, full-color magazine called *World's Finest Comics*, in which a Superman story prominently appeared (though a coloring error rendered his hair blond on the magazine's cover). In the tale, Clark and Lois are sent to cover the World's Fair. On arrival, Clark overhears that an exhibit to benefit infantile paralysis won't be finished by the time the fair opens. What follows are two pages of the strangest how-to booklet ever—Superman springs into action, excavates the plot, drives pilings into the swampy ground, mixes and spreads a cement floor, constructs the exhibit, and even indulges in a bit of super-landscaping by transplanting trees, just so.

The next year, DC comics released a second commemorative comic, this time called simply *New York World's Fair Comics 1940 Issue*. On the cover, a beaming, waving Superman is joined by Batman and Robin. Inside, Clark and Lois are once again sent to the World's Fair and manage to find time to foil a gang of jewel thieves between marveling at the exhibits.

On July 3, 1940, Superman, Inc., publicist Ducovny organized "Superman Day at the World of Tomorrow," a daylong event at the World's Fair to promote the comic. The fair's admission price was lowered from 25 cents to a dime for the day. Children competed in athletic events, Charles Atlas judged a contest to bestow the title of "Super Boy and Super Girl," and the Superman radio show broadcast an episode live from the fair's Assembly Hall, after which there was a parade: "12:45—Superman Day parade of floats, elephants, midget autos, Boy Scouts, Super-boys, and the Superman himself from Theme Center through the grounds to Empire State Bridge. 10,000 balloons, some containing coupons entitling holders to Superman prizes, will be released."

"The Superman himself" was actor Ray Middleton, dressed up in the first Superman outfit ever made. It didn't quite match the comics version—the tunic had the word *Superman* emblazoned above the insignia, and Middleton wore laced wrestler's boots—but it served. Middleton strutted around the fair shaking hands and posing with children and adults alike. Tall and skinny, sporting red shorts that fit his form like an adult diaper, Middleton managed (with some judiciously arranged foam padding) to exude he-manliness whenever he posed in what had already become the classic Superman pose: legs wide apart, hands on hips, chest thrust out.

Later that year, for the first time, an eighty-foot-long Superman balloon soared over the Macy's Thanksgiving Day Parade.

Fleischer Cartoons

In 1940, Republic Pictures approached Maxwell with an idea for a live-action movie serial, but the timing wasn't right just yet. Republic reportedly had trouble conceiving of ways to bring the character's ability to leap tall buildings to life. Paramount approached Maxwell, offering to have Fleischer Studios produce a series of animated shorts. The combination of Fleischer's reputation (the animation studio was known for Betty Boop and Popeye shorts) and Paramount's distribution network was too good to pass up, and a deal was struck.

Max and Dave Fleischer were wary of the challenge, however. Betty Boop and Popeye were broad cartoons, but Superman demanded close attention to the unexaggerated details of human anatomy. Yet these fears were allayed, or at least mollified, by the budget for each short—an astonishing $50,000, making them by far the most expensive animated shorts that had ever been produced. (The budget for an average Popeye cartoon, for example, was closer to $14,000.) The radio actors supplied the voices, and Sammy Timber, the composer of Popeye's theme song, prepared a bright, stirring brassy theme for the opening titles. (The theme was soon adopted by the radio show, although notes that sounded valiant and vigorous when played by an orchestra tended to sound less so when hammered out on the radio show's pipe organ.)

Paramount threw its marketing might behind Superman. Teaser trailers were released—the first time any animated short had merited that treatment. The first short, titled simply *Superman*, appeared in theaters in September 1940. The animation was striking: rich, eye-popping colors, shadows that lent characters an unusual depth and weight, an Art Deco design scheme, and backgrounds that appeared three dimensional.

A pre-title sequence briefly retells Superman's origin ("In the endless reaches of space there once existed a planet known as Krypton, a planet that burned like a green star in the distant heavens"), before it considerably tightens the radio show's opening and adds striking visuals: "Faster than a speeding bullet!" (a gun fires) "More powerful than a locomotive!" (a train speeds toward the viewer) "Able to leap tall buildings in a single bound!" (A figure soars over an Art Deco skyscraper) "The infant from Krypton is now the Man of Steel—*Superman*. To best be in a position to use his amazing abilities in a never-ending battle for truth and justice, Superman has assumed the disguise of Clark Kent, mild-mannered reporter for a great metropolitan newspaper."

It's in this introduction that the phrases "Faster than a speeding bullet" and "never-ending battle" enter the Superman chronicles for the first time. Fleischer studios produced nine shorts in all, which were released on a roughly monthly schedule between September 1940 and July 1941.

It was the Fleischer shorts that added another element to the Superman canon that has infiltrated the collective cultural memory: the phone booth.

In both *The Mechanical Monsters* (which appeared in theaters on November 28, 1941) and in *The Bulleteers* (March 27, 1842), Clark ducks into a phone booth to make the change. Only rarely did the Superman of the comics avail himself of a phone booth, preferring out-of-the-way store rooms and dark alleys. On the rare occasions he did use a phone booth for expediency's sake, he made a point of complaining about it: "This definitely isn't the most comfortable place in the world to switch garments," Superman says in a Sunday comic strip panel in 1941. "But I've got to change identities—and in a *hurry!*"

In the Fleischer shorts, Lois Lane shares with her radio and comic book counterparts their propensity for getting into trouble, but she's also considerably more tenacious and resourceful. In the first Fleischer short, she seethes when Clark is assigned to cover a story she feels she could do a better job on, so she commandeers a plane and flies herself to a lonely island to investigate a mad scientist's "electrothanasia ray." Rays, robots, and meteors from outer space are Superman's primary foes in these first nine shorts; after the United States entered World War II, eight more Superman shorts would be made (albeit not by Fleischer Studios), and they would focus almost exclusively on Axis threats.

The Fleischer shorts depict Lois taking impulsive but decisive action, again and again: she climbs on the back of a giant robot, empties a machine gun at train robbers, sneaks aboard a rocket-car that's threatening the city and attempts to sabotage it, and throws herself between a rampaging gorilla and a scared little girl. In the Fleischer shorts, she is her own woman—and one hell of a reporter.

Meanwhile, Back in the Comics

By the time 1941 was drawing to a close, *Superman* and *Action Comics* were selling a combined 2.5 million copies every month. Superman had set off a comic book boom, and newsstands teemed with costumed superheroes.

Superman still went after petty crooks, crooked politicians, and those who exploited the honest working man. For the first two and a half years of his existence, he dangled racketeers out of windows and threatened wealthy industrialists with murder after they skimped on construction materials. "Either answer my questions," he bellowed at one luckless warmonger, "or have your brains dashed out on that wall!"

During this time, he is partial to crusades; in *Superman* #5, he preserves the virtue of a group of young boys by destroying all of the city's one-armed bandits, then turns to sternly warn the readers not to throw their money away on slot machines. In this same issue, the Man of Steel infiltrates Luthor's inner circle by employing an odd, now-forgotten superpower for the first time. He kidnaps Luthor's lackey, a portly middle-aged man named Mosely, and then, "Studying Mosely's figure closely, Superman contorts his features so that they are identical." For the next few years, the character will only infrequently avail himself of the power to "twist his plastic features" to alter his appearance, but this ability never makes it into the permanent roster of superpowers, disappearing from the comics after 1947.

In *Action Comics* #16, Superman declares war on all gambling and, sneering at one hapless casino denizen, tells him to give his money to charity instead.

The moralizing didn't stop there: In the same story, he prevents a man from hanging himself. The man is stunned to find himself saved: "Who . . . *what* are you?" "Someone who thinks life is too precious to be destroyed!" snaps our hero, whom readers had just seen in the previous issue murdering an airplane full of enemy agents by sending it plummeting to a fiery doom.

The specter of suicide finds its way into many of these early, prewar stories. Again and again, the Man of Steel foils the efforts of hapless men to off themselves. In *Superman* #2, he prevents a boxer from doing himself in, and he does the same for a bank president in both the comics and the newspaper strip shortly afterward. In *Superman* #4, he finds the body of a guilt-ridden, suicidal scientist, and when, in *Superman* #11, he arrives too late (a man who's been swindled out of his fortune by crooked stockbrokers has taken his own life), Superman's outrage inspires him to go to great lengths to mete out justice.

At about this point, though, Superman's New Deal social consciousness begins to fade, and his cavalier attitude toward evildoers "getting what they deserve" softens. DC created an editorial advisory board to assure that content met standards of morality and wholesomeness.

From the very beginning, the correspondence between Siegel and DC was marked by acrimony. Publisher Jack Liebowitz expressed exasperation at Siegel's repeated demands for more money ("As I have pointed out to you many times, our company has very little to gain in the monetary sense from the syndication of this material"), and editor Whitney Ellsworth delighted in finding fault with the artwork:

In the first panel, Superman's physique is a bit on the lah-de-dah side, and I particularly like his big fat bottom.

It was necessary for me to spend a day, with my mediocre talents, trying to shorten a number of ape-like arms, remove extremely curly forelocks from Superman's forehead, and to de-sex Lois.

[Lois] looks pregnant. Murray [Boltinoff] suggests you arrange for her to have an abortion or the baby and get it over with so that her figure can return to that of the tasty dish she is supposed to be. She is much too stocky and much MUCH too unpleasantly sexy.

I have written you repeatedly about the manner in which his jock strap is drawn, and absolutely nothing is ever done about it.

The First Supervillian

Gradually, Siegel and Shuster began to add more and more science-fiction conceits into the stories. Watching Superman toss mobsters around was fun, and it was still thrilling when bullets ricocheted off that big red S—but it was time to raise the stakes, to provide Superman with something he'd never truly faced: a challenge. That's why, one year after his debut, Superman was confronted with his first—and, strictly speaking, *the* first—supervillian, a brilliant scientist known only as the Ultra-Humanite. (To create Superman's opposite number, Siegel needed to look no further than the nearest thesaurus: Super = Ultra, Man = Human.)

The adventure begins prosaically enough—with Superman setting out to crush a protection racket that is targeting the city's cab companies. Then the action takes an unexpected turn when Superman trails the head gangster to a remote cabin, only to find himself ensnared by a bald scientist whose "fiery eyes . . . burn with terrible hatred and sinister intelligence" and who indulges in villainous monologues to tent your fingers by:

So we meet at last, eh? It was inevitable that we should clash! [I am] the head of a vast ring of evil enterprises . . . You have interfered frequently with my plans, and it's time for you to

be removed. . . . You may possess unbelievable strength—
you are pitting yourself against a mental giant!

I am known as the Ultra-Humanite! Why? Because a
scientific experiment resulted in my possessing the most
agile and learned brain on Earth! Unfortunately for mankind, I prefer to use this great intellect for crime. My goal?
Domination of the world!

Superman breaks free, but Ultra escapes to plague the Man
of Steel another day. The villain proves hard to kill—Superman
subsequently exposes his extortion of a subway manufacturer and a
shipbuilding company, but both times Ultra gets away. Ultra seems
to meet his end, however, when he threatens to destroy the city with
a disease that causes purple festering lesions and death (the story
provides what is perhaps the most wonderful caption of the Golden
Age, "A fantastic airship of Ultra's creation wings out over the city,
to spread its cargo of purple death!"), but even though his body dies,
Ultra's evil brain lives on.

While visiting Hollywood, Clark finds himself on a cruise ship
that is being hijacked by the beautiful movie starlet Dolores Winters.
When Superman confronts her—well, the gleefully B-movie dialogue speaks for itself:

Superman: Those evil blazing eyes! There's only one person
    on earth who could possess them . . . Ultra!
Ultra-Dolores: My assistants revived me via adrenalin [sic] . . .
    and placed my mighty brain in her young, vital body.

There you have it: Superman's first real nemesis has a mind like
Mengele and gams like Grable. You might imagine that a writer
in Siegel's position, cranking out story after story to keep up with
increasing demand, would appreciate the endless narrative possibilities of such a creation.

You would be wrong: within two pages of revealing her identity, Ultra-Dolores throws herself into the crater of a volcano.
Comics being comics, the character will return, but not for several
decades—and only after undergoing another, even more extreme
physical transformation.

Enter . . . Luthor

Just two months after the Ultra-Humanite commits suicide by lava, the character who will become Superman's greatest foe enters the chronicles. In many ways, the Ultra-Humanite was a first-draft version of Luthor; both were mad scientists, and both came factory-installed with the basic mad scientist motivation package— the desire to rule the world. Yet where Ultra had been all about seething hatred and wild-eyed cries for vengeance, Luthor's first appearances were characterized by his icy, sneering intellect. If Ultra was a *mad* scientist, Luthor was a mad *scientist*.

In April 1940 (*Action Comics* #23), Superman, while attempting to stop a terrible war between the European nations of Galonia and Toran, discovers that an evil mastermind called Luthor (he would not receive a first name for another twenty years) has sparked the war for his own nefarious purposes. Superman finds Luthor's lair—a vast city suspended in the air by dirigible—and is taken to the villain's throne room.

Ever the scientist, Luthor forces Superman to submit to a series of tests to gauge his invulnerability.

Superman soon foils Luthor's plan, rips his dirigible apart with his hands, and sends it—and Luthor and thousands of Luthor's henchmen—crashing to earth. "So much for Luthor!" Superman says, though it's doubtful either he or the reader believed it.

A few months later, in *Superman* #4, Luthor is back, kidnapping a scientist to learn the secret of his earthquake machine. Once again, Luthor is determined to test the Man of Steel's abilities and proposes a series of challenges pitting Luthor's technology against Superman's might. Superman races the mad scientist's planes around the world and into the stratosphere, lifts heavy boulders more easily than Luthor's most advanced technology, and withstands everything thrown at him—grenades, cannon fire, poison gas—all without getting a single hair out of its Brylcreemed place.

The city dirigible had been only the beginning. From this point on, Luthor's presence gave Siegel and Shuster leave to indulge in bolder, wilder flights of high fantasy and science fiction. In the same issue, Luthor's headquarters are revealed to be an ancient undersea city he has encased in "glassolite" and made into an enormous submarine. As if that weren't enough, he sets his pet dinosaurs loose on the Man of Steel. When Superman destroys the floating city, Luthor is thought dead.

The next time he appears, he is revealed as the evil architect of nothing less than the Great Depression itself.

In summer 1940 (*Superman* #5), Metropolis's wealthiest men have been exposed to a drug that makes them Luthor's willing slaves. Through them, he manipulates stock prices and causes record unemployment. Superman foils Luthor's plot and sends his escape plane plummeting into the sea. "The end of Luthor!" he observes, very wrongly.

Luthor would return to dog the Man of Steel four more times in the months that followed. In May–June 1941 (*Superman* #10), he comes with rocket-powered planes and invisibility fields—and a newly bald pate, to match the Luthor appearing in the daily newspaper strip. In September–October 1941 (*Superman* #12), he returns with scientifically altered beasts and a mysterious island. In November of that year, he is back again, with still another floating city, disguised as Zytal, an explorer from another universe. And in November-December 1941 (*Superman* #13), he returns again, disguised as the masked criminal the Light, who hypnotizes powerful men—including Superman—with colored rays.

The Turning Point

While *Superman* #13 was on the stands—an issue whose cover depicted Superman punching the prow of a German battleship—the Japanese attacked Pearl Harbor. That act drew the United States into a war that would irrevocably change how the country viewed itself and its place in the world. Superman would change along with it.

He began as an adolescent power fantasy of two nebbishy boys who aspired to something more. Now it was time for him to grow into the power fantasy of an entire beleaguered nation.

3

... AND THE AMERICAN WAY
(1942–1945)

Milestones

1943: *Adventures of Superman* novelization

1944: First appearance of Superboy in *More Fun Comics*; Lois Lane gets a back-up feature in *Superman*

First appearance of Kryptonite (in the radio serial); Fortress of Solitude (mentioned); the Toyman; Superboy; Mr. Mxyztplk (spelling changes to "Mxyzptlk" in 1955); the Prankster

Power creep: flight, "super-brain" added; strength increases

In a series of newspaper strips that ran the week of February 16, 1942, Clark Kent reports to his local U.S. Army recruitment center, eager to enlist. Yet when the exam is over, the doctor delivers a crushing blow.

> Clark: There must be some mistake! Did you say the army *doesn't want me*?
> Doctor: You're physically superb—except that you're obviously blind as a bat. When I asked you to read the eye chart aloud, you muffed every line!

Clark had mistakenly peered through the examination room's wall with his X-ray vision and read the eye chart in the next room. The doctors declare him 4F, consigning Clark—and Superman—to remain stateside for the war's duration.

That sequence was created to solve a problem *Time* magazine called "Superman's Dilemma":

> Superman is now in a really tough spot that even he can't get out of. His patriotism is above reproach. As the mightiest, fightingest American, he ought to join up. But he just can't. In the combat services he would lick the Japs and Nazis in a wink, and the war isn't going to end that soon. On the other hand, he can't afford to lose the respect of millions by failing to do his bit or by letting the war drag on.

Siegel and Shuster felt strongly that Superman should participate in the war effort but were worried about how to go about it. In the pages of *Look* magazine, they'd already demonstrated how he could win the war by himself; in other stories, he'd simply brought warring generals together to settle their disputes in person. Yet now that the lives of U.S. soldiers were on the line, Superman couldn't be so cavalier. German bullets didn't bounce off the chests of GIs, and stories of a grinning Man of Steel effortlessly routing Nazi gun nests could be easily construed as trivializing the grim work that soldiers faced.

Thus, it was decided to turn Superman into a symbol, an icon to boost morale, leaving the war to be fought and won by what he called "the greatest of all heroes, the American fighting man!"

Birth of a Super-Patriot

During the war years, Superman encouraged readers to buy war bonds and saving stamps, to plant Victory gardens, to give blood, and to collect scrap metal. In the comics, he visited military bases and took part in war games. In *Superman* #23 (July/August 1943), his arrival at an army base is met with cheers, and he is humbled ("American soldiers cheering me, when all the civilized peoples of the world are cheering them! It's the grandest tribute I've ever had!").

The process of becoming a symbol smoothed Superman's rough edges and shaped him into something safer, more trustworthy. His social conscience morphed into boosterism. His sardonic smirk became a genial grin. Once hunted as a vigilante "mystery man," he now began working alongside the police ("What would the police force do without you?" asks a sergeant in *Superman* #16, May/June 1942).

There was a war on, so the time for social crusades was over. Where once he agitated and chafed against the status quo, Superman was now determined to reinforce it.

As comics historian Gerard Jones points out in his book *Men of Tomorrow*, Superman—and the costumed heroes he'd inspired— assumed this very different role during the war for a reason: "Superheroes turned anxiety into joy. As the world plunged into conflict and disaster almost too huge to comprehend, they grabbed their readers' darkest feelings and bounded into the sky with them. They made violence and wreckage exciting but at the same time small and containable."

The American Way

Comics boomed during the war, selling more than 25 million copies every month, thanks to a hungry readership composed of kids and servicemen. Comics were suited for the "hurry up and wait" nature of military life—easily portable and tradable, with outlandish, whimsical stories that both cheered the spirit and could be devoured quickly. The *New York Times* reported at the time that one in four magazines shipped to GIs overseas every month was a comic—thirty-five thousand of those were *Superman* comics.

On the covers of those comics, U.S. servicemen found stirring, patriotic imagery to rally around. *Superman* cover artists had begun to produce propagandistic depictions of the Man of Steel even before the United States entered the war; on the cover of *Superman* #12 (September/October 1941), he walks proudly, arm-in-arm, with a U.S. soldier and sailor.

Now that the war was on, the artists didn't hold back. On the cover of *Superman* #14 (January/February 1942), Superman poses in front of a giant shield bearing the stars and stripes, while an American eagle alights on his muscular forearm. On *Superman* #17

(July/August 1942), he stands astride the Earth, lifting Hitler and Hirohito by the scruffs of their necks and looking as if he's about to bash their heads together. On the next issue's cover, he rides a bomb as it whistles toward some unseen enemy encampment ("War Savings Bonds and Stamps Do the Job on the Japanazis!" blares the copy). *Superman* #23 (July/August 1943) boasts one of the most famous images of wartime Superman: we are inside a German U-Boat, watching a pair of Nazi soldiers panic as the periscope reveals both the boat they've just sunk and Superman swimming toward them, a look of murderous rage on his face. In the next issue, he simply stands in his by-now-iconic pose, holding the American flag.

Over on the covers of *Action Comics*, Superman tears through German tanks and gun placements, ties gun barrels and U-boat periscopes in knots, and cranks out enormous jingoistic war stamps on a printing press ("Superman Says . . . You Can Slap a Jap with War Bonds and Stamps!").

On the covers of *World's Finest* comics—the New York World's Fair comic had become a quarterly ninety-six-page anthology of DC's ever-growing roster of superhero stories—Superman, Batman, and Robin plant a Victory garden, hawk savings bonds, glad-hand servicemen, and ride astride the barrels of a battleship's heavy-caliber guns.

The images on those covers—the way they deftly conflate Superman and America, finding affinities between the cape and the flag, and between the red, yellow, and blue and the red, white, and blue—infiltrated the American consciousness. When the war began, Superman was a wildly popular children's character. By the time it ended, he was an American icon.

Taking the Good Fight to the Silver Screen

The last of the first nine Fleischer Superman cartoon shorts, *Terror on the Midway*, appeared in theaters on July 24, 1942. Most of this first batch featured Superman facing larger-than-life science-fiction foes—monsters, giant robots, death rays, and so on.

Yet in the second and final batch of eight short films, which was produced by Famous Studios after Paramount ousted the Fleischers from the studio that bore their name, several tackled the war head-on.

In the first, *Japoteurs*, which debuted in theaters on September 18, 1942, Superman foils Japanese spies' attempt to sabotage a U.S. bomber. In *The Eleventh Hour*, which appeared in theaters on November 20, Clark and Lois go to Japan on assignment, and Superman sinks Japanese warships. In March 26's *Jungle Drums*—a short that features a cameo by Adolf Hitler—Superman discovers that an African temple is really a Nazi headquarters. In the final Superman short produced, *Secret Agent*, which debuted on July 30, 1943, Superman saves the life of a woman who's gone undercover to foil a ring of saboteurs.

Radio Days

In February 1942, almost two years after production began and after completing 325 syndicated episodes, the *Superman* radio show came to a halt. By this time, *Superman* was airing on 85 radio stations across the country, but Robert Maxwell had always hoped the show would get picked up by a national radio network. Now the Mutual Broadcasting Company came calling with a hole in its line-up; it wanted a Superman series.

On Monday, August 31, 1942, that new series—now called *The Adventures of Superman*—premiered. Maxwell tweaked the cartoon's prelude, adding a line about the character being able to "change the course of mighty rivers."

Maxwell made another small change to reflect the mood of the times—but that change would become an indelible part of the character for decades. (This new version of the prelude is the one Maxwell would return to years later, when scripting Superman's televised adventures.)

The Superman cartoons had begun with a narrator intoning the phrase "Superman fights a never-ending battle for truth and justice!" Maxwell's emendation was "a never-ending battle for truth, justice, and the American way!"

Episodes of *The Adventures of Superman* lasted fifteen minutes and aired Monday through Friday evenings during the five o'clock hour. Kellogg's Pep Wheat Flakes signed on as a sponsor and urged the producers to soften the Man of Steel's few remaining hard edges. Between the deadly serious business of busting up saboteurs and spies, humor became more prevalent, with more airtime devoted to Perry White's bluff bluster ("Great Caesar's ghost!" became his catchphrase) and young Jimmy Olsen's feckless nincompoopery.

A Meteoric Rise . . . and Fall

On June 3, 1943, a new story arc called "The Meteor from Krypton" began on the radio show.

When he'd written the *Superman* novelization in 1942, George Lowther, the show's head writer, had been given access to DC Comics' house files. There, he came across the script for a story that Jerry Siegel had submitted to his editors three years earlier, only to have it rejected. In the tale, "The K-Metal from Krypton," a strange meteor turns Superman into an ordinary man—and bestows his superpowers on nearby Earthlings. At the time, Siegel's editor had turned down the story because it hinged on a scene in which Clark reveals his secret identity to Lois.

Inspired by the conceit of a powerless Man of Steel, Lowther penned a script in which a scientist discovers a glowing meteor with a strange effect on Superman. "As he came within five feet of the mass of metal, which glowed like a green diamond, he suddenly felt weak, as if all his strength had been drained from him . . . here was an enemy far more deadly than anything human."

The metal also gives Superman visions of a gleaming city of bejeweled towers, which trigger a stunning realization. "Doctor, it's all coming back to me now! This city! It's Krypton!"

The notion that kryptonite was introduced to render Superman unconscious and thereby allow Collyer to take a vacation, has become a persistent legend—but this first kryptonite arc lasted for just seven episodes, and all of them featured Collyer.

Lowther had discovered a way to have Superman learn something that his listeners and readers had known from the start—his origin. "I know now, for the first time, who I really am, where I came from."

Yet the price for that self-knowledge is dear—in this case, the introduction of a substance with the power to accomplish what nothing he had ever encountered, nothing else on Earth, could do: kill him.

A Glowing Green Symbol

From a storytelling perspective, kryptonite or something like it would have come along sooner or later. Up to this point in his life, Superman lacked an Achilles' heel, and a hero who goes unchallenged is no hero at all. Sooner or later, the Man of Steel would have to encounter a threat more daunting than petty gangsters and their ineffectual handguns.

Yet aside from its narrative inevitability, kryptonite's presence makes a kind of larger, symbolic sense.

Siegel and Shuster had created the Man of Steel as the ultimate immigrant, the personification of the promise America represented to them. His abilities are metaphors for limitless potential and opportunity, for new horizons stretching out before us: the American Way.

It seems fitting, then, that the only thing capable of harming him would be a reminder of the Old World he left behind, a past that is irrevocably gone. Only the past—our past—can hurt us.

Years later, Superman's longing for his doomed homeworld would fuel some of his most enduring stories. Yet no matter how tragic and emotional the tale, Superman's fondness for contemplating the past will always carry a bitterly ironic sting: all that remains of his long lost, beloved Krypton is a substance that is lethal to him.

To this day, kryptonite functions in the Superman mythos as the physical manifestation of both survivor's guilt and a particularly toxic kind of nostalgia, a reminder that when we dwell on what we've lost, we can kill what we have.

After this brief, seven-episode introduction, kryptonite isn't mentioned again on the radio show until after the war is over. One reason for that absence: national security.

Superman and the Supersecret Super-Collider

During the war, Superman radio scripts were submitted to the U.S. War Department for review. Discussion of radioactive elements was a sensitive issue, and the government let the show's producers know it. Kryptonite wouldn't make another appearance until September 1945.

Censorship wasn't an issue only for the radio show. In 1944, representatives from the War Department visited the DC office to discuss a scheduled Superman story that featured Luthor employing a fantastic device he called an "atomic bomb." The DC editors agreed to scuttle the story, though it was published after the war was over, in *Superman* #38 (January/February 1946).

A story for the newspaper strip that involved an imaginary device called an "atom-smasher" was also censored, and the War Department officially asked the McClure newspaper syndicate to avoid any mention of atomic energy.

Escapism . . . on the March!

Though the covers of Superman comics boasted patriotic images meant to stir the blood and steel the spine, the content of the books generally shied away from mentioning the war. In the months following the United States' entry into the war, stories gradually but perceptibly took on an increasingly whimsical, juvenile tone. Superman had always been about wish fulfillment, but the character had always performed his amazing feats in familiar, even mundane surroundings. Now his world expanded to include slapstick gags, groan-inducing puns, and increasingly outlandish, gimmicky plots, which pushed the character into the realm of pure escapist fantasy.

This was no accident. Superman's handlers were mindful that an increasing proportion of their audience consisted of worried and world-weary GIs and felt strongly that Superman should offer a diversion. Given that the newly instituted editorial board frowned on acts of violence, Superman grew less aggressive, allowing his mere presence to sway evildoers, where once he'd relied on ugly threats. (Sometimes Superman manages to thread the needle of whimsy and war, as when, in one newspaper comic strip storyline, he rescues Santa Claus from the clutches of vile kidnappers Hitler, Mussolini, and Hirohito.)

Captain Marvel: The Big Red Cheese

Superman's publisher couldn't help but notice that despite the Man of Steel's rampant and continuing popularity, a usurper had appeared on the newsstands. Since this upstart, published by rival comic book publisher Fawcett, had made his debut in 1940, his sales had soared to the point where he was now selling millions more comics every month than the Man of Steel.

The reasons for the character's runaway success were many, including some dazzling art from a stable of illustrators led by C. C. Beck. Yet unlike the Man of Steel, Captain Marvel rarely tackled problems such as real estate scams and crooked politicians—his comics exuded a lighter, breezier tone and were written specifically for ten-year-old boys.

To that end, their hero's secret identity wasn't simply a symbolic stand-in for the reader—he *was* the reader: plucky ten-year-old Billy Batson.

If kids empathized with the way Clark transformed into Superman, seeing in that act something like the kind of transformation they wished to undergo themselves, Captain Marvel was markedly less coy about its element of wish-fulfillment. What was subtext in Superman was Captain Marvel's text: no fumbling around in supply closets and dark alleys for him—Billy Batson literally *spoke a magic word* to become a muscular, superpowered adult in a flash of lightning.

Operation: Whimsy

Siegel, for his part, embraced the new, more whimsical direction. He and Shuster had always intended for Superman to be a humorous comic, and if the humor could no longer come from having the Man of Tomorrow toss gangsters around like rag dolls, Siegel could adjust. He'd loved writing comedy back when he was working on the *Glenville High Torch*; now he threw himself into the challenge. The books' sardonic humor brightened, and the gimlet-eyed tone became wilder and more kid-friendly.

While this was going on, Superman was undergoing another species of change: he was getting stronger. Where once Earth's weak gravity allowed him to leap tall buildings, now he openly defied the laws of physics by flying through the stratosphere, hovering in midair, and attaining speeds "so that he equals the pace of light itself!" (*Superman* #16, May/June 1942). Where once he was content to heft cars over his head and bend steel bars, now his strength was such that he was capable of barreling through a mountain using only his fists (April 1942, *Action* #47). In July 1943 (*Action* #62), the first mention is made of the Man of Tomorrow's possessing a "super-brain."

Send in the Clowns

Given this steady increase in his physical and mental formidable-ness, Superman's creators began to introduce foes who existed to pester and annoy him rather than match his might.

Action Comics #51 (August 1942) introduced the Prankster, the first of Superman's irksome clownish foils. A villain with a vaudevillian bent, the Prankster is a short, rotund man given to straw hats, big bowties, and checkered suits who delights in making the Man of Steel look foolish.

In *Superman* #19 (November/December 1942), Siegel and Shuster indulged in some particularly playful meta-commentary. In one story, Superman squares off against Funnyface, a floating cartoon head who brings villains from newspaper funny pages to life— to commit crimes. Again and again, he outwits the Man of Steel, until the redoubtable Lois Lane uses Funnyface's mysterious ray device to bring comic-strip *heroes* to life to even the odds. Superman defeats the bad guys and unmasks Funnyface, who turns out to be . . . an embittered creator of unsold comic strips who bears a striking resemblance to Jerry Siegel.

In the same issue, Clark and Lois attend a movie matinee together, at a theater that happens to be playing one of the Fleischer Superman cartoons, *The Mechanical Monsters*. "I hear that Paramount did an outstanding job," chirps Clark, in one of the first recorded examples of cross-platform synergizing. Seconds later, the words "Superman appears each month in *Action Comics* and *Superman* Magazine" appear on the screen. Lois's reaction: "I don't believe I've ever seen those magazines."

To his dismay, Clark quickly realizes that the cartoon will reveal to Lois his secret identity, so he distracts her by knocking Lois's pocketbook to the floor so that she'll miss onscreen Clark's changing into Superman; later, he fakes a dizzy spell to prevent her from seeing the coda.

Siegel and Shuster waved away the logical questions this story raises by inserting a blurb on the first page: "Our Very First *Imaginary Story!*" It was by no means the last. The Imaginary Story conceit would swiftly become one Superman writers would return to often, allowing them to explore a breathtaking array of "What if . . . ?" possibilities, from a Superman-Lois marriage to a heroic

Lex Luthor. As we will see, Imaginary Stories recurred so often in the fifties and sixties that they effectively grew into wholly separate, ongoing storylines.

Birth of a Notion

During the first few years of their acquaintance, Lois Lane had suspected that Superman might have another identity and had even, in July/August 1941 (*Superman* #11) idly speculated that it might be Clark Kent. Yet it was not until a year later (Superman #17) that the penny really dropped for the first time, in a way that would forever alter the Lois-Clark dynamic.

When Clark scoops Lois on a story that involves Superman saving a subway train, Lois grows suspicious. She confronts Clark, whose stammering protestations only fuel her conviction. "I'm still not convinced by Clark's explanation," she says to herself. "He looked very agitated—as tho he were trying to conceal something. Come to think of it, it's mighty peculiar that Clark is never present when Superman goes into action, and on more than one occasion I've noted a faint resemblance between the features of Clark Kent and Superman! Clark Kent really Superman? The very thought seems absurd. And yet . . ."

By story's end, Superman has accomplished a series of faster-than-the-eye-can-follow identity switches that seem to throw Lois off the scent—until, in the last panel, she finds herself scooped again on a Superman story. "But are Lois's suspicions of Clark's true identity completely allayed?" asks the concluding caption. "Only future releases of your favorite strip will tell!"

The answer, of course, is no, not by a long shot. The suspicion that Clark Kent is secretly Superman will become an obsession that will come to define the character of Lois Lane in the decades to follow—and will supply hundreds of Superman tales with narrative grist.

A Changing of the Guard

In 1943, Jerry Seigel was drafted. (Joe Shuster's failing eyesight kept him out of military service for the duration.) DC brought in a stable of writers to replace him, including Don Cameron, Alvin Schwartz, and Bill Finger, though Siegel would continue to submit stories from Fort Meade, where he was stationed. Shuster's studio of "ghost" Superman artists continued to grow and eventually included Paul Cassidy, John Sikela, Stan Kaye, Jack Burnley, and others.

By now, Shuster's hand was injured from overwork (his doctor prescribed an immobilizing glove), and he delegated more and more art duties—to Wayne Boring, especially. Shuster's familiar scratchy line work had by now disappeared from the comics, replaced by stronger, thicker inking, which imbued Superman with a sense of reassuring stolidity and dependability.

Gradually, Superman's physique changed. Shuster's infatuation with bodybuilding had inspired him to give the Man of Steel a body that would win any posedown he'd enter: large, round deltoids; thick, saucerlike pectoral muscles; a torso that narrowed to the waist in a drastic V. Under Boring's pencil, Superman began to grow burlier. In the fifties, Boring's barrel-chested, thick-waisted Superman would become the standard.

The Legion of Super-Pests Expands

In September 1943 (*Action Comics* #64), another whimsical foe made his first appearance. The Toyman, an elderly toymaker, vows to make the world pay for thinking him a "harmless old eccentric" and proceeds to commit crimes using toy soldiers, a toy truck, and remote-controlled dolls with poisoned, needle-sharp fingers. Superman captures the Toyman, but the twisted genius vows revenge: "How the world will laugh when Superman is defeated by a toy! Ha ha ha ha ha ha ha ha!" Like the Prankster, he would often return to plague the Man of Steel, creating havoc that would endanger innocent lives and distract Superman long enough for the Toyman to commit his crimes.

In January/February 1944 (*Superman* #26), the Man of Steel faces Metropolis's most notorious con man, J. Wilbur Wolfingham, for the first time. With his top hat, monocle, and ever-present cigar, Wolfingham visually invokes both W.C. Fields (on whom he was based) and the fat-cat industrialists Superman used to toss around. Yet his attempts to swindle innocents out of their hard-earned money always come to naught—and tend to benefit the very people he attempted to bilk.

In the fall of 1944 (*Superman* #30), the fifth-dimensional imp called Mr. Mxyztplk (the spelling would later change to Mxyzptlk) made his first appearance in the comics. Though he had already appeared in the newspaper comic strip earlier in the year, his debut within comics continuity depicts his meeting Superman for the first time. In his first appearances, he wears a purple suit, a green bowtie, spats, and a bowler hat—years later, he will favor a more outlandish orange-and-purple tunic/dress outfit that owes a great deal to schlocky science fiction.

Myxztplk's presence introduces a concept to the Superman universe that will help define the character for decades by establishing his number-two vulnerability, right behind kryptonite: magic.

Myxztplk possesses powers with no meaningful limits, thanks to his fifth-dimensional origin. The mischief he makes in his first comics appearance, for example—animating a statue of Rodin's *The Thinker*, causing water to squirt out of radios—is harmless enough, but it quickly becomes clear that in his zeal to get a rise out of the Man of Steel, he routinely wreaks havoc without regard to innocent lives.

Mxyztplk tells Superman that in his home dimension, he is a court jester who stumbled on two magic words—one, "Mxyztplk," which, when spoken aloud, transports him to our dimension, and another, Klptzyxm (the first word spelled backward), which sends him home. "And when do you intend to return to your world?" Superman asks.

"Never!" says the imp. "I find this backwards three-dimensional world of yours most amusing! With my extra-dimensional powers, I could easily conquer and rule it!"

Appearances by Mxyztplk allowed artists to draw wildly whimsical feats of magic and gave writers the chance to showcase something besides Superman's sheer strength. To defeat Mxyztplk, Superman has to trick the sprite into saying his name backward, which returns the imp to his home dimension for a set period of time (eventually, the creators settled on ninety days). With each subsequent appearance, Superman is forced to avail himself of increasingly elaborate ruses to get Mxyztplk to say his name backward.

Enter . . . the Boy of Steel

Superman was by far DC Comics's most popular creation, but by now, most of the costumed heroes he'd inspired had teamed with kid sidekicks—Batman's Robin, Green Arrow's Speedy, the Sandman's

Sandy, Mr. Scarlet's Pinky. Kid sidekicks, publishers believed, gave kids a character with whom they could identify. Even Captain Marvel—who went the extra mile by having his alter-ego be a kid himself—had Captain Marvel Jr.

Back in 1941, Jerry Siegel had pitched to his editor a comic book series starring Superman as a young boy. It would offer readers a glimpse of what the Man of Tomorrow was like before he'd dedicated himself to fighting for truth and justice, when he was instead a super-mischief-maker with a fondness for using his great powers to pull practical super-jokes on hapless Earthlings. The proposal was rejected. Siegel tried again two years later with a more detailed outline, but was again turned down.

Yet then, while Siegel was serving in the army, the January/February 1945 issue of *More Fun Comics* #101 included a brief, five-page story about a character called Superboy, introduced with typical comic-book brio:

> Thousands of followers of the great Superman have asked the answers to these questions: "What is the story of Superman's origin?" "What was Superman like before he grew to Man's Estate—was he just an ordinary boy, or was he a 'Superboy'?" In this story you will find the answers to those questions—and, we believe, you will look forward to the further adventures of the youth who was destined to become the idol of millions as the great Superman! For these stories will deal with . . . Superboy!

The story retells the origin: Krypton, rocket, orphanage. No mention is made of a "passing motorist" who discovers the rocket ship. From this point on, that element of the Super-origin disappears. In subsequent retellings, it will be the Kents themselves who find and hide the baby's rocket.

The Kents adopt the infant, and he gradually discovers his super-abilities as he becomes a child. When he lifts a car off a man pinned beneath it, young Clark decides that if people knew what he could do, "that knowledge might be dangerous." In the panel's final story, we see Superboy for the first time; the caption reads "Clark Kent secretly fashions a colorful red-and-blue costume—and thus is born—Superboy."

Comics historian Bob Hughes has noted that except for the last two panels, the script for this story is lifted directly from a version of Superman's origin written by Siegel for the Sunday comic strip. Hughes believes that without Siegel's knowledge, DC had Shuster draw the story and got another writer to fill in the final panels that actually show Superboy in costume.

The character would move from a back-up feature in *More Fun Comics* to star in *Adventure Comics* in April of the following year and would get his own comic in 1949. In these early adventures, he seems to be a ten-year-old; his adventures consist of doing good deeds around his hometown (not yet in Kansas, not yet named Smallville, but merely a "suburb of Metropolis.")

Superman the Phenomenon

During the course of the war years, references to Superman began to saturate American popular culture.

Superman, Inc., helped generate much of that buzz. In addition to churning out metric tons of Superman merchandise, DC changed the text of its company logo in November 1941 from "A DC Publication" to "A Superman-DC Publication" to ensure that readers would know who owned the Man of Steel.

In 1942, George Lowther, the writer, narrator, and director of the Superman radio program, published a novelization called simply *Superman*, the first time a character created for comic books had inspired a prose novel. In the book, Lowther made tweaks to the Superman origin; some of these amendments would last (he changed Superman's parents from Jor-L and Lora to Jor-El and Lara), and some would not (he gave the elderly Kents the names Eben and Sarah).

Meanwhile, Superman's name became a shorthand for a host of different meanings. Crime reporters could signify to readers that a notorious mobster such as Anthony "Dukey" Maffetore was subliterate by mentioning his fondness for *Superman* comics. In the 1942 film *All through the Night*, Humphrey Bogart tries to convince a skeptical cop that he's stumbled across a Nazi spy ring, causing the cop to reply, "You're scarin' me. Sounds like the next installment of *Superman*. My kids'll enjoy this."

It didn't take long for Superman to become an object of satire. In March 1941, the Merrie Melodies cartoon short *Goofy Groceries* included a scene in which the costumed mascot for "Superguy Soap Flakes" comes to life and leaps from the package to charge into action, only to be terrified by a lion's roar—and get transformed into an infant in the process.

In 1942, a character called Supersnipe, written and drawn by George Marcaux, began to appear in comics produced by Street and Smith Publications. The Supersnipe stories starred ten-year-old superhero-fan Koppy McFad ("The Boy with the Most Comic Books in America! He reads 'em! He breathes 'em! He sleeps 'em!"), who dresses up in long underwear and a cape and tackles neighborhood crime. In a spoof on Superman's Man of Tomorrow moniker, Supersnipe was called the Man of 1953—the year that young Koppy would reach manhood.

That same year, the cartoon short *The Mouse of Tomorrow* introduced the character of Super Mouse, a flying rodent in a blue-and-red costume given to singing light opera as he saves the day (after seven shorts, the character's costume changed, as did his name—to Mighty Mouse.) Publisher Standard Comics introduced an unrelated character called "Supermouse, the Big Cheese" in the pages of its *Coo Coo Comics* anthology. Supermouse gained his powers by eating super-cheese.

Yet the Man of Steel really hit the big time when Bugs Bunny himself took a swipe at him. The first time Bugs dresses up in the super-suit occurs on the comics page in the 1942 *Looney Tunes and Merrie Melodies Comics* #5 story "Super-Duper Rabbit." Yet the very next year, the Merrie Melodies animated short *Super-Rabbit* appeared in theaters, which began with a shot-for-shot parody of the Fleischer/Famous Superman shorts:

Voice 1: Look! Up there in the sky!
Voice 2: It's a boid!
Voice 3: Nah, it ain't a boid, it's a dive-bommah!

The 1944 Popeye animated short *She-Sick Sailors* finds Bluto dressing up as Superman to impress Olive Oyl (the Man of Steel is "My super-duper dream man!" says Ms. Oyl, as her eyes turn into a pair of thumping hearts). Because Famous Studios produced both

Superman and Popeye, musical phrases from the Fleischer's official "Superman March" are liberally quoted.

Also in 1944, Warner Bros. produced the cartoon *Snafuperman* as part of its Private Snafu series of animated shorts commissioned by the U.S. Army to train and entertain low-literacy enlisted men. In *Snafuperman*, Private Snafu—a perennial screw-up who never reads his field manual and is always doing the wrong thing—is given the power, and the costume, of Superman. Eagerly, he takes a bomb and heads to Berlin—without a map. By the time he is done, he will have nearly bombed Washington, D.C., attacked a U.S. tank, and gotten himself blown up by German bombers.

The War Ends; the Never-Ending Battle Continues

With the dropping of atomic bombs on Hiroshima and Nagasaki, the world suddenly found itself inside one of the bizarre science-fiction tales Siegel and Shuster used to pore over as kids. Science had created an actual doomsday weapon. Eerie metals radiated disease and death. Many thousands of human beings could be reduced to dust in an instant.

The Axis threat was over, and a wave of triumphant glee seized America—but the shadow of the newer, less-localized, less-apprehendable atomic threat loomed. While the war had raged, Superman offered a garishly colorful distraction. Yet the Atomic Age dawned with anxieties of its own, and now Superman, like everyone else, would have to change to cope with them. Even a cursory glance at a U.S. newsstand during the closing months of 1945 would make something very clear: the era of the super-hero was ending.

4

"STRANGE . . . I . . . I FEEL ALL THE STRENGTH DRAINING OUT OF ME . . ." (1946–1949)

Milestones

1948: *Adventures of Superman* live-action movie serial

1949: *Superboy* comic debuts. In the daily *Superman* newspaper strip, Clark Kent marries Lois Lane. The marriage is never acknowledged in the *Superman* comics and, two years later, is revealed to have been a dream.

First appearances: Arctic Fortress of Solitude (named), time travel, first Superman robot, heat vision

There was no GI Bill waiting for the Man of Steel after the war, though the guy could have used it. The nation's fascination with Superman was fading fast.

It was inevitable. More than 125 new newspaper comic strips were launched in 1946 alone, and as the funny pages grew more crowded during the postwar years, newspapers began to drop *Superman* to make room for *Steve Canyon*, *Pogo*, and others. Something similar was happening on newsstand shelves: sales of *Superman* and *Action* dropped 20 percent between 1944 and 1946 and would continue to slide.

Yet for comics themselves, it was a boom time.

Publishers Weekly reported that 540 million comic books were published in 1946, and a study by the Market Research Company of America revealed that about one half of the U.S. population—70 million people—was reading them: fully 95 percent of boys and 91 percent of girls ages six to eleven. Adults, too: 41 percent of men and 28 percent of women ages eighteen to thirty counted themselves comics readers.

So why was Superman left behind?

The Incredible Shrinking Audience

For one thing, with the war over, Superman's huge GI reader base dried up. The very thing that had made him a hit in the barracks—his colorful, patriotic, easily readable adventures packaged in such a portable, tradable format—only served to remind the weary men now returning home of a grim and difficult time. The comparatively pleasant work of building a family and entering the workforce demanded no candy-colored distractions, and if it did, that's what radio and this new fad called "tele-vision" were for. If the nation's men ever found themselves with a spare minute to read, they'd just as soon reach for the latest issue of *Collier's*, the *Saturday Evening Post*, or *Life*.

Meanwhile, the ten-year-old kids who'd bought those first issues of *Action Comics* back in 1938—the ones who'd fueled Superman's runaway success and that of the costumed heroes who came after him—now found themselves in the throes of puberty. Superman was kid stuff. They preferred to sample some of the other comics genres now flooding newsstands—teen humor like *Archie*, teen romance like *Katy Keene*, horror titles like *Eerie Comics*, and, especially, lurid crime comics like *Crime Does Not Pay*.

As for the current batch of ten-year-olds, they'd also cooled to the appeal of costumed crusaders, opting for newly launched Western and "funny animal" titles. The last new DC superhero to really catch on had been Wonder Woman, all the way back in 1941. Green Lantern got sidelined in his own comic by Streak, the Wonder Dog, in 1948, and sales of titles featuring other superheroes continued to slide. Superman, Batman, and Wonder Woman would manage to tough it out, but many of their less-popular compatriots—Sandman, Hawkman, the Flash, Green Lantern, and the Boy Commandos—would not live to see the end of the decade.

Atomic Anxieties

During the war, Superman and his fellow costumed crime fighters offered colorful diversions, but they also served to distill American anxiousness about the state of the world—and make it punchable. There was good (the Allies), and there was evil (the Axis), and every time Batman delivered a haymaker to some goon's jaw, or Superman toted a garishly dressed villain off to the hoosegow, it was warfare-by-proxy, engineered to reassure. Issue after issue after issue, the good guys won.

Yet the atomic threat wasn't so reducible or clear-cut. Now we ourselves had the power to destroy the world, and soon the Russians—who'd helped us defeat Hitler!—stood revealed as a less theatrical but slyly sinister villain, with agents lurking in our very communities and—gasp—our public schools.

At first, Superman directly reflected the nation's increasingly conflicted feelings about the atom bomb. In October 1946 (*Action Comics* #101), Superman, driven temporarily insane by an evil cabal's secret chemical formula, forges a path of destruction around the world until a nuclear test blast in the Pacific Ocean clears his head. The striking image on the issue's cover ("In this issue!! Superman covers atomic bomb test!") is of Superman flying up to an enormous mushroom cloud and snapping a photograph "as a warning to all men who talk against peace!"

In September 1948 (*Action* #124), Superman is caught in an explosion at a nuclear reactor and becomes temporarily radioactive, forcing him to keep his distance from Metropolis—which sets off a crime wave. It was still possible for writers to attempt to equate atomic power and the Man of Steel, presenting both as incredibly powerful forces harnessed for the betterment of mankind—while acknowledging the danger such power represented. Yet soon the Russians would have the bomb, too—and the threat of nuclear annihilation would become too horrible for Superman to tangle with directly. Eventually, Superman would deal with the specter of the atom bomb only rarely and at oblique angles.

Domestic Hijinks

Instead, in these years immediately after the war, Superman tangled with his usual rogues' gallery of pests and whimsical threats—including the low-rent magicians Hocus and Pocus and Lois Lane's troublemaking, fib-spinning niece, eight-year-old Susie Tompkins. Con man J. Wilbur Wolfingham, Mr. Mxyztplk, the Toyman, and the Prankster put in frequent appearances. Storylines involved Superman baby-sitting, adopting a son, capturing criminals by using a television camera ("the most modern of scientific miracles"), and meeting celebrities, such as *Truth or Consequences* host Ralph Edwards and screen starlet Ann Blyth. Robots and extraterrestrials began to appear more frequently, presaging the science-fiction onslaught to come. For the most part, however, no significant new adversaries, allies, or locales were added to the chronicles during these postwar years; it was a time of narrative lassitude.

Of course, it was the image on a given comic's cover that determined whether it got thumbed through and purchased or returned to the publisher, and with the *Superman* books, DC was betting on whimsy.

Super-slapstick grew steadily broader—many covers depicted Superman playing the fool: juggling bowling pins, playing in a one-man band, getting a pie in the face from the Prankster, or being squirted with seltzer as he stands in an apron, holding a feather duster.

The public had rejected superheroes, so Superman's writers altered his fuel mixture, downplaying the super to play up the man. Gradually, images of Superman in situation-comedy settings became more common, reflecting the postwar state of American manhood, just as covers showing a martial Man of Steel had reflected wartime. GIs had returned home and were slowly adjusting to the everyday duties of heading up households. Thus, more and more covers played up the Lois and Superman romantic relationship ("Does Superman Prefer Lois as a Blonde, Redhead or Brunette?" "Can You Blame Lois for Being Jealous When Superman Meets *the World's Most Perfect Girl?*") and involved imagery that evoked domestic bliss or something very like it. On the cover of *Superman* #36 (September/October 1945), the Man of Steel helps Lois defrost her refrigerator; in issue #51 (March/April 1948), she drops one of her homemade muffins on his foot, causing him to leap around in great pain.

These images of Lois in an apron, attending to various domestic chores, contrast sharply with the tough-as-nails girl reporter of the late 1930s. Yet in fact, during the course of the war years, the Lois depicted in the comics had grown increasingly infatuated with the notion of getting Superman to marry her. Though she was still written as a brave and impulsive reporter, her lovesick fixation on Superman was beginning to figure in the text more frequently; often she grew jealous of perceived rivals, and Superman began to use his powers to "teach Lois a lesson." This dynamic would become the central, driving feature of their relationship during the fifties and sixties, when Lois's transformation from Rosalind Russell to Doris Day would become complete.

Unhappy Trails

Jerry Siegel and Joe Shuster were bitterly unhappy with DC. They knew their contract was up in 1948 and strongly suspected DC wanted them out of the way. They were right.

That knowledge only fueled a resentment that had been building for years. Both felt that they had been taken advantage of, that DC was hiding profits from Superman and Superman-related merchandise so as to avoid paying them what they were owed. They also felt very strongly that they should get compensated for creating what seemed to them (if not to the publisher) the wholly different character of Superboy.

The problem, as comics historian Gerard Jones put it, is that "Writers and artists believe in ownership that transcends money and contracts, but salesmen and accountants do not."

In April 1947, Siegel and Shuster filed a lawsuit against DC for $5 million and the return of all rights to Superman. They would lose the case—DC's pockets were deeper, its lawyers more numerous and highly skilled at protecting its interests. In May 1948, the court ruled that Siegel and Shuster had no claim to Superman but urged the parties to reach a settlement on Superboy; ultimately, Siegel and Shuster received $100,000 for the rights to Superboy, much of which was eaten up by legal fees.

Their tenure at DC was over, their byline summarily removed from Superman comics. Joe Shuster left comics for good, and artistic duties fell to Wayne Boring, Al Plastino, John Sikela, and other artists DC had hired away from the Shuster studio years earlier. Jerry Siegel would return, years later, to DC to write stories that would enrich the Superman mythos in significant ways, but his and Shuster's legal battles with DC were only beginning.

New Blood

Siegel and Shuster had been gone for a year, but the post-Jerry-and-Joe era officially arrived with a flourish in *Superman* #53 (July/August 1948)'s tenth anniversary story called "The Origin of Superman!"

It wasn't the first time the character's origin had been told, of course, and it would be far from the last. Yet it served as a sort of Superman Year Zero, signaling the cleaving of ties to Siegel and Shuster—and their scrappy, smiling, wiseguy Superman.

To this day, whenever a superhero's origin is retold, it serves as a de facto statement of principles, a chance for the new creative team to put their stamp on the character. Reiterating the origin every few years has become an important means by which publishers keep a given character alive. Over the decades, for example, the details of Superman's youth—cultural touchstones such as the model of the car the Kents were driving when they found Kal-El's rocket, the fashions worn by young Clark's schoolmates, the music he listened to as he contemplated his future—have been steadily updated with each retelling.

This first major retelling of the Super-origin, however, had little to do with temporal fixes and had everything to do with taking the character in a new direction. Bill Finger, the co-creator and writer of Batman, was by now a regular Superman writer, and Wayne Boring, who'd been drawing the comic strip and comics for years and subtly altering the character's look, handled the art. When they were done, Superman would never feel—or look—the same. Years later, in the era of personal computers, the act of redefining a character by wiping the slate and starting from scratch would come to be called a "reboot," after the act of shutting down an electronic device and powering it up again. No comic book character has been rebooted more often than the Man of Steel.

The drastic change in mood is evident on the story's splash page. We see the now-familiar rocket (colored, for the first time, an iconic red and blue) speeding away from Krypton as it destructs—but there is something different. We see an image of Jor-El and Lara framed inside the exploding planet, like a photo encased in some kind of cataclysmic cameo locket. They are beaming as they watch their son fly to safety; Lara raises a delicate hand in farewell.

Meanwhile, in the foreground, we see a Superman we have never seen before—one we never could have guessed existed. He sits slumped forward, head in his hands, wracked with sorrow. His eyes are downcast, soulful, brimming with tears, as he remembers the home and the family lost to him forever. (Boring was indulging in a bit of artistic license there, because although the readers knew of his extraterrestrial origins, the comic-book Superman had yet to learn of these himself—that would take another year.)

The first page of the retelling takes the now-familiar form of a litany of super-deeds: flight and strength ("The whole world knows of Superman's titanic strength!" reads the caption, as the Man of Steel flies a city bus to safety), invulnerability, and X-ray vision. He defeats a giant robot of Luthor's, and in an homage to *Action Comics* #8, he is seen flying a tenement building into the air ("I'll rebuild this area so people don't have to live in slums!"). Tellingly, however, instead of depicting this act as Siegel and Shuster had—as a willful act engendered by Superman's social reformist zeal and one that would mark him as an outlaw—the caption couches it quite differently: "He has used his wonderful powers to aid worthy causes!"

The era of the super-citizen had arrived.

New Origin for a New Era

The pages that follow hit the usual beats—Krypton, orphanage, discovery of superpowers, pledge to fight evil. Yet Finger devotes half the story to exploring Krypton more fully than ever before—presaging the increased role Superman's doomed homeworld would assume in the years ahead.

Boring's Krypton is a world of towering minarets and distant, mysterious midcentury-modern obelisks. Flying walkways describe wide curves as they snake between, and through, buildings. Kryptonians dress in regulation Flash Gordon drag: the men wear brightly colored, short-sleeved tunics with chest insignias and foam shoulder hoops with their tights and boots; the women wear futuristic prom dresses. Headbands and capes are worn by some, but not all, and thus may signify class, professional achievement, political status—or simply a fondness for accessorizing.

After Finger sets up Kryptonians' advanced mental gifts, he shows two scientists calculating that a Kryptonian who found himself on the distant planet Earth "could almost defy its weak gravity entirely!"

We are then inside "the Hall of Wisdom" where "the Council of Five awaited the arrival of Jor-El, Krypton's greatest scientist."

Suddenly, Jor-El stands before them in a green tunic, his yellow cape flapping theatrically behind him. His chest emblem is a red planet inside a yellow circle. Boring draws Jor-El exactly as he draws Superman—stout, barrel-chested, sober of mien—and supplies a yellow backlight around his head so that his literally fateful words seem to split the darkness of the council room: "Gentlemen . . . Krypton is doomed!"

Jor-El explains to the incredulous council that Krypton's core is composed of uranium, "which has been setting up a cycle of chain-impulses, building in power every moment! Soon . . . very soon . . . every atom of Krypton will explode in one, final terrible blast! Gentlemen . . . Krypton is one gigantic atomic bomb!"

This is one of Bill Finger's tweaks to the tale—a new explanation for Krypton's destruction, perfectly suited to the Atomic Age.

Jor-El is laughed out of the council, but even as he heads home to break the news to his wife, Krypton enters its death throes. Once again, Lara refuses to join Kal-El in the experimental rocket ship; once again, the infant is sent off into space moments before "nature's fury gathered for one final cataclysmic eruption . . . the once mighty planet Krypton exploded into stardust!"

The rocket lands in a field on Earth, where it's found by the Kents (no first names are given) as they pass by in their jalopy (Boring draws them as a clearly elderly couple straight from central casting). As they take the child to their car, the rocket ship bursts into flames, leaving no trace. They take him to a "home for foundlings," expressing their interest in adopting him. At the orphanage, the requisite super-tot shenanigans ensue ("Doctor, come quickly! It's that *baby* again!"), and adoption papers are hurriedly processed. "At last," says Ma Kent. "We've a son of our very own!"

During the course of the next page, young Clark grows into a teenager as various powers manifest. (No mention is made of the Superboy identity. It's certainly true that the Boy of Steel's light-hearted adventures would clash with Finger's somber tone, but it nonetheless stands as a glaring oversight that would not be tolerated had it occurred even a year later, once editor Whitney Ellsworth and assistant editor Mort Weisinger started to devote themselves to cor-ralling the burgeoning Super-industry and creating a more consistent universe.) A runaway tractor collides with him—and gets destroyed in the process. He runs home late for supper to discover he can outrace the express train. He attempts to hurdle a fence, only to find himself sailing over the house as well. In addition, he discovers his X-ray vision when his mother loses her spectacles behind a cabinet.

The story's tenth and final page is devoted to the death of his fos-ter father (Ma Kent passes away off-panel). Clark kneels at his father's deathbed, and Pa delivers a speech that future writers of the charac-ter will return to often:

> No man on Earth has the amazing powers you have. You can use them to become a powerful force for good! There are evil men in this world . . . criminals and outlaws who prey on decent folk! You must fight them . . . in cooperation with the law! To fight those criminals best, you must hide your true identity! They must never know that Clark Kent is a . . . super-man. Remember, because that's what you are! A *Superman*!

In Finger's telling, Superman's motivation is to live out his father's dying wish. The kernel of Siegel and Shuster's "fighter for the oppressed" remains, but Clark's decision to dedicate his life to good now comes weighted down with more patrilineal emotional baggage than Siegel and Shuster ever brought to the table. The specters of his parents, both biological and adopted, will take on a greater importance during the fifties and sixties, giving the sto-ries greater psychological depth—even as they chase from public memory any trace of Siegel and Shuster's rakish, Robin Hood inter-pretation of the Man of Steel.

In the story's next-to-last panel, Clark makes a nighttime visit to his foster parents' graves and muses aloud about his career prospects.

"A job as a reporter on a big newspaper will keep me in touch with those who may need my help! I'll wear glasses, pretend to be timid."

In the final panel, Boring's Superman stands revealed, hands on hips, feet wide apart, cape fluttering in the wind; "but when I'm needed I'll wear this costume, and the world will know of . . . *Superman*!"

The Boring Superman

Now that Shuster was gone, Boring could make Superman more completely his own. So just as Finger had fleshed out the origin story, Wayne Boring set to fleshing out the Man of Steel's physique.

He'd always thought Shuster—and the artists under him—drew Superman too short and compact, like Shuster himself. Superman, Boring thought, shouldn't be average height. No, a Man of Steel needs a more commanding presence. Boring made Superman tower over all of the other characters and kept him broad at the shoulders. At his best, Boring's less cartoony, more photorealistic Superman conveys stolidity and honest American good sense. He can, however, seem posed, stiff, diffident, because although a Wayne Boring panel is artfully composed, it lacks the immediacy and roughness, the sense of dynamism and danger, of Shuster's work.

Shuster and his ghosts depicted Superman in flight, for example, as a hurdler lunging at the top of his leap. Boring's Superman doesn't have to try so hard. Often, he seems to be out for a light jog through the air on an invisible floating sidewalk.

Kryptonite Comes to Comics

Boring would become the signature Superman artist for the next decade, but several other artists made their mark on the Man of Steel. Al Plastino was one of the most prolific and influential.

His square-jawed, clean-cut Superman looked a lot like the G.I.s who had returned home to start families, don gray flannel suits, and like Ike. Gone were Shuster's laughing eyes, replaced by a pair of piercing blues capable of conveying concern for us, his charges. Plastino's Superman looked slightly older than that of Shuster or Boring—he was America's Dad, albeit one who opted for boots and a cape over slippers and a pipe.

In the November/December 1949 issue of *Superman* (#16), Plastino drew a Superman story written by Bill Finger that would cast a long shadow over the history of the character and pave the way for the many changes to come.

The story's splash page is remarkably similar to Boring's retelling of Superman's origin a year earlier: Krypton explodes in a green inferno, and a superimposed image of Superman reacts with a look of shock and dismay. The introductory blurb makes it clear that this story is different, though: "Everyone now knows that Superman came from another planet, Krypton, that exploded shortly after Superman's birth there! Yes, *we* have known that, but, naturally, Superman has not! But now, in this sensational story of a baffling crime, the Man of Tomorrow unwittingly tracks down his past! Yes, it finally happens, when . . . Superman returns to Krypton!"

Two years earlier, the September/October 1947 issue of Superman (#48) marked the first instance when Superman traveled back in time by flying faster than the speed of light. In this issue, he pulls the same trick to trace the history of a mysterious meteorite that saps his strength. He finds its source, "a planet far outside Earth's solar system!" and lands on it. (An editor's note explains that the temporally displaced Superman is invisible to the planet's inhabitants "because he is not of their time and doesn't exist for them. He can only view them as he would a silent film, but he can read lips.")

He is surprised to see a man who looks exactly like him and follows the man home. He watches this green-tunicked scientist and his wife place their infant son in a rocket and send it into outer space, and the planet explodes. "The death of a world!" thinks Superman, his super-brain oddly slow on the uptake. "I wonder if this infant will survive? I've got to know!"

Still a ghost, Superman follows the rocket ship to Earth and sees his young self getting rescued by the Kents. Finally, the penny drops. "Now I understand why I'm different from Earthmen! I'm not really from Earth at all—I'm from another planet—the planet Jor-El called Krypton!!"

Once he's disposed of the kryptonite meteor at the bottom of the Metropolis river, Superman looks heavenward. "Somewhere out in trackless space there must be more particles of kryptonite!

I hope none falls to Earth again! Perhaps it may never happen . . . but perhaps it may . . . "

Yeah, you think?

Operation: Intolerance

If Superman was getting steadily nudged aside on the country's newsstands, he could take comfort in the fact that in living rooms from coast to coast, he was a bigger hit than ever—and was about to get even bigger. In the months after the war ended, more than two hundred radio stations in the Mutual network carried *The Adventures of Superman*; more than four hundred million listeners were tuning in.

During the war years, kids had thrilled to Superman facing off against countless Axis spies and saboteurs, as well as a host of nemeses who never made the crossover to the comics or the newspaper strips, such as the Vulture, Baron Kronk, Der Teufel, the Scarlet Widow, the Scorpion, and Atom Man.

Now that the war was over, producers of the radio show began to look around for a new scourge for Superman to fight. A change was in the air.

Sharp eared listeners likely picked up on the nature of that change on February 5, 1946, the first time the show's introduction included a small but significant revision. There was the usual "Faster than a speeding bullet" litany and then:

Narrator: Yes, it's Superman! Strange visitor from another planet who came to Earth with powers and abilities far beyond those of mortal men.

So far, nothing out of the ordinary, but then came the twist.

Narrator: Superman! Defender of law and order, champion of equal rights, valiant courageous fighter against the forces of hate and prejudice!

According to some reports, it was Kellogg's advertising agency, Kenyon and Eckhardt—perhaps sensing the growing disquiet among parents' groups complaining about Superman's tendency to solve problems with his fists—that had proposed altering the show so that Superman taught lessons about the dangers of racism and the importance of tolerance. "We're not in the business of education. We're selling corn flakes," advertising VP William B. Lewis said. "But we'd like to do both. We sure would like to do both."

Superman, Inc.'s Robert Maxwell remembered it quite differently, and in press interviews he gave in the wake of the success enjoyed by the show's new direction, including an April 29, 1946, issue of *Newsweek*, he made a point to mention that he had to convince both Kellogg and the Mutual network to let Superman tackle social ills.

Producers reached out to experts on child welfare and education, as well as to religious organizations, to help them craft messages children would understand and respond to. They also launched a publicity campaign to raise awareness among newspaper editorial boards of their high-minded purpose, earning them laudatory editorials in trade publications (which dubbed the effort "Operation Intolerance"), as well as favorable advance coverage in the *New York Times*.

On April 16, 1946, the first arc of the new initiative—"The Hate Mongers Organization"—premiered. (To signal the new direction, the show included music for the first time, though it would take a handful of episodes before that music would take the form of the Fleischer shorts' familiar "Superman March.")

In the story, which ran for five full weeks, an interfaith youth center is threatened with violence by a gang of juvenile delinquents that calls itself the Guardians of America. Jimmy Olsen goes undercover and exposes the gang, learning that it is secretly led by a former Nazi.

Buoyed by praise from social organizations and the mainstream press, ratings climbed steadily; by the time this first story concluded, *The Adventures of Superman* was again the top-rated children's show in the United States.

Yet although the Hate Mongers' story hedged its bets by revealing the villain of the piece to be a Nazi, a subsequent storyline took aim at the Ku Klux Klan. Technically, the racist organization Superman faces in the story is called the Clan of the Fiery Cross, but the descriptions of robes, hoods, flaming crosses, and midnight meetings are unmistakable.

The first episode of the sixteen-part story aired on June 10, 1946. Producers made the hero of the story a Chinese-American boy who is targeted by the Grand Scorpion of the Clan of the Fiery Cross. In a clever twist, the listener ultimately learns that the true purpose of the Clan is to recruit gullible new members who will fork over good dough to pay for robes and hoods—that is, to make money from "jerks who go for that 100 percent American rot. . . . We deal in one of the oldest commodities on earth—hate."

Newsweek praised the story, declaring "Superman is the first children's program to develop a social consciousness." A *New Republic* piece asserted that the Superman broadcasts included KKK code words that had been passed to the producers from author and activist Stetson Kennedy, who had infiltrated the organization. "As a result, Samuel Green, Grand Dragon of the KKK, had to spend part of his afternoon with his ear pressed against the radio. As soon as Superman used a KKK password, Green had to send out urgent orders for a new one." Although there is evidence that Kennedy passed along details of Klan meetings, nothing that seems likely to have been a codeword was broadcast in the actual episodes.

The praise continued to pour in—a Citation of Merit from the VFW, an Official Commendation from the American Veterans Committee, the Award of Distinguished Merit from the National Conference of Christians and Jews, salutatory notices from the Boy Scouts, and so on.

In subsequent radio stories, Superman repeatedly faces down Big George Latimer, Metropolis's crooked political boss, an anti-Semite who refuses to hire veterans. He tackles a white-supremacist secret society known as the Knights of the White Carnation. Bud Collyer went on the lecture circuit, giving speeches about tolerance to public school audiences.

In time, however, ratings cooled. In 1949, the decision was made to move from a daily fifteen-minute format to self-contained half-hour episodes that aired only three days a week.

Sixty of these half-hour episodes aired but did nothing to invigorate ratings. Another change in format was decreed—and a new Saturday evening time slot to go with it. A press release announcing the drastic change in tone read, "*Superman*, originally slanted at young listeners, will emerge as a mystery and crime-detection show aimed at adults when it bows on ABE October 29, 8:30–9:00 p.m."

The emphasis shifted away from Superman and onto the Clark Kent persona; the Man of Steel tended to show up to save Lois and Jimmy from a horrible fate at what was always pretty close to the literal last minute. *Variety* complained that "there is nothing particularly 'adult'" about the new incarnation and expressed doubt that the "shift to sherlocking" would be enough to find a mature audience.

It wasn't; ratings sank, and after thirteen weeks the adult-targeted *Adventures of Superman* was not renewed.

The Man of Steel would mount one final return to the radio airwaves—in his old, thrice-weekly, kid-friendly afternoon time slot—on June 5, 1950, but the fight had left him. Budget cuts forced the show to let go of its three highest-paid actors and to hire a new announcer, a new Jimmy Olsen, and, in a move that signaled to anyone paying attention that the end was near, a new Superman, in the form of Michael Fitzmaurice. After an additional sixty episodes, all of which consisted of the new cast reading previously broadcast scripts, the last episode of *The Adventures of Superman* radio show aired on March 1, 1951.

Yet Robert Maxwell didn't mind. For one thing, Superman had enjoyed a longer run on radio—eleven years—than most of his compatriots. The Atomic Age was dawning. Radio was the past.

Television, he decided, was the future. What better place for a Man of Tomorrow?

From Cereal to Serial

Back in 1940, a deal with Republic Pictures to get a live-action Superman into the nation's movie houses had fallen through, but Robert Maxwell kept trying. Finally, in 1947, a deal was struck with Columbia Pictures for a fifteen-chapter movie serial titled, simply, *Superman*. Even if the comics weren't selling as much as they had during the war, the toys were going like gangbusters, the Fleischer/Famous shorts had been runaway hits, and the radio show was then at the height of its popularity. Superman's exploits seemed, to the Columbia execs, preternaturally suited to the action serial format. Production took barely two months, a remarkably short period of time to produce four hours of film. By the time it was released in February 1948, it would cost more than $350,000—the most expensive serial yet produced.

Not that you could see it on the screen.

The first twenty-minute chapter, "Superman Comes to Earth," is notable for the deadly gravity with which it imparts Superman's origin, borrowing heavily from George Lowther's 1942 novelization. The scenes of Krypton have an agreeably hokey air to them; when Jor-El swans into the conference chamber of the Ruling Council in a flowing toga to deliver the news that Krypton is doomed, the members of the council—most of whom sport pencil-thin mustaches that make them look as if they got lost on their way to a gangster movie being shot on the next lot—laugh cruelly. Stock photography of volcanoes is spliced into scenes of Jor-El and Lara lurching across the room as if tossed by an earthquake. The destruction of Krypton and the flight of baby Kal-El to Earth are both depicted using animation.

Once on Earth, the rest of Clark's origin story is hilariously condensed. To save time, the Kents (named Sarah and Eben here, as in Lowther's novel) simply take the child in themselves, without going through an orphanage. As young Clark ages, he is shown in a rapid succession of scenes pulling a tractor, finding his mother's watch in a haystack using his X-ray vision, and saving his father's life during a tornado.

When the time comes for the Kents to send their adopted son out of the nest, they do so in a scene stuffed to the gills with exposition. Eben Kent delivers a speech to Clark, who's wearing glasses for no readily discernible reason:

> Pa Kent: You came to us out of the sky, from what distant place we can't even imagine. You're different from other people. Your unique abilities make you a kind of . . . superman. Because of these great powers—your speed and strength—your X-ray vision and super-sensitive hearing—you have a great responsibility.

Years later, Stan Lee would distill this sentiment, which lies at the heart of the superheroic ideal, into the considerably pithier "With great power comes great responsibility."

> Clark: I know what you're going to say, Dad. I must use my powers wisely.

For a guy who's just learned he's an alien living among inferior beings, Clark is one cool cucumber.

Ma Kent tells him, "Here's a uniform I made for you out of the blankets you were wrapped in when we found you. It's a strange kind of cloth that resists both fire and acid. I hope it will protect you always."

This isn't the first mention of Ma Kent making the super-suit—that was back in Lowther's original novel, when she made young Clark a costume for a costume party—but it is the first time it's made clear that she made it out of his indestructible Kryptonian swaddling clothes. (The image of frail old Sarah Kent, with her cameo brooch and her gray hair in a bun, running a battery of tests involving fire and acid is a fun one.)

As Superman, Kirk Alyn looks the part. He was a former Broadway chorus boy who'd worked his way up to become a Columbia day player, and his athletic form required little in the way of muscle padding. (If he doesn't quite live up to the illustration on the serial's movie poster—Superman as a downright steroidal mountain of muscle—few men of the day could.) For a man with an extensive dance background, however, he moves stiffly; when the script requires him to run, he does so with ungainly, loping strides that make the Man of Steel seem gangly. Chalk some of that up to the constricting costume—a heavy wool track suit colored brown and gray to suggest Superman's bold colors on black-and-white film—and the need to evoke the Superman of the comics: chest out, shoulders back at all times, whether in or out of repose.

Unlike radio's Bud Collyer, Alyn's Clark and Superman don't seem like two distinct characters. In attempting to emulate Collyer's vocal drop when switching identities, Alyn only succeeds in making it seem as if Clark is trying to disguise his voice, not revert to his true one. Yet when it comes to portraying wholesome sincerity in a deadly serious manner, Alyn nails it.

Like Krypton's explosion and the rocket's journey to Earth, Superman's flights are animated (test footage of Alyn suspended from wires was deemed unconvincing, and the idea was scrapped). The live-action-to-cartoon transitions are handled smoothly, and the quality of the animation is remarkably high; the result is an effect that isn't remotely realistic—but is believable nonetheless. It's easy to imagine a movie theater full of kids cheering the first time "Superman" takes to the air.

Noel Neill plays Lois Lane in a manner that's meant to suggest the sardonic wit of *His Girl Friday*, but that comes off onscreen as mere grouchiness. Onetime child actor Tommy Bond (he'd played Butch in the old *Our Gang* shorts) brings the requisite gee-willikers guilelessness to his Jimmy Olsen.

The serials were heavily promoted via ads in the comics and on the radio show—DC was uniquely positioned to hype Superman's live-action cinematic debut to exactly the target market most eager to see it.

When the first chapter debuted in theaters in February 1948, Columbia knew that it had a hit on its hands. Eventually, the combined grosses for all fifteen chapters of *Superman* would net more than $1 million, making it the most successful movie serial up to that time. Plans for a sequel—with a budget big enough for flying effects—were set into motion.

Meanwhile, Back in the Comics

If Superman was king of the silver screen, that fact did nothing to reverse a worrisome trend on newsstand shelves. Sales of Superman comics were still falling, even as sales of horror, crime, war, and Western comics continued to thrive. The Man of Steel's creators made halfhearted attempts to glom onto this new publishing vogue. The cover of July 1949's *Action Comics* shows Superman in a cowboy hat performing rope tricks for a small crowd of onlookers at a dude ranch ("Yee-ha! New thrills in the Old West when Superman becomes a Super-Cowboy!"). Clearly, the Man of Steel was looking over his shoulder.

Yet he was looking in the wrong direction. A real threat was stirring, far greater and more serious than mere market competition, a threat that would not only deal a serious blow to comic books as a medium, but sully Superman's name and come very close to turning the entire country against him.

This new, real-world foe was still biding his time, consolidating his power, gathering acolytes. In March 1948, he presented a talk at the Association for the Advancement of Psychotherapy called

"The Psychopathology of Comic Books." That same month, a *New York Times* article took his crusade against comic books to a national readership. He pleaded his case again in the May 29 issue of the *Saturday Review of Literature.* The eager audience his words found was large and growing: across the country, communities, parents' groups, and religious organizations were passing measures to ban or restrict the sale of comic books, and they saw in this man an articulate and impassioned leader.

His name was Dr. Fredric Wertham, and he was about to make Lex Luthor look like Shirley Temple.

5

POWERS AND ABILITIES FAR BEYOND THOSE OF MORTAL MEN (1950–1959)

Milestones

1950: *Atom Man vs. Superman* live-action movie serial debuts

1951: *Superman and the Mole Men*

1953: *The Adventures of Superman* television show premieres

1953: Superduperman parody in *Mad* magazine, by Kurtzman and Wood

1954: *Superman's Pal, Jimmy Olsen,* debuts; Kovacs's *Superclod* sketches

1957: Superman (George Reeves) guest stars on *I Love Lucy; The Adventures of Superpup* TV pilot produced

1958: First issue of *Superman's Girlfriend, Lois Lane,* released

First appearance of Krypto the Superdog; Supergirl; the Bottle City of Kandor; Bizarro; Brainiac; Beppo the Super-Monkey; Lana Lang; Lori Lemaris; Legion of Super-Heroes; Legion of Super-Pets; Jimmy Olsen's Superman signal watch, red kryptonite

By 1950, the Man of Steel was featured in no fewer than five different titles—his adult self in *Action, Superman,* and *World's Finest,* while "Untold Tales" of the Boy of Steel graced the pages of *Adventure* and

Superboy. (It was during this period, in fact, that readers first learned that Kal-El had been dogged by a nosy, pestering love interest even as a youth, in the form of a pretty young miss named Lana Lang.) Yet the combined sales of those five books paled next to the readership *Action* and *Superman* alone had enjoyed, back during wartime.

The absurdist flights of fancy of the postwar years now gave way to more prosaic storytelling. More and more, the Superman of the comics and the newspaper strip turns his attention to matters domestic, even quaint: fending off the amorous attention of Lois Lane, devising elaborate ruses to preserve his secret identity, and—almost as an afterthought—fighting crime.

Luthor puts in his occasional appearances, but the criminals with whom Superman now concerns himself—even as he grows steadily faster, stronger, and more powerful with each issue—are generally on the order of jewel thieves, bank robbers, and con men. As narrative impulses go, it was a return to the dynamic of the early days of the Siegel and Shuster era, when the mere fact that Superman so completely overmatched his adversaries was considered a sufficient story engine.

One notable exception was the July 1950 story "The Three Supermen from Krypton!" in *Superman* #65, in which writer William Woolfolk introduces, for the first time, the notion that others similar to Superman survived the destruction of Krypton. It is a concept that will go on to fuel countless tales in the fifties and sixties and will forever alter the Superman mythos.

A spaceship lands in Metropolis, bearing three brothers in Kryptonian garb—down to the matching shoulder hoops and headbands. On Krypton, brothers Kizo, Mala, and U-Ban were evil members of the Ruling Council who were placed in suspended animation and launched into space after they attempted to seize control of the government. Superman battles them to no avail, until he outsmarts them by using his super-ventriloquism to trick them into fighting one another until they exhaust themselves. He places them into suspended animation and launches them back into the inky blackness of space.

By contrasting Superman's altruistic, levelheaded use of his powers against the Evil Three's heedlessly destructive lust for world domination, the story underscores something fundamental about the Superman of the 1950s: his resolve to use his tremendous abilities to defend the status quo. He may have started life as a New Deal Democrat, but in twelve years of life, that reformist zeal had cooled to a normative breed of Eisenhower Republicanism, a pallid rage for order.

As comics writer and historian Mark Waid points out, this was the time when he first got slapped with the "big blue Boy Scout" epithet—by a society that meant it as a compliment. In panel after panel, there was something reassuring about Plastino and Boring's blandly handsome Superman; he was what a nation of American men wanted to see themselves as—a coolly paternal presence who always knew best.

Superman Stays Stateside—Again

One of the things Superman knew best was how to stay the hell out of Korea. During World War II, he had helped the nation localize its anxieties by reflecting America's view of itself as the Good Guy who must always triumph over Ultimate Evil.

Yet the police action that began in Korea during the summer of 1950 didn't lend itself to such a Manichean mind-set. Although Superman's presence had offered coded reassurance to the nation during World War II, now the symbolic connection between Superman and the American fighting man had grown feathery and abstract. The young kids who were once again Superman's primary audience had only the faintest grasp of the nature of the conflict, and older kids no longer needed to look to costumed crusaders to be their bloodless proxies. Now they now had reams of hard-bitten war comics, such as Harvey Kurtzman's *Front Line Combat*, that tackled the conflict head-on.

So Superman never stormed Pyongyang. Instead, he contented himself with teaching Lois another lesson about being nosy and rescuing Jimmy from his latest passel of kidnappers—still, again, some more. The Korean War erupted in earnest, and Superman paid it no heed.

Television: The Serial Killer

The *Superman* newspaper strip carried on, albeit in fewer cities than before, and the radio serial was entering its death throes. Columbia produced a sequel to the wildly successful 1949 Kirk Alyn movie serial called *Atom Man vs. Superman*, based, as was the original serial, on a story arc of the radio show.

The plot involves a sinister scheme of the Atom Man (who is in reality Luthor wearing a glittery oversize papier-mâché head—the effect is that of a sinister team mascot). Once Luthor gathers the materials necessary to make synthetic kryptonite, he consigns the Man of Steel to a ghostlike existence (accomplished by double-exposing the film so that Alyn seems to pass through solid objects). This netherworld, called "The Empty Doom," is the direct precursor to what will be one of the strangest additions to the Super-mythos when it is introduced into the comics more than a decade later: the Phantom Zone.

Atom Man vs. Superman is a different, more idiosyncratic beast than its predecessor. Producers improved somewhat on the first serial's flying effects via basic camera tricks, though extended flight scenes were still rendered with animation. Lyle Talbot spices his Luthor/Atom Man performance with a plummy, vaguely Transylvanian accent, and Noel Neill's Lois is notably less tetchy this time out. Yet the plotting is looser, the cliff-hangers less suspenseful, and the pacing suffers as a result.

Atom Man vs. Superman received a cooler box office reception than its predecessor. Movie serials, similar to radio serials, were increasingly seen as products of another, less enlightened age. Television, on the other hand, promised the excitement of the movies in the comfort of your living room.

Superman and the Mole Men

Superman, Inc.'s Robert Maxwell established a Hollywood beachhead to take the Man of Steel to the small screen. He resolved not to use a production company but to oversee the creation of a sixty-minute black-and-white Superman television pilot himself. If the pilot was successful, DC would have a series on the air over which it would exert complete editorial control.

Maxwell began assigning scripts to the writing staff of the radio show, confident that the TV version of *The Adventures of Superman* would fly. He also reached out to Superman editor Whitney Ellsworth, who came on board as a cowriter and a story editor. This would ensure that the comics and the television show worked in concert.

Yet such autonomy came at a literal cost. Without a production company to invest in the project, the budget would have to be shoe-string tight. Compared to sumptuously filmed television fare such as *The Lone Ranger* and *The Cisco Kid*, *The Adventures of Superman* would have to be made on the cheap—about $15,000 per episode—and at a lightning pace (five episodes every two weeks).

After a long casting search that involved musclemen of various stripes, George Reeves was hired. At the time, Reeves was a beefy thirty-seven-year-old actor who had been plugging away in Hollywood with modest success for years, waiting for his big break. That it came with a pair of thick wool long johns outfitted with twenty pounds of rubber muscles left Reeves deeply conflicted. After a long day of preproduction spent having his prematurely gray temples dyed black and getting fitted for a foam chest plate that chafed his skin, he took his newly hired Lois Lane—costar Phyllis Coates—out for drinks. He offered a toast: "Well, babe, this is it: the bottom of the barrel."

The script that would become the pilot was titled "Nightmare" and involved the remote town of Silsby, "Home of the World's Deepest Oil Well." When horrific looking mole creatures crawl up out of the well, the town panics; only Superman's intervention prevents an angry mob from murdering the creatures in cold blood. The mole people return to their realm beneath the Earth's crust, destroying the oil well behind them to ensure that the two societies go about their business without contact. Tolerance prevails.

Yet by the time "Nightmare" made it to film, the script's terrifying mole creatures had become little-people actors in cheap bald wigs with tufts of fur above the ears that brought to mind Larry, the middle Stooge. When they descended on the town as a group, they looked as threatening as a gang of tiny, vaguely dyspeptic notary publics. Sometime after the first dailies were screened, the pilot's name was discreetly changed to the more matter-of-fact *Superman and the Mole Men*.

The flying effects are largely limited to having Reeves jump on- and off-screen, accompanied by wind noise; this gambit and the accompanying wind noise would become one of the television show's signature elements.

In a scene requiring Superman to outrace an angry mob, the director simply mounted the camera high above the street and dollied past the walking crowd—as if looking down from the Man of Steel's point of view. Another brief scene involving Superman rescuing a falling Mole Man is accomplished with a few brief frames of animation far shoddier than would ever have made it into the Alyn serials. Times had changed.

The flying effects on the pilot and the subsequent series were modest but did require Reeves to be suspended from wires—which snapped on several occasions, injuring the star.

Filming of the original sixty-minute pilot wrapped in just eleven days, on Saturday, July 21, 1951. Just two days later, production began on *The Adventures of Superman*, the series.

The remaining twenty-four episodes of the first season were filmed at a breakneck pace. To save time, each member of the main cast of characters was assigned only one signature outfit. This enabled all scenes taking place in the same location—the *Daily Planet* set, for example—to be filmed back-to-back, regardless of which episode they belonged to. It was disconcerting for the actors—John Hamilton, who played Perry White, was known to include script pages in the sheaves of papers on his character's desk, just to keep his lines straight. Yet Reeves was deeply grateful for *Daily Planet* scenes—it meant he didn't have to suffer and sweat in what he and the crew had already taken to calling "the monkey suit."

It shows in his performance: Reeves's Clark Kent is no milksop. Where the Superman of the comics, the newspaper strips, and the radio enjoyed play-acting the meek, mild-mannered—even occasionally cowardly—reporter, Reeves will have none of it. His Clark is a masculine, quick-tempered, no-nonsense guy—an all-around good Joe. It's Lois Lane who (loudly, forcefully, repeatedly) imputes a cowardly motive to the fact that Kent is never around when danger arises, a notion Reeves's Clark finds highly amusing.

Reeves dispenses with his predecessors' vocal and physical distinctions between Kent and Superman, opting to make the Man of Steel a slightly more matter-of-fact version of his Clark. Because, for budgetary reasons, Superman tends to show up in the final act, Reeves gives him the brusque, all-business manner of an emergency room doctor—he attends to the matter at hand and flies off. Whenever a hapless, thickheaded goon fires a gun at him, we see a medium shot of Superman standing there, rolling his eyes as the bullets ricochet off his chest—"Oh, *please*," he seems to be thinking. "This demeans us both."

Our Flag Was Still There

After the pilot, episodes in the first season would feature an opening narration in line with the radio show—the whole "Faster than a speeding bullet" catechism—but they would do away with the radio's tolerance-oriented tagline ("Defender of law and order, champion of equal rights, valiant courageous fighter against the forces of hate and prejudice!") and once again adopt "Truth, Justice, and the American Way."

It's not difficult to guess why. Although the anti–comic book movement had quieted somewhat following Dr. Wertham's opening national salvos in 1948, a new wave of violent crime and horror comics was touching off a second round of hostilities in the culture war. Parents and church groups were holding public comic-book burnings, and Wertham hadn't gone anywhere—he'd merely sequestered himself to work on his magnum opus, biding his time.

Meanwhile, Congress's Kefauver Crime Commission was beginning to sniff around the edges of the comics industry. Now seemed as good a time as any to remind readers of Superman's All-American bona fides. It was as if Maxwell and Ellsworth were holding up Superman's scrapbook for inspection: Remember during the war that issue with the cover of Superman waving the flag? Remember when he sold war bonds? Remember when you couldn't tell where his cape ended and the flag began? Remember that?

Selling Superman

Now that Maxwell had twenty-six episodes completed, work began to find sponsors that could help get *The Adventures of Superman* on the air. Kellogg came on board—but as it had years earlier on the radio show, the company had . . . some notes.

The writers of that first season, unfettered by feedback from anyone besides themselves—and perhaps spurred by the depictions of violence in the crime comics of the day—wished to secure an adult time slot. What they'd produced, as a result, was a remarkably dark, gritty set of Superman adventures, reminiscent of the radio show. To underscore a bad guy's criminality, for example, they'd depict him throwing his gun moll onto a bed and striking her repeatedly. Drive-by shootings were common. Thugs fell to their deaths, screaming in fear. In one episode, Superman leaves a pair of gangsters to starve to death on a remote island.

The makers of children's cereal blanched and asked for reedits. The changes were made—but only on temporary, duplicate negatives, not on the original masters. The versions that survive are the original, quite dark versions—the bowdlerized cuts are lost to history.

The first episode of *The Adventures of Superman* aired on an ABC affiliate in Chicago on Friday, September 19, 1952, at 7:30 p.m. Gradually, other, smaller, stations followed. In February, a Los Angeles station began to air episodes, followed by New York. Jack Larson, who played cub reporter Jimmy Olsen, was living in Manhattan when the show began to air there and soon found himself unable to go to breakfast without getting mobbed by schoolchildren.

The Adventures of Superman was a hit.

Changing of the Guard

When the second season of *The Adventures of Superman* began pre-production, Robert Maxwell was replaced as producer by comics editor Whitney Ellsworth, ushering in an era of kinder, gentler, kid-friendly scripts more closely in line with the increasingly domestic turn the *Superman* comics had taken. Indeed, several *Superman* comics tales were simply recycled as TV episodes; often, a single storyline would weave through the comics, the newspaper strip, and the television show. Ellsworth felt that the show should be a simple translation of the comics—and, given the modest special effects budget he had to work with, that meant the comics should scale back their ambitions as well.

Now that Ellsworth had decamped to Hollywood full time, writer Mort Weisinger stepped up to edit *Superman* comics back in New York. He seemed only too happy to allow the Man of Steel to devote his attention to petty goons. Most stories turned on Superman's efforts to protect his secret identity from Lois—and, beginning in October 1952 (*Superman* #78), from his childhood sweetheart, Lana Lang, who arrives in Metropolis and secures herself a job at the *Daily Planet* by sweet-talking an uncharacteristically credulous Perry White.

In June 1953, filming began on *The Adventures of Superman*'s second season. The scripts were lighter, the budget larger, and the shooting schedule a comparatively leisurely six episodes every three weeks. Because Phyllis Coates had accepted a role in a sitcom during the long break between shooting, the original serial's Noel Neill stepped back into Lois Lane's feathered hat.

Fawcett Fallout

It was during this second season that Superman slowly began to regain something akin to the cultural currency he'd enjoyed during the war. Producers began to send Reeves out on personal appearances in the Superman costume (Reeves detested these events). In magazines and on news programs, child welfare experts debated the merits of the show's positive messaging versus its depictions of criminality and violence, and the legal system handed Superman a victory that raised his profile even further.

DC Comics had first filed suit against Fawcett Publications—alleging that Captain Marvel infringed on Superman's copyright—back in 1941. The case had dragged on for years, only to be finally settled in federal appellate court, presided over by Judge Learned Hand. Fawcett agreed to pay a sum of $400,000 in damages and cancel publication of all Marvel Family titles.

The case drew the attention of two cartoonists at a fledgling humor magazine called *Mad*. In the April/May 1953 issue (#4), Harvey Kurtzman and Wally Wood wrote a blistering eight-page parody in which nebbishy Clark Bent fights crime as the great hero Superduperman, whose chest emblem changes from panel to panel—here the Good Housekeeping Seal of Approval, there a FOR RENT sign, there the EC comics logo. Kurtzman and Wood get in plenty of jabs at some of the character's touch points (the phone booth identity switch goes wrong, "Lois Pain," and so on) before revealing that the villain of the piece—the "Unknown Monster" who has been terrorizing the city—is none other than Captain Marbles. (Young reporter Billy Spafon speaks the magic word "Shazoom!"—Strength! Health! Aptitude! Zeal! Ox, power of! Ox, power of another! Money!") Ultimately, Superduperman wins the day by tricking Captain Marbles (whose chest emblem is a golden dollar sign) into punching himself in the face.

The Superduperman parody helped put *Mad* on the map and set the new magazine's satirical tone—it would go after specific targets in the popular culture. When DC inevitably sued over the parody, *Mad* successfully invoked "fair use," a doctrine that would provide the magazine with the legal cover it required to function for more than three decades.

The Doctor Is In

Dr. Fredric Wertham had begun his campaign against comic books in the late 1940s, writing editorials, speaking before parents' groups and psychology conferences, and providing impassioned expert testimony in hearings before state legislatures and Congress. Yet all of those efforts failed to win the sweeping reforms he'd hoped for. In early 1954, he took his case to the people, with the four-hundred-page screed *Seduction of the Innocent*, in which he placed blame for the nation's juvenile delinquency problem squarely on comic books.

One can quibble with his reasoning here: in preparing the book, Wertham had interviewed "troubled youths" and asked them whether they read comic books. Most of them said yes—in an era when somewhere between 80 and 90 percent of kids read comics, whether or not they spent their afternoons smoking Lucky Strikes behind the boys' gym. The contemporary equivalent would be to survey anyone who'd ever had suicidal thoughts and ask whether they had ever seen an Adam Sandler movie.

Wertham's list of indictments against comics is potent: they promote violent behavior and sexual deviancy (one of the book's most infamous lines, regarding the life of Bruce Wayne and Dick Grayson: "a wish-dream of two homosexuals living together") and harm literacy. He lifted truly gruesome panels and racy dialogue from crime and horror comics to illustrate his points, but—oddly—reserved some of his strongest, most inflammatory language for the few superheroes who were still managing to hang on in a world grown increasingly indifferent to them. Superman was his main target—to Wertham, the Man of Steel was clearly a super-fascist:

Superman (with the big S on his uniform—we should, I suppose, be thankful that it is not an S.S.) [a line that seems engineered to set Superman's Jewish creators' and caretakers' teeth on edge) needs an endless stream of ever-new submen, criminals and "foreign-looking" people not only to justify his existence but even to make it possible. Superman has long been recognized as a symbol of violent race superiority. The television superman, looking like a mixture of an operatic tenor without his armor [Is that a fat crack?] and an amateur athlete out of a health-magazine advertisement, does not only have "superhuman powers," but explicitly belongs to a "super-race."

At last, Wertham's invective reached its desired audience and single-handedly transformed a medium most people had considered merely disposable into something disreputable, even twisted.

Ladies' Home Journal and *Reader's Digest* funneled his rhetoric to millions of readers; church groups started up comic book burnings again in earnest; consumer groups urged parents to complain to their local grocers about the comics they stocked, in a successful bid to convince those grocers that the lousy pennies' worth of profit they made off a comic wasn't worth the headache. There were more congressional hearings, and, in states and communities across America, bills were introduced to curtail the sale of comics.

All of this took place while comics were struggling to compete for attention with television and the relatively new publishing phenomenon of paperbacks. Comics publishers knew what the combination of regulation and shrinking audience spelled and resolved to self-police their wares, rather than let the government step in. They created a Comics Code (technically, they added stricter regulations to a loose set of guidelines they'd instituted a few years earlier).

The new Comics Code was to comics what the Hays Code had been to movies—an attempt to ensure that content was wholesome and above reproach. From now on, Crime Would Under No Circumstances Pay, and Moral Turpitude Would Be Punished.

For publishers of crime and horror comics, this move spelled doom. For DC and *Superman*, it simply extended and solidified the trend toward increasingly kid-oriented stories.

In a way, it was an official acknowledgment of something Ellsworth had decided on taking over the TV show, a truth everyone at DC knew but rarely acknowledged:

From now on, Superman and comics were for little kids.

The Predawn of a Silver Age

The television show enabled Superman comics to weather the newly hostile environment and drove steady readership such that the sales figures stabilized at about 1 million per month.

To capitalize on the success of the television show in general and its breakout character in particular, in 1954 DC launched a new title, *Superman's Pal, Jimmy Olsen*, written by Otto Binder and penciled by Curt Swan, who was making a name for himself with his highly detailed ("tight," in industry parlance) pencil work on a special Superman 3-D comic, as well as on several Superboy stories.

"Cocky, courageous and clever, that's Jimmy Olsen, cub reporter for the *Daily Planet*," reads the intro to the first story in issue #1. "You've seen him on television as Superman's plucky pal. Now join his exciting adventures when he goes in quest of sensational scoops on his own!" This issue introduces three elements that will quickly become a permanent part of the Superman mythos: the *Daily Planet*'s "Flying Newsroom"—an oversize helicopter that ferries reporters to the scene of the action; Jimmy Olsen's penchant for ingenious disguises; and the most famous timepiece in comics, the Superman signal watch. A twist of his wristwatch's winder sends an ultrasonic signal (rendered, always, as "zee—zee—zee—zee") that only Superman's hearing can detect, to alert the Man of Steel that the young reporter is in trouble again.

In the pages of the comics, amid the street-level hijinks that have become Superman's lot, several notable firsts take place. Although they'd appeared in separate stories in the *World's Finest* title for fourteen years, it wasn't until issue #76 of *Superman* (June 1952) that Batman and Superman appear in a story together. Bruce Wayne and Clark Kent embark separately on the same ocean cruise, only to find that due to overcrowding, the two men must share a cabin (why millionaire Bruce Wayne is mixing with the hoi polloi at all, instead of setting off on his own yacht, goes curiously unaddressed). That night, when danger threatens, the two men attempt to switch into their heroic identities in the dark—but at that moment a bright light shines through the porthole, revealing all. The two men solemnly resolve to guard each other's secrets, and that's exactly what they set out to do, beginning with *World's Finest* issue #71 (July 1954), which switched its format to feature team-up stories between the two superheroes—as had often occurred on the radio show.

Over in the March 1955 issue of *Adventure Comics* #210, the Boy of Steel has his first encounter with the breed of super-nostalgia that would come to consume the Super-titles in a few years' time. A superpowerful pooch stages a mass breakout from the Smallville dog-catcher's paddy wagon; the pup is ultimately revealed to be none other than Kal-El's boyhood pet, Krypto.

Return of the Superheroes

Meanwhile, DC editor Julius Schwartz decided that the field of superheroes had gone fallow long enough. He became determined to launch a series of books aimed squarely at the Baby-Booming juvenile market, starring new heroes specifically created for the Atomic Age. To accomplish this daunting task, he created a title called *Showcase* in March 1956, which would serve as a testing ground for new characters, a chance to gauge interest for possible solo titles.

Schwartz cannily encouraged his writers to create new, science fiction–based heroes using the names of old World War II–era heroes over which DC retained the copyright. Thus, a roster of new crime fighters gradually joined Superman's ranks—the Flash, Green Lantern, the Atom, and many more.

Issues 9 and 10 of *Showcase* (August and September 1957) featured a heroine whose only superpowers were courage, quick wits, inquisitiveness—and a perennial need for super-rescue: "Superman's Girl Friend, Lois Lane." In a series of stories, Lois vies for Superman's affections on meeting the adult Lana Lang for the first time (their 1952 "first meeting" was not mentioned); attempts to deduce his secret identity; dreams of being "Mrs. Superman"; attains superpowers by opening a Kryptonian box she should not; and attempts to make Superman jealous by pretending to be married.

Where previous solo stories starring Lois Lane had belonged to the era of postwar whimsy and humor, these new tales hurled themselves onto the romance comics bandwagon. They played up heartache, misunderstandings, and cruel rejections and featured more (choke!)s and (sob!)s than an episode of *Queen for a Day*. They also proved popular enough to earn Lois Lane her own title in April 1958.

Superman (on Television) Goes Dark

By the time Lois earned her 1957 spotlight in *Showcase*, five seasons of *The Adventures of Superman* had aired; what would turn out to be the show's final season was filmed in late September through early November of that year.

In the five years since the show had begun to air in 1952, the number of U.S. houses with televisions had more than doubled; the world had changed. Even so, ratings were down from the previous year's peak, though the show remained one of television's most popular syndicated series. The comfortably formulaic nature of the show meant that producers could slip episodes from earlier seasons into the run and still hold onto viewers—a phenomenon that encouraged DC to package old episodes together for distribution to movie houses across the United States.

With every passing year, Reeves had grown huskier—the foam muscles had been dispensed with, though he now filled out the super-suit in a way altogether different from how he had in the Mole Men days. He'd developed the bread basket of a wrestler and looked more like Wayne Boring's barrel-chested Man of Steel than ever. Now that he was forty-three, the gray at Superman's temples was more difficult to hide.

Reeves's Superman, too, had changed. The evolution he'd undergone mirrored that of his comic book self. In the first season, Superman is a tough-talking scrapper; he brawls with gangsters and is only too eager to toss kidnappers around. Yet the outcry over television violence had turned Reeves's Man of Steel into a passive, reactive hero, content to let his enemies knock themselves out—literally. At most, he'd deliver a quick karate chop capable of KOing the kind of pudgy, arteriosclerotic gangsters who challenged him nowadays.

Reeves had kept up the schedule of personal appearances in costume, despite his considerable misgivings, and made a memorable cameo appearance on an episode of *I Love Lucy* that aired on January

14, 1957. The net effect was potent: to a generation of kids, Reeves had become Superman, and vice versa.

The actor was only too aware of this state of affairs. Despite the considerable free time that *Superman*'s concentrated shooting schedule allowed him, he'd seen other acting gigs dry up. Perhaps, then, his decision to join the Director's Guild of America and direct what would turn out to be the last three episodes of the series can be seen as an acknowledgment on his part that he needed to readjust his Hollywood ambitions.

Once filming on the sixth season wrapped, the actors and the crew waited for sponsors to determine their fate. Most of them expected that there would be a seventh season, but no official word had come down. A draft script for a possible Superman movie, to be called *Superman and the Secret Planet*, had been written. On April 28, 1958, the final episode of *The Adventures of Superman* aired.

More than a year later, on June 16, 1959, Reeves was found dead in his Hollywood home, the victim of a gunshot wound to the head. The coroner ruled it a suicide. "TV's Superman Kills Self," read the *New York Post* headline. In the months and years that followed, a persistent urban myth would arise that Reeves had jumped off a building in his Superman suit. Those who loved and worked with him and who knew just how constricting he found the costume— literally, artistically, and professionally—dutifully spent the next few decades slapping down that myth every chance they got.

In the weeks after shooting what would become the series' final episode, Ellsworth had turned his attention to developing what stands as one of the weirdest footnotes in the annals of Superman's history: a television pilot for a show called *The Adventures of Super Pup.*

He's No Krypto

Ellsworth's idea was to create a show targeted to an audience even younger than that of *Adventures of Superman*. Filmed on the set of the Superman television show—but without dialogue or sound effects (which were dubbed in later), the Super Pup pilot posits a Metropolis (sorry, "Pupopolis") entirely populated by dogs that walk upright.

This effect was—one hesitates to use the word *achieved*—by hiring little people as actors and outfitting them with giant, adorable dog-head masks. The plot, such as it is, involves Bark Bent, a newspaper reporter, who turns into Super Pup when girl reporter Pamela Poodle is kidnapped by the twisted Professor Sheep-dip.

DC had not given Ellsworth and his producers much money to produce the pilot, so Ellsworth beefed up the show's budget out of his own pocket. When he showed it to DC, they immediately took it off his hands—and wasted little time consigning it to the deepest recesses of the DC vaults for perpetuity.

In 1958, Ellsworth's assistant editor Mort Weisinger officially took control of the Superman titles. His ascendancy triggered a wave of sweeping, permanent changes to *Superman* comics. These changes had little to do with Superman himself—he would remain the same barrel-chested big blue Boy Scout drawn by Wayne Boring for years to come. Yet the world around him was about to expand and enrich itself at an unprecedented pace. The Last Son of Krypton would suddenly find himself the harried patriarch of an extended, obstreperous family, all clad in tight long johns. New loves would entice him, new enemies would dedicate themselves to his utter destruction.

And where once there were no monkeys, now there would be monkeys. In abundance.

After long years of narrative lassitude, the Silver Age had come to the Man of Steel.

Traumas, Tricks, and Transformations: The Silver Age of Superman

The end of the TV show meant that the Superman of the comics could unclip his wings. No longer need he scale back his exploits to the kind of prosaic thug-nabbing and kidnapper-foiling that could feasibly take place on a studio back lot. Petty foes who merely annoyed the Man of Steel, such as the Prankster and the Toyman, disappeared. After all, the comics medium came factory-installed with an unlimited special effects budget—anything that could be imagined could be depicted on the page.

What Weisinger and writers such as Otto Binder, Edmond Hamilton, Robert Bernstein, Leo Dorfman, and others were imagining, now that the shackles were off, was a huge science fiction spectacle. The Space Age was just around the corner, and Weisinger helped ensure that Superman was ready for it by infusing his adventures with rocket ships, flying saucers, monsters, aliens, and exotic planetscapes, all in service of the kind of sweeping intergalactic sagas that beggared Hollywood.

No studio makeup department could assay the kind of grotesque physical transformations that begin to bedevil Superman and his inner circle on a monthly basis. Lana Lang receives a ring that enables her to transform various parts of her body into those of any insect or spider (she wastes little time designing a costume and adopting the nom-de-superhero Insect Queen); Lois Lane becomes "The Fattest Girl In Metropolis!" when exposed to a ray that encourages plant growth ("What if Superman, the man I love, saw me now? I must avoid him at all costs!").

It is Superman's pal Jimmy Olsen, however, who undergoes the most extreme metamorphoses. A typical adventure would see young Olsen turning invisible or transformed into a merman or developing a giant bald head to house his "super-evolved" brain or growing a Rip Van Winkle beard overnight or switching bodies with a gorilla or becoming a human skyscraper or gaining the power to stretch himself to fantastic lengths (and promptly assuming a superhero identity by donning a purple leotard with the words "The Elastic Lad" emblazoned on the chest) or growing a lie-detecting Pinocchio nose or turning into a green-scaled alien from Jupiter or breathing fire or growing four extra arms or becoming a genie, a wolf-man, a rampaging giant turtle-man, or a human porcupine.

At the same time, over in the pages of *Adventure*, a new element— literally—was quietly introduced that would go on to fuel countless stories for years to come. In September 1958 (*Adventure* #252), Superboy encounters "red-K," a particularly lethal form of kryptonite. Just three months later, however, in *Adventure* #255, red kryptonite attains the quality that will allow it to become synonymous with Silver Age Superman comics.

When an alien uses the strange element to split Superboy into two beings—an evil Clark Kent and a good Superboy—we learn that red kryptonite was formed when a shower of green kryptonite passed through a "strange radioactive cosmic cloud" on the way to Earth, imbuing it with the power to produce unpredictable (albeit predictably weird) effects on Kryptonians.

In red kryptonite, the Silver Age had been given its trickster god. For the next few decades, exposure to red-K would transform Superman in hugely inconvenient ways for a period of twenty-four to forty-eight hours, and the effect was always different. As plot-complicating story engines go, red-K has it all—it sparks elaborate protect-my-secret-identity shenanigans, and it practically demands that writers tweak the usual story formula to account for the transformation-du-jour. Mostly, though—as detailed in the next chapter—it just looks cool.

To Be Continuity-ed

Although writers such as Hamilton had served up glimpses of Kryptonian life for years, they were only glimpses. A fanciful new character might get introduced in January, but by February he or she was gone, likely for good. At the end of each issue, characters dutifully returned to their original states, like dancers resuming first position, and the status quo continued.

The difference, in the Weisinger age, was that from now on writers weren't to think of Superman's monthly adventures as a series of one-offs but as disparate parts of a greater interconnected whole. Weisinger and his team set out to build a cohesive, ever-expanding universe of recurring characters and places, where the past informed the present and pointed the way to the future—a grand fictive universe that would come to be known, in the growing fan community, as continuity.

Weisinger's tighter hand on the editorial reins meant, for example, that writers of *Superman* or *Action* would no longer be permitted to ignore the existence of Superboy. Yet it also meant that a major new character introduced in one title could—and undoubtedly would—cross over into others.

Weisinger ensured that the influx of new characters, enemies, and places that began in 1958 was a controlled explosion. "I would introduce a new element every six months to keep the enraptured kids who were our audience involved," he said years later. To help keep him on top of just how enraptured those kids were—or weren't—he routinely surveyed his young son and the children living in his neighborhood; he also added the first monthly letters pages to appear in a DC comic, starting with *Superman* in

September 1958 (#124). He used the letters page to respond to readers' questions and actively solicit more—and to hawk the other titles he edited to the expanding generation of Boom kids. In this regard, lifelong science-fiction fan Weisinger took as a guide the long-running traditions of science-fiction pulp magazines.

By instituting both a cohesive narrative continuity and a public forum whereby readers could quibble over mistakes and oversights or entreat creators for the return of a favorite character, Weisinger had created a beast capable of feeding itself. Superman's world would grow steadily larger, and fans would be part of the process of painstakingly mapping its many, increasingly complicated, interconnections.

This was the era that began to offer answers to questions raised in the text—raised, it should be noted, only in the minds of those who took the text *very* seriously. The kids who'd read Superman's adventures in the forties never bothered to consider wonky questions such as where he hid his Clark Kent clothes or why Clark's glasses didn't melt when he used heat vision in his secret identity. Yet now those questions could be answered—either in the letters column (as in issue 127, when Weisinger explains to young Earl Zubkoff of Greenbelt, Maryland, that "Superman conceals his entire Clark Kent outfit in a secret pouch in the lining of his cape. Natch, he uses super-pressure to compact his street duds into a small, compact bundle") or during an adventure (as when, in the January 1959 issue of *Superboy* [#70], we learn that Ma Kent made young Clark's lenses out of the indestructible shards of the windshield of the rocket that sent him to Earth).

The Fortress Goes North

The June 1958 issue of *Action Comics* (#241)—the character's twentieth anniversary issue—is regarded by many as the official birth of Silver Age Superman. Certainly, the story "The Super-Key to Fort Superman" is structured like a classic Silver Age tale, with a central mystery that turns on a seemingly sinister act (Who has broken into the Fortress and learned Superman's secret identity?), only to be revealed as an elaborate ruse conducted for an innocent reason (It's Batman! And he's just playing a prank for Superman's birthday!).

Yet what makes this story so quintessentially Silver is the way its manifold colorful, kid-friendly conceits tap directly into the subconscious hopes and fears of the ten-year-old mind. (The terms "the Golden Age" and "the Silver Age" were coined by readers in the 1960s to distinguish the heyday of classic, World War II–era superheroing [Golden] from the then contemporary era of whimsical science fiction [Silver].)

Superman's Fortress of Solitude had been mentioned in the comics earlier—readers had visited it several times when it was simply a mountain retreat in the hills outside Metropolis; beginning in 1949, he'd begun to refer to it as the Fortress of Solitude, "built . . . in the polar wastes because the intense cold keeps away snoopers." Yet it's not until 1958 that the reader gets the guided tour.

We see Superman flying toward an enormous yellow metal arrow that stands on an Arctic mountaintop. "From above," he thinks, "this looks like a luminous arrow marker to guide planes over this lonely region! No one would suspect it's really a key—a super-key that weighs tons—and that no one else can lift!"

We learn that Superman spends his free time creating extravagant gifts for his friends—a necklace of exquisite pearls he's harvested himself for Lois; a sports car for Jimmy; a crime-solving computer for Batman—and stores them in rooms dedicated to those friends, replete with life-size wax statues of them.

"I've even made a Clark Kent room!" he thinks and follows it up by blurring the thin line that separates precaution from paranoia. "Clark is known to be a friend of Superman, and if some unexpected earthquake ever opened my secret cave to a stranger, that wax Clark would help preserve the secret of my identity!"

The tour continues: a room where he paints Martian landscapes, a laboratory, an interplanetary zoo, a room invitingly marked "Forbidden Weapons of Crimedom," and a giant diary of metal pages, on which he engraves his entries with his fingernails.

Despite its name, the Fortress of Solitude would not stay lonely for long. The very next month, the Kryptonian population explosion began.

There Goes the Neighborhood: The Kryptonian Influx

In the June 1958 issue of *Action* (#242), the Bottle City of Kandor is introduced into the chronicles. The plot closely follows a story arc of the *Superman* newspaper strip that ran from April through August of the same year. Superman encounters an alien named Brainiac (named Romado in the newspaper strip) and his pet, Koko (a white monkey with antennae), who travel the galaxy in a flying saucer, miniaturizing great cities and placing them in oversize bell jars.

Superman is shocked to learn that one of the cities in Brainiac's collection is none other than Kandor (in the strip: Dur-El-Va), which was once the capital of the planet Krypton. After thwarting Brainiac's scheme, Superman rescues the bottle city and gives it a place of honor in his Fortress. "The miniature Krypton city will keep safely here! Perhaps I'll find a way to restore it to normal size . . . and live with my people again . . . someday! Who knows?"

Here was a city full of Kryptonians—a thriving population of potential plot complications for writers to play with. As soon as any one of them left the bottle—as became a regular occurrence within a matter of months—that Kryptonian would become as powerful as Superman. Here, suddenly, was an entire Municipality of Steel.

In one sense, it was inevitable—Superman's powers had by now grown to godlike dimensions. Just one year earlier (*Superman* #110, January 1957), he'd tossed around an entire planet like a medicine ball and used his telescopic vision to find his quarry on a planet millions of light-years away (*Action* #226, March 1957). The days of Siegel and Shuster—when stories could consist of little more than Superman performing some fantastic stunt or showing off his strength—were over. If having a few thousand superpeople on hand could open up plot possibilities—and it could—then uniqueness be hanged.

Kandor swiftly became a major element of Superman stories, both as a source of new foes (several "rogue Kandorian scientists" matched wits with the Man of Steel) or as a setting for adventures (during the 1960s, the bottle city would become a prime vacation destination for both Superman and Jimmy Olsen).

"Great Krypton!"

The genie had left the bottle in an experimental rocket ship; where once years could pass without even a passing reference to Krypton, now, each and every month, the specter of Superman's doomed planet hung over the comics—and with it, the notes of tragedy and mourning grew steadily louder and more plangent. Superman's longing for his lost homeworld would swiftly become the Silver Age's dominant theme.

In August 1958 (*Superman* #123), Jimmy Olsen uses a magic totem to make a series of wishes on behalf of Superman. He starts by wishing "that a *super-girl*, with super-powers equal to Superman's would appear and become his companion!" In the next instant, a girl with short blond hair and a costume based on Superman's (with a short red skirt, instead of trunks) appears and sets about aiding the Man of Steel in his never-ending battle. Soon, however, she sacrifices her life to save Superman's. (The story served as a test balloon; a blond Supergirl [no hyphen] in a skirt would become a member of the growing cast of characters less than a year later.)

Jimmy uses his final wish to transport Superman to Krypton before it exploded to allow the Man of Steel to meet the young man and woman who are destined to become "my future dad and mom [*choke!*]" It will not be their last meeting. A little more than a year later, in *Superman* #132 (October 1959), writer Otto Binder and artist Wayne Boring offer up the most in-depth exploration of Krypton yet, in a three-part story that sees Superman conducting a computer simulation of what his life would have been like if Krypton had never exploded. This story, with its gleefully gee-whiz images of Kryptonian life laced with tragedy ("In this other life, my parents escaped the doom of Krypton exploding . . . only to meet the same end on an exploding asteroid! So in either life I was destined to be an *orphan!*") is the Silver Age polished to a dazzling gleam.

"Me Hate Lois! Hello Forever!"

Meanwhile, in the pages of *Superboy* #68 (November 1958), Binder and artist George Papp had created a character who would come to embody the Silver Age: take a goofy concept (a baby-talking Frankenstein's monster in a Superman outfit), add pathos ("Me want to make friends, but people against me!"), and you get Bizarro.

When a scientist's "duplicator ray" accidentally strikes the Boy of Steel, it creates an imperfect copy of him "made of *nonliving* matter!" with chalk-white, rocklike skin.

> Superboy: Gosh, that creature is *bizarre*!
> Creature: Him call me [*mumble*] *bizarro*! Is . . . is that my *name*?

A series of misadventures follows, in scenes that play to a child's deepest subconscious fears of being misunderstood and lonely ("Wait! Bizarro not harm you! Why you scared of me?" "Me not bad! Why they hate me?" and, not to put too fine a point on it: "She hate me too? . . . My own Mom? . . . She turn me away . . . [*sob*]!").

Less than a year later (July/August 1959, *Action* #254 and #255), Bizarro would return, when Luthor re-creates the Smallville scientist's duplicator ray and tricks Superman into standing before it. By the time this story is through, a quick-thinking Lois Lane has created a Bizarro version of herself, and Bizarro and Bizarro-Lois fly off together.

Adding Melo- to the Drama

There is a formula to Silver Age storytelling.

On a plot level, the mechanics are those of situation comedy, the humor of misdirection and misapprehension. We observe someone acting wildly out of character—seeming suddenly cruel or aloof, for example. Complications arise, feelings are hurt until, on the story's last page, the bizarre behavior is revealed to be a misunderstanding or an elaborate ruse that was perpetrated for the noblest of reasons (read: to save a life) or to teach a lesson (read: stop snooping, *Lois*).

Each issue was a new puzzle to solve—and that simple fact helped drive sales. "Mort wasn't interested in a story if it didn't have a compelling cover scene," Silver Age writer Jim Shooter told comics historian Michael Eury. "To get a story approved, or to sell one, first and foremost, a writer had to pitch a cover idea." Generally, these covers depicted the surprising-development-du-jour in enticing detail, causing eager readers to snap up the issue to learn why Superman was acting like such a complete tool.

Yet beneath all of the gimmicks and whimsy, the heart of any given Silver Age Superman story is big, soft, and wet. The Weisinger era is in touch with its feelings—in fact, it can't seem to stop touching its feelings. Overwrought emotions are the story engines, constantly buffeting hapless characters about—guilt ("If not for my super-abilities, Mother and Dad would be alive today!"), loss ("I stood on the cliff alone, looking for the last time at the only woman I'd ever asked to marry me!"), isolation ("If she saw my *face*, she be scared of me too, like all others! Me can never have *real* friend . . .

[*sob!*]")"), jealousy ("That hussy—kissing Clark in public! Hasn't she any *manners*?"), grief ("Futuro made a *space memorial* in honor of Kal-El's family! [*choke!*]"), and melancholy ("I . . . I wish I were *more* than a close friend . . . a *wife!* [*Sigh*]!")

During this period, when the increasingly moody, introspective Superman's thought balloons grew thick with (choke!)s and (sob!)s and sundry passions *to which he dared not give utterance*, artist Wayne Boring—still the go-to Superman artist, especially for high-profile stories—made subtle tweaks to Superman's face. The melodramatic turn that Silver Age stories had taken meant the Man of Steel needed to emote, so Boring deepened Superman's brow and thickened his eyebrows (the better to smolder with), narrowed his chin, and elongated his features to allow all of those brooding expressions of super-melancholy to land with readers.

This is why, in a story such as "The Girl in Superman's Past," (*Superman* #129, May 1959), in which we learn that while in college, Superman met and fell in star-crossed love with a girl named Lori Lemaris, the Man of Steel moons about, bearing a striking resemblance to Montgomery Clift. (Lori, you see, is a mermaid on a mission from Atlantis and must return to her people. [*Choke*]!)

The soft, salty emotionalism of the Weisinger era is already in full force in the April 1958 issue of *Adventure* (#247), when Superboy meets three teenagers from the future who belong to a club called the Legion of Super-Heroes. When he fails a series of initiation trials, they tease him mercilessly—and not a little misogynistically ("You lost . . . to a *girl!* Is this the great Superboy we learned about in school?" "Ha, ha! Only the backward 20th Century people could think him a super-hero!"), causing the Boy of Steel to nobly choke back tears—only to learn that the trials were fixed, and the true initiation test turned on how well he handled defeat.

Over in the pages of the *Superman's Girl Friend, Lois Lane* comic (which launched in April 1958), the Man of Steel spends more time fending off the man-hungry Lois's matrimonial advances—and schemes to expose his secret identity—than alien threats or giant robots. This called for a Superman who looked more like a conventional romantic lead, the kind of dreamboat readers could see Lois tying herself in knots over.

Artist Kurt Schaffenberger drew his Superman to be just that, using clean, thick lines to lend the Man of Steel's handsome face a forceful, uncomplicated, and confident look reminiscent of Cary Grant.

Yet the Superman of the *Lois Lane* comic is even more commitment-phobic than he is in his other titles and a good deal more cruel, playing constant tricks on her to make her appear foolish before her colleagues at the *Planet* in ways that would ruin a real-life reporter's professional reputation. Each time, he rationalizes his vindictive bad-boyfriend behavior by employing the Silver Age's go-to rubric: "To teach her a lesson!"

Lois, for her part, grows more needy and more demanding, as her schemes to make Superman jealous constantly backfire. To read multiple issues of *Superman's Girl Friend, Lois Lane* is to watch, in horror, as the world's most toxic relationship plays out in excruciating, repetitive detail. George and Martha in blue tights and pillbox hat.

The pseudo-screwball, romantic back-and-forth that Clark and Lois had enjoyed in the postwar era was gone for good, replaced by a simmering disdain. Yet this, too, plays directly to the budding psychosexual emotional landscape of the very young: to boys who think girls whiny, simpering, helpless, and sly; and to girls who regard boys as thoughtless, cruel, insensitive, and dumb.

Daily Planet of the Apes

There is one last ingredient present at the dawning of the Weisinger-era Superman, one last element that gave the Silver Age in singular, burnished gleam: Apes. Monkeys, too.

In just the first two years of Weisinger's editorship, Superman tangled with King Krypton (dubbed "The Super-Gorilla from Krypton!" March 1958, *Action* #238) and Titano the Super-Ape (*Superman* #127, February 1959), who is no ape at all, but a chimp launched into orbit that grows to mammoth size on his return, among other, even more credulity-defying, out-of-nowhere changes ("Heavens! Those green rays from Titano's eyes . . . somehow, he has acquired *Kryptonite vision!*").

There was Koko, of course, Brainiac's space monkey. And in *Superboy* #76 (October 1959), the world learned that the rocket ship that had delivered Superman to Earth harbored a stowaway—one of Jor-El's laboratory animals, Beppo.

Or as he would come to be known: Beppo, the Super-Monkey. Blue shirt, red cape, red diaper.

The Silver Age had arrived.

"Look Again, Superman! It's Me . . . Supergirl! And I'm real!"

Three villains, a dog, an ape, a monkey, and the population of an entire city—Earth was lousy with Kryptonians. In May 1959, in *Action* #252, still another arrived—and this one would go on to effect the biggest changes in *Superman*'s ongoing storyline since the appearance of kryptonite. For the first time, Superman would have a true companion, a confidant—a *family*.

Her name was Kara. She went by Supergirl. And although she arrived in 1959, her story belongs to the next decade.

6

NOT A DREAM! NOT A HOAX!
NOT AN IMAGINARY STORY!
(1960–1969)

Milestones

1961: *Superboy* live-action TV pilot produced, never aired

1962: *Legion of Super-Heroes* comic launched

1966: Broadway musical *It's a Bird! It's a Plane! It's Superman* debuts; *New Adventures of Superman* cartoon debuts

1967: First Superman vs. Flash race around the world in the pages of *Superman;* Kinney National Company buys DC Comics, buys Warner Bros. two years later.

First appearance of the Phantom Zone, Bizarro World, Superman-Red/ Superman-Blue, Nightwing and Flamebird, kryptonite (blue, white, gold, jewel, and so on), the Parasite

"The Superman mythology." When he met a new writer, that's how Mort Weisinger described the burgeoning, interconnected network of characters and gimmicks and history he had set into motion in 1958. By 1960, the controlled burst of narrative innovation was chugging along at a fast clip and gaining speed.

What's more, it was working. Western, war, and romance comics were still popular, but superhero books once again far outpaced them—and though Julius Schwartz's roster of "new" heroes had helped drive this capes-and-cowls resurgence, it was the Man of Steel who sold more comics than any other character. When sales of *Superman* titles overtook those of Disney comics—which had been largely spared the wrath of the Werthams of the world and had languished comfortably on the top of the sales charts for a decade—other publishers took notice and began to churn out their own heroes.

Schwartz's heroes joined together to form a "Justice League of America" in *The Brave and the Bold* #28 (February/March 1960) and got their own title in October of that year. Weisinger fretted that having Superman on the team would overexpose the character, conveniently overlooking the fact that that particular super-horse was already out of the barn. The Man of Steel was appearing regularly in an unprecedented seven titles a month (*Action, Superman, Adventure, Superboy, Lois Lane, Jimmy Olsen, World's Finest*, as well as in special *Superman Annuals*). It's more likely that Weisinger simply didn't want to let another editor (even his close friend Schwartz) play in the Superman sandbox. A compromise was brokered: the Man of Steel's presence in Justice League stories was minimal; he appeared on JLA covers only occasionally.

Writer Otto Binder had a large role in establishing the rapidly expanding Superman mythology's bright, whimsical tone and many of its most gleefully goofy aspects. Years earlier, at Fawcett Comics, Binder had helped create some of the most indelible (and gleefully goofy) aspects of Captain Marvel's universe, from a despotic worm with tiny spectacles named Mr. Mind to a genteel, nattily dressed talking tiger called, unapologetically, Mr. Tawky Tawny. So a Super-Monkey named Beppo? Stories featuring an infant Superman—aka Superbaby ("Me can fly! Me feel strong, too!")? All in a day's work.

Binder left DC in 1960 (Weisinger's reputation as a mean-spirited boss reportedly played a role), but by now the super-infrastructure was in place, and other writers such as Leo Dorfman, Bill Finger, and Ed Hamilton were on hand to extend and enrich it further.

Weisinger called it a mythology, but what it really was, of course, was a family.

Before he left, Binder ensured that Superman's family would be a quite literal one, at least where one character was concerned.

Enter: Supergirl

When Supergirl is introduced to readers in *Action Comics* #252 (May 1959), the story cuts to the chase. A rocket crashes outside Metropolis. Superman arrives to find a chipper blond teenager in a Super-costume greeting him, unharmed amid the wreckage. Flash back to the explosion of Krypton, when "a large chunk of the planet was hurled away intact, with people on it." (Later, this floating chunk of Krypton would earn the name Argo City.) "We may be orphans," Superman says, embracing his young charge, "but we have each other now! I'll take care of you like a big brother, cousin Kara!"

A bossy big brother who doesn't want his sister to cramp his style, anyway. In the very next panel, Superman explains that Supergirl can't come to live with him, because it might jeopardize his secret identity. His weirdly Dickensian solution: Kara will adopt a secret identity of her own and go to live at an orphanage. "Someday the outside world will hear of you as *Supergirl*! But for a long time to come, you'll live here quietly as an 'ordinary' girl until you get used to Earthly things!"

That's the dynamic the two will share during the Silver Age, as Supergirl gets her own backup feature in *Action*—Superman as Father-Knows-Best, Supergirl as his worshipful, dutiful daughter. Before her first adventure is done, a perky Kara has donned a brown, pigtailed wig and the name Linda Lee and set happily about her life at the orphanage. For three years, Superman will keep Supergirl's identity a secret, setting up several issues' worth of hijinks whereby characters find their lives mysteriously aided by a "guardian angel" and in which the rather baroque notion of a secret identity having its own secret identity will fuel many stories.

Lest her young girl readers harbor any doubts that Supergirl stories were aimed squarely at them, she was soon joined by Streaky the Super-Cat (a housecat given superpowers in *Action* #261 [February 1960]) and a Super-Horse named Comet (*Action* #292, October 1962), who is actually a centaur-turned-horse-turned-human, who, in human form, becomes Supergirl's boyfriend.

It was, after all, the Silver Age, when every emotion—even a girl's fondness for horses—could provide a story with its murky Freudian substrata.

Here Comes the Sun

In the same issue that introduced Supergirl (and the villain Metallo, a cyborg powered by a chunk of kryptonite where his heart should be), Kara's mother mentions that her Super-costume "will *become* indestructible *super-cloth*" on Earth" (emphasis added).

This is the first oblique mention of a major revision to Superman's power-set. For thirty-two years, the comics had stuck with Siegel and Shuster's original explanation that Superman's abilities were due to his status as a member of Krypton's "super-race" of beings capable of leaping tall buildings and learning calculus while still in the nursery—and to Earth's lesser gravity. Yet in *Action* #262 (March 1960), the notion of a Kryptonian "super-race" goes away for good— (Had Wertham's accusations of fascism stung?)—and is replaced, for the first time, by another explanation. As Superman explains to Supergirl, their powers now derive *partly* from Earth's lesser gravity and partly from "*ultra solar rays* that penetrate Earth day and night!"

The idea that a yellow sun gives superpowers (and that a red sun takes them away) was a late development in Superman's history, but one that has remained with him ever since—even as many other Weisinger-era innovations have fluttered in and out of continuity. This strange, detailed, pseudo-scientific apportioning of powers— the need to pore over and explain, to take nothing as read—is a major theme of Weisinger-era Superman. On letters pages, a new, more sophisticated readership caviled and nitpicked and debated fine points that readers ten years earlier had never bothered to consider. These readers delighted in the Easter eggs Weisinger and his writers kept throwing into the texts, the most famous—and frequently mentioned—being the recurrence of the initials "L.L." around the Man of Steel (Lois Lane! Lana Lang! Lori Lemaris! Lucy Lane! Lyla Lerrol! Linda Lee! Lex Luthor!). A new desire to categorize and subdivide and classify was emerging among fans, which likely helps explain why, before the sixties were over, kryptonite would come in green, red, blue, white, yellow, gold, silver, jewel, "anti-," "magno," and "plus"—each with a different effect.

Apart from the lethal green variety, it was red kryptonite—which produces an unpredictable, never-repeated effect in the Man of Steel with each exposure—that writers and readers loved best. It could give Superman long hair and a beard or telepathy or the head of a giant ant or turn him into a flying Kryptonian monster or cause him to shoot flames from his mouth. Readers ate it up and demanded more, so weirder, non-kryptonite-related transformations proceeded apace throughout the Superman titles; sooner or later, every Superman cast member developed a super-brain, for example, and an enormous bald head to hold it in.

By far the most bizarre Silver Age development—the one that seized the imaginations of readers and gave writers and artists the greatest opportunity to indulge themselves—grew out of that 1959 *Action Comics* story that had ended with Bizarro Superman and Bizarro Lois flying off into the sunset.

It's Bizarro's World, and We're Just Livin' in It

In *Action* #263 (April 1960), the reader learns that the two creatures have settled on a world in a far-off solar system, which Superman, using a "super-large bulldozer attachment," later turns into a giant cube.

A kid-friendly, "Opposite Day" logic rules Bizarro World (actual name: Thrae), and stories set there exude a goofy charm that's easy to get caught up in. Restaurants serve dessert first! They take baths in dirt!

And all of the residents of Bizarro World—be they Bizarro waiters, Bizarro mailmen, or Bizarro gardeners—live by a code: "Us do *opposite* of all Earthly things! Us *hate* beauty! Us *love* ugliness! Is big *crime* to make anything *perfect* on *Bizarro World*!"

A Bizarro World story is essentially an earnestly presented series of broad, dumb jokes strung together by inverse logic. So it makes sense that many of them were written by a guy with a good deal of experience writing Superman stories, who also knew his way around a good, corny gag.

Jerry Siegel was back.

Back to the Salt Mines

Since he and Shuster had left, Jerry Siegel had been working as an art director for magazine publisher Ziff-Davis but had run into some financial difficulty. Siegel's wife, Joanne, reached out to Weisinger—in some versions of the story she stormed into Weisinger's office and demanded that he hire her husband back—and in 1959 Superman's cocreator once again began writing stories for various Super-titles. He did so, however, at standard pay and without a byline.

If the situation was galling, Siegel could take comfort in the fact that during the years of his return, he wrote some of the most important, signature stories of Silver Age Superman and added to the continuity several elements that still endure.

In April 1960 (*Adventure* #271), Siegel contributed his second major lasting alteration to the Superman myth (the first being his notion of Superboy, years earlier). Such changes would come to be known, years *later*, as "retroactive continuities" or "retcons." In this story, he revealed that before they became archenemies, Superboy and Luthor had grown up together in Smallville.

Not only did this story supply the villain with his first name ("Lex! Lex *Luthor*! Meeting you, Superboy, is about the most thrilling thing to happen to me!"), but it also provided him with a motivation for his seething, lifelong hatred of the Man of Steel. A *deeply weird* motivation, to be sure, but a motivation just the same.

When Superboy uses his super-breath to douse a fire in the teenage Luthor's laboratory—where the redheaded youth has been secretly working on a kryptonite antidote as a surprise for his bosom chum—he is surprised to see Lex emerging from the smoke, shaking a pale fist: "You rat! Your puff of super-breath blew an acid bottle against the antidote bottle! They broke, and their contents *destroyed* the formula for my great discovery! Not only that—the gas fumes made my hair fall out! *I'm bald!*"

There you have it. What caused a brilliant young mind to dedicate itself to cruelty, hate, and world domination? An accidental cranial depilatory. Had the accident occurred today, when shaven heads are little more than a fashion choice, Luthor might still have become a humanitarian.

Of course, the story is careful to show there's a bit more to it—Luthor is convinced that Superboy is "jealous of my genius"—but it's fun to imagine Siegel, who held onto his hair to the very end, smiling quietly to himself while submitting the script to the demanding and billiard ball–pated Weisinger.

Baldness and badness were often linked, in the Weisinger era. Perhaps fearing that readers might confuse the evil Brainiac, another hairless hero-hater, with Luthor, the alien villain was eventually revealed to be an android. In subsequent appearances, the top of his cranium was outfitted with electrodes, like a kind of solid-state yarmulke.

Return to Krypton

It was just a few months later (*Superman* #141, November 1960) that Siegel penned, and Wayne Boring drew, one of the most elegiac, emotional epics of Superman's Silver Age. In the three-part story "Superman's Return to Krypton," Superman flies through the time barrier and finds himself on Krypton before it exploded. Under Krypton's red sun, he's lost his powers and resigns himself to perishing along with the rest of the people when the planet is destroyed.

He falls in with a Kryptonian film crew making a science-fiction movie and is taken for one of the film's extras. He falls in love with movie actress Lyla Lerroll and befriends his parents while doing his best to keep his surging emotions in check ("[*Choke!*] Neither they, nor anyone on else on this world, has long to live."), becomes Jor-El's lab assistant, manages to engineer his Earth foster parents' romance from across millions of light-years, and takes in the local flora and fauna to boot. Siegel introduces the reader to Krypton's Rainbow Canyon, Jewel Mountain, Gold Volcano ("Unfortunate, isn't it, that gold is so common on Krypton! It's worthless!"), Fire Falls and Meteor Valley.

Just as Superman resigns himself to marrying Lyla and perishing with his planet, a strange happenstance (or a "cringeworthy contrivance," depending on the reader) propels his movie-prop rocket ship into outer space, where he regains his powers. "Fate can't be changed! It's impossible for me to save Lyla or my parents! Earth needs me!"

The combination of Siegel's swooning emotions and Boring's boldly exotic Kryptonian scenescapes supplies "Superman's Return to Krypton" with a haunting, melancholic power.

One year later, Siegel wrote another ingeniously structured, three-part epic filled with emotion that would be remembered fondly for decades to come (*Superman* #149, November 1961).

In it, he would do what no other Superman writer had dared to do—something only Superman's creator could attempt: he killed the Man of Steel.

The Valiant Taste of Death but Once. Twice. Okay, Three, Maybe Four Times, Tops.

To accomplish this feat of super-manslaughter, Siegel availed himself of a conceit that swiftly became a Weisinger-era mainstay: the Imaginary Story.

Siegel had invented the concept back in World War II, in a story that showed Clark and Lois taking in a Superman animated short—and a harried Clark attempting to distract Lois Lane, lest the onscreen action reveal to her his secret identity (in *Superman* #19 (November/December 42). Yet that had been mere metafictional playfulness.

What Siegel is up to in the Imaginary Story "The Death of Superman" is altogether different, in that it grapples with the most basic logistical tenets of superhero comics.

All superheroes have origins, but none of them have endings. That's where the Imaginary Story comes in—it offers writers a chance to simulate the closure that they are denied by the demands of comics' ongoing, open-ended narrative. In providing an ending, it supplies a shape to Superman's life of endless adventure and turns it into a *story*. What's more, it's not definitive—here's *an* ending, the Imaginary Story says, but it's not *the* ending—next month everything goes back to normal.

The first chapter of "The Death of Superman" opens with a jail-bound Luthor, who is granted permission to use the prison hospital's laboratory and promptly creates a serum that cures cancer. Moved by this altruistic turn, Superman testifies on behalf of Luthor before his parole board, and the once-mad scientist is set free. As he shows the Man of Steel his secret hideout—in a nice touch, "Luthor's Lair" includes a gallery of statues of Attila the Hun, Genghis Khan, Captain Kidd, and Al Capone—the two men reminisce fondly about their previous tangles. When Metropolis's criminal underworld turns against the reformed Luthor, Superman acts as his bodyguard. To protect him, Superman constructs a lab for Luthor in orbit, outfitted with a distress signal—"this jet-rocket, which resembles you," Superman explains. (He's right on that score—in a touch of implacably weird Silver Age logic, the tip of the missile is outfitted with a facsimile of Luthor's bald head.)

Later, Luthor fires the missile, causing Superman to race to his defense, only to realize too late that he has fallen into the not-really-reformed scientist's death trap.

What follows is fascinating. Siegel relishes this opportunity to kill off his creation and takes his sweet time doing so. Luthor has never been more vindictive and cruel as when he fires powerful green kryptonite rays at the unsuspecting Man of Steel, straps him onto a table using "bands of metal containing *kryptonite*" (thus gilding an already malevolent lily), and pulls a switch: "See, *Superman*! That wall is rising! There's a thick glass partition behind it, separating us from your dear friends . . . Lois Lane, Jimmy Olsen and Perry White! They can't possibly break through that glass and rescue you! . . . Ha, ha. . . . You've begun to *turn green* as *kryptonite fever* rages with you! . . . Now to raise the *kryptonite* power in these rays to *full-strength*!"

The Man of Steel turns completely green and dies. (His last words: "*Owww! Ohh-hhhh . . .*") Anticipating his readers' doubts, Siegel has Luthor examine the body to determine that the body is that of the real Man of Steel and not a Superman robot.

Siegel and artist Curt Swan give Luthor a panel of his own to relish the victory he's been denied for twenty years—he stands in his lab coat, fists raised above his head, and seems to glow: "*At last*! After all these years of vainly trying, I've finally succeeded in killing *Superman*! I've destroyed the mightiest man in the universe! What a glorious achievement!"

In the story's third and final chapter, no twist arises, no quint-essential last minute Silver-Age deus ex machina saves the day. Superman is dead, and Siegel takes nine pages to fully imagine how the world would say its farewells.

In the pages that follow, everyone—but *everyone*—gets a moment by the catafalque to express his or her (or its) grief in thought balloons that practically sop with heavy tears. Siegel stops at nothing in his attempt to tug his readers' heartstrings so hard they snap.

Even the damn dog gets an encomium: "I will never know another master like you! [*choke*]" thinks Krypto. "Goodbye!—When I think of all the adventures we had together . . ." When the Superman *robots* get in on the act ("There's not a one of us who wouldn't have died gladly, in his place"), the story turns from grim to emotionally grotesque.

The scene then abruptly shifts to a party thrown by "the underworld" for Luthor. Again, Siegel delights in Luthor's evil glee. "Callously, *Luthor* has decorated the great banquet hall with exhibits mocking the final death of *Superman*."

The party is busted up by Superman—but not the real one, of course. To provide the story with a light psychosexual punch, Siegel reveals that it's Supergirl, whose Superman disguise flies off when she "flexes mighty muscles." Luthor stands trial in Kandor: "You *killed* a Kryptonian, so you will be *tried* by Kryptonians!"

As the trial proceeds, and a tearful Lois, Jimmy, and Perry provide their testimony, "*Luthor*'s icy, arrogant composure still doesn't crack." "The puny ants!" thinks Luthor, because he is Luthor.

The villain surprises the court by pleading guilty—but offering to restore Kandor to its full size if they let him go immediately. "Naturally," he thinks. "They won't refuse! Being made normal-sized again has been their greatest desire!"

Yet the Kandorians have a surprise of their own: "We Kandorians don't make deals with murderers! Executioner, send this wretch into the *Phantom Zone*, immediately! He is the greatest villain since Adolf Eichmann!" intones the Kryptonian judge, pulling an Earth reference with remarkable facility.

In the story's final panel, Supergirl and Krypto fly through the clouds, as a ghostly image of the Man of Steel waves in farewell: "[*Choke*] All I feel is a great sorrow at the passing of the strongest, kindest, m-most powerful human being I've ever known! [*Sob!*] M-my cousin *Superman*."

"Well, let's not feel *too* badly!" the comics' closing narration pipes up. "After all, this was only an *imaginary* story, and the chances are a *million to one* it will *never* happen! See the next issue for new, great stories of the mighty *Superman* you know!"

The specter of Superman's death would be evoked countless times, in stories both imaginary and in-canon. For decades, Swan's image of Superman lying in state, surrounded by superhero mourners, has been adapted and iterated by comic book artists, every time a hero dies—or seems to.

Just a year later, in *Superman* #156 (October 1962), another three-part story by Edmond Hamilton finds Superman mistakenly convinced he has been stricken by a Kryptonian virus. Up until the last-minute reveal (it's a small lump of kryptonite and not a virus that has weakened him; once the pebble is disposed of, he recovers completely), the story recalls the somber, reflective tone of "The Death of Superman."

Of course, death is only one kind of grim fate that Weisinger-era Imaginary Stories explored. The other was marriage.

A Levittown of Solitude

Many Imaginary Stories examined what would happen if Superman settled down and had a kid or three—if the Man of Steel became a Man in the Gray Flannel Suit. Images of Superman as a sort of ultimate suburban dad—Ward Cleaver in circus tights—adorned many covers of the period.

One of the most fondly remembered of these—"The Amazing Story of Superman-Red and Superman-Blue!" by Leo Dorfman (*Superman* #162, July 1963)—begins with the citizens of the Bottle City of Kandor delivering unto the Man of Steel a mammoth guilt trip (pointing out that he has failed to restore Kandor to its normal size, failed to find a kryptonite antidote, and failed to wipe out evil on Earth), followed up by an ultimatum: accomplish those tasks in six months' time, or step aside and let some other Kandorian take a shot at them.

Superman builds a "brain-evolution machine" powered by "all varieties of kryptonite" that makes him a hundred times smarter but splits him into two identical Supermen—one wearing an all-red costume and one wearing an all-blue costume.

With their phenomenal brainpower, the two of them figure out how to enlarge Kandor—and reassemble planet Krypton from all of its fragments scattered throughout the universe. Happy with their home on "New Krypton," the Kandorians ask to be returned to their home galaxy, under its red sun.

They find a new homeworld for Lori Lemaris and her Atlantean people and build satellites that project "anti-evil rays" that, true to their name, "erase all thoughts of evil from the minds of the world's criminals!" During the course of the next several panels, bank robbers return the loot they've stolen, shoplifters come clean, escaped prisoners return to the pen, and certain enemies of America repent their godless ways:

Man who looks a lot like Khrushchev: You heard me! Dump
   all missiles into the sea! Notify President Kennedy we
   agree to disarmament with full inspection!
Man who looks a lot like Castro: Open the jail doors! Release
   all prisoners at once!

Brainiac retreats, Luthor creates a serum that cures all diseases
(and restores his hair!), the Phantom Zone criminals go straight
and depart for New Krypton—with Supergirl. Suddenly, a thought
occurs.

Superman-Blue: Our hypno-beam is working perfectly!
   Now that crime and evil are abolished, we can fulfill
   another ambition! We can get married!
Superman-Red: You're right! The woman we love is no
   longer in danger from the evil plots on [*sic*] the criminal
   world!

Separately, Blue proposes to Lana Lang, while Red does the
same to Lois. Each woman accepts with delight but expresses regret
that her rival will be brokenhearted. When they realize what has
happened, both women are astonishingly game: "Now each of us
can have a *Superman* for a husband!"

A triple wedding follows (not to be outdone, Jimmy proposes
to Lois's sister, Lucy), and Lois and Red depart for New Krypton.
With crime a thing of the past, Blue decides to retire and devote
himself to science, leaving his robots to handle any natural disasters
that may arise.

The story ends with Jimmy and Lucy gazing at wedding photos
of both super-couples, marveling at how everyone has found the
happiness they hoped for. The narration concludes: "What's *your*
opinion, readers? Suppose this Imaginary Story *really* happened!
Which couple do you think would be happiest? The end." The
almost desperate insistence on closure and happiness in Imaginary
Stories such as this one is reminiscent of the last act of a Shakespeare
comedy—*you* get married! And *you* get married! Everybody dance!
Happy, happy, happy!

Before long, Imaginary Stories were coming so fast and furiously that readers grew to expect them. Yet the Silver Age reliance
on featuring wildly contrived puzzles on their covers meant that

in-canon stories were forced to defensively assert the veracity of their contents, often with the soon-to-be-famous phrase: "*Not* a Dream! *Not* a Hoax! *Not* an Imaginary Story!"

A series of Imaginary Stories that began in *Superman's Girl Friend, Lois Lane* #19 (August 1960), also written by Siegel, imagined the married life of "Mr. and Mrs. Clark (Superman) Kent." As drawn by Kurt Schaffenberger, they made for a strikingly handsome couple as they dealt with domestic super-scrapes in their bright, immaculate split-level suburban paradise. Although Lois, vacuuming the den in her apron and pearl necklace, looked like June Cleaver, she acted more like Lucy Ricardo; many stories ended on a bittersweet note, due to some jealousy or foolishness on Lois's part.

Over in the pages of *World's Finest*, several Imaginary Stories (including *World's Finest* #157, May 1966) involved Superman and Batman attempting unsuccessfully to wrangle their willful super-heroic kids in green, well-manicured backyards.

It's telling that when Superman's writers gave themselves license to dream up anything they could, they invariably dreamed the American dream of the fifties, opting for the normative closure of marriage and family, of keeping house, cookouts, campouts, and, ultimately, a peaceful retirement. Most of Superman's Imaginary Stories, whose very reason for being was to explore how radically the setup could get upset, ultimately offered their readers assurance that Superman would remain forever an Eisenhower Republican, and the status would remain comfortably, quietly, permanently quo.

Meanwhile, just a few city blocks from Mort Weisinger's office, another comic book publisher was putting the finishing touches on its own answer to DC's *Justice League of America* comic. It was called *The Fantastic Four*. More about them later.

(Another) New Origin for a New Age

In 1961—the same year that saw the addition of the Phantom Zone (a limbo where Kryptonian criminals lived on, condemned to an eternal, ghostlike existence), white kryptonite (deadly to plant life), and Mon-El (a character introduced in *Superboy* #89 (June 1961), who, like Halk Kar before him, is at first thought to be the Man of Steel's brother, but who turns out to be from a different planet entirely)—a script from Otto Binder and artist Al Plastino took stock of where the character stood.

"The Story of Superman's Life" (*Superman* #146, July 1961) begins exactly as Bill Finger and Wayne Boring's "Origin of Superman" had, thirteen years earlier, by evoking the scene from 1939's *Action Comics* #8, in which Superman willfully destroys slums to force the city to build new homes. Yet where the 1948 origin had cleaned up Superman's motivations for the act ("I'll rebuild this area so people don't have to live in slums!"), this new version scrubs the history to an almost Orwellian degree, presenting the act as an officially mandated public works project and the Man of Steel as a civic-minded super-citizen ("*At the mayor's request* [italics mine], I'll remove these ugly tenement buildings and build decent homes for the poor!").

The origin goes on to hit the now-familiar major points, albeit in more exhaustive detail, introducing all of the disparate threads that Weisinger and his writers had so furiously spun during the previous three years and painstakingly tying them together. As Finger had before him, Plastino visually quotes the image of Clark standing over his parents' graves at night. Then, for the first time, we see Superman granted "honorary citizenship in all the countries of the United Nations!"

"What an honor," Superman says, taking care to add, "But of course my main loyalty will always be to the United States, where I grew up!" In 1961, at least, you couldn't take the super-patriot out of the Superman.

There was no question that Superman's origin had been deepened and enriched since the day Krypton was simply referred to as "a distant planet"—but it was also growing increasingly complicated. What had taken Siegel and Shuster a single page to depict now took thirteen.

Our Numbers Are Legion

With the three hundredth issue of *Adventure Comics* (September 1962), the Legion of Super-Heroes—which had made twelve sporadic appearances throughout the Super-titles since its first, four years earlier—earned a regular slot in the back of the comic. With each subsequent appearance, the Legion membership roster had grown, and now its ranks continued to swell with more and more superpowered teenagers from the future.

Legion stories, whether or not they involved Superman, Superboy, or Supergirl, appealed to boys and girls alike with their combination of derring-do and melodrama. The thirtieth-century setting freed the stories from the constraints of Weisinger's closely monitored continuity and, given the huge cast of characters, allowed writers such as Jerry Siegel and Edmond Hamilton to raise the stakes. In a Legion tale, major characters could—and did—die. New characters could join or, if they failed to live up to Legion standards, be relegated to "Substitute Hero" status. Love could bloom and fade. A hero could lose his or her power, only to gain a new one. Triplicate Girl, for example, who had the power to split into three identical selves, could suffer a tragedy, dust herself off, and reemerge as Duo Damsel.

Fans embraced the giddy, roiling mix of powers, planets, and pathos provided by Legion tales, but these stories offered something specific to the Superman mythos that would shape him for decades to come.

Superman had time-traveled many times by now, but what Legion stories established—and underlined—was Superman's ultimate fate. In the Legion universe, the Superman of the twentieth century has gone down in history as the greatest hero of all time—indeed, the Legion was formed to honor his memory. Some of the best Legion stories play off the notion of a young Superboy learning to come to terms with the legend he is destined to become. Still others offer tantalizing glimpses of Superman's future and add cosmic-level, time-hopping villains who will bedevil the heroes of the DC Universe for years.

Swan Dives In

Early on, John Forte handled art chores on *Legion* tales, while penciller Curt Swan and inker George Klein handled covers. Yet gradually, the Swan-Klein team assumed the art duties for the *Legion*—and for several other Superman titles as well.

As artist Wayne Boring had defined the Superman of the forties and fifties, Curt Swan would establish the signature Superman look of the sixties through the early eighties. "I wanted to show strength, of course, and ruggedness," Swan said. "And *character*." Thus, Swan's Superman is both less moody and less burly than Boring's. His waist is narrower, his shoulders bigger and rounder, and Swan drops the

Man of Steel's body fat percentage precipitously, eliminating the barrel chest for a torso with greater muscle definition.

It's the face of Swan's Superman, though, where the true difference arises. It's less stylized than Boring's deep-browed, emo take ("Mort told me early on that he wanted to soften [Boring's] jaw line," Swan has said). But neither does his Superman seem coolly paternal, like Al Plastino's. Swan splits the difference, creating a more illustrative, realistic Superman whose face in repose looks handsome in a vague, unthreatening way and—more than anything else—*kind*. "He had to be the kind of person you'd *want* to have on your side," Swan said.

Where Swan truly excels, however, is in his characters' "acting"—he unshowily captures shifts of facial expression and body language with directness and subtlety. "I felt it was necessary to put lines in the face to show pain, or whatever. Mort . . . thought they made Superman look too old." When Swan's pencils were being inked by Klein, relatively few of the facial lines he'd drawn made it into the final panels, which is why a Swan/Klein Superman seems like a notably younger man than either Boring's or Plastino's.

Swan shows great economy of form—where Boring's line work could make a page seem heavy, a Swan/Klein page has a lightness and a simplicity to it that invite the eye in. It's under Swan's reign that Superman's S-curl is reduced to a signature squiggle—and attains its iconic status, becoming as much a central part of the character as the boots or the cape.

While we're talking coiffure, it should be noted that Swan's Superman, especially in these early years, bears an ever-so-slightly receded hairline, compared to Plastino and Boring's. This is Superman as your favorite, compassionate uncle.

Meanwhile, Marvel Comics was on a roll. They had just introduced yet another new superhero, and this one was everything Superman wasn't—a guilt-ridden teenager with an inferiority complex who'd only blundered into superheroing after his selfishness got someone he loved killed. Where Superman contended with sundry secret-identity hijinks, this Parker kid couldn't afford medicine for his sick old aunt, had girl trouble, and was forever rejecting his role as a hero and whining about wanting to be normal. If Superman was America's uncle/superego, this punk was America's ungrateful stepson/id.

They called him Spider-Man. More on him later.

With Great Power Come Limited Possibilities

Now that it was established that Superman loses his powers under a red sun, more and more stories featured a depowered Superman forced to make do with his wits. It was an inevitable development in a era when the Man of Steel's power levels had ballooned to a degree that he need only knit his brows to peer through the time barrier (as he had in *Superman* #127 (February 1959) and could pulverize an entire planet with a head-butt (*Superman* #154, July 1962).

In January 1963 (*Superman* #158) and again in August 1964 (*World's Finest* #143), Superman and Jimmy Olsen travel to the Bottle City of Kandor (where Superman loses his powers) and adopt the identities of Nightwing and Flamebird, a masked crime-fighting dynamic duo named for a pair of Kryptonian birds. Any similarities to Batman and Robin are intentional, and, if Batman was feeling litigious, actionable: as Nightwing, Superman wears a mask and a dark blue costume (complete with Prussian blue pixie boots), while Jimmy's outfit is red and yellow. Both men wear jet-belts that enable them to fly but also avail themselves of a "Nightcar" and a "Nightcave." In the decades to come, several characters will adopt these crime-fighting identities.

In October 1963 (*Superman* #164), Lex Luthor challenges the Man of Steel to a boxing match "without his super-powers to help him." Superman swiftly accepts and—in a single panel—constructs a spaceship to fly them both to a planet that revolves around a red sun.

There, the two men strip to the waist and engage in a few rounds of bare-knuckle boxing. (At which point, it becomes clear that Luthor, whom artists have depicted for years as a portly, double-chinned figure in a blousy lab coat, has evidently found time to hit the gymnasium and toss the ol' medicine ball around.)

Later, a chase through a weird forest of living cacti separates the two enemies. Superman wanders, lost in the desert, while Luthor finds a populous city and convinces the people that he is a hero who could locate them a new source of water—and that Superman is a villain. Though his plan begins as a mere ruse, by the end of the story Luthor has come to care for the people of this planet and convinces Superman to secretly provide them with water. The people revere Luthor, building a statue to him.

During the Silver Age, an era that is fond of up-is-down Bizarro logic as a story engine, Luthor will make several sojourns to this planet that so reveres him its natives rename it Lexor, in his honor— while shunning Superman as a cur and a dastard. In November 1964, Luthor will take the lovely Lexorian Ardora for his wife.

Camelot

When Superman finally presents his cousin Supergirl to the world in *Action* #285 (February 1962), President John F. Kennedy greets her warmly. "I know you'll use your super-powers not only to fight crime, but to preserve peace in our troubled world!"

It wasn't the first time Superman had rubbed elbows with a U.S. president in the comics pages. He'd thwarted an attempt to assassinate President Dwight D. Eisenhower three years earlier (*Action* #256). Yet Superman's relationship with Kennedy was unprecedented, although the timing was ghoulish. In the issue cover-dated February 1964 (*Action* #309), which was the issue on newsstand shelves when Kennedy was killed on November 22, 1963, Superman gets himself in a tight spot: A live television show honoring the Man of Steel requires Superman and Clark Kent to share the stage at the same time. The Man of Tomorrow appeals to the leader of the free world for help, and POTUS agrees to don a rubber Clark Kent mask and glasses and pass himself off as Superman's alter ego.

"I knew I wasn't risking my secret identity with you!" a beaming Superman confides. "After all, if I can't trust the *president of the United States*, who *can* I trust?" 1964, ladies and gentlemen.

Kennedy was originally scheduled to make a return appearance just two months later (in *Action* #168, an issue cover-dated April 1964), in a story dedicated to promoting the President's Council on Physical Fitness. Yet in the wake of the assassination, the story was pulled and replaced with another "Luthor, Hero of Lexor" story.

The letters page scheduled for that issue was pulled as well and replaced with an In Memoriam written by Weisinger, which featured a clipping from a *New York Times* article about the planned story.

Later, President Lyndon Johnson contacted the DC offices and urged that the story see print; the Kennedy family concurred. Lacking Curt Swan's original art, however—which had, in fact, been donated to the Kennedy estate—Al Plastino stepped in to redraw it. The Kennedy tale, looking a good deal more rushed and crudely drawn than Plastino's coolly composed norm, finally appeared as the lead story of *Superman* #170 (July 1964). DC felt it best not to picture the president on the issue's cover, opting instead to feature an Imaginary Story that explored what would happen if Luthor were Superman's father.

The Silver Age Begins to Tarnish

By 1964, it was clear that change was coming. Situations and characters that had produced an endless stream of inventions, inversions, and innovations now offered up mere iteration. Another form of kryptonite appeared—jewel kryptonite, this time, which allowed Phantom Zone villains to mentally manipulate people in our dimension (*Action* #310, March 1964)—but by now readers had seen green, red, blue, white, and gold versions of the stuff, to say nothing of not one but two "hoax" kryptonites, yellow and silver; the conceit and others like it were beginning to pall.

The tone changed, too. Just as the kids on the leading edge of the Baby Boom hit their late teens, *Superman*'s middle-aged writers (Siegel was fifty, Hamilton sixty, Robert Bernstein forty-five) began to make tin-eared attempts to reach this new breed of American youths.

The guileless whimsy of the previous years had produced an unself-consciously vibrant, loopy assortment of characters and situations, but now it was clear that Superman was looking over his shoulder. Writing for kids was one thing; they'd been doing that for years. Yet how could they write for this thing the newsmagazines were calling "the growing youth culture"?

A story in the September 1964 issue of *Superman's Pal, Jimmy Olsen* (#79), written by the then fifty-year-old Leo Dorfman, offers an interesting case study in the new note of self-consciousness threading through the Super-books. It's called "The Red-Headed Beatle of 1,000 B.C.!" On the cover, Superman flies over ancient Judea and spies Jimmy Olsen in a toga and a red Beatle wig tootling away on a shofar and beating a drum. "Great Krypton!" he thinks. "Jimmy has started a Beatle craze here in the ancient past! He's become as popular as Ringo!"

The story begins with our intrepid cub reporter dancing alone in his apartment as he watches the Beatles on television. "Man! Those Beatles are a blast! And I always seem to enjoy their music more when I wear my personal Beatle wig!" A sinister time-traveler arrives from the future and tricks Jimmy into guiding him to the ancient past.

There, he meets the ancient world's resident superhero, a muscular boy in a turban and a toga who calls himself Mighty Youth. The boy swiftly rescues Jimmy from the villain's clutches, but the cub reporter is still stranded in ancient Judea. He finds a job as a sheep shearer, although it doesn't pay well. So he takes a little extra wool, buys some black dye, makes several Beatle wigs, and starts hawking them in the public square, performing Beatles songs to draw a crowd.

> Boy: Who is this strange fellow who twists and twitches like a beetle on a hot stone?
> Girl: That catchy drum-beat! I can't keep my own feet from twitching!
> Jimmy: Hold everything, kids, You can't do the Beatle Dance without a Beatle wig! . . . *Yeah! Yeah! Yeah!*

Later, Mighty Youth reveals his secret identity—the biblical Samson, naturally. When the time-crook steals into Mighty Youth's secret headquarters in the middle of the night to cut Samson's hair and rob him of his strength, Jimmy foils the attempt by substituting a Beatle wig for the boy's luxurious mane.

Superman arrives and all is made well—but not before Jimmy gives one last command performance for his pal, causing Superman to opine, in the squarest manner imaginable, "You've really started a '*Beatle*' fad here, Jimmy! You seem to be as popular as *Ringo*, the *Beatle* drummer!"

The Times, They Are a-Changin'

Even as Superman's creators nervously began to avail themselves of more and more ham-fisted pop culture references, that same popular culture was changing around them at a faster and faster pace. As it changed, so did the popular attitude toward the Man of Steel.

The kids who had grown up on Kirk Alyn and George Reeves were teenagers now, with the reflexive adolescent compulsion to reject the trappings of their youth as "kid stuff." Adolescence is, after all, a process of defining oneself by deciding what one is not—and Superman was a handy symbolic representation of everything staid and square and little-kiddy that they wished to leave behind.

Thus it was that the kids who had once worshiped the Man of Steel now began to delight in parodies of him. Underground comics starring Gilbert Shelton's gleefully pornographic, superpowered Wonder Wart Hog, the World's Awfulest-Smelling Super-Hero, had begun to appear in a variety of humor magazines three years earlier. On October 3, 1964, NBC began to air a cartoon parody of Superman that would infiltrate the public consciousness and live on in syndication for decades to come. The show's Superman proxy is an ineffectual, clumsy goof who succeeds in spite of himself. He is voiced by the great character actor and quintessential nerd Wally Cox.

Also? He's a dog. A dog with one of the grooviest theme songs in cartoon history, granted, but a dog nonetheless.

In one narrow sense, *Underdog* is everything the ill-fated *Adventures of Superpup* pilot had hoped to be, six years earlier, only with wit and wordplay in place of little people and mascot-heads.

Affectionate though its parody may have been, the tale of humble and lovable Shoeshine Boy and his bumbling canine super-self was only the beginning. More Superman parodies were on the way. Many more.

Aprés Underdog, le deluge.

In March 1965, the popular American Comics Group character Herbie became the flying superhero the Fat Fury. In April, Disney's Goofy became *Super Goof*. In October—exactly one year after *Underdog*'s debut—the first episode of *Atom Ant* appeared on NBC. The flying, superstrong, invincible member of the family Formicidae even had a catch phrase ("Up and at 'em, Atom Aaaaant!") similar to the Man of Steel's.

That same month, America's favorite tic-tac-toe-headed teen, Archie Andrews, gained superpowers and a skintight outfit to clean up the not-even-remotely-mean streets of Riverdale as Pureheart the Powerful. Soon, Reggie, Jughead, and Betty adopted their own superheroic identities.

Before long, these parodies would be joined by the animated spoofs *Super Chicken*, *Mighty Mouse*, *the Mighty Heroes*, and the truly bizarre *Super President* (who fights crime from his secret lair beneath the Oval Office); the bumbling sitcom heroes *Captain Nice* and *Mister Terrific*; and the *Monty Python's Flying Circus* sketch "Bicycle Repairman," which features a mild-mannered mechanic who fixes bikes in a world full of Supermen.

Amid the glut of parodies and knock-offs on the comic stands, DC sought to enhance its brand identity. Beginning in February 1965, the top edges of all DC books featured a strip of black-and-white checkerboard boxes—dubbed "Go-Go Checks" to tie them into the pop-art movement ("Don't Hesitate! Choose . . . The Mags with the Go-Go Checks!")—and to help the books stand out on crowded spinner racks.

How to Make Comics the Marvel Way

The only branding element Marvel Comics needed was bound up in the glad-handing persona and cornball brio of its editor, Stan Lee. That persona—more so than the words "A Marvel Pop Art Production" emblazoned across Marvel titles—had by now become Marvel's identity. Lee's editorial voice and blusterin', back-slappin', hyperbolic energy saturated every panel. On letters pages, he whipped his fans into a Marvel-loving frenzy and disparaged the "Distinguished Competition" (also dubbed "Brand Ecch"). He delighted in offering readers behind-the-scenes glimpses of his "Bullpen" of writers and artists, never letting readers forget that these stories they were reading came from a very specific place, that these characters were products of his and his team's "ever-lovin' minds!"

As to those characters—well, they were a fractious bunch.

Just as Superman's universe underwent a population explosion at the beginning of the decade, that same time period saw a shared fictive Marvel Universe suddenly teeming with its own brand-new costumed heroes: the Fantastic Four, the Hulk, Spider-Man, Thor, the X-Men, Doctor Strange, Daredevil, and the Avengers had all appeared within a brief span of three years and were gaining readership—and, more important, cultural cachet.

Writers and rock musicians—and even filmmakers such as Federico Fellini and Jean-Luc Godard—were stopping by the Marvel offices, a state of affairs Lee would breathlessly detail in his letters pages. *Esquire* noted that Marvel heroes had become a phenomenon on the country's college campuses. More than fifty thousand college students had become members of the Mighty Marvel Marching Society and listed Spider-Man among their favorite "revolutionary icons." Stan Lee became a fixture on the college lecture circuit.

The secret to Marvel's success wasn't strictly one of content—the books were just as much about characters in tights punching one another as any DC book—but of mind-set. Where DC was content to simply have characters reference the music kids loved, Marvel had captured how those same kids were feeling. The approach was just as cynical but far more effective.

Stan Lee and Jack Kirby took the overwrought, childlike emotionalism of Weisinger's Superman mythology and aimed it squarely at teenagers. They knew that narcissistic adolescents wanted to read about themselves, so they created a universe of characters that were, or behaved like, narcissistic adolescents; every page practically exuded Clearasil.

DC heroes were adults with established careers: Green Lantern was a test pilot, the Flash was a police scientist. Yet Peter Parker was a whiny, outcast, put-upon teen. What's more, he actually *was* a nerd, not merely posing as one, like a certain Man of Steel. Over in the X-Men, teenage feelings of loneliness and isolation were given freakish flesh, in the form of mutations.

Many readers and comics historians have noted that these new Marvel heroes exhibited something DC heroes lacked—definable personalities. It's true that Superman and other DC heroes operated out of a completely unexamined sense of duty and altruism. It was true, also, that writers didn't concern themselves with using dialogue as a tool for characterization—unless it was to give a goon a Brooklyn accent or to force self-consciously "hip" lingo into the mouth of a teenager ("I like to swing, but these cats are too much, dig? Strictly weirdsville!").

The key difference, however, was that the pervasive emotionalism of Weisinger-era Superman—all of those chokes and sobs—grew directly out of situations; they were a function of plot. Lois sees Lana kissing Superman, cue slough of despond.

Marvel characters, on the other hand, each met the world with a unique, preinstalled set of emotional hair-triggers. It's tempting to call these "personalities"—but they were far more primal and outsize than that. What they truly were, of course, were personality disorders.

Thus, Johnny Storm, the Human Torch, is an egotistical hothead given to throwing tantrums over tiny perceived slights. The Hulk is literally a creature of pure rage. When Spider-Man isn't acting out of an overriding sense of guilt over his uncle's death, he's wallowing in self-pity. (It's no coincidence that self-pity, the dominant feature of the adolescent emotional landscape, motivates reluctant Marvel heroes such as the Thing, the Hulk, Beast, and a good five-sixths of any given X-Men roll call.)

The very notion of a reluctant hero—Marvel's stock in trade—had no place in a DC book. In fact, every non-super character in a Superman title longed to slap on tights and fight crime—and by now, most had gotten their chance. Lana Lang's first impulse, for example, on learning that she had acquired the ability to transform herself into enormous insects, was not to hide under the couch like Gregor Samsa (*clearly* a Marvel character) but to sew herself a bee-themed costume.

Lee had set out to create a study in contrasts, and it wasn't lost on readers. If, in DC books, superheroes had team-ups, in Marvel, they would brawl.

If Superman worried about disembodied alien criminals exposing him to gold kryptonite, Spider-Man would worry about school, money, and girls.

It was a canny bet Lee had made, pitching stories squarely at the beating heart of the hormonal American teenager. He knew that readers would opt for Marvel id over DC superego, and it was already beginning to pay off. Marvel sales surged; by 1967, they were edging dangerously near DC's numbers. Superman still ruled the comics sales charts, but he was about to be dealt a one-two punch that would leave him a marginalized figure of fun for years to come.

Superman Goes to Camp

1966 was the year of the camp superhero.

The culture had always found the concept of superheroes juvenile—they were children's' entertainment, after all—and they'd certainly come in for their share of light mockery over the years, the way one might make fun of a fondly remembered kiddie show host. Yet it took an unprecedented television phenomenon for the popular imagination to begin to view the superhero as something truly, abjectly ridiculous, to equate "costumed hero" with "campiness" so completely, it would take more than a decade to recover.

In January 1966, *Batman* debuted on ABC, starring Adam West and Burt Ward as the Dynamic Duo. Filled with intentionally garish pop-art colors, unusual visual effects (*Pow! Zap!*), and inventive cinematography (the camera was slightly tilted for all scenes set in villains' lairs, to subtly unsettle the viewer), the show became a sensation. Yet the show's runaway popularity had less to do with its production design and more to do with its simple central conceit: taking comic-book superhero conventions, characters, and situations and playing them with deadly seriousness.

The kids who loved the show didn't clue into its humor—to them, it was a straightforward superhero adventure—but their parents hooted at Adam West's Batman, a squeaky clean super-citizen who'd never think of parking the Batmobile without feeding the meter.

The show burned itself out after two and a half seasons and a theatrical movie, but in that brief time, it so infiltrated the American mind-set that today, almost half a century later, one of its signature elements ("*Pow! Zap!*") has become a cliché as detested by comics readers as it is loved by lazy feature editors trying to find a headline for articles about graphic novels.

The Smell of the Greasepaint

When the musical *It's a Bird . . . It's a Plane. . . It's Superman*, produced and directed by Harold Prince, premiered on Broadway in March 1966—just three months after *Batman*'s television debut—the country was still deep in the grip of Bat-mania.

Cowritten by David Newman and Robert Benton (both of whom would later work on the screenplay for *Superman: The Movie*), with music by Charles Strouse and lyrics by Lee Adams (the team behind 1960's *Bye Bye Birdie*), *It's a Bird* attempted to thread *Batman*'s mock-serious, high-camp needle, but its status as an old-fashioned sing-your-guts-out Broadway spectacle, filled with splashy dance numbers, meant its humor couldn't help but come from a broader, showier place.

The muscular Bob Holiday made a striking Superman and handled the role's many stunts with aplomb—lifting a bleacher full of spectators, swooping over the footlights on a wire.

Song-and-dance man Jack Cassidy received top billing as Max Mencken, a slick *Daily Planet* columnist who makes a play for Lois and conspires with mad scientist Dr. Abner Sedgwick (Michael O'Sullivan) to unmask Superman. The *King and I*'s Patricia Marand, playing Lois Lane, did her best with the show's unremarkable love ballads. Holiday's Superman had three solos in the show and handled them well—though any Superman fans in the audience may have bristled at the elbow-in-the-ribs jokiness of the show's lyrics, as in the opening song "Doing Good":

> It's a satisfying feeling
> When you hang up your cape
> To know that you've averted
> Murder, larceny, and rape.

In an inevitable nod to the Batman craze, Holiday's final number, in which Superman effortlessly beats up a gang of evil Chinese acrobats, is called "Pow! Bam! Zonk!"

The show's breakout number (which would live on as an audition song and become a minor cabaret standard) was sung by *Daily Planet* gossip columnist Sydney, played by Linda Lavin. "You've Got Possibilities" finds Sydney reevaluating the schlubby Clark Kent as a possible suitor:

> Hair cut—simply terrible.
> Neck tie—the worst.
> Bearing—just unbearable.
> What to tackle first?
> Still, you've got possibilities,
> Though you're horribly square.
> I see possibilities;
> Underneath there's something there.

On the word *underneath*, Lavin would seductively undo Holiday's necktie and open his shirt, while Holiday scrambled to recinch and rebutton, lest she glimpse his Superman costume.

The show received lukewarm reviews, with the *New York Times*'s Stanley Kauffmann noting, "It is easily the best musical so far this season, but, because that is so damp a compliment, I add at once that it would be enjoyable in any season." (To place that in context: *Man of La Mancha* and *Sweet Charity* had opened scant months before; *Mame* would open two months later.)

At first, ticket sales were brisk. Soon, however, producers noticed that the audience was composed of a great number of kids, so matinees were added. Cassidy, O'Sullivan, and Marand were nominated for Tony awards on June 1, but by then the show was fighting off a growing public perception that it was a piece of "children's theater," and the nominations did nothing to help ticket sales. Some have conjectured that the timing simply wasn't right—in interviews, writer David Newman has said he believes the show was a victim of "capelash" caused by the television Batman's wild popularity. The show closed on July 17, after just 129 performances.

DC's *Superman* editor, Mort Weisinger, attended several performances of *It's a Bird.* . . . He'd been involved with licensing the Superman name and could get tickets easily. When he wanted to impress a new writer, he'd take him to dinner and then to the show.

One evening in late June 1966, Weisinger sat in the audience with a hot new writer from whom he'd bought several *Legion of Super-Heroes* stories. Weisinger had big plans for him—the *Legion* was tremendously popular, popular enough to take over the *Adventure Comics* title completely, and Weisinger thought this guy might be just the writer to run with it.

He hadn't actually met the writer in person before, had only corresponded and talked on the phone. Yet now the writer had come to New York for a visit, so Weisinger had set him up at a nice hotel, showed him around the DC offices, and taken him out to see the Superman musical.

The writer's name was Jim Shooter. He was fourteen years old.

The Fanboys Are Coming

A year earlier, in 1965, the then thirteen-year-old Jim Shooter had set his sights on DC: "I wrote and drew, as best I could, a Legion of Super-Heroes story for . . . *Adventure Comics* and sent it off. I picked that one because I judged it to be the worst comic book published, and therefore, the place where I had the best chance to sell a story."

Weisinger, thinking Shooter a college student, wrote back a letter of encouragement, and Shooter sent off two more stories, introducing new characters Karate Kid, Princess Projectra, and others, which Weisinger duly bought. During the following five years—while attending high school—Shooter would contribute stories to many *Superman* titles, but the *Legion of Super-Heroes* would fast become his baby.

Though Weisinger maintained a tight grip on his burgeoning Superman continuity, the mere fact that many different writers were involved resulted in stories that felt interchangeable, even generic, with endings that returned everything to the starting position. Yet *Legion* stories, set in the thirtieth century, had their own wholly separate continuity, and writers such as Siegel and Hamilton delighted in introducing lasting changes like death, dismemberment, and betrayal. When Shooter became the *Legion*'s regular writer, he was effectively ceded control over the *Legion*—and by extension, the distant future of the entire DC Universe—and made the *Legion*'s intersecting storyline even more addictively complex.

He expanded Legion membership, introducing more and more characters, and this wider canvas gave him the chance to develop romantic relationships and storylines to an unprecedented degree, introducing elements that would pay off only many months later.

He was at the vanguard of an entirely new phenomenon—an entire generation of writers entering the field who'd grown up on comic books and were writing about their favorite heroes in the fan press. They approached their duties as custodians of the characters they so adored with a kind of gleeful reverence. For Shooter—and writers such as Roy Thomas and Cary Bates, as well as Paul Levitz and Elliot S. Maggin a few years later—writing Superman was not merely a paycheck, but a dream come true. The low status of comics among the literary establishment might have rankled the Siegels and the Hamiltons of the world; these new kids saw it as a point of pride.

Speaking of paychecks: in 1965, Jerry Siegel parted ways with DC for a second time. DC's Superman copyright was up for renewal in 1966, giving Siegel a chance to challenge it in court. This time, Shuster did not join him. Siegel's challenge was denied by the court, and he filed an appeal. The case would drag on for almost a decade.

A Job for Bud Collyer

In 1966, an animated series called *The New Adventures of Superman* premiered on CBS. Each episode featured two six-minute Superman shorts and one six-minute Superboy segment. As was typical for a Filmation Association production, the animation was strictly bargain-basement—stiffly composed, with character movement kept to the barest minimum before constantly recycled backgrounds. Yet the stories and characterizations were better than the format's standard, because the writing staff included several longtime DC writers. In a move that delighted longtime fans, producers also cast radio show veterans Bud Collyer, Joan Alexander, Jackson Beck, and Jack Grimes as Superman, Lois Lane, Perry White, and Jimmy Olsen, respectively. An entirely new generation of kids would grow up on Collyer's voice and revel in his signature tonal drop when Clark Kent became the Man of Steel.

The show was a success in its Saturday morning time slot. For the 1967 season, the format was expanded to sixty minutes, half of which were devoted to the undersea adventures of DC's Aquaman. In 1968, *The Superman/Aquaman Hour of Adventure* became *The Batman/Superman Hour*. In all, sixty-eight Superman shorts were produced.

I Am I Am I Am Superman

Even as Superman—or satiric facsimiles thereof—proliferated on television, the Man of Steel was enjoying some serious radio airplay. In July 1966, Scottish folk singer Donovan released a single that quickly made its way to number one on the *Billboard* charts. The song, a bouncy, lustful boast/proclamation of love, was called "Sunshine Superman" and became the title track of an album that was released a few months later. The Man of Steel got name-checked in the verse, alongside another DC hero ("Superman or Green Lantern ain't got nothin' on me").

A year later, the 5th Dimension, a group who took their name from the home of Superman's pesky foe Mr. Mxyzptlk, scored a sunshine-and-bubble-gum pop hit inspired by Superman's "Up, up, and away" catch phrase, a paean to hot-air ballooning written by Jimmy Webb that combined close harmonies with a brassy dose of Broadway. In 1969, the Austin-based band the Clique released the single "Sugar on Sunday," which enjoyed modest Top 40 success. Seventeen years later, REM would cover "Sugar on Sunday's" obscure, garage-rock B-side, "Superman."

Silver Wear and Tear

Sure, he was all over the airwaves. On the comics pages, however, Superman's never-ending battle had taken a worrisome turn. Sales of Superman titles were down, and Marvel was surging.

As the sixties drew to a close, so did the Silver Age of Superman. The boom time of ideas, gimmicks, and new characters at the start of the decade had faded, in recent years, into rote repetition. The mood of the country had darkened considerably, and the Superman who could blow out distant stars with super-breath and withstand "a thousand H-bombs" without a scratch (*Adventure* #366, March 1968) was no longer attuned to the times.

In 1970, Mort Weisinger retired. During the first half of his twelve-year tenure, he had taken the Man of Steel to unprecedented heights of popularity. The latter half, however, saw that same popularity fading. In fact, during those years of decline, only one new element was added to the Superman mythos that evinced any real staying power.

It was a villain named the Parasite, introduced in 1966 (*Action* #340). His gimmick: draining Superman of his powers, leaving him weak and exhausted, a shell of his former self.

Looking back, it seems a little on-the-nose.

7

KRYPTONITE NEVERMORE! BRIEFLY! (1970–1977)

Milestones

1970: Jack Kirby takes over *Superman's Pal, Jimmy Olsen*; begins his Fourth World saga

1972: *Super Friends* cartoon premieres

1974: *Superman Family* comic debuts

1975: *Superman vs. the Amazing Spider-Man* collector's edition

1976: Jerry Siegel and Joe Shuster's bylines return to the Superman logo

1977: *Superman vs. Muhammad Ali* collector's edition

First appearance of Darkseid and the New Gods; Morgan Edge, Galaxy Communications; Steve Lombard

Having spent much of the previous decade merely observing from the cultural sidelines, the now thirtysomething Superman was hit hard by the disillusionment that seized the country in the 1970s. This was the era of the Man of Steel's midlife crisis: a new job, a new wardrobe, and a newly defined relationship with Lois Lane, freshly minted women's libber. It was also the age of "relevance" in comics—which meant Superman's dance card would quickly fill up with issues such as pollution, famine, gang warfare, and racism.

Meanwhile, as Vietnam and Watergate further soured the national mood, the public regarded authority figures with a new breed of cynicism, if not outright contempt. With his close-cropped hair, clean-shaven face, and literally muscular defense of the status quo, Superman had now come to represent the capital-E Establishment.

Marvel heroes bickered and questioned and agitated—they were agents of chaos, and they looked like the kids who read them.

Superman, on the other hand, dutifully imposed order, and he looked like a cop.

"There's a New Kind of Superman Coming!"

With Mort Weisinger gone, his vast kingdom of Superman titles was divvied up among several editors. Weisinger's longtime assistant E. Nelson Bridwell took over *Lois Lane*. Murray Boltinoff took the reins of *Action*, *Superboy*, and *Jimmy Olsen*. Mike Sekowsky took over *Adventure*. Julius Schwartz—the man who'd orchestrated the Silver Age resurgence of DC heroes, was brought in to edit *Superman* and *World's Finest*. And he was none too happy about it.

Schwartz was frank with his fellow creators about his inability to "get his head around" the character he'd inherited from his friend Weisinger. His first act was to bring in writer Dennis "Denny" O'Neil, who'd spent the previous years contemporizing characters such as Wonder Woman and Green Arrow and attempting to wrest the character of Batman from under the long shadow of the sixties TV show.

O'Neil shared his editor's ambivalence, because he figured that such a high-profile character would come with too many corporate strings attached. He also found it difficult to get excited about a character who could see through time and blow out a star. "How do you write stories about a guy who can destroy a galaxy by listening hard?" O'Neil famously joked.

Schwartz and O'Neil resolved to depower the Man of Steel, taking him back to World War II–era levels. The key, they decided, was to let readers see him struggle again.

Fortress of Lassitude

Off in the pages of *Adventure*, meanwhile, Supergirl attended college and experimented with new Super-outfits, settling on a mini-skirt with a chain belt and a pair of red thigh-high boots in October 1970

(*Adventure* #397). It was the first of many costume changes the Maid of Might would experience. Unlike Wonder Woman or Batgirl, whose looks remained largely unchanged for decades, concerted efforts were made to ensure that Supergirl reflected the fashions of the times. Yet, of course, those times, and hemlines, continually changed, necessitating a constant cycle of new Supergirl looks and hairstyles. As the years progressed, miniskirt would give way to hot pants, a tunic to a V-necked blouse, short blond locks to a riotous perm.

The Man of Steel had a harder time keeping up with the fashions—and the social issues—of the day. His writers' uneasy relationship with the new passion for relevance in storylines is never more clearly displayed than in Robert Kanigher's Lois Lane story "I Am Curious (Black)" (*Superman's Girl Friend Lois Lane* #106, November 1970). Looking past the appropriateness of the title—a nod to a then scandalous 1967 film full of nudity and sex—this tale of Lois Lane is a well-meaning but ham-fisted puzzle.

Lois decides to visit Little Africa, "Metropolis' black community" in the hopes of "get[ting] the Pulitzer Prize for telling it like it is! The nitty-gritty no newspaper ever printed before!" Arriving in the black neighborhood, she finds herself shunned by locals. "Look at her, brothers and sisters! She's young and sweet and pretty! But never forget. *She's Whitey*!" Undaunted, Lois gets Superman to expose her to a narratively convenient piece of Kryptonian technobabble.

> Superman: Are you *sure* you want to step inside the *plastimold*, Lois? Do you know what's going to *happen* when I pull the switch of the *Transformoflux pack*?

The machine turns Lois into a black woman, and she returns to the community that wouldn't speak to her before, only to have a taxi refuse to pick her up and to suffer the suspicious stares of white people on the subway. She sees firsthand both the appalling conditions of life in Metropolis's slums and the selfless warmth of its residents. Her eyes opened, Lois confronts Superman.

And proceeds to make it *all*. About. Her.

> Lois: Look me straight in the eye! And tell me the truth! Do you *love* me? Suppose I couldn't change back? Would you *marry* me? Even if I'm *black*? An *outsider* in a *white man's world*?

Superman, showing superhuman restraint, politely points out to her that he himself might know a *little* something about being an outsider—what with the whole being from another planet millions of light-years away and all—before giving her his standard speech about not wanting to put her in danger from his many enemies.

"Let's Rap!"

In 1970, a survey appeared in the pages of DC's comics, with Superman and the Flash soliciting reader feedback. What's striking—and what speaks to just how disconnected the publisher felt from its readers—is that the two heroes talk in such tin-eared, self-consciously hip lingo.

"Let's Rap!"
Answer all the questions so we know who you are and what you think is groovy. Just because you helped us out and we love you for it we're giving away big gifts including a portable color TV set. We're drawing the names on September 30, 1970.
DIG!

Amid questions about the readers' ages, hobbies, where they bought their books, and whether they read advertisements in comics, the survey includes this question:

(Q5) How interested are you in reading about: (For each question check [Very interested, Fairly Interested or Not interested]).

a. Pollution
b. Black People
c. Space Flights
d. National Problems
e. City Problems
f. Sports (which one)
g. Hobbies
h. Romance
i. Astrology

Pollution, city problems, astrology, and black people. The seventies had arrived in force.

"Kirby Is Coming!"

In the waning years of Weisinger's tenure, furious negotiations had gone on behind the scenes. For two years, DC had been trying to woo Jack Kirby, the legendary artist whose cosmic-powered ideas, plots, designs, and layouts had established the visual language of Marvel's ascendancy. In 1970, the deal was made, and the news stunned comics fans. (The professional comics community, which had been hearing for years about Kirby's contentious relationship with Marvel in general and Stan Lee in particular, was perhaps less surprised.)

In a move that left many fans of Kirby's work scratching their heads, he decided to take over the writing and art chores on a DC book languishing near the bottom of the sales charts—*Superman's Pal, Jimmy Olsen*. A lackluster teen book such as *Jimmy Olsen* seemed a supremely odd fit for such a distinctive, ingenious creator—imagine Salvador Dali stepping in as showrunner on *Hannah Montana*—but Kirby had his reasons. Unlike other, more prominent titles, the *Olsen* book lacked a regular creative team, and Kirby didn't want to kick established creators off a book.

Kirby soon took over the editing of *Jimmy Olsen* and launched an interconnected series of books (*Forever People*, *New Gods*, and *Mister Miracle*) to chronicle his sprawling intergalactic myth-soaked "Fourth World" saga. In these tales, godlike beings locked in eternal struggle exploit amazing technology to decide the fate of existence itself. Many concepts from Kirby's run on these books would go on to become key elements of the mainstream DC Universe, none more so than his impossibly powerful intergalactic dictator Darkseid, who would, in just a few years' time, supplant Luthor as the Man of Steel's greatest foe.

Behind the scenes, however, Kirby's carte blanche deal with DC rubbed some fellow creators the wrong way. What's more, it showed in the work. He churned out pages and pages of comics he considered finished, more at home with dynamism and spectacle than in the more prosaic narrative business of characterization and, especially, dialogue. Although the concepts are boldly innovative, the execution is, to be kind, clunky—as in *Jimmy Olsen* #139 and #141 (July and September 1971), which for no discernible reason feature "Goody" Rickles, a Don Rickles look-alike given to dressing up as a superhero.

"You give somebody too much freedom," said artist Neal Adams to interviewer Michael Eury in 2006's *The Krypton Companion*, "[and] very often they screw themselves. And that's what Jack did. And yet nobody came to Jack and said, 'Jack, we gotta redo this thing. . . . I really have to give this to some professional writers and have them flesh it out because we're not getting whole stories here . . . it's just not working.'"

Because Kirby's way of drawing Superman was so completely his own, it differed markedly from the official DC model sheets supplied by Curt Swan. Too markedly, the publisher decided, and tapped Adams and other artists to take Kirby's pages and redraw the faces of Superman and Jimmy Olsen to bring them in line with the company's standards. DC also tasked Al Plastino and Murphy Anderson to soften Kirby's characteristically angular figure work. It was uncomfortable for the artists, who felt as if they were disrespecting a master draftsman and an already legendary creator, and it fueled Kirby's resentment. By 1972, many of the Fourth World titles would be canceled.

"Kryptonite Nevermore!"

Finally, in the January 1971 issue of *Superman* (#133), Schwartz and O'Neil revealed their new Superman status quo. A striking Neal Adams cover announces one of the changes in no uncertain terms: the Man of Steel stands, feet apart, thrusting out his massive chest and bursting a set of green kryptonite chains. His look is confident, even euphoric, as the text at his feet blares "*Kryptonite nevermore!*"

The splash page text: "Beginning . . . a Return to Greatness!"

As the story begins, a massive explosion of an experimental "kryptonite engine" leaves Superman unconscious—and also causes a chain reaction that turns all kryptonite on Earth to ordinary iron. At first, Superman is elated—until he realizes that he now possesses only a fraction of the power he once did. By the time the tale is over, he will face a duplicate version of himself spawned by that explosion, which will siphon off even more of his strength.

Meanwhile, the Galaxy Broadcasting System has bought the *Daily Planet*, and its slick, shady president Morgan Edge taps Clark Kent to be WGBS-TV's newest television reporter. A concerned Clark speaks for thousands of readers when he worries, "Will *Superman* always have to wait for commercials?"

The move to TV meant Clark Kent had to ditch the blue suit, white shirt, red tie ensemble he'd been sporting for most of his thirty-something years. Penciler Curt Swan and inker Murphy Anderson (credited as "Swanderson") widened the lapels of his suit jacket and added bold stripes, polka dots, and bright, retina-sizzling colors into his wardrobe. (Clark's kicky new togs were featured in an issue of *Gentlemen's Quarterly*.)

The Swan-Anderson team began to let some of the turbulence of the times show in the Man of Steel's face. His blue-black hair grew slightly longer (slightly!), his sideburns began to creep farther and farther down those granite cheekbones, and Swan adopted a more photorealistic approach that let readers begin to see more lines in his face. He looked less cartoony—but also older, more careworn, than before. This Superman, it was clear, stood not with America's wayward youth, but with their worried parents and guidance counselors.

Kryptonite? Some More!

O'Neil lasted less than a year on Superman, during which time he threw everything but the kryptonite sink at the Man of Steel. He turned the public against him, had him become a kind of Typhoid Clark, carrying a plague that turned the people of Earth into monsters, and, not to put too fine a point on it, sent Superman to Hell.

Despite Schwartz and O'Neil's ambitions to humanize the Man of Steel by bringing him low, the new editorial status quo—with multiple editors controlling different titles of the Superman mythos—meant that Weisingerian-level coordination and control were no longer possible. Without every creative team on board, readers turning from *Superman* to *Action* would be greeted by a character possessing far greater strength—and technology (Schwartz's "No more Superman robots" edict didn't reach writer Cary Bates, whose August 1971 [*Action* #403] story contained a deus ex machina that was an actual Super-machina).

Or they might encounter a Superman whose sensibility seemed jarringly different from that of O'Neill's Man of Steel. It's tough to imagine the thirty-three-year-old O'Neil writing a howler of a story like *Action* #398's "The Pied Piper of Steel" (written by a fifty-seven-year-old Leo Dorfman), the cover of which depicts Superman demolishing a building and inciting an angry mob: "Come on you cats! The university is next!"

In the story, Clark Kent becomes a roving TV reporter, gets outfitted with a sweet RV ("Wow," he thinks. "Now there's a freaky set of wheels!"), and covers a Woodstock-like event ("Those rock festivals are the big thing now!"), where a nefarious concert promoter uses music to mind-control throngs of dirty hippies ("Too bad I can't broadcast that music, folks! It's really turning those youngsters on!").

After O'Neil left Superman, and it became clear that the bold experiment hadn't boosted sales, the changes Schwartz and O'Neil had wrought began to unravel. As early as December 1971 (#208), the cover of *World's Finest* depicted Superman hitched to an enormous space harness, pulling planet Earth out of its orbit. Before long, kryptonite returned to plague the Man of Steel. O'Neil and Schwartz's most lasting change to the Superman status quo would turn out to be Clark's new job as a television reporter, but even that wouldn't endure forever.

Behold the (Super) Man

Meanwhile, Superman was turning up in toy stores more than ever. Aurora model kits featuring Superman beating down a brick wall— or Superboy and Krypto greeting a small dragon—were popular, and when, in 1973, the toy company Mego kicked off its World's Greatest Heroes line of eight-inch action figures, Superman was the first character to hit store shelves.

By now, money from licensing Superman's likeness eclipsed the income from comics sales, as the launch of the action figure line touched off a boomlet in licensed games, jigsaw puzzles, coloring books, play sets, stickers, and related merchandise. Superman imagery by artists such as Neal Adams and Jose Luis Garcia-Lopez soon began to turn up with increasing regularity on all manner of merchandise. Superman had always been both a character and a commodity, but during the early seventies, the iconography of the Man of Steel became a wholly separate entity, with its own appeal to millions who didn't read the comics.

It wasn't just kids; parents, too, soon began to see Superman turn up in unexpected places. Jim Croce name-checked him, as did the shroom-inflected lyrics of the New Riders of the Purple Sage. The Jesus character in the 1970 Broadway musical *Godspell*—and in the subsequent 1973 film adaptation—sported a shirt emblazoned with the trademark "S" shield. This playful invocation of an affinity between Jesus Christ and Superman would not be the last; in 1978, the writers of Superman's first big-screen incarnation would find occasion to strike the same chord, more loudly.

Taking It Seriously

The move toward a new photorealistic approach to comic art, ushered in by artists such as Neal Adams, merely echoed a growing thirst among comics fans—who were older and more sophisticated than their Silver Age counterparts—for "realism" in their comics. They now wanted to dissect and discuss every possible aspect of Super-lore. Fans would no longer let writers get away with cutting narrative corners or availing themselves of wacky contrivances— they interrogated stories with a new zeal. They wanted numbers, metrics, to quantify and fuel their endless discussions about which hero could kick which other hero's nigh-invulnerable butt. They performed thought experiments to investigate the unforeseen—or, at least, unexplored—limitations and ramifications of powers such as heat vision, supercold breath, superhearing, and superstrength. How, they wondered, could Superman hear things happening halfway across the globe, when the vibrations of those sound waves would attenuate long before they could make the journey overseas?

In an essay written for the girlie magazine *Knight* later collected in his 1971 book *All the Myriad Ways*, science fiction writer Larry Niven humorously and graphically tackled a question that had been asked only privately, sniggeringly, in the backs of school buses and in the occasional punchy/tipsy/raunchy editorial meeting: What about sex?

What would happen if invulnerable, superstrong Superman ever did get his super-freak on with the very human, and thus comparatively fragile, Lois Lane? The answer, as far as Niven was concerned, was so obvious he made it the title of his essay on the topic: "Man of Steel, Woman of Kleenex."

The essay details Niven's (*remarkably* thorough) theories about the problematic nature of Krypto-terrestrial coitus, the difficulties of artificial Super-insemination ("We may reasonably assume that kryptonian sperm . . . are capable of translight velocities.") and possible solutions (expose the sperm to gold kryptonite!) and ponders whether, if the fetus uses X-ray vision, it would render Lois sterile. The ultimate answer to the question of super-fetus gestation—namely, that Superman should carry the fetus inside his own invulnerable abdomen—is presented as a QED.

The gag, of course, is the deadpan, painstaking manner in which Niven lays out his thought process. This is where you end up if you take this stuff too seriously, he seems to say: killer sperm from outer space.

Looking back on Niven's humorous essay today, it's impossible to see it as anything but a chilling harbinger of the high-level, weapons-grade nerdery that would seize comics in the decades that followed. All too soon, legions of fans and creators adopted Niven's let's-pin-this-to-the-specimen-board approach and proceeded to leach humor and whimsy and good old-fashioned, Beppo the Super-Monkey–level goofiness out of superhero comics, leaving in their place a punishing, joyless, nihilistic grittiness.

Even in the pages of *Superman* comics, the new crop of writers who'd grown up on the character were beginning to grapple with this new "realism" and "relevance." In January 1972 (*Superman* #247), the then twenty-two-year-old-writer Elliot Maggin explored Superman's place and purpose in a story called "Must There Be a Superman?" The story, inspired by an idea from future Superman scribe Jeph Loeb, would form what Maggin called "the pivot point" on which his understanding of the character was based.

The story opens with Superman performing a special mission for the Guardians of the Universe—a group of immortal, impassive galactic overseers who "survey and safeguard the 100 billion stars in the Milky Way galaxy and the lives that grow in their light." Afterward, the manipulative, passive-aggressive, vaguely bitchy Guardians "casually" mention to the Man of Steel that his presence on Earth is stunting human social growth and causing a "cultural lag." When Superman asks what they mean, they wave the question away like the Mean Girls they are—having successfully placed the nagging self-doubt in his mind.

"For years I've been playing *big brother* to the *human race!*" he thinks. "Have I been *wrong*? Are they depending on me *too much . . . too often*?"

Back on Earth, he encounters a farmer abusing a young field-hand. The excited workers rally around the Man of Steel: "Now you can solve all our problems!" they say, in case the reader has somehow missed the story's thesis. Superman explains that they can redress their problems on their own, by striking, and melodramatically announces that he will do "Nothing! *Nothing at all!*" to help them.

Just then, an earthquake destroys their village. Superman rebuilds their homes—leaving the villagers understandably confused. Patiently, the Man of Steel lays out his new mission statement: he will help when humans are up against something they cannot defend against, but when the problem is more manageable, "You don't need a *Superman*! What you need is the *super-will* to be *guardians* of *your own destiny!*"

The Terra-Man with No Name

Two months later, the cover of *Superman* #249 made a grandiose promise: "Introducing . . . the Man of Steel's Latest and Greatest Foe. . . . *Terra-Man!*" The "latest" bit is hard to argue with: Cary Bates's laconic future cowboy—who, for good measure, rides a winged horse—was the first major new villain introduced into Superman's rogues' gallery since the Parasite five years earlier. But "greatest"? That was a promise the character just couldn't keep. Though not for lack of trying.

Inspired by Clint Eastwood's Man with No Name character in a string of spaghetti Westerns, Cary Bates created a villain who'd challenge Superman with a combination of advanced technology and Old West tropes—for example, a device that explodes into a sky-written warning to Superman that reads (wait for it) "Earth's not big enough for the two of us."

Meanwhile, in the pages of *Superboy*, the Legion of Super-Heroes was undergoing a revitalization. Artist Dave Cockrum, a onetime protégé of inker Murphy Anderson, took over penciling chores, imbuing Legion stories with a bold, ultramodern design aesthetic utterly unlike the quaint sixties retro-future look the stories had evinced for years.

He also radically redesigned the costumes of several Legionnaires, infusing the characters (especially the female characters) with a bracing, unapologetic sexiness that gave readers fodder for enthusiastic debate. (When it came to Saturn Girl's new bikini-esque uniform, for example, there was a good deal more enthusiasm than debate.)

In all, Cockrum worked on just twelve Legion issues, but during his tenure, the sexy superpowered teens from the future managed to relegate Superboy to backup stories in his own title.

Easy Like Saturday Morning

On September 8, 1973, a nation of pajama-clad kids tuned in to ABC to watch the premiere episode of a new hourlong animated program produced by Hanna-Barbera. They were greeted by Ted Knight's stentorian baritone, declaiming the stirring words of the show's opening narration. (The show's theme song—a driving, martial anthem that breaks into a joyous fanfare—would infiltrate the minds and hearts of a generation, as would Knight's idiosyncratic pronunciations ("*Ack*-wuh-man! *Wun-duh Wuh-mun*!").

The hugely successful *Super Friends* would run on ABC—in a variety of formats, with an ever-changing roster of heroes and villains—for more than a decade. For a new generation of American kids, the show would represent their first encounter with the concept of superheroes in general and Superman in particular. DC Comics, sensitive to this fact, made sure to devote special episodes of the show to retelling each hero's origin stories—powerful, time-tested narratives with the proven ability to capture kids' hearts, even if those kids were buzzed out of their minds on Sugar Smacks.

Los Angeles DJ and commercial voice-over star Danny Dark, the rich baritone behind the "Sorry, Charlie" Sunkist tuna and "Raid kills bugs dead" ad campaigns, was tapped to play Superman. Dark's Man of Steel had a deep, authoritative baritone but lacked a true emotional range—his voice seemed perfectly suited to the stiff Hanna-Barbera animation.

The comic relief provided by the addition of teenage sidekicks Wendy and Marvin and their caped canine was a thin gruel indeed. It remained so, even when they were given the boot and replaced by shape-shifting teenage alien twins Zan and Jayna—and their space-monkey, Gleek.

The decision to focus the action on kid sidekicks leached drama from the proceedings, and this lack of narrative momentum was only exacerbated by the heroes' TV-watchdog-enforced passivity. In an era when concern over TV violence turned even Tom and Jerry into a pair of blandly chummy milquetoasts, the Super Friends never quite got around to hitting anything.

For the first few seasons, in fact, the heroes rarely faced off against actual villainy. Instead, many of their foes were driven to extreme measures by a desire to conserve natural resources or make life easier for mankind. (In 1978, the series introduced the Legion of Doom, full of cackling, sinister supervillains, and more sophisticated plots borrowed from the comics.)

Man of Tomorrowland?

On January 21, 1972, the Ohio River town of Metropolis, population seven thousand, in southeast Illinois, began to call itself "the Hometown of Superman." The whole town got in on the act, angling to attract tourist dollars. In May, the local paper changed its name from the *Metropolis News* to the *Metropolis Planet*.

On Saturday, May 26, 1973, the "Amazing World of Superman Exhibition Center"—an eleven-thousand-square-foot former roller rink painted blue, red, and yellow—opened to the public. Exhibits included a cinema showing Superman cartoons and serials, a model of Superman's boyhood home, displays of various forms of kryptonite, George Reeves's costume, and a series of photos depicting how a comic book is made.

DC Comics prepared a special comic for the occasion, *The Amazing World of Superman: Metropolis Edition*, which featured a map of Krypton, hints on drawing the Man of Steel, reprints of several old Superman tales, and a brand new "Origin of Superman" drawn by Swan and Anderson and written by DC's resident Superman continuity expert, editor E. Nelson Bridwell. In writing the origin,

Bridwell decided the time had once again come to wrestle divergent storylines into order.

"It was decided that the only thing to do was throw out part of the tales and work the rest into a consistent whole," he told readers, but the tweaks were mostly minor. For the sake of a planned Superman theme park, he made two significant changes: In all previous versions of the origin, the rocket ship that had piloted Kal-El to Earth had self-destructed, but Bridwell had the Kents keep and hide it, to explain why "Superbaby's rocket ship" could be on display in the park. He also included a scene in which Clark stands over his foster parents' graves in the backyard of their house, because the headstones were also to be features of the park's replica Kent home.

A May 23, 1973, UPI article with a headline straight out of the comics, "Superman Honored by City," suggests the town—certain members of it, anyway—wasn't kidding around.

> Mike Forbes, 26, a Marion high school English and psychology teacher, will quit his job to take the role of Superman on a full-time basis. He says he regards it as a "challenge."
>
> A former Marion, Ill. high school football star and shot putter at Murray State College in Kentucky, Forbes is 6 feet, 6½ inches tall and weighs 250 pounds. He wears a 52 extra-long coat and size 14e shoes. And he is mild-mannered, like Superman's alter ego, reporter Clark Kent.

DC Comics, sensing an opportunity—and noting with interest the success of the newly opened Disney World—commissioned Neal Adams to come up with some concept sketches for a vast theme park to be called the Amazing World of Superman (or, informally, Supermanland) built on the outskirts of Metropolis. The design was loosely based on a 1955 *Action Comics* story called "Superman in Superman Land" and featured several elements from that tale, including a "Voyage to Krypton" ride and a Disney-like "Main Street" of Smallville.

Attendees would enter the park through the legs of a giant Superman statue. A Bizarro playground would be filled with backward or upside-down swing sets, jungle gyms, slides, and games. Visitors would stroll through a full-size Bottle City of Kandor and marvel at the Rainbow Falls of Krypton, a Hall of Science, and the capital city of Kryptonopolis itself. Towering over the entire park would be the Fortress of Solitude, complete with Giant Golden Key—and a restaurant overlooking the park.

The oil crunch of the early seventies had driven gas prices through the roof, however, and when the planned interstate that would pass near the park was beset by delays, the hugely ambitious Supermanland project was abandoned.

The town of Metropolis did not give up on Superman, though it would take years for the sting of this high-profile failure to fade.

The Saga of the Super-Sons!

In the January 1973 issue of *World's Finest* (215), writer Bob Haney and artist Dick Dillin attempted to do something many before them had tried but failed: they tackled the ever-widening generation gap between Superman (who was lately putting "the Man" in "the Man of Steel") and his adolescent readers head on—and leaped across it.

The result looked a lot like what Denny O'Neil had tried to create, a year earlier. Here was a Man of Steel who was less power-ful and more relatable—who was, in fact, a creature who should not exist: a Superman of pure, adolescent id, a Man of Steel perfectly suited to the Marvel Age.

The Superman in question wasn't *the* Superman, technically. Yet it was *a* Superman.

In point of fact, it was Superman Jr.—a snot-nosed, rebellious teen given to tantrums and peppering his speech with outdated, hippie-dippie locutions. This was the *Saga of the Super-Sons*, a series of profoundly, stubbornly odd stories that whirled together a broody, teen-baiting, Marvelesque emotionalism with a tincture of old-school DC Silver Age weirdness.

Imaginary stories? Not according to Haney. No, the story's nar-rator assures us, these tales are "not imaginary, not fantasy but *real, the way it happened.*"

And *what* tales! In the first, Superman Jr. and Batman Jr. pres-sure their fathers to let them fight crime, but their fuddy-duddy dads fear their sons will get hurt. To test them, Superman travels to a city on the San Andreas Fault and causes an earthquake, the vibra-tions of which somehow create a second city that's displaced in time (it exists one day in the past), for the unwitting super-sons to defend.

It is one of the least weird things to occur in a series of eleven *Super-Sons* stories published during the course of the following three years. The boys set off across the country on a shared motorcycle to find themselves, face biker gangs and crooked coppers, join an "Encounter Camp" with their fathers to "work out their generation gap," and encounter female separatists, all the while emoting like X-Men ("Look, I'm sorry I was born with super-strength! It's a big responsibility . . . and it doesn't give me super-happiness!") and spouting "youth culture" catchphrases like sitcom hippies straight from central casting.

Haney's assertion that the stories were "real" was allowed to go unchallenged for a surprisingly long time, but weirdness of the kind on display in these stories must be contained. In *World's Finest* #263 (July 1980), a full four years after the last *Super-Sons* tale had been published, Denny O'Neil wrote a story that tied a tidy bow on the Jrs., revealing that the stories had simply been part of a computer simulation taking place at the Fortress of Solitude.

Ch-Ch-Ch-Changes

At first, Jack Kirby's *Jimmy Olsen* title had exposed a seamier, grittier side of Metropolis, but now every page roiled with more cosmic concerns—the palace intrigues, familial struggles, and mind-bending technology of a great and terrible pantheon of New Gods, whose very fingertips crackled with enough raw power to consume planets, shatter galaxies, and rend the very heavens themselves in twain.

It didn't sell.

Not enough, anyway. Kirby left the book with issue 148 (April 1972) to concentrate on his other Fourth World books, along with the futuristic *OMAC* (*One Man Army Corps*) and the post-apocalyptic *Kamandi, Last Boy on Earth*, but it didn't take long for all of them to fall under the ax, and Kirby returned to Marvel in 1975.

Writers such as Leo Dorfman did their best to keep the *Jimmy Olsen* title alive, but the book was canceled with issue 163 in March 1974. In October of that same year, with issue 137, the bell tolled for *Lois Lane*'s book, as well as for *Supergirl*'s solo title, which had survived for only ten issues.

With Kirby's departure, the Fourth World characters and concepts Kirby had developed during his DC stint would now begin to thread their way through the background of the entire DC Universe, forming an intricate network of narrative connections between *Legion*, *Justice League*, and *Superman* tales.

For *Jimmy Olsen*, *Lois Lane*, and *Supergirl*, however, cancellation was a much less dramatic event, because their adventures were simply folded into a new anthology title.

Superman Family debuted in April/May 1974, beginning with issue #164 (having simply adopted the numbering of *Jimmy Olsen*, the longest-lasting book of the three it had subsumed). The book was coedited by Julius Schwartz and Murray Boltinoff.

By now, Schwartz had taken over the editing of *Action Comics*, too, and would eventually become editor or coeditor of all of the Super-titles DC published, with the exception of *Superboy Starring the Legion of Super-Heroes*, which would remain in Boltinoff's hands alone. Schwartz had effectively united the kingdom of Superman under his banner, much as Weisinger had done, but he was a more benevolent ruler. It was during his tenure that comics storytelling subtly but irrevocably changed. In Weisinger's time, it was rare for a story to take two issues to tell; now story arcs occasionally began to stretch out over three, four, or five months.

Until this era—which would come to be known as the Bronze Age—a comics script read much very like a radio script. "Great Scott!" Superman might say, in a panel depicting him using his telescopic vision to spot a giant meteor hurtling toward Metropolis, "My telescopic vision has spotted a giant meteor! And it's hurtling toward Metropolis!"

Panels without narration or dialogue were rare enough that when one occurred—as it did in the story introducing Terra-Man, when Swan and Anderson depicted the villain and his winged horse diving through a break in the clouds, limned by the rays of the rising sun—the effect was striking. Yet gradually, during the course of the decade, the relationship between text and image would change, with writers trusting artists to convey more and more information visually.

Sp-Sp-Sp-Speedos

After Dave Cockrum's brief term on *Superboy Starring the Legion of Super-Heroes*, during which he'd brought a sleek, unapologetically sexy aesthetic to the book, Mike Grell inked Cockrum's pencils for one issue and then officially took over the art chores with the next (#203, August 1974), where he proceeded to up the sexy even more.

Grell believed that in the more enlightened thirtieth-century DC universe, skin would be in. What's more, his costume designs testified to the fact that both female Legionnaires and their male counterparts felt comfortable exposing plenty of flesh. (They were, after all, hormonal teenagers.) Detractors have dinged Grell's designs for their Ming-the-Merciless collars, bikini bottoms, and pixie boots (and that's just on the *men*)—and it's true that in some panels, Legion HQ crowd scenes seem more like the VIP lounge at Studio 54, but his designs made the book look like nothing else on the shelves.

The downside to Grell's ultraglam Legion (Cosmic Boy, for example, wore what was essentially a bustier cut to the navel) was that it made Superboy's familiar blue-and-red number look comparatively square. And this at a time when the Boy (and Man) of Steel was fighting the growing public perception that he was a glorified policeman who wielded heat vision instead of a billy club—a caped cop, if you will. A super-pig.

If the Man of Steel seemed a bit conservative standing among his salaciously attired fellow Legionnaires, they were nothing compared to Vartox, the Speedo-clad superhero from outer space. Next to that guy, Superman looked downright Victorian.

Superman first meets Vartox in *Superman* #281 (November 1974). Writer Cary Bates had a very specific look in mind for the character and gave artist Curt Swan several stills of Sean Connery in the film *Zardoz*, which had been released the previous February.

Swan delivered. Like Connery, Vartox wears a skimpy leather vest over his hairy, muscular chest, a pair of trunks that the term *banana hammock* was invented to describe (which are at least an improvement over the red diaper-esque loincloth Connery sports in the movie), and leather thigh boots with tiny jets attached to them. The vest, it feels important to note, sported shoulder pads.

Unfortunate sartorial choices aside, the character of Vartox—who would make several return appearances during the next ten years—introduced something wholly new to the Superman universe: the concept of an older hero in whom the Man of Steel believes. For a hero defined by the dense network of relationships he shares with his sprawling cast of characters, it was no small thing to introduce someone to whom the Man of Steel defers.

Even Superman, we learned, has a Superman.

Vindication, of a Sort

In 1975, a Warner Bros. lawyer contacted Jerry Siegel in an effort to make his lawsuit over ownership of Superman go away. There was, Siegel learned, a Superman movie in the works, and it could not proceed unless they put this unpleasant business behind them. A modest annual stipend was preliminarily agreed to.

Yet for months after that opening conversation, Siegel didn't hear anything—until he read in the trades that Warners had bought the rights to Superman from DC for $4 million.

Siegel was incensed. He wrote a ten-page, single-spaced screed against the executives who had nickel-and-dimed him for decades even as they pocketed huge profits from his and Shuster's creation. "I, Jerry Siegel, co-originator of *Superman*, put a curse on the *Superman* movie!" He sent it to newspapers and radio and television stations across the country. Eventually, his story appeared on the front page of the *Washington Times* (where it was read by Superman artist Neal Adams), which led to an appearance on Tom Snyder's *Tomorrow Show* (which was seen by veteran comics artist and Joker-creator Jerry Robinson, then president of the National Cartoonists Society [NCS]).

Adams and Robinson decided that they would circumvent the courts and take Siegel and Shuster's case to the people, essentially shaming Warner Bros. and DC into doing the right thing. Adams spearheaded a media blitz; Robinson gathered the support of the NCS, the Screen Cartoonists Guild, the Writers Guild of America, and other associations; eventually, an agreement was reached.

Siegel and Shuster would each receive $20,000 every year for the rest of their lives, and the words "Superman created by Jerry Siegel and Joe Shuster" would henceforth return to all printed material and the credits of television programs and movies.

The money, of course, was an infinitesimal fraction of the fortune their creation had made for DC, but Siegel and Shuster were tired and broke, and their medical expenses were growing. And for the first time in years, the character they'd brought into the world would bear their name.

That night—Christmas Eve—on the *CBS Evening News*, Walter Cronkite signed off his broadcast with the story of the settlement, concluding: "Today, at least, truth, justice and the American way have triumphed. And that's the way it is, December 24, 1975."

Superman on the Air

Between new episodes of *Super Friends*, old episodes of the Filmation cartoons, the 1950s George Reeves show (which still did well in syndication), and commercials for all manner of Superman merchandise—everything from action figures to Underoos to bath foam (which came in a canister equipped with a nozzle such that the foam dispensed from Superman's mouth)—the Man of Steel was all over the airwaves.

A series of U.S. Air Force recruiting ads featured sports figures interacting with Superman, played by bodybuilder-actor Peter Lupus. Later, after a nude pictorial of Lupus appeared in *Playgirl*, he was replaced in the ads by blond actor Denny Miller (star of 1959's *Tarzan, the Ape Man*) in a black dye job.

On Friday, February 1, 1975, ABC aired a ninety-minute adaptation of the 1966 *It's a Bird . . . It's a Plane . . . It's Superman* Broadway musical, as part of its late-night *Wide World of Entertainment* programming block. The program aired opposite the juggernaut that was the *Tonight Show* and received poor ratings and even worse reviews.

It's easy to see why. The production was done on the ultra-cheap. Sets were constructed and painted to seem like black-and-white comic-book panels, but the net effect looked more like an elementary-school play. Four of the musical's songs were chopped to accommodate the program's ninety-minute time slot, and the original script's troupe of Chinese acrobats was changed to a squad of "dese-and-dose" gangsters in pinstripe suits.

The show is available on DVD and online and is of interest today as a curiosity, albeit a hilariously dated one. Where the Broadway show had ensconced itself squarely in the established musical theater tradition, which imparts a sense of timelessness, the 1975 TV adaptation is awash in the bell-bottomed, wah-wah pedal zeitgeist of its time. The comedy is seventies variety-show broad, the performances constantly wink at the audience, and scenes move with a sluggishness that borders on the narcotic.

In a representative example of the show's fundamentally mis-thought nature, the Broadway show's only standout song, the bright, tinkly "You've Got Possibilities," in which gossip reporter Sydney flirts with Clark, is now a low, slow, and fuzzy funk number, full of saxophones and electric guitars. Imagine "Tea for Two" arranged by Barry White.

"Who Took the Super out of Superman?"

Superman had a villain problem.

If that wasn't readily apparent in *Action Comics* #458 (April 1976), when Superman tangled with his "newest, most fantastic foe," a villain named Blackrock who was secretly a television network executive with the power to convert television signals into energy blasts, it became painfully clear the following month, in *Superman* #299, the conclusion of a four-part story arc called "Who Took the Super out of Superman?"

In the issue, Superman uses his telescopic vision to check in on Clark's apartment, only to spy, to his horror, "Nine of the most fearsome super-villains I've ever *fought*! *Terra-Man*! *Toyman*! *Luthor*! *Brainiac*! *Mr. Mxyzptlk*! *Prankster*! *Amalak*! *Parasite*! And from my *super boy*-hood—*Kryptonite Man*! Lolling around in *my apartment* . . . as if it were a *super-villain hangout*!"

Swan renders the gathering amusingly, depicting the vile android Brainiac, scourge of the galaxy, sitting on Clark's ottoman and chatting away with Luthor as if he's at some kind of Stitch-n-Bitch-of-Doom. Yet the group turns out to be just an illusion, much like the notion that Terra-Man, Toyman, and Prankster belong on anyone's "most fearsome" list, to say nothing of Amalak—a low-rent, mustachioed space pirate Superman had faced only once since the villain's first appearance, ten years earlier.

When it came to worthy adversaries, Superman couldn't match Batman's or Spider-Man's roster of intriguing, psychologically damaged foes. No, the Man of Steel's archvillain bench was just two characters deep—Luthor, a mad scientist driven by hatred, and Brainiac, a computer driven by cold, merciless logic.

So in the landmark "Who Took the Super Out of Superman?" story, cowriters Cary Bates and Elliot Maggin (Bates plotted, Maggin wrote the dialogue) pitted Superman against himself.

The Superman vs. Clark storyline was already a fixture of the comics. Every year, in one title or another, some mechanical device, magical imp, or chunk of red kryptonite was forever splitting Superman and Clark into two people. This time, however, the divide is psychological. It begins when Superman suddenly realizes that whenever he assumes his guise as Clark Kent, his powers go away.

As an experiment, he decides to remain in the Clark Kent identity for a while, to see what life as a full-time human feels like. The experience changes Clark in subtle ways: he stands up to a bully at work, realizes that the Metropolis Fire Department can handle crises without his help, and—in the story's truly significant (and controversial) development—consummates his relationship with Lois Lane.

It happens when Lois, intrigued by Clark's new confidence and assertiveness, invites herself over to his apartment to cook him dinner. "In the next hour or so," a caption informs us, "Clark finds out what a good cook Lois is—and that there's a *lot* they didn't know about each other."

Yet soon, Clark starts to have nightmares about all of the crimes and crises he hasn't been helping to avert, so he decides to try being Superman full time—only to realize that trying to be everywhere for everybody is an impossible task, and that, as Superman, he can no longer relax around his friends, who believe he should always be off saving someone.

Ultimately, he learns that "the split-effect" was caused by a sinister alien being called Xviar, an agent who has been tasked with destroying the Earth to make way for an intergalactic transportation route (two years *before* Douglas Adams' *The Hitchhiker's Guide to the Galaxy*). Xviar has disguised himself as Clark's mysterious neighbor Mr. Xavier (who'd been introduced into the comics four years earlier) and has treated Clark's suits with a chemical that blocked out the sun's yellow radiation.

The villain sorted, Superman's powers restored, he resumes his dual role, reverting Clark to his former timid disposition, much to Lois's dismay. "Poor Lois!" he thinks. "I tried to decide whether *Clark* or *Superman* is more important . . . and realized that to do away with *one* would be to *kill* half of myself—*whoever* I really am!"

That "whoever I really am" reads, at first, like a throwaway line, but, of course, it's the question that's resided at the heart of the character since *Action Comics* #1. Thirty-eight years earlier, Siegel had answered that question one way; ten years later, John Byrne would answer it in another; Mark Waid still another eighteen years after that, and it will continue to be answered by different writers in different ways for as long as Superman exists in any form.

For now, however, Superman resolves, "Meek, mild-mannered *Clark Kent* will still walk the streets of the city—while up in the sky . . . the world will still watch and thrill to the sight of . . . *a job for Superman!*"

The Battle of the Century

The etiquette of the DC Universe was markedly different from that of Marvel's. DC heroes formed groups and subgroups with the eager enthusiasm of public policy project managers. Marvel heroes, on the other hand, tended to attack one another, both on first meeting and periodically thereafter. Stan Lee knew that "Who would win in a fight?" was more than a simple story engine; it was a question that stoked fannish fervor into a blazing buying frenzy.

Yet fighting wasn't Superman's style. Oh, he'd race the Flash around the world—for charity—but to him, violence was a last resort. Plus, he was Superman. Who would fight him?

So, it took some doing—both behind the scenes, and on the page—for the Man of Steel to face off against Spider-Man, but in 1976, a massive joint project between Marvel and DC, *Superman vs. The Amazing Spider-Man*, hit the stands.

As befitting the epic nature of the event, the book was printed as an oversize, ninety-six-page Treasury Edition. It wasn't the first time the two rival companies had copublished a book—that distinction belongs to a comic book adaptation of MGM's *The Wizard of Oz*, published in 1975—but it was the most fraught. Both publishers were committing their flagship characters to the venture, so the process of making the book was a legal, financial, and editorial mine field.

It was decided that every stage of the project would involve contributions from both DC and Marvel. DC's Gerry Conway wrote, and Marvel's Ross Andru penciled the book. DC's Dick Giordano inked, and Marvel's Glynis Oliver colored. Neal Adams tightened Andru's Superman figures and faces for DC, John Romita did the same on Peter Parker for Marvel. The book was edited by the two companies' editors in chief, Stan Lee and Carmine Infantino, with input from a committee of assistant DC and Marvel editors.

Getting the two heroes into a brawl involved a higher-than-usual number of villainous machinations on the part of the Luthor–Doctor Octopus team: Luthor disguises himself as Superman and kidnaps both Lois Lane and Spider-Man's girlfriend, Mary Jane Watson. He then fires a raygun at Spider-Man, which conveniently imbues the web-slinger's costume with red sun radiation, so that he and Superman can fight each other on roughly equal footing.

Out of deference to the fans, in the ensuing battle both heroes get their licks in—first Spidey sends Superman hurtling toward the pavement, then Superman delivers a haymaker that sends Spider-Man sailing across several city blocks. Soon, however—too soon for many rabid readers—the two heroes realize they have been duped, and they join forces to rescue their sweethearts and defeat the Luthor–Doc Ock team.

Conway's characterization underlines the distinctions between the two heroes; Spider-Man is all little-guy wit and wisecracks, while Superman comes across like a steroidal but affable Eagle Scout. The book, as both publishers expected, was a hit; a second print run of five thousand was signed by both Infantino and Lee and would inspire several more super-battles—although Superman would keep things a little closer to home for the time being.

An Unserious Book Takes Superman Seriously

The 1977 novel *Superfolks*, by Robert Mayer, represents the first time the capes-and-cowls set came in for anything approaching serious literary treatment. Mayer's tale of a faded superhero—a blue-haired Superman analogue named David Brinkley, the lone survivor of planet Cronk—contains graphic sex scenes, raunchy humor, and pop-culture references by the cubic ton, but it's also a carefully crafted work of fiction that locates the human in the superhuman.

The book's dryly ironic, introspective tone helped inspire comic-book writers who read it in their formative years—such as Kurt Busiek—to take a more realistic look at their superheroic charges. Yet echoes of Mayer's seminal book also turn up in the work of Michael Chabon, Jonathan Lethem, and others, because what Mayer wrestles with in *Superfolks* is an essential truth: the superhero is America in full—its noble ideals, its brutal violence, its garish spectacle.

Explosion and Implosion

The 1970s were an era long before entertainment news became a massive industry unto itself, and entire television networks could devote themselves to reading industry tea leaves with breathless enthusiasm twenty-four hours a day. Today, when a studio announces that a big-budget movie is going into production, websites, television shows, and magazines roil with speculation and hype. Yet in the 1970s, all of the day's entertainment news could fit inside "Hollywood Minute" segments on local evening news broadcasts.

It's likely, then, that many comics readers first learned of their hero's upcoming live-action cinematic debut when they picked up their comics in the summer of 1977 and saw the cover banner proclaiming, "*You* can be in the *Superman movie*! Details inside."

"The Great Superman Movie Contest," as DC called it, asked readers to clip out letters appearing in special coupons inside DC Comics to spell the words *Superman* and either *Kal-El* or *Clark*, glue them to a card, and send them to DC. The contest offered two first prizes—cameo roles in the upcoming Superman movie (plus an expense-paid trip to the DC offices)—and five thousand second-place prizes, including one-year comics subscriptions.

DC was pinning a great deal of hope on the Superman movie. In advance of what it deemed would be an event that would dramatically raise the profile of, and demand for, comic books, DC had already instituted sweeping changes. It increased the page count and the cover prices across its entire line, and the number of different titles it offered had ballooned; DC added sixteen titles in 1975, twenty-one in 1976, and twelve in 1977. These new books included several fantasy, war, martial arts, and horror titles, plus TV tie-ins such as *Isis*, *Super Friends*, and (for reasons lost to history) *Welcome Back, Kotter*.

"We've been calling all of this *the DC Explosion*," publisher Jenette Kahn wrote in an editorial, "and that's what it truly is—an explosion of new ideas, new concepts, new characters and new formats. We now have near limitless opportunities to experiment, to do longer and indeed better stories, to be more flexible in the type of material we're presenting. The best is getting better."

Hopeful words, but the passion for "new concepts" and "experiments" passed Superman by entirely. Instead, DC looked to the Man of Steel to do what he'd always done—to remain the company's dependable sales leader, racking up solid, if unspectacular, numbers—while the DC Explosion writers and artists desperately sought to find new audiences that would revitalize a stalled industry.

They wouldn't find that new audience, and in 1978, the DC Explosion would be followed by a staggering implosion, with the cancellation of no fewer than sixty-five DC comics when the shake-out was over. It knocked the already struggling comics industry back on its heels and helped chase comics out of the nation's grocery store spinner racks and into specialty stores devoted entirely to comics.

Yet Superman, as was his wont, emerged from it all without a scratch. In fact, 1978 would prove to be the best year he'd had since the Golden Age.

8

THE YEAR OF
SUPERMAN (1978)

Keenly aware that *Superman: The Movie* would premiere in December, DC (and Warner Bros., its parent company) spent 1978 attempting to raise the Man of Steel's profile by pumping out an unprecedented number of Superman products.

An *Official Superman Quiz* book by Bruce Nash contained hundreds of trivia questions covering Superman's fifty-year history. Michael Fleisher, a former writer and editor for *Encyclopedia Britannica*, published *The Great Superman Book*, a phonebook-thick chronicle of every character, place, power, and idea that had appeared in a *Superman* comic between the years 1938 and 1964. The result of a five-year effort, *The Great Superman Book* is an astonishing accomplishment and stands as the most rigorous and exhaustive examination of the character ever published. Without Fleisher's efforts, countless books that came afterward—including this one—would not be possible.

In April, the *Chicago Tribune/New York Times* Syndicate launched a new daily newspaper comic strip called *World's Greatest Superheroes*, featuring Superman, Batman, Wonder Woman, and other DC heroes. Several DC writers and artists worked on the series during its seven-year life span, including Martin Pasko, Paul Levitz, and Gerry Conway, with art from George Tuska, Vince Colletta, and others.

The Man of Steel's first video game incarnation, *Superman*, was released for the Atari 2600 console. Crude even by the day's standards—with pixels so large that characters appear to be multicolored stacks of boxes—the game was essentially a race against time. A green stack of boxes (Lex Luthor) destroys a bridge, so a blue stack of boxes (Clark) must change into a blue stack of boxes with a red squiggle (Superman), reassemble the bridge, capture the Lex stack of boxes and his henchstacks, and avoid glowy green boxes (kryptonite). If touched by kryptonite, Superstack loses his ability to fly and can regain it only by getting a kiss from a stack of boxes in a dress (Lois Lane).

Easily the most ignominious pseudo-tie-in, however, was the disco song "Superman" released by Celi Bee and the Buzzy Bunch, which went to number 3 on the *Billboard* dance chart and later became a more modest hit for Herbie Mann. ("You get so deep inside and, wow/You warm me up, it's super/Do it to me Superman-man-man.")

Meanwhile, the town of Metropolis, Illinois, undaunted by the failure of its Superman theme park initiative, held the first annual Metropolis Superman Celebration, featuring displays of memorabilia, live music, costume competitions, and a host of activities for kids in the town square.

Super-Smackdowns

With a major motion picture on the way, the contemporary reader might reasonably assume that in the months leading up to the premiere, DC Comics editors and writers dedicated themselves to coordinating their storylines, characters, and perhaps even various design elements with the film production. Certainly, the last time the character had enjoyed a similar chance to reach beyond the comics shelves to a mass audience—during the run of the fifties television show—the comics had moved in lockstep. Yet that had been an inevitable result of DC holding creative control over all aspects of the television program, and this was a different era.

In 1978, the film production and the comics occupied wholly separate fiefdoms. Neither Warner Bros. nor DC bothered much with the notion of "branding" Superman to create consistency among the various iterations of the character available to the public, the way they would today. Instead, DC concentrated on filling the shelves with as many books featuring the Man of Steel as they would bear.

The year in comics began with the release of an oversize Collector's Edition comic inspired by the success of *Superman vs. Spider-Man*. This time, however, the Man of Steel's foe was closer to home: Wonder Woman.

This issue takes place on Earth-2, an entirely separate continuity from that of the ongoing *Superman* titles (which, as all fanboys and fangirls knew, takes place on Earth-1). Earth-2, introduced by editor Julius Schwartz during his run on the *Justice League* book, exists in a parallel dimension and is championed by Siegel and Shuster's less powerful, Golden Age version of Superman—and other heroes who were around during World War II.

In *Superman vs. Wonder Woman*, set during World War II, a horrified Diana Prince learns that the United States is developing an atomic bomb and resolves to destroy the project. Superman is equally determined to stop her, lest the Axis powers gain the technology before America does ("I trust my adopted country, and from the briefing I was given by the Secretary of War, I know we don't have a choice but to [develop the bomb]"), and the two come to super-blows.

Of course, it isn't long before they unite to face common enemies, the hilariously on-the-nose Sumo the Samurai of Japan and Baron Blitzkrieg from Germany. After the villains are defeated, writer Gerry Conway provided a faintly subversive, downbeat coda, in which Superman and Wonder Woman meet Franklin Roosevelt, who assures them that the United States will never use the atomic bomb to kill innocent people.

Even Marvel couldn't resist writing about Superman, in its own way. The February 1978 issue of *Thor* (#280) finds the Thunder God tangling with what he thinks is Hyperion, a villainous analogue of Superman that had been introduced into the Marvel Universe by writer Roy Thomas in 1969. The twist, in the two-part 1978 story plotted by comics historians Don and Maggie Thompson and scripted by Thomas, is that the Hyperion in question is actually a *heroic* version of the character from an alternate universe—and one that is the subject of an upcoming major motion picture. In the tale, we meet his arch-nemesis, a riff on Lex Luthor. If all of this isn't layered enough with allusions to Super-lore, the story was penciled by the seminal Superman artist of the postwar era, Wayne Boring.

In March, another oversize Collector's Edition of *Superboy and the Legion of Superheroes* features the wedding of Saturn Girl and Lightning Lad, along with the Legion traveling back to 1978 to prevent the United Nations from disbanding.

Also in March, in *Action* #481, Superman temporarily loses his powers when waves of red sun radiation pass over the Earth. Undaunted, the ingenious Man of Steel repairs to the Fortress of Solitude to fashion a flying rocket-car out of the universe's strongest metal, Supermanium. The resulting flying vehicle, called the Supermobile, is equipped with all of Superman's powers—including two metal extendable arms for punching giant robots—and is featured in only two issues and, coincidentally enough (note: not coincidental at all), on toystore shelves. Toy company Corgi released die-cast metal versions with a pair of red plastic fists that would shoot from the car at the press of a button.

Float Like a Kryptonian Snagriff, Sting Like a Kryptonian Fire-Snake

April saw the publication of one of the weirdest throwdowns in comics history. Weird, and weirdly compelling: *Superman vs. Muhammad Ali*.

The cover of this oversize Collector's Edition depicts the Man of Steel and the Louisville Lip trading blows before an arena filled with hundreds of 1970s celebrities. (*What* celebrities, you ask? Sweathogs Ron [Horshack] Palillo and Robert [Epstein] Hegyes! Wolfman Jack! Wayne Rogers! Liberace! Donny! Marie! Andy Warhol! Tony Orlando! Phyllis Diller! And, in ringside seats, Lucille Ball, Sonny Bono, Lex Luthor, and Batman!)

The conceit of the tale: Aliens threaten to destroy the Earth unless an Earthling can defeat their champion in combat. Superman volunteers, but Ali points out that Superman is not an Earthling—so the honor of defending the planet belongs to him. The two duke it out to settle the issue, on a faraway planet under a red sun, in a setup much like Superman's bare-knuckle boxing match with Luthor, back in the sixties.

In July, DC launched a new book starring Superman. Every month, *DC Comics Presents* featured the Man of Steel teaming up with a different hero from across the DC Universe. With the new title, Superman now appeared in nine different monthly comics—*Action*, *Adventure*, *DC Comics Presents*, *Justice League of America*, *Super Friends*, *Superboy*, *Superboy Starring the Legion of Super-Heroes*, *Superman Family*, and *World's Finest*.

Red vs. Blue

The journey that led to the third and final oversize *Superman vs.* Collector's Edition of 1978—*Superman vs. SHAZAM!*—was a long and strange one.

Back in 1954, a DC lawsuit had succeeded in chasing Fawcett's Captain Marvel—and the rest of the Marvel family—out of comics. In the decades since, Fawcett's trademark on the Captain Marvel name had lapsed, prompting small publisher MF Enterprises to introduce a Captain Marvel of its own in 1966 (he could make bits of his body split off and fight crime, simply by shouting, "Split!" and recall them by shouting, "Xam!" No, seriously). Not to be outdone, Marvel's Stan Lee and Gene Colan introduced their own Captain Marvel in December 1967 (*Marvel Super-Heroes* #12), an alien military captain named Mar-Vell, and promptly trademarked the name. Eventually, writer Roy Thomas would introduce the concept that Mar-Vell trades places with Earth teenager Rick Jones when danger threatens, a playful tweak on the Billy Batson/Captain Marvel dynamic.

In 1972, Fawcett licensed the original Captain Marvel character, along with several members of the Marvel Family and attendant villains, to DC. Given Marvel's trademark on the Captain Marvel name, the book that brought the World's Mightiest Mortal into the DC universe was named after the hero's magic acronym: SHAZAM!

On the cover of *SHAZAM* #1, February 1973, Superman introduces readers to Captain Marvel; he stands at the edge of a curtain, hand extended in a polite "May I Present?" pose. There is, in the smile that artist Nick Cardy gave Superman, the suggestion of smug satisfaction. Here is the Man of Steel, introducing a generation of readers to the hero who consistently outsold his own titles during the forties. Yet those days were over. The Big Blue Boy Scout had beaten the Big Red Cheese (in court, if never on the newsstands), and now Captain Marvel was back—but on Superman's terms. If you look carefully, you can almost see Superman's thought balloon:

"This? Is *my house. My house.*"

Thus, the Supes vs. Cap rivalry that had been a staple of school-yard debate in the 1940s got the opportunity to flare up again, with a new twist. In the years of Cap's absence, the notion that magic was one of Superman's key vulnerabilities—second only to kryptonite—had become a canonical tenet of Superman lore. And Captain Marvel was a creature of magic. So if the two heroes were ever to come to blows . . .

Finally—in the 1978 oversize issue *Superman vs. SHAZAM!*—it happens. We learn that Captain Marvel et al. live on yet another parallel earth dubbed, prosaically enough, Earth-S. An evil alien sorcerer resolves to smash the two Earths together and use the resulting energy for his own sinister purpose. He sets a plan in motion that involves doubles of Superman and Captain Marvel—and a ray gun capable of enraging its targets—to get the heroes to fight each other, while he goes about destroying their worlds. Artist Rich Buckler created panoramic two-page spreads of the heroes fighting across America—ultimately, however, Superman is the victor. (Writer Gerry Conway provided die-hard Cap fans with an out by stipulating that on Earth-1, where the battle takes place, Captain Marvel's magic-based powers are weaker than they would be on Earth-S.)

Vivisecting the Unicorn

In October, on the comics pages of the nation's newspapers, the recently launched *World's Greatest Superheroes* strip changed its name; the words *World's Greatest Superheroes* shrank to make room for the new words "Presents Superman," and the strip would revolve around the Man of Steel for the rest of its run.

In *Superman* #330, an issue with a cover date of December 1978, the story "The Master Mesmerizer of Metropolis" provided an answer to a question that had been asked on letters pages—and by stand-up comedians—for years. The question: "How does Superman fool everyone just by putting on a pair of glasses?" The answer?

Well, the answer is *complicated.*

In fact, as presented in this tale, it's so hilariously, goofily complicated that it seems at first glance to belong to Weisinger's Silver Age, that whimsical era of Superman robots and flying monkeys. Yet a closer reading reveals how thoroughly it's motivated by something decidedly more mundane, serious—and troubling.

It's no surprise that the story in question, by Martin Pasko, was in fact "based on a story concept by Al Schroeder III," a Superman super-fan who was a perennial presence on the letters pages of Superman comics.

Clark Kent wakes from a dream in which his *Daily Planet* colleagues impatiently urged him to go off and save the day because his Clark disguise isn't fooling anyone. This puts the Man of Steel in a literally reflective mood as he gazes into his bedroom mirror.

> Is my *Clark Kent disguise* really that bad? Even if I do *change* my *voice* slightly when I pose as Clark. . . . Can my dual identity really be *that easy* to *see through*? [He brushes back his forelock, puts on glasses.] . . . Hmm. . . . Now that I stop to *think* about it . . . that's the *dumbest disguise I've ever seen*! What am I *supposed* to look like? A *totally different person*? Unh-*unh*! *Superman wearing glasses* is what I look like! But *what should I expect*? Ordinary people start wearing glasses, do their friends say "*Who are you*?" No! They say "Oh— You've got *glasses*." Who was I trying to *kid* when I dreamed up that ridiculous disguise?

Meanwhile, a villain named the Spellbinder is hypnotizing citizens to commit crimes for him. Superman builds a fleet of giant flying television screens and, as a prophylactic measure, hypnotizes the entire population of Metropolis to make them immune to any further hypnosis. Because, sure.

Later, Lana Lang walks into the *Daily Planet* storeroom and catches Superman donning his Clark Kent disguise. Just as in his dream, she's having none of it. "*That's* supposed to be *Clark*?" she asks. "Oh come *on*, luv. I admit there's a *superficial* resemblance—but you're too *heavily built*—and you're much too *handsome*! No, forget it! You don't really look like Clark at all!"

Once the Spellbinder is defeated, and Superman releases Metropolis from its resistance to hypnosis, Superman follows a hunch and asks the *Daily Planet*'s courtroom artist to draw a picture of Superman and a picture of Clark Kent. The drawing of Superman is accurate. But the drawing of Clark? "Look[s] frailer!" he notes. "And not terribly handsome!"

Clark is being generous here—as rendered by penciler Curt Swan and inker Frank Chiaramante, the "Clark," as seen by the eyes of Metropolis, is thin, almost gaunt, and his hairline is receding. He looks, in point of fact, a lot like David Brinkley:

> Apparently, my power of *super-hypnotism* is *always* working— at *low power*—even when I'm not *willing* it! It automatically projects my *subconscious desire* to be seen as a *weaker* and *frailer* man than I really am! . . . Some unknown property of the *Kryptonian Plexiglass* [in my eyeglasses] must *intensify* the low-level effect of my *eyes*! So when people look at *Clark*— *what they see is the image of Clark I try to project*!

Kryptonian Plexiglas?

Mercifully, this notion of Superman performing a kind of ambient Jedi mind trick on the population at large without their consent didn't hang around for very long, but it's noteworthy here because it is emblematic of a troubling tendency in comics writing that would, in just a few short years' time, become the dominant mode.

The question "How can he disguise himself just by putting on glasses?" exists at the very beginning of an endless and ultimately pointless line of questioning that can only serve to leach the color out of Superman. How *does* he fly, exactly? How *can* he see through walls? What's that heat vision *about*?

The Clark Kent disguise is an essential conceit, no more and no less. It is a base principle. Yet a new fannish compulsion to constantly search for ways to defend and justify whimsical propositions that demand neither defense nor justification—let's call it Vivisecting the Unicorn—was on the rise. And it wasn't going away.

And even as the comic tied itself in tortuous knots to explain why nobody realized that Clark Kent and Superman are the same guy, the actor Christopher Reeve supplied a different, simpler, truer answer, simply by squaring his shoulders.

You Will Believe a Man Can Fly

It had been Ilya's idea.

His father, Alexander Salkind, didn't go in for science fiction and didn't see the appeal of a children's movie about an alien who can do anything he wants. What's more, he was certain no one else would either. It was 1973, and superheroes were low-rent, Saturday morning schlock best left, Alex believed, to the peddlers of kiddie-fare, to the Disneys and Hanna-Barberas of the world.

The Three Musketeers—now *those* were what real heroes looked like. Alex should know; the Salkinds had just finished producing a movie about them—in fact, they'd made that movie and its sequel at the same time, which had saved them millions of dollars but earned them the enmity of the Screen Actors Guild. Something about paying the cast for one film without mentioning that they were actually making two separate movies had rankled. Actors—so sensitive.

In response, every agent in Hollywood had taken to inserting into their clients' contracts a new proviso that swiftly came to be known as the "Salkind clause," which required producers to specify exactly how many projects they were contracting for.

Yet that didn't bother the Salkinds. *The Three Musketeers* was a hit, as, no doubt, would be *The Four Musketeers*, so now, while the money and good reviews were still pouring in, the father and the son were looking around for their next project. Of course, there were the usual complaints from the Musketeers cast, crew, and investors that the money they'd been promised hadn't quite made its way into their bank accounts yet—but that, as far as the Salkinds were concerned, was just how business was done. Things take time.

A dubious Alex contacted his European investors with the silly Superman idea, and they greeted it warmly. Heartened, the Salkinds and their producing partner, Pierre Spengler, contacted Warner Bros. Studios—owner of DC Comics—to see about buying the rights to Superman. The Warner Bros. production team was only too eager to sell the rights to a property that would be so expensive and risky to produce, but when word of a possible sale trickled down to the DC offices, the editors made it known that they felt fiercely protective of their best-known, best-selling, and longest-running character.

They knew a successful film could help bolster the declining comics readership, while a bomb could damage the character's brand in a way that would take years to shake off. The specter of campy sixties *Batman* still hung over the DC bullpen. Superman's editors felt strongly that a successful film had to be true to the character, and that meant they had many questions for the Salkinds.

Ultimately, the producers tired of this nattering—and of having to constantly assure DC that their intention was to take the material seriously and imbue the film with an epic sweep—and made an end-run around Schwartz and company, securing the rights to Superman from DC's higher-ups at Warner Bros. publishing, for $4 million.

An Offer He Couldn't Refuse

Mario Puzo, fresh off *The Godfather*, attacked the problem with passion, meeting with DC writers to sound them out, review some of the Man of Steel's complicated history, and get his head around the character. Superman writer Elliot Maggin—who is a student of folklore and who, like many of his generation, considers the Man of Steel an American mythic hero—recalled:

> Before I knew it Mario Puzo, of all people, is in the [DC Comics] library with [DC editor] Nelson Bridwell looking through old Superman comics. Cary [Bates] and I ended up spending two days in a conference room with Mario puffing on those enormous Cuban cigars and talking. . . . Then sometime on the second day Mario furrowed his forehead and looked at the both of us and said "Well, this thing is a Greek tragedy," and Cary and I looked at each other and then looked at Mario and then one of us said, "That's what we've been trying to tell you." It was a scene out of a 50s sitcom.

Maggin had completed his own treatment for the Superman film, but the producers' resolve to go with a known screenwriter meant it hadn't been given serious consideration. Maggin would later adapt that treatment into the novel *Superman: Last Son of Krypton*, which was released as the Superman movie debuted. The mass market paperback featured a photo of Christopher Reeve's Superman and photos from the film; many who purchased it expected a straight-ahead novelization. What they got was something very different. Maggin begins by retelling Superman's origin but spins a grander, more cosmic tale, suffusing his plot (which involves ancient galactic prophecies, Albert Einstein, the Guardians of the Universe, and an alien minstrel) with a puzzling religiosity in the process. At the same time, he provides Lex Luthor with a remarkably nuanced, clever, and empathetic characterization.

In October 1975, Puzo delivered a massive, more-than-three-hundred-page script that the Salkinds felt was unfilmable. They asked him to pare it down, but Puzo had had his fill of the Man of Steel and bowed out. The producers reached out to David Newman and Robert Benton (who'd cowritten the book for the 1966 Superman Broadway musical), and later, when Benton dropped out, Newman's wife, Leslie, was asked to work on Lois Lane's dialogue. First, they set about dividing the Puzo script in two, saving a battle with Kryptonian villains for the second movie. Then they went about excising some of Puzo's jokier elements (Superman straightening the Leaning Tower of Pisa? That would *never* work!), while inserting a few of their own.

Meanwhile, the Salkinds searched for a director. Steven Spielberg expressed interest, but Alexander Salkind thought him untested for such a big project and wanted to wait to see how his little "fish movie" turned out. (Once *Jaws* became a blockbuster, the Salkinds' calls to Spielberg went pointedly unreturned.) Many directors, including *The Godfather*'s Francis Ford Coppola, *Jesus Christ Superstar*'s Norman Jewison, and *The Three Musketeers*' Richard Lester, were approached but declined outright or cited scheduling conflicts. Ultimately, the producers settled on veteran James Bond director Guy Hamilton.

A Streetcar Named Dinero

Yet it was the next decision the Salkinds and Spengler made that created international news and attracted the attention—both good and bad—of the industry. They hired Marlon Brando to portray Jor-El for a record-breaking $3.7 million, plus 11.3 percent of the domestic gross and 5.6 percent of the foreign gross. He would work a total of two weeks. The presence of Brando—and the paycheck he'd receive—helped net the production the services of Gene Hackman as Luthor, for a tidy $2 million.

Yet it also caused the first of a series of logistical snags in production. The Krypton sets, where Brando would film, were originally scheduled to be constructed in Rome, but the Italian government had declared his film *Last Tango in Paris* obscene. If Brando showed up in Italy, he would be arrested.

So filming moved to London—but this, too, created its own crisis. The British Guy Hamilton was a tax exile; were the director to remain in the UK for longer than a month every year, he'd see little of the money he stood to make for his work on the film. Given the choice between losing Brando or Hamilton, the Salkinds let Hamilton go.

Just as they'd nearly signed *Earthquake* director Mark Robson, Ilya was asked by his wife, Skye, to watch Richard Donner's hit film *The Omen*. The producers admired the film's moodiness—and its strong box office returns. After some vacillating, Donner agreed to direct the film for $1 million. When he arrived in London in 1977, the film was already behind schedule.

Donner's first item of business was hiring Bond screenwriter Tom Mankiewicz to tighten the latest draft of the script and expunge as much of the lingering campiness as possible. Out went Lex Luthor's habit of eating Kleenex nervously, as well as a scene in which Superman scours Metropolis in search of Luthor and, spying him, swoops down and seizes the villain—only to realize that he's nabbed actor Telly Savalas, who removes a lollipop from his mouth and intones, "Superman! Who loves ya, baby?"

Some of the Newmans' arch jokes would remain, but Donner's watchword was *verisimilitude*—he hung it on signs around the Superman offices—and he expressed to all who would listen the need to play the material straight.

In this, he met some resistance from the eccentric Brando, who delighted in playing up his larger-than-life persona and making his director sweat. Why, he asked Donner at one meeting, should Jor-El look like a human being at all? He's an alien being, so, really, he could look like anything—a bagel, a suitcase, anything—and that way, Brando could simply provide the voice. Donner dutifully explained the character's long history, though he suspected he was just being tested by the actor.

Star Search

Now it was time to hire a Superman. The net was cast throughout Hollywood, New York City—and beyond. Hordes of actors, body-builders, and at least one dentist were considered:

- Robert Redford: First to be offered; first of many to turn it down.
- Paul Newman: Laughed it off; was subsequently offered the role of Jor-El; turned it down.

- Arnold Schwarzenegger: The 1975 Mr. Olympia—and star of 1970s *Hercules in New York*—campaigned for it but was not offered the role. Became convinced his accent soured the deal.
- Sylvester Stallone: Campaigned hard but was considered "too Italian."
- Bruce Jenner: Was flown to Europe for a screen test. Came across as too young and too stiff.
- Clint Eastwood: Begged off, citing "scheduling conflicts." But come on.
- Steve McQueen: Flatly refused. Unsurprisingly.
- Christopher Walken: Considered wrong for Superman but right, had things worked out differently, for Luthor.
- Warren Beatty: Tried on the tights, felt ridiculous in them; declined.
- Muhammad Ali: A notion only briefly, albeit enticingly, entertained by Ilya Salkind but never followed up on.
- Charles Bronson: Too "earthy."
- Burt Reynolds: Too recognizable; not temperamentally suited to the role (read: a wise-ass).
- Patrick Wayne: Was in the running; took himself out of contention when his father, John, became ill.
- Kris Kristofferson: Not right.
- James Caan: No.
- Ryan O'Neal: Not quite.
- Sam Elliott: Nah.
- David Soul: No.
- Jan-Michael Vincent: Nope.
- Jeff Bridges: No.
- Lyle Waggoner: Too TV.
- Neil Diamond, yes, *that* Neil Diamond: Wanted to break into acting, met with producers, told interviewers he balked at the time commitment that would be required. According to actor Jack O'Halloran, who played Kryptonian villain Non, other considerations may have factored. "He went into the interview with [the producers] and I remember when he was coming out. People were laughing like hell."
- Ilya Salkind's wife's Beverly Hills dentist: Got a screen test. A handsome, square-jawed Southern California fitness nut, Don Voyne looked the part. On film, however, his lean face appeared

gaunt and wrinkled, and he evinced a menacing quality that wasn't right.

In the end, there were three front-runners: TV actor Perry King, Nick Nolte (who'd been part of the pitch the Salkinds had made to Donner), and Jon Voight. Voight came closest; his enthusiastic embrace of the trappings of the role impressed producers but not quite enough to close the deal. They signed him to a contract, stating that he would be their Superman if they couldn't find someone else.

Finally—just a few weeks after the dentist had gotten ready for his close-up, and less than a month before a Superman was needed on set—Donner turned again to a headshot he'd dismissed twice before: that of Juilliard graduate Christopher Reeve. When Donner had met him months earlier, he considered the actor too skinny, too young, and—oddly, it must be said—too handsome for Superman. The Salkinds and the casting director were adamant, and Reeve was flown to London for a screen test. (To accommodate the whirlwind move, the Superman producers bought every seat in the house of Reeve's off-Broadway play during the weekend he was away.)

In a padded Superman suit that caused him to sweat so profusely (like a stuck pig, Donner recalls) that dark circles blossomed at his armpits, Reeve performed an early version of the interview scene on Lois Lane's balcony. It was a tricky one to pull off but crucial—it's in this exchange that the viewer first sees the man in the Superman, first catches a glimpse of what the "strong streak of good" Luthor mentions in the movie actually looks like. The actor has to nail the guileless sincerity of a line such as "I never lie," without turning it into children's theater.

Reeve nailed it. There is, even in this early performance, something new about Reeve's Superman, something he adds to the character that feels like it's been there for the last fifty years, and we just never noticed it: a calmness. In his squared shoulders and compassionate blue gaze, Reeve's Superman is unhurried, unforced; his very presence soothes and reassures. Where George Reeves possessed a roguish confidence, Kirk Alyn a by-the-numbers serial-action-hero dynamism, and Bud Collyer the clipped matter-of-factness of a trained crisis manager, the Salkinds and Donner could tell from this brief dialogue that Reeve's Superman would be the kind of leader the neurotic 1970s so desperately cried out for. When Reeve tested as Clark Kent, he managed to sell the movie's make-or-break conceit—that somehow no one would guess that Clark was Superman, albeit four-eyed and in a cheap suit.

Only one major role still needed to be cast, that of Lois Lane. Once again, the producers and the director considered name stars such as Barbra Streisand, Liza Minnelli, and Jill Clayburgh. Several actresses tested before the cameras, including Stockard Channing, Anne Archer, Lesley Ann Warren (dialing down the Betty Boop voice she'd brought to the 1975 TV musical role), and Margot Kidder. Donner liked Channing's forceful Joan Blondell energy, but worried that she was too assertive, too theatrical. The producers saw something very of-the-moment in Kidder's fragile, neurotic Lois, and she was hired.

Tensions and Timetables

Production was beset by delays and steadily ratcheting up tensions between a methodical director and budget-and-time-conscious producers, who found themselves overextended financially before a single frame had been shot. Donner had nixed the production team's designs for Krypton, which were based on the comic's Art Deco/Disney Tomorrowland vision of the future. He tasked *Star Wars* designer John Barry to create a stark, cold, crystalline Krypton. A blackout in New York City during the extensive Metropolis location shooting held up production for days. In London, film equipment suffered water damage. A wing of the film's replica of Air Force One broke off and killed stuntman Terry Hill. The most difficult, expensive, time-eating aspect of production, Reeve's practical effect flying sequences—which found the actor suspended for hours from wires before a blue screen—were the film's most important set pieces, and they needed to be done right.

Communications broke down between Donner and the producers. Midway into filming, Salkind brought Richard Lester to the set and summarily instructed him to shadow Donner, acting as a second director who would serve as go-between for Donner and the Salkinds. If the Salkinds had been hoping for a blow-up from Donner, he did not provide it. Instead, Lester uneventfully took over second-unit filmmaking, and the two directors formed an odd but effective partnership. For a while. Time was running out until the night of the premiere, so both agreed to focus on finishing the first film, leaving the remaining 50 to 60 percent of the work until after the first film was released—work on what would be called *Superman II.* There was a financial, as well as a logistical, reason for this: if the first film bombed, they could cut their losses and leave the second film unfinished.

Finally, on December 10, 1978, at the Kennedy Center in Washington, D.C., *Superman: The Movie* had its official premiere.

Superman: The Movie

The film's essential narrative structure is one that would be iterated again and again by every superhero movie to follow:

1. Origin: "Who he is and how he came to be!"
2. Training: The hero develops his abilities and prepares for his destiny.
3. Ta-dah!: An extended montage of various super-deeds and rescues, as the hero makes his first public appearance.
4. Face-off: The plot kicks in, the hero and the villain finally meet, and our hero experiences his first true challenge.

Donner ensures that *Superman: The Movie*'s origin section proceeds at a stately—and at times sluggish—pace, but he does so for a very specific reason: verisimilitude. For his 1978 audience to buy in to the story he has to tell, he must first chase from their minds all thoughts of Adam West and Underdog and Super-Grover, not to mention the stubborn image of an embarrassed-looking George Reeves standing around like a burly trapeze artist on a smoke break. So he sets out to frontload the film with epic sweep and grandeur; he wants his audience to be thinking John Ford, because he knows so many of them have settled into their seats thinking *Gunsmoke.*

"This is no fantasy," says a voice. "No careless product of wild imagination." It's difficult not to read these, the first words spoken by any character in the film, as anything but the film's mission statement: This ain't no party. This ain't no disco. This ain't no foolin' around.

The speaker of those words is Marlon Brando's Jor-El, wearing a ludicrous white wig with a spit curl that is evidently carried, in the

El family, on a dominant gene. On his chest he sports the familiar S-symbol. (The notion that the S is a crest of some kind is a hold-over from the Puzo script; Puzo felt that the S-shield should be the symbol of Krypton itself, stamped on every table, floor, and wall. In the final film, however, other Kryptonians sport different symbols on their chests, denoting family, title, or occupation—this is one of many concepts introduced by the film that writers of Superman comics have since incorporated.)

Following the destruction of Krypton, the film shifts to Smallville, Kansas, swapping one vast, empty landscape for another. Kirk Alyn and Noel Neill make their cameos as train passengers whose daughter can't seem to convince them that she's seen a boy running alongside the train. "Oh, Lois Lane!" Neill says. "You've got a writer's imagination! I'll say that for you!"

What follows is a scene in which Pa Kent imparts fatherly advice to his adopted son. It is easily the most important scene in the film's origin segment—one that has nothing to do with what Superman can do or why he can perform these feats, but that defines who he is. It's fitting to note, here in the most leisurely paced section of a film that some consider overlong and even ponderous, how ruthlessly efficient this scene is. The movie has to establish that Clark, though born an alien, has gone native—that he is now thoroughly a child of the American Midwest, and that his values are those of a humble farm boy, not a cold, advanced race. It does all of that in a single, unbroken, one-minute take that begins at the end of the Kent driveway and ends at their farmhouse. Pa Kent tells his son, "There is one thing I do know, son, and that is you are here for a reason. I don't know whose reason, or whatever the reason is. Maybe it's because . . . well. I don't know. But I do know one thing. It's *not* to score touchdowns."

The film then promptly metes out its second father death, as Pa Kent collapses of a heart attack. That the attack occurs because Clark urges Pa to race him to the top of the driveway is a twist of the narrative knife so gratuitous and guilt-soaked, it'd make more sense in a Spider-Man movie.

Next, with a simple toss of a Kryptonian crystal into polar waters, pillars of ice shape themselves into a taste of home, a vast shimmering palace. One that comes with a kickin' entertainment center capable of summoning Jor-El's ghost—or at least a reason-able computerized facsimile thereof—to answer Clark's questions.

"Here in this . . ." Jor-El's image pauses, considering, "this fortress of" (tiny pause; what's the word?) "solitude, we shall try to find the answers together." It could be argued that by making such an unabashedly hokey concept sound so matter-of-fact, so *inevitable*, Brando earns his $3.7 million right here.

Following a series of lectures, including an admonishment that "It is forbidden to interfere with human history," which drips with foreshadowing, Jor-El concludes with a bit of paraphrased gospel that was the last thing on Siegel and Shuster's mind when they created their rabble-rousing costumed bruiser. Nonetheless, it's a message Donner and Mankiewicz choose to embrace with a literally messianic fervor: "They can be a great people, Kal-El, they wish to be. They only lack the light to show the way. For this reason above all, their capacity for good, I have sent them you. My only son."

Now, more than forty-five minutes into the film, we are treated to our first glimpse of Superman. "Treated" is perhaps too strong—call it "amuse-bouched"—we get a long shot of Superman standing on a ledge in his fortress, from at least a football field away. He takes to the air, and, as soon as it began, the scene is over.

Suddenly, we are in Metropolis. This, we sense, is what the last forty-five minutes have been about—this is where all those empty sprawling colorless landscapes have been heading, to this bustling, crowded, colorful city. This is the home Clark has been yearning for, without knowing it—the place he will find his destiny.

The *Daily Planet* scene in which we meet Lois, Jimmy, and Perry possesses an energy the film hasn't shown us before, filled with throwaway lines and crisp banter deliberately reminiscent of *His Girl Friday*, *The Front Page*, and, visually, at least, *All the President's Men*.

Yet the real revelation of this scene is Reeve's Clark Kent. We've only gotten that fleeting glimpse of his Superman so far, so the true magic of the performance isn't yet apparent, but we instinctively know what this Kent is about. Reeve shows us Superman behind the glasses, having fun with the bumbling Clark pose, without camping it up or winking to the audience. Even in a primarily comic scene in which Clark pretends to faint while protecting Lois from a mugger's bullet by being sufficiently faster than it, he shows us the Russian-nesting-doll nature of his Superman, the performance inside the performance.

Luthor's Lair—an abandoned train station two hundred feet below Park Avenue—is an impressive set, and scenes in which Valerie Perrine's Miss Teschmacher trades barbs with Gene Hackman's pompous, cravat-sporting Lex Luthor are jokier and campier than the *Daily Planet* scenes but share their screwball-lite pacing and energy. Hackman, who begged off playing the character in a bald cap, except in his final scene, creates a Luthor possessed of an odd, ingratiating charm: he's not the stark-raving-mad scientist of the comics, he's a kind of slick, sociopathic car salesman. Complete with pinky rings.

In the film's most overt (and smarmiest) wink to the audience, Clark, seeking a place to change to Superman and save Lois Lane, gives a modern, boothless payphone a quick, annoyed look. Next comes the money shot—Clark ripping open his shirt to reveal the S-symbol—as he steps inside a hotel's revolving door to emerge in the bright, primary-color costume of the Man of Steel.

"Say, Jim," says the cringeworthy Huggy Bear stereotype standing nearby. "That's a bad out*fit!*"

Superman rescues Lois, effortlessly, and delivers a self-consciously square bromide about the safety of air travel.

"Who *are* you?" the reporter asks.

"A friend," he says. No longer the big brother of the thirties and forties or the father figure of the fifties or the out-of-touch uncle of the sixties but a colleague, a compatriot. A friend.

The interview scene in Lois's palatial penthouse garden—the scene used in the screen tests that earned both Reeve and Kidder their roles—is the moment the film's disparate (and at times disjointed) tones and themes come together seamlessly. As in the screen test, Reeve's Superman is calm and steady, while Kidder's Lois is a frayed nerve. Their chemistry is real, and Reeve lets us see a knowing sense of humor inside the suit, which keeps such a fundamentally decent character from edging over into square.

Superman takes Lois on a flight over the city. If, in musical comedy, the moment when the two lead characters dance together is a metaphor for sex, then this scene carries a similar emotional and symbolic weight. It's here that the now-infamous "Can You Read My Mind (Love Theme from Superman)" enters Superman lore. The original plan was to have Kidder sing it, but this was quickly reconsidered once the director heard her vocal track. Instead, we hear Kidder simply reading the lyrics as we watch Superman and Lois flying through clouds, buzzing the Statue of Liberty, and terrifying geese. The treacly phrases—which sound like lines ripped from a sixth-grader's diary—effectively transform Lois from a tenacious reporter into a hormonal schoolgirl and eat up eight minutes of screen time to simply underline the connection between our two leads that has already been well established. (A sung-through version was released by Maureen McGovern and became a minor hit.)

After Superman flies off, Clark arrives to pick up a very distracted Lois for their date. While Kidder goes to the bedroom to freshen up, Reeve removes Clark's glasses and, simply by straightening his posture and steadying his gaze, becomes Superman before our eyes.

It is this moment—the magical, seamless instant of transition—that has always defined the character. Back on the radio show and in the sixties cartoon, Collier managed it by dropping his voice. Yet here, for the first time, we *see* it happening. More than the effects, the costume, the script, or the set pieces, Reeve's ability to sell us on the dual nature of the character is why the movie works.

Near the end of the film comes perhaps the most controversial moment in Superman lore. The setup: A Lex Luthor missile lands atop the San Andreas Fault, causing classic seventies disaster-movie havoc—earthquakes, car crashes, dam breaks, and so on. Superman flies into the crack in the earth and lifts what is essentially a continent back into place. The earthquake has caused damage throughout California, however, and he sets about doing what he can—saving a schoolbus full of children, inserting his indestructible body over a damaged railroad track, preventing a flood caused by a burst dam.

Yet he's too late to save Lois, whose car has been swallowed by a fissure in the earth. Standing over her dead body, the Man of Steel screams his fury at the heavens and launches himself into the air.

In the years that followed, the melodramatic "Skyward Scream" would become a much-used—and much-parodied—cinematic trope. But this was one of the first—if not the first—uses of it, and it works for two reasons: (1) Reeve sells it, and (2) it spurs action, not self-pity.

In most films, the overhead "Nooooo!" is an expression of impotent rage, of helplessness. Here, and here alone, it is followed up immediately by decisive action that will right the grave wrong in question: Superman resolves to turn back time.

At that moment, the image and voice of Jor-El appear to admonish Superman that "It is forbidden for you to interfere with human history"—but this is immediately followed by Pa Kent's voice: "You are here for a *reason*." The battle lines are drawn: Jor-El/intellect vs. Pa Kent/emotion. Because it's Superman's heart that's broken, not his brain, there's no question which side will win, and that Superman will implicitly reject his Kryptonian heritage and embrace his Earthly existence—especially when we hear Young Clark's voice as he decides: "All those things I can do. All those powers . . . and I couldn't even save him."

What happens next is, to many, the point at which the film asks too much of its audience, when our disbelief, suspended successfully for almost two hours, comes crashing to the ground: Superman orbits the Earth at super-speed, until suddenly, for no reason the film will point to, the world begins to spin backward. As it does, time moves backward as well. We watch the river unflood, the dam unbreak, and Lois's car right itself.

Time travel had been a staple of Superman stories for most of the character's existence, but this, to many viewers, was different. This was cheating.

Yet how different is it, really? Why is it any more difficult to believe than the notion of an alien who can fly or a beat reporter being able to afford a penthouse apartment in Midtown? There is, after all, another explanation for what happens at the film's climax.

The *Superman* comics have long established that for Superman to break the "time barrier," he must travel faster than the speed of light. What if—some fans of the film posit—that's what we're seeing? What if Superman decides to break the time barrier—but knows that if he simply does so as he does in the comics, by flying out into space and away from the Earth, he'll arrive in the past and then have to fly back to Earth at subliminal speed, wasting precious seconds. Inefficient!

Instead, he stays closer to home by flying around and around the Earth until he reaches the necessary speed. So, what we see on screen—as the Earth seems to rotate backward—isn't really the Man of Steel *turning back* time, but instead *traveling back in* time.

To adherents of the Back in Time Exegesis, it *appears* that the river unfloods, the dam unbreaks, and so on, because we're seeing it through his eyes. Superman saves Lois, though the film remains silent about how; Lois mentions the earthquake, so it's clear the missile landed, even if Superman seems astonishingly blasé about it.

"You Will Believe a Man Can Fly"

Superman: The Movie became a huge hit, one of the top box-office winners of the 1970s. Worldwide, the $55 million movie grossed more than $300 million. Critics singled out Reeve's performance ("a performer who manages to be both funny and comic-strip heroic without making a fool of himself," said the *New York Times*) and the spectacular effects.

Amid the success, the Salkinds' reputation took a beating, as Mario Puzo, Marlon Brando, Richard Donner, and eventually Christopher Reeve slapped them with separate lawsuits demanding more money. Puzo, for his part, saw his suit as nothing more than a tried-and-true Hollywood negotiating tactic, but the Salkinds, who'd spent a lot of time in court in disputes over money, were stung. When it came to Donner, who'd lambasted them in media interviews, they were incensed.

Incensed enough to take an action they'd been wanting to take for some time. With filming on *Superman II* somewhere between 40 and 50 percent done, shooting was scheduled to resume in August 1979.

In March, the Salkinds fired Richard Donner.

9

SUPERMAN AGONISTES
(1979–1986)

Milestones

1981: *Superman II* premieres

1983: *Superman III* premieres

1985: *Crisis on Infinite Earths* maxiseries begins

1986: *Dark Knight Returns;* "Whatever Happened to the Man of Tomorrow?"

The Man of Steel didn't know it yet, but he was headed for a reckoning. As was the grocery-store spinner rack where he'd lived for half a century.

In 1979, mass market retailers (supermarkets, newsstands) were still responsible for the vast majority of all comic book sales, but that was changing. Comic-book buyers who wanted to have access to all the issues on sale in a specific month would have to search many different newsstands to find what they were looking for. So-called specialty stores—mom-and-pop comics shops—had begun to spring up, providing comics-seekers with one-stop shopping and access to an impassioned community that kept them in the know. So, if they could find such a comics shop, fans began to frequent it to feed their habit.

This caused newsstand sales to drop—which in turn made it harder for supermarkets to justify giving over any shelf space to low-pricepoint, low-markup, low-selling items such as comic books. At the same time, comic book publishers were realizing that the specialty stores (called the "direct market") provided a no-risk distribution channel through which they could tailor print runs precisely to demand. They no longer needed to print five copies to sell one. That meant DC and Marvel could lower their production costs by concentrating on the comics shops and leaving the supermarket checkout to Archie and the gang.

The New Normal

When the 1970s had begun, the stable of Superman writers still teemed with old-guard, cigar-chomping veterans of the Weisinger era, such as Leo Dorfman, Robert Kanigher, and Bob Haney—men in their fifties and sixties who'd fallen into the comics racket and cranked out yarns because it was their job. By 1979, most had been replaced by a generation of long-haired, mustachioed kids who'd grown up on comics, and who saw writing these characters as the fulfillment of dreams they'd nurtured during childhood and adolescence and—in the case of Elliot Maggin and others—lovingly dissected in college courses on folklore and mythology.

A sequel to the blockbuster film was in the works, and a major milestone had been reached as well. In October 1979, *Action Comics* would become the first comic book in history to reach issue 500, and plans were begun for still another major retelling of the Super-origin.

First, though, it was time to put Superman's house in order. A three-issue storyline that had been scheduled for a planned *Showcase* comic—another victim of the great DC implosion—focused on the life of Jor-El, pulling together the disparate elements of his backstory that had entered the canon over the years. In July, the story, called *World of Krypton*, became the first-ever comic book miniseries, borrowing the strange-sounding moniker from a new television format that had recently given the world *Roots* and *Rich Man, Poor Man*.

Grow for Me

In August, a twenty-year storyline came to its end, when Superman finally freed the Bottle City of Kandor from its wee glass prison. The story, in *Superman* #338 ("Our 40th Anniversary Super-Spectacular! An Explosive Extra-Length Novel"!)—shamelessly called "Let My People Grow!"—involves Superman duping Brainiac into shrinking the Man of Steel. This allows Superman to test on himself the "expanding energy" he's just collected from a sun going supernova; to his delight, he finds that it reverses the effect of Brainiac's shrink ray. He and Supergirl fly the Bottle City to a remote planet revolving around a red sun, eager to fulfill a promise he made to the people of Kandor two decades earlier.

To readers of the day—a time when any such permanent, sweeping changes to a superhero's status quo were exceedingly rare—it was a big deal. What's more, the knowledge that Kandor would one day be restored to normal size and given its own planet had been an element planted in Legion of Superheroes stories as far back as May 1967 (*Adventure* #356). It should be noted here that the fact that the ray Superman uses to enlarge the city looks like nothing less than some kind of cosmic caulk-gun, and that the sound effect it produces is "*Skwah-wah-whoom!*" do nothing to undercut the power of the moment. If anything, they make it that much cooler.

Alas, the "expanding energy" works only on animate objects, and the city promptly crumbles to dust. Yet the citizens of Kandor are remarkably chipper nonetheless: "Look around you, Kal-El . . . a primitive *wilderness*, waiting to be *tamed, conquered.* . . . You may have *destroyed* our *city*, my friend . . . but you have given us a *world!*"

It could have ended there—with a primitive civilization of restored, nonsuper Kryptonians on a planet millions of light-years away. Lest even this caveat-filled existence deal a blow to Superman's uniqueness, we learn at the story's conclusion that the planet on which the Kandorians find themselves is a "phase world" that Brigadoons in and out of our dimension at regular intervals.

Many years later, in a 2006 interview with Michael Eury recorded in *The Krypton Companion*, writer Len Wein expressed regret for the decision to enlarge Kandor and offered insights about the nature of writing for characters who persist for decades:

> All of us, at some point in our careers as editors and writers, have said, Oh god I'm so tired of *that*, whatever *that* is, so we changed or dropped it. But I don't think any of us realized at the time that what was old to *us* was new to somebody just coming in. . . . So I came to Kandor thinking, I'm so tired of

this. It's 20 years . . . of that stupid city. So I came up with a story I thought might have some emotional impact. . . . And I regret that, because the idea of a bottle city of tiny people is a much cooler idea than what I left it as.

On his website, Confessions of a Superman Fan, writer David Morefield eloquently sums up why this major event left a bad taste in the mouths of many fans:

> The shrunken Kandor served as a living connection to Superman's alien heritage and a potential seed for Krypton's eventual rebirth. Its presence was at once a painful reminder that even his powers had limits and a refuge, a source of solace when his longing for lost Krypton became acute. In short, I liked it better in the bottle. . . . Somehow this story manages to enlarge Kandor and make it smaller at the same time.

Origin, Again: Last Stop before the *Crisis*

Finally, in October 1979, *Action Comics* #500 arrived. Once again, it was time to review the accumulated history and create an up-to-date, comprehensive, yet streamlined origin that would define the character for new and old readers in the years ahead. As every retelling of the origin had done since the very first, it would serve as a way for the new creative team to put their mark on this corporate-owned, narratively static character who had been handed down to them over the decades.

The central conceit of "The Life Story of Superman" is the opening of the Metropolis Superman Museum, with the Man of Steel walking the public through rooms dedicated to different facets of his life. In a remarkably ill-thought gesture for anyone possessed of a secret identity, he allows the museum curator to hook him up to a "mind-prober ray helmet" that will transmit his memories to the waiting crowd.

While Superman is reliving these memories, the mind-prober helmet relays them to a sinister laboratory below the museum, where a mysterious figure is growing a clone of Superman that sees and feels Superman's memories. Eventually, the mysterious figure stands revealed (Luthor, duh, who else?) and replaces the real

Superman with his evil clone. But, of course, there's no keeping a good Man of Steel down, and Superman uses his super-breath to expose the Super-clone to gold kryptonite (which is conveniently, if foolishly, on display) and permanently rob him of his powers. Luthor and the clone are arrested.

As narrative loose ends go, an exact (albeit nonpowered) duplicate of your hero, who is possessed of all of his memories and secrets, is an awfully big thread to leave unpulled. Yet it would take two full years (*Action Comics* #524) for the Super-clone to return, only to find his attempts to take over the Clark Kent identity thwarted.

This issue is notable for its take on the Clark/Superman dynamic. It's clear—as it was in the 1976 "Who Took the Super Out of Superman?" story arc—that the relationship between the Man of Steel and his secret identity has become significantly more nuanced than Siegel and Shuster originally conceived it. Once, Clark was merely a pose. In 1979, well, it was a good deal more complicated: "I *need* being Clark . . . [He] is as much a part of what I am as Kal-El from Krypton is! Ma and Pa Kent . . . the way they raised me . . . my boyhood in Smallville . . . they made me what I am . . . and I'd sooner die than give it up!"

Enter . . . Mongul

During this time, writer Martin Pasko began to campaign Schwartz for the chance to tell longer Superman stories, similar to those that were unfolding over in *Legion of Super-Heroes*. There, multi-issue story arcs were the default, and "one-shots" (single-issue stories) were used to fill in gaps between them. It wasn't Schwartz's preference, but gradually, *Superman* stories began to take longer to tell. Yet increasingly, in Pasko's view, they also started to take on some of the gimmickiness of the Weisinger era—and that rubbed the younger generations of writers, who sought to infuse a more naturalistic approach and who tossed around phrases such as "character-driven," the wrong way.

"Julie would never have bought into the idea of trying to create something 'sophisticated,'" Pasko said. "His generation held that comics were strictly for pre-teens. . . . After thirty years of editing comics, Julie was pretty jaded. Consequently, his efforts to be original . . . led him to embrace ideas that were over the top."

Yet Pasko had other concerns besides characterization. He and his fellow writers felt strongly that Superman needed to sweat more. They brought back kryptonite with a vengeance and set about attempting to beef up Superman's villains—or to create new ones.

DC Comics Presents #27 (November 1980) introduced the hulking, immensely powerful alien tyrant Mongul, created by Len Wein and designed—from the top of his yellow cranial ridge to the tip of his purple, hero-stomping boots, by Jim Starlin. In this first appearance, it's clear that Mongul is more than a physical match for the Man of Steel (only the timely intervention of the hero Martian Manhunter saves the day), but the villain would not fully come into his own as a threat for another five years, when he would fall into the hands of writer Alan Moore.

"So Fresh-Roasted! So *Creamy*! So Yummy!"

In 1981, with the release of *Superman II* slotted for June (in the United States, at least—it had premiered in Australia the previous December, with a staggered release around the world), Superman's licensed image began to appear on a wide variety of merchandise. A *New York Times* article that came out the day after *Superman II* opened reported that Warner Bros. had "awarded 200 licenses for more than 1,200 products on the two movies, including belt buckles, underwear, watches, pillowcases, soap packaged like a telephone booth and expensive velour sweatshirts at Bloomingdale's."

For some of these items, the tie-in made sense, such as the Superman pinball game in the nation's arcades and a special comic available free at Radio Shack. (In this comic, titled *The Computers That Saved Metropolis! Starring the TRS-80 Computer Whiz-Kids!* Superman averts natural disaster with a little help from two plucky sidekicks, the Tandy Corporation and 16K of RAM.)

For other Superman items, the connection was tenuous at best. Take, for example, Superman Peanut Butter. In an animated commercial, Lex Luthor interrogates a caged Man of Steel, weakened by kryptonite:

> Luthor: *Now* you'll tell me why Superman Peanut Butter
>   tastes so great!
> Superman: N-never!

Meanwhile, New York multimedia performance artist Laurie Anderson had achieved the impossible—she had combined a minimalist monotone tape loop with lyrics that paid winking homage to an aria from an 1885 Massenet opera, gave the whole thing an electronic acid bath, and sent it up the music charts. "O Superman (for Massenet)," with its insistent, affectless humor, became the number two single in the UK by conflating images of authority ("O Superman/O judge/O mom and dad") with the motto of the U.S. Post Office. Much more than a novelty song, the absurdly infectious "O Superman" has since been covered, sampled, and mashed up countless times by musicians ranging from Canadian hip-hop groups to post-punk German DJs to David Bowie.

On comics shelves, writer E. Nelson Bridwell traced Superman's family tree in a three-issue mini called *The Krypton Chronicles*. Kent is assigned the task of digging into Superman's ancestral roots for a TV miniseries, giving Superman and Supergirl an excuse to travel to the distant phase-planet where the recently enlarged Kandorians reside to investigate the El family vault. The ensuing story contains little in the way of superheroics but serves to flesh out Krypton's cultural, military, and scientific history—with the aid of an extensive glossary of Kryptonian terms. It was an impressive achievement that would, just five years later, be wiped from continuity.

Once again, a Superman movie in theaters meant a mass-market paperback Superman novel by Elliot Maggin in bookstores. And once again, the book, *Miracle Monday*, had absolutely nothing to do with the Warner Bros. movie. Maggin's plot involves a time-traveling historian and a demon tasked to break Superman's spirit by threatening the lives of his friends and exposing his secret identity. Ultimately, the demon is tricked, and order is restored in a manner that makes spinning the Earth backward seem like a legitimate narrative choice—via a magic wish.

Superman II: The Adventure—and the Headache—Continues

Donner was out, Lester was in, and when production ramped back up on *Superman II*—about half of which was already in the can—the director confronted some tough decisions.

First, he was faced with a movie that had no beginning or end. Originally, the film opened with the Phantom Zone criminals speeding toward Earth, having been freed at the end of the first movie by the nuclear missile Superman had sent hurtling into space. A new opening was needed that would somehow show the three Kryptonian criminals escaping from their mirror-tile prison. In addition, the second film's scripted ending—Lois dying, and Superman turning back the Earth/traveling back in time to save her—had been used as the emotional climax of the first.

David and Leslie Newman returned to script a new opening that involved nuclear terrorists at the Eiffel Tower and reworked the coda, changing the manner in which Superman causes Lois to forget his secret identity, from a drugged cup of water to a hypnotizing super-kiss.

Lester also had to finish the film without Brando and Hackman. In Brando's case, the decision was financial: if he appeared in the second film, he'd have to get paid and get a percentage of the gross. The decision was made to reshoot the scene between Reeve and Brando in which Superman confesses his love for Lois and surrenders his powers. Another scene in which the now-powerless, penitent Clark returns to the Fortress of Solitude to ask for his powers back would also need to be reworked completely—as written and shot, Jor-El returns Superman's powers by reaching out to him in a tableau deliberately reminiscent of the Creation of Adam on the ceiling of the Sistine Chapel, but doing so means Jor-El surrenders his existence.

It was exactly the kind of shameless, open-hearted myth making that Donner loved but that rubbed the sardonic Lester the wrong way. The first scene—the discussion of love—would be reshot with Susannah York taking Brando's place, and the return of Superman's powers would take place offscreen.

Hackman, out of loyalty to Donner, refused to return for pick-ups and reshoots, necessitating the hiring of a stand-in and a voice double for several scenes.

The scenes that remained to be shot—including the terrorists in Paris and the climactic super-brawl on the streets of Metropolis—involved a great many units filming at once. Where Donner took tremendous pains to get a shot exactly right and often ran his actors through additional takes just to be sure, Lester worked at a breakneck pace, constantly shuttling from set to set in a golf cart. The producers were happier, but the editors at DC Comics were still worried about the sex scene between Lois and non-super-Clark, which had been a part of the script since Mario Puzo's very first draft. We do not know but can reasonably infer that they were equally concerned about the raft of noncanonical superpowers on display, about which more later.

Lester asked Donner if he wished to have his name listed as codirector in the credits. Donner emphatically declined. *Superman II* opened in the United States and Canada on June 19, 1981.

You Will Believe a Man Can F***

The film's opening set-piece, involving the Eiffel Tower, a hydrogen bomb, and a passel of actors speaking English with outrageous Charles Boyer accents, is a nimble bit of business that hints at the lighter, jokier tone to come. In the end, Superman saves Paris by flinging the terrorists' hydrogen bomb into outer space, where the shockwaves of its explosion shatter the Phantom Zone prison (in a display of cheap animation that unintentionally recalls the flying scenes in "Superman and the Mole Men").

In a scene shot by Donner, the three criminals, General Zod (Terence Stamp), Ursa (Sarah Douglas), and Non (Jack O'Halloran), land on the moon, slaughter three astronauts, and realize—or, rather, expositionally intuit—that the closer they get "to an atmosphere with only one sun—a yellow sun," their "dense molecular structure" gives them tremendous powers. They set off toward a place called Houston.

In Niagara Falls, Lois and Clark have gone undercover to expose a hotel's honeymoon scam—and when Superman shows up to rescue a kid who falls into the falls, Lois finally begins to suspect that Clark and Superman are one and the same. The Niagara Falls scenes, shot mostly by Lester, have a pleasant snap; Kidder is particularly strong, imbuing Lois with a world-weary quality that contrasts nicely with Reeve's naiveté.

Lois throws herself into white-water rapids, daring Clark to change to Superman and save her. Instead, Clark discreetly uses his powers to send a floating log her way, allowing her to rescue herself.

The three villains alight by a bucolic lake, and the viewer gets a better sense of them. Non is the brute, Ursa takes wicked delight in her powers, and Stamp's Zod is cool and impassive. If *Superman II* belongs to anyone, it's to Stamp's icy and imperious Zod. In the first film, when bargaining for his life, he was a creature of desperation and fury. Yet here, possessed as he is of the great power he believes is his right, his attitude is aloof and more than a little bemused by the primitives around him.

Back at the honeymoon hotel, in a plot contrivance that Mort Weisinger himself would consider too gimmicky, Clark trips over a pink polyester bearskin rug and ends up with his hand in the middle of a roaring fireplace. When it emerges unharmed, Lois is shocked—and Superman stops pretending. "Let's go to my place," he says.

The Kryptonian trio begin to terrorize a small town; Lester's fondness for slapstick makes these scenes seem longer than they are. In the film's first of many departures from the canonical list of Kryptonian superpowers, a beam of white light emerges from the tip of Zod's finger, capable of lifting a local man off the ground. Super-kinesis?

Stamp, in a subtle touch, lets us see that Zod enjoys the sight of himself on the television. "Is there no one on this planet to even challenge me?" Zod asks a news crew's camera.

Superman and Lois, however, are canoodling in the fortress over dinner and champagne. While she slips into something more comfortable, Superman asks the image of Lara, his mother, about love. She informs her son that if he wishes to be with a woman, he must live as a mortal, forsaking his powers forever. She must have been spending the afterlife reading Larry Niven essays.

Purists may quibble over the film's relaxed attitude toward Kryptonian power-sets, but it's what Superman does next that completely contradicts the character's single, overriding principle, the one constant in his seventy-five years of existence. Superman isn't about the powers or the costume—he's about selflessness and determination. The battle he fights for Truth and Justice and the American Way is called never-ending because it never ends. For all of his triumphs and the reassurance he offers us that good will conquer evil, there is about him a note of Sisyphus. His work is never done, so neither is he.

Thus, the notion that Superman would ever give up his powers—would ever give up, for that matter, for the sake of his personal pleasure—that he would place his own interests above those of humanity, may satisfy the narrative demands of a screenplay and allow the film's three-act structure to pay off, but it represents a fundamental misread of the character. Spider-Man would give up his powers; in fact, he seems perennially eager to do so. Superman would not.

And yet, he does: Superman enters a special crystal chamber that has "harnessed the powers of the red sun." One cheesy light-show later, he emerges depowered in a sensible white oxford shirt and black trousers; the Man of Steel is no more, and in his place stands Clark Kent, cater-waiter. Who promptly leads Lois to his shiny silver bed/bounce house.

In a pair of Donner scenes, Zod, Non, and Ursa invade the White House and get the president to "kneel before Zod" (a line that quickly entered the cultural lexicon), and Clark gets thrashed by a bully in a roadside diner. Bloodied and beaten, Clark sees the president of the United States surrendering to Zod on the diner's television and resolves to go back to the fortress and somehow get back his powers.

There, after admitting to the empty, darkened fortress that he has failed, he is granted a reprieve—the green crystal that called to him in the first film glows anew.

Superman returns, setting off a showdown on and above the streets of Metropolis. Amid the carnage and the product placement (during the course of the Metropolis fight, signage for Coca-Cola, Marlboro, and Kentucky Fried Chicken gets prominently smashed), director Lester again indulges a fondness for broad slapstick. A scene in which the three villains use super-breath to keep citizens at bay features a toupee flying off, a man continuing his conversation even after his telephone carrel tips over, a backward roller-skater, an inside-out umbrella, and, in the absence of a local cream pie franchise, an ice cream cone flying in someone's face.

The ensuing battle in the Fortress of Solitude rankles ardent Superman fans, who object to its kitchen-sink approach to Kryptonian powers. Non flies at Superman, who disables him with what to all appearances is a giant, S-shield-shaped Fruit Roll-Up. The villains then "combine their strength" by . . . pointing at

Superman. The white beams that emerge from their fingers have no comic-book precedent, but their effect seems to mimic heat vision. It's possible the director felt that having characters point at Superman was more cinematically interesting than having them simply stare at him.

There follows a sequence in which the four Kryptonians seem to teleport around the fortress, winking in and out of existence. It's possible to rationalize this distinctly non-Super superpower by assuming they are using super-speed, moving faster than the eye (Lois's or the camera's) can follow.

Superman's ability to create doubles of himself—be they image projections or animate ice-statues—also has a comic-book anteced-ent, but one has to go all the way back to the kind of Kryptonian super-science Superman practiced during the Weisinger Silver Age era, and that hadn't really been seen in the comics for more than a decade. Fans eager to forgive the film's more egregious depar-tures from canon can find comfort in the possibility that Superman retreated to the fortress because he wanted to make certain special preparations for the villains' arrival, and that it's the fortress defense systems, and not Superman himself, producing these duplicates.

Superman tricks the villains into surrendering their powers and sends Zod hurtling down a bottomless pit. Non sends himself into a similar chasm, and Lois unceremoniously lands a haymaker on Ursa's jaw that causes her to meet the same fate. (The nature of that fate is somewhat muddy; in an extended cut of the film the Salkinds released to video two years later, we see a U.S. "Polar Patrol" crew arresting the villains and Lex Luthor. In the theatrical cut, however, the viewer is left with the conviction that both Superman and Lois have committed first-degree murder, and that Superman abandons Luthor at the North Pole.)

For all the critical kvetching about the film's resolution of the Lois-Clark relationship—the "super-kiss" that removes her memory of his secret identity—the notion of super-hypnotism, howsoever goofy, is one with a long comic-book pedigree. In fact, it's one that has been used countless times to wipe Lois's memory of Superman's secret identity.

Clark returns to the truck stop to give the bully a taste of his own medicine, and, in the film's most shamelessly go-for-broke shot, Superman flies a new American flag to the White House, to replace the one destroyed by Zod.

The closing credits begin with a promise: "Coming Soon: *Superman III*."

The film broke box-office records on its opening weekend, and although it ended up making $108 million—significantly less than *Superman: The Movie*'s $134 million—and finished third for the year (behind *Raiders of the Lost Ark* and *On Golden Pond*), the film was a major hit.

One of the film's biggest fans was comedian Richard Pryor, who released what would be his last live comedy album in 1982. Titled *Supernigger*, its cover featured a cartoon of a muscle-bound Pryor flying through the air in an ersatz super-suit and included a brief bit in which Pryor enacts a scene between Perry White and Clark Washington, mild-mannered custodian of the *Daily Planet*.

Pryor appeared on *The Tonight Show with Johnny Carson* and raved about Superman in general ("I love that dude") and *Superman II* in particular. The segment was seen by David and Leslie Newman, who made a fateful phone call.

(Not So) Enormous Changes at (Almost) the Last Minute

In the comics, it was a time of change for Superman and his colleagues, but the nature of those changes was small; it's fair to characterize them as fussy. With the cancellation of *Superman Family*, Supergirl moved to Chicago and enrolled in the psychology department at Lake Shore University. The book, titled *The Daring New Adventures of Supergirl*, could not live up to its title (which changed to the more matter-of-fact *Supergirl* with issue 13) and would be canceled at issue 23, cover-dated September 1984. Despite its short life span, this book was the one in which the always fashion-conscious heroine reached her sartorial nadir, sporting a "Dynamic New Costume!" that included a billowy skirt, a frizzy blond perm, and, in issue 17, a red cloth headband ("[the] symbol of citizenship on Krypton!"), which made her look like she'd just shoulder-danced her way off the set of the "Love Is a Battlefield" video.

In the *Legion of Super-Heroes* title, Paul Levitz and Keith Giffen wrote a five-issue story arc in which the superpowered teenagers call on every ally in their space-Rolodex, in order to confront a mysterious, immensely powerful foe who turns out to be Jack Kirby's Darkseid himself. This story, called "The Great Darkness Saga," imbues the Darkseid character with a grander, more sinister presence and helps raise his profile, turning him from just another space-opera villain to a truly menacing, implacable enemy for Superman and his friends.

Over in the pages of *Justice League of America* #195–#197 (October–December 1981), Superman's very first comic nemesis—the body-switching mad scientist called the Ultra-Humanite—returned. Before, his evil brain had resided within the comely form of 1940s movie star Dolores Winters. This time, however, he had exchanged that body for one with a bit more comic-book oomph: that of an enormous, mutant, albino ape.

The New Luthor-Brainiac Team

Yet such whimsy wasn't welcome in the main Superman titles, where writers Cary Bates and Marv Wolfman felt it was time to revamp Superman's classic bald baddies, Luthor and Brainiac. In *Action* #544 (Superman's forty-fifth anniversary), Bates gave Luthor an armored green jet-suit that allowed him to go toe-to-toe with the Man of Steel. Wolfman, for his part, took a more extreme route: he dispensed with the green-skinned, bald-headed, diode-crowned robot alien look altogether. "I wanted to make [Brainiac] cold and deadly," he told Mike Eury in 2006.

His solution: Transform Brainiac into a true artificial intelligence. Make him a disembodied consciousness equally capable of inhabiting an android shell and a vast spaceship. He was given a new look, too. The Brainiac spaceship is a gleaming metal skull atop hundreds of squirming tentacles, as if the android were taking design advice from HR Giger.

"Superman vs. the King of Computerized Crime!"

Months before Richard Pryor had appeared on *The Tonight Show* extolling his love of the Man of Steel, Ilya Salkind had prepared a treatment for the film that would eventually become *Superman III*. In it, the evil computer Brainiac does what villains have done to the Man of Steel countless times in the comics—splits him into a good

Clark Kent and an evil Superman. The ambitious (read: expensive) science-fiction-focused treatment also brought in Supergirl (with the intention of spinning her off into her own franchise) and the fifth-dimensional pest, Mr. Mxyzptlk.

Warner Bros. nixed the idea, citing budget concerns and their worries that characters such as Brainiac and Mxyzptlk were too inside-baseball for the casual viewer. They reasoned that hard-core Superman fans would see the film anyway, so there was no need to cater to their specialized knowledge; what the movie truly needed was a broader appeal.

After Pryor's *Tonight Show* appearance, David and Leslie Newman wrote a script that picked up on the idea of a computer villain, with a part for the wildly popular comedian. Unfettered by the need for *Superman: The Movie*'s epic sweep or *Superman II*'s set-piece battle sequences—and freed as well from the nagging tendency of Donner and Mankiewicz to cut their biggest, corniest gags—the Newmans decided not to try to top the first two films. Their film, with the working title *Superman vs. Superman*, would not be about myth making. It would be lighter, campier, and more slapsticky— they'd even get a chance to dust off that Leaning Tower of Pisa gag Donner had cut from the original movie's script.

The Salkinds were miffed at actress Margot Kidder's tendency to badmouth their pecuniary ways to the press, although their public position was that the first two films had taken the Lois/Clark relationship as far as it could go. Whatever the reason, Annette O'Toole's Lana Lang steps in as the romantic interest this time around, when Clark returns to Smallville for a high school reunion.

Robert Vaughn was hired to play ruthless computer tycoon Ross Webster, and the part the Newmans wrote for Pryor was considered a skeleton, because the screenwriters fully expected him to ad-lib like crazy. When the time came to shoot, however, Pryor stuck to the script.

Yet at several points during the shoot, Lester grew concerned that Pryor's physical comedy (as when he slaps on a pair of skis, ties a blanket around his shoulders, and flies off a roof) was eating up too much screen time, but Warner Bros. was adamant that the public wanted as much Pryor as it could get.

Which, unfortunately, is exactly what they got.

Superman III

Lester wasted no time at all communicating to his audience that this Superman film was his and his alone. The movie's opening shot is no homage to the character's rich history (*Superman: The Movie*) or a supraliminal flight through the vast, interstellar dark (*Superman II*) but something entirely more earthbound and prosaic: a close-up of Richard Pryor's face as his character, Gus Gorman, waits in line at the Metropolis unemployment office.

Partway through the film, at an event honoring Superman in Smallville, Gus shows up dressed as a general (Pryor does a Patton impression, extolling the virtues of plastics for some reason) and awards the hero a chunk of synthetic kryptonite. The substance does not harm the Man of Steel, but later he begins to behave oddly—ignoring cries for help, putting the moves on his high school sweetheart, straightening the Leaning Tower of Pisa, and blowing out the Olympic Flame.

Just as Reeve manages to telegraph the difference between Clark and Superman simply by squaring his shoulders, he locates his "Evil Superman" in a slight softening of the features, a louche sneer on the lips.

The drunken, reprobate Superman ends up in a junkyard, where he splits into two—evil Superman and good (and superpowered) Clark Kent. The resulting fight scene is easily the film's high point—and, in point of fact, the whole hinky "synthetic kryptonite" plot that has made this set piece possible is classic Silver Age Superman storytelling—long on contrivance, short on logic, but ultimately serving to turn the story's emotional conflict into a purely physical one.

Superman III premiered on June 17, 1983, and went on to make nearly $60 million, about half of the money *Superman II* made and one-fifth that of *Return of the Jedi*, released just three weeks earlier.

Reeve had had enough of the role—or so he told *Omni* magazine, when asked whether he'd return: "No, I guarantee you I won't. Because I don't want these films to become like a series, where they become formula stuff. . . . But you should quit while you're ahead, you know? . . . You've got to move in your life. . . . We all had a good time in senior year in high school, but you can't stay there." He would, of course, return to the role a final time, and it wouldn't be the money, but the message, that enticed him.

The Salkinds, meanwhile, figured that if audiences weren't responding to a Man of Steel, perhaps it was time to offer them a Maid of Might.

Standout Stories

Even as the chintziness of *Superman III* dealt a blow to the Man of Steel in the public consciousness, making everything about him—his powers, his adversaries, his very presence—seem small, low-rent, and risible, the creators of *Superman* comics were desperate to return a sense of grandeur and gravitas to the character.

For the four hundredth issue of *Superman* (October 1984), writer Elliot Maggin and editor Julie Schwartz staged a massive salute to the Man of Steel, inviting twenty-three different artists to illustrate Maggin's short stories or produce pinup images of Superman in their distinctive styles; these artists included Will Eisner, Steve Ditko, Moebius, Bernie Wrightson, Frank Miller, Brian Bolland, Walt Simonson, Bill Sienkiewicz, Howard Chaykin, Wendi Pini, and *MAD*'s Jack Davis. John Byrne provided an early iteration of a Man of Steel very similar to the one he would use to reboot Superman two years later, and Jack Kirby offered a smiling, joyous-looking take—one that likely reflected his own sense of satisfaction in knowing that, this time at least, no other artist would redraw his Superman to ensure that it comported with DC's style sheets.

In his introduction to the issue, Ray Bradbury wrote of his affinity for the clumsy Clark Kent, and avowed, "As we slip, slide and catapult ourselves, yelling, into the future, Clark Kent will go with us to make sure Superman will catch us."

Maggin's collected stories depict the near and distant future of the DC Universe, when Superman's exploits have passed into legend. As historians debate the minutiae of Superman's life, we see his tale continuing to inspire different generations. Jim Steranko produced a five-page illustrated story on his own, which shows the sons and daughters of Superman spreading through the stars and giving rise, via a dimensional implosion, to a future civilization or to ancient Kryptonians or possibly to mankind itself (Steranko's art is gorgeous, but his narrative gets a bit opaque).

Over in the pages of *Action Comics* #554 (April 1984), writer Marv Wolfman paired with legendary artist Gil Kane for a stylish tale that explored what would happen if Superman didn't exist. In the story, ancient aliens visit the prehistoric Earth, only to find humanity a warlike species that would be difficult to conquer. They install a secret technology that renders humanity docile by preventing it from engaging its imagination and embracing "the heroic ideal." When the aliens return to Earth in a few thousand years, they find a populace huddling in mudhuts, ripe for the picking. That is, until two young boys named Jerry and Joey, who are ostracized by their fellows ("They're always making up those *dumb stories*! . . . Stories can't plow the fields or make your life any better!"), hatch the idea of a Super Man.

As long-overdue salutes to Superman's creators go, the story is heartfelt, if less than deft ("Jerry, I keep feeling inside that we're . . . something *special* . . . We've just got to *believe*!"). When Joey scrawls the figure of Superman on a cave wall, the aliens panic ("Sir! The *heroic concept* exists! *Mythic belief* is returning!"), Superman is summoned into being, and "true" reality reasserts itself.

Who Runs the (Super)World?

The Superman film franchise's reboot, if reboot it was, came with a chunky heel.

Superman III had performed poorly, and Reeve had sworn off the spit curl, but no matter: the Salkinds had cannily licensed the entire Super-oeuvre—anyone and anything in Superman's nearly fifty-year history was fair game. Supergirl, Superman's perky blond cousin, was the logical choice.

The producers wanted to do it up big—an epic interplanetary adventure that would finally bring the evil computer Brainiac to the big screen, in a team-up with a powerful sorceress. Initially, Ilya Salkind even got Reeve to agree to brief cameo appearances in the film—an aerial ballet-duet with Supergirl when she arrives on Earth and later as a victim of a magic spell whom only Supergirl can save.

Ultimately, Reeve begged off, and the ambitiously expensive script was rewritten to excise Superman, Brainiac (whom Warner Bros. still considered too niche a villain), a lengthy opening sequence revealing how Supergirl's Argo City survives the destruction of Krypton, and—for budgetary reasons—any off-world adventures at all.

Demi Moore tested for the title role, and Alexander Salkind pushed—strongly—for Brooke Shields, but in the end, the part of Kara Zor-El/Supergirl went to a nineteen-year-old unknown, Helen Slater, who impressed the producers with her combination of grace and self-assurance.

Settling on an actress took less time and effort than it took to settle on her costume. Endless iterations were produced, tested, shot, and reshot; between production meetings, the hemline of Supergirl's skirt rose and fell and rose again. At first, costumers tried to reproduce the recently redesigned look she was sporting on comic book pages at the time—complete with an S-shield that crept over the shoulders and a timely, albeit ghastly, perm/headband combination. Ultimately (and, for the sake of the film's longevity, thankfully), they went for a more timeless (read: generic) look based on her first comic book appearance.

The role of Selena the Sorceress went to Faye Dunaway, with Brenda Vaccaro as her brassy sidekick; Peter Cook played Selena's mentor Nigel (who doesn't figure in the film largely enough to justify his character's presence), and Peter O'Toole looks sheepish as the wise Argo City artist Zaltar—in his quieter moments, he adopts the faraway expression of a man anticipating cocktail hour. Hart Bochner played Ethan the Hunky Landscaper (although the studio pushed for Peter Gallagher), and Marc McClure reprised his Jimmy Olsen to provide some tenuous continuity to the Reeve films. Reeve made only a virtual cameo—a poster of Superman on a dorm room wall.

Director Jeannot Zwarc imbued the movie with a softer, more overtly fantasy-tinged tone than the Reeve films possessed. Apart from the scenes between scenery-chewers Dunaway and Vaccaro (who's campier than a drag queen in a pup tent), the humor is quieter, gentler.

Too gentle and—at an initial running time of 135 minutes—too long for test audiences. Producers chopped twenty minutes out of Zwarc's edit, and *Supergirl* premiered on November 21, 1984.

Licensed tie-ins were few and far between—a children's activity book, a coloring book, and the soundtrack, by Jerry Goldsmith. The Salkinds couldn't even look to DC to hype the movie to the character's hard-core fans—because the *Supergirl* comic had been canceled due to low sales with the September 1984 issue.

"Her First Great Adventure"

The film begins in Argo City, looking like an odd cross between a Sedona commune and the Mall of America, where young Kara Zor-El (Slater) visits her friend Zaltar (O'Toole), an artist who, we learn, "founded" this last remaining vestige of doomed Krypton. He's borrowed an omegahedron, a spinning, glowing globe that powers Argo City. Via leaden dialogue, he exposits to Kara that their city "exists in inner space" and that he's getting ready to leave ("In that! Through there!").

In a bizarre series of events involving a giant dragonfly (this is a very odd movie), the omegahedron hurtles away from Argo City; Kara, feeling guilty, steals Zaltar's spacepod and pilots it "through the binary chute" to chase and retrieve the power source before Argo City perishes. Zaltar, for his role in the loss, exiles himself to the Phantom Zone.

Kara arrives on Earth (in costume, suddenly) and proceeds to experiment with her newfound powers. An extended, quietly lovely sequence that features Supergirl describing graceful arcs and somersaults through the trees and over the water suggests the elegiac, fantastical mood the rest of the film only aims for.

Eventually—and for no reason the film attempts to explain—Supergirl decides to adopt a secret identity. This being a Salkind film, yet another noncanonical Kryptonian superpower puts in an appearance, when Supergirl somehow manifests a complete Midvale School for Girls uniform and a brown wig. A face-off with Dunaway's Selena, who has claimed the power of the omegahedron for herself, lands Supergirl in the Phantom Zone. While Selena begins her reign of terror (which, truth be told, consists of little more than tootling around the town of Midvale in a limo), the now powerless Supergirl is found by Zaltar, who informs her that there *is* a way out of the Phantom Zone. "But it's impossible."

Escape turns out to be not quite as impossible as he makes it out to be, though it is fairly inconvenient—especially for Zaltar, who gets swallowed up by a tornadolike piece of hokum called the "quantum vortex." Supergirl returns to Earth and faces off with Selena, who conjures an especially cheap-looking shadow demon. Supergirl turns the demon on Selena, saves the omegahedron, and flies back to Argo City, which reignites with light and warmth as she approaches.

End(s) of an Era

If the poor performance of *Superman III* had been worrisome, the anemic box-office returns on *Supergirl*—a mere $14 million in total, on a film that cost $35 million to produce—were kryptonite. The Salkinds, who still retained the rights to the characters in the Super-universe through 1999, felt that they wanted to get out of the business of making films about primary-colored Kryptonians. They weren't prepared to sell their license completely—they had some ideas they considered ripe for television—but they began to look for someone interested in temporarily taking over the Superman license for a specific film project or two.

Meanwhile, in the offices of DC Comics, a momentous decision had been made. They were wiping the slate clean and starting over.

The *Crisis* Approaches

A clever gimmick Schwartz and writer Gardner Fox had introduced in the 1961 story "Flash of Two Worlds"—the notion that on an alternate Earth in a parallel dimension, the original World War II–era versions of DC's heroes still fought crime—had spread like a virus, over the years.

By the time the 1980s rolled around, readers of DC Comics might encounter stories set on Earth-1 (the main continuity); Earth-2 (the Golden Age heroes); Earth-3 (heroes are villainous despots); Earth-C (funny animals); Earth-S (Marvel Family); Earth-X (Nazis won World War II); or Earth-Prime (our Earth, where superheroes are mere comic-book characters). What's more, many Earths contained different versions of the same hero. The DC Powers That Be, nervously eyeing a steady decline in sales and print runs, convinced themselves that this state of affairs was too confusing and was keeping hordes of new readers away.

The word came down to the writers on all DC titles: Get your ducks in a row. Big changes were coming. All of the Earths would be collapsed together, and the entire history of the DC Universe streamlined. Going forward, there would be one and only one version of each character. It would all take place over the course of a twelve-issue miniseries to be called *Crisis on Infinite Earths*, scheduled to launch in April 1985. Every book would have to tie into the event. No title would emerge from the event unchanged, and some titles would not emerge from it at all.

In today's comic-book climate, which is rife with reboots, retcons, *New Universes*, and world-shattering crises of various stripes turning up every summer like algal blooms, it's difficult to grasp what a monumental and unprecedented decision this was. Marvel had enjoyed a boost in sales with its own massive, all-hands-on-deck crossover events called *Secret Wars*, but they were simply excuses for roiling, issue-length fight scenes that could have been drawn by Hieronymus Bosch. This was different—this would change things. Although DC felt certain that dispensing with decades of confusing and often contradictory continuity would help new readers, hardcore fans took tremendous nerdy pride in being able to distinguish Earth-1 Superman from his Earth-2 twin with a quick glance at his sideburns; they delighted in mapping the DC Multiverse, and when it came to navigating the many narrative dead ends and cul-de-sacs that had piled up over the years, they didn't resent them—they *lived* in them.

As if a wholesale universal collapse wasn't enough, DC also let creators, both in and out of the company, know that the Big Three were on the table for radical revamps. In the wake of the *Crisis*, they would be relaunching Superman, Batman, and Wonder Woman and wanted to see proposals, the bolder the better. The goal was to make the heroes more contemporary, more colorful—and to appeal to the more sophisticated (read: older) readers, who were demanding more and sticking around longer.

Steve "Howard the Duck" Gerber submitted a Wonder Woman proposal. So did artist George Perez. Frank Miller's Batman proposal was turned down, so he changed its setting from the present day to the future and pitched it as a miniseries; it became *Batman: The Dark Knight* (which, once collected, was called *Batman: The Dark Knight Returns*). Howard Chaykin submitted a plan for Superman, as did John Byrne. Ultimately, Byrne's pitch won out.

A newly launched Superman meant new writers, new artists— and a new editor. Julius Schwartz was informed that when John Byrne's Superman would be launched in a year's time, Andy Helfer would take the editorial reins of all Superman books. Schwartz, seventy years old, announced his plans to retire in 1986 and become an unofficial editorial adviser. During the final year of his sixteen-year reign, he set plans in motion to give "his" Superman a proper send-off.

Unbeknownst to Schwartz, Bob Rozakis, Elliot Maggin, executive editor Dick Giordano, and others produced an entirely different September 1985 issue of *Superman* from the one he believed to be in production. *Superman* #411, "The Last Earth-Prime Story," is an issue-length tribute to Schwartz for his seventieth birthday.

That same month's issue of the team-up book *DC Comics Presents* (#85) sees the Man of Steel's oddest team-up yet, in "The Jungle Line," an odd, trippy story penciled by Rick Veitch and written by Alan Moore.

Clark Kent becomes infected by a lethal Kryptonian fungus that has hitchhiked to Earth on a meteor. A fever descends on him, his powers vanish, and he begins to hallucinate. He resolves to die alone and begins to drive south. Eventually, he reaches the Louisiana bayou and succumbs to the fever, driving off the road. There, he is found by Swamp Thing, the walking mountain of muck who starred in DC's highly acclaimed horror title. By communing with both the fungus and Superman's fevered brain, Swamp Thing saves the Man of Steel's life. The fever breaks, and a healthy Superman flies off, believing his encounter with Swamp Thing to be a simple hallucination.

For the Man Who Has Everything

In an odd coincidence, September 1985 also saw the publication of another Alan Moore story involving Superman and a hallucinatory plant. *Superman Annual* #11, by the *Watchmen* team of Moore and artist Dave Gibbons, is titled "For the Man Who Has Everything." It begins with Wonder Woman, Batman, and Robin arriving at the Fortress of Solitude to celebrate Superman's birthday. They find their friend in a catatonic state, an enormous alien plant form attached to his chest. The plant, called a Black Mercy, "attaches itself to its victims in a form of symbiosis, feeding from their bio-aura . . . it reads them like a book, and feeds them a logical simulation of the happy ending they desire."

The "happy ending" Superman envisions is that of the life he would have led had Krypton never exploded: that of a successful archaeologist, happily married to former actress Lyla Lerrol (a reference to Siegel's "Superman's Return to Krypton" from *Superman* #141, November 1960), with two kids.

Back in the Fortress, Wonder Woman tangles with the evil space tyrant Mongul, while Batman and Robin attempt to free Superman from the plant's control. Moore's skill at characterization gets a nice workout—his Mongul is a roughly equal mixture of brute force and cool intelligence, with a cruel, cunning sneer.

Yet the vision the Black Mercy supplies to Superman isn't all warmth and wonder. Superman's will is fighting the plant's mind control, and the vision sours. We learn that his elderly father, Jor-El (drawn burly and white-haired to resemble *Superman: The Movie*'s Marlon Brando), was kicked off the Science Council when his theory of Krypton's destruction was proved wrong, and he is now a member of an extremist religious group that rails against modern Kryptonian society. Meanwhile, a political movement protesting the continued use of Phantom Zone imprisonment grows violent.

Superman finally fights himself free of the Black Mercy's grip, and Moore and Gibbons show us a rare sight: the Man of Steel driven to an almost murderous rage. After a fierce fight, the day is ultimately saved by Robin, who tosses the Black Mercy at Mongul.

In the years since its publication, "For the Man Who Has Everything" has been widely acclaimed and anthologized; in 2004, it was made into an episode of the animated series *Justice League Unlimited*. The reasons for its enduring appeal include its status as a snapshot of a simpler time, just before the *Crisis*—there's a special breed of chumminess to the Batman/Superman relationship, for example, which the reboot dispensed with. There's Gibbons's exquisite character work—the gloating expression on Mongul's face, the way, just before a turn in the battle, Superman's eyes blaze red, though his face remains hidden in shadow, the many homages to classic Superman tales scattered throughout the fortress's trophy room.

Yet there is something more primal, more simple at work here, too. Moore shows a Man of Steel whose fondest wish is to undo the very cataclysm that brought him into being, the event that sets him apart. He wants—Moore posits—a normal life, a family, a wife. When that is revealed to be a fantasy, it is as if he has lost Krypton again. In the rage that seizes him, Moore offers us a fleeting and ultimately chilling glimpse of something that hasn't existed for forty-six years: a Superman who is dangerous.

"You Turn in Battle, Girl? That Is a Fatal Mistake!"

On the cover of the October 1985 issue of *Crisis on Infinite Earths* (#7), artist George Perez presents the reader with the kind of shocking "death of a hero" image that misled many a ten-year-old during the Silver Age—but this was different. This was not a dream, not a hoax, not an imaginary story.

Superman stands in classic Superman pose at the very center of the cover, limned by a distant sun as throngs of heroes stand behind him, heads bowed. The Man of Steel's arms cradle the bloody, battered, lifeless body of his cousin, Supergirl.

Of course, the very first image of Superman in action was that crude 1938 panel depicting him cradling the blond murderess Evelyn Curry in his arms, an image shot through with pulpy adolescent glee. Yet this image—this super-pieta—is its antithesis and offers uncomprehending readers a surprisingly wrenching portrait in spandexed grief.

For *Crisis* writer Marv Wolfman, this was a necessary sacrifice.

> Before [the] *Crisis*, it seemed that half of Krypton had survived the explosion. We had Superman, Supergirl, Krypto, the Phantom Zone criminals, the bottle city of Kandor, and many others. Our goal was to make Superman unique. We went back to his origin and made Kal-El the only survivor of Krypton. That, sadly, was why Supergirl had to die.

In the story, Supergirl is one of a team of heroes assaulting the asteroid-fortress that belongs to the villain of the piece, an evil entity called the Anti-Monitor who wishes to fuse the few remaining Earths together and destroy them utterly. Superman locates the "solar collector" machine the Anti-Monitor is using to merge and destroy the Earths but is felled by a devastating blast.

Supergirl hears her cousin's scream and flies to his side, at which point Wolfman kicked up the foreshadowing so much ("And Supergirl rushes ahead, knowing full well that whatever could bring such pain to her powerful cousin . . . could certainly destroy her. But Supergirl is a hero . . . and her concerns are not for herself . . . But for the one she loves."), it's technically fiveshadowing.

Wolfman proceeded to slather on the pathos, gilding the emotional lily so fervently it makes Dickens's death of Little Nell read like an expense report. Supergirl pauses along the way to rally her fellow heroes ("There's *always* hope. You *can't* give up hoping. Not ever!") and hurtles into battle, giving herself the world's most self-critical pep talk: "I may never be as good as [Superman] is, but Kal always taught me to do my best. Nothing else matters. Be true to yourself, be the *best* you are able to . . . don't ever give anything *but* your best. I've lived with his ideal, and heaven knows I've tried my hardest to live *up* to it. And I think for the most part I have."

Supergirl shouts for her fellow heroes to abandon her—to save themselves and the Earths, but that moment of selfless inattention is all the Anti-Monitor needs to fire up an energy blast ("*Thooommm*") that rips through her body.

The Maid of Might is no more, and the Anti-Monitor escapes, but his infernal machine is destroyed, and the Earths are safe—for now.

Dark Knight vs. Blue Stooge

In February 1986, while heroes fought and worlds died in the pages of *Crisis*, and the final fate of the DC Universe was yet to be determined, Frank Miller introduced a wholly separate reality in a four-issue prestige-format miniseries now known as *The Dark Knight Returns*. Existing as it did outside DC Universe continuity, the events of the *Crisis* played no role in the *Dark Knight*'s story line. Yet Miller's stand-alone, hard-bitten slice of superhero noir would throw a long shadow over DC's post-*Crisis* continuity—and over the entire superhero comics genre—for decades. Because where the *Crisis* merely changed DC Universe history, *The Dark Knight Returns*—along with grim-and-gritty sister comic *Watchmen*—changed the essential mood of superhero storytelling.

The Dark Knight Returns is set in a future Gotham City in which Bruce Wayne, now fifty-five years old, has not ventured out as Batman for ten years. The public no longer trusts superheroes; one by one, the government has rounded up members of the Justice League or forced them to retire. Upon the return of the villain Two-Face (and, subsequently, the Joker), Bruce Wayne dons the cape and cowl once more, and his vigilante actions attract the attention of the president of the United States—and his secret weapon, Superman.

In his depiction of the Man of Steel, Miller captured both the surface and the essence of the character. On one level, he presented Superman as many readers at the time doubtlessly saw him—an agent of the status quo, a dutiful, fascistic stooge of the military-industrial complex. Miller underscored this point with his introduction to the character: a series of panels zooms in on the American flag until, in a single transition, we realize that the billowing red-and-white stripes have become the red-and-yellow curve of the S-insignia on Superman's chest.

Superman, we learn, has made a deal with the government: "I gave them my *obedience* and my *invisibility*," he thinks to himself, while dispatching Soviet battleships. "They gave me a *license* and let me *live*. No, I *don't* like it. But I get to save lives . . . and the *media* stays quiet. But now the *storm* is growing again . . . they'll hunt us *down* again . . . because of *you*."

The inevitable climax of the series is a brutal slugfest between Superman (weakened by synthetic kryptonite) and Batman (in an armored exoskeleton). To the readers of the time, such a hero vs. hero brawl seemed novel, at least in the pages of DC Comics, where Superman and Batman had spent decades as bosom pals, distinguishable only by their respective color schemes.

Yet the battle spoke to the changing mood of the times; as far as widespread public perception went, Superman's star was fading, and Batman's was on the rise. The 1980s had begun with a blockbuster Superman film that mixed bright, sunlit science fiction with fantasy; the decade would end with a blockbuster Batman film steeped in director Tim Burton's gothic-horror shadow and murk. Heroes were out, as was altruism as a believable motivation; in came antiheroes and sociopathology. The fight scene in the fourth and final chapter of *The Dark Knight Returns* marked the handoff of the baton.

Waiting Out the Clock

In the twelfth and final issue of *Crisis on Infinite Earths* (March 1986), one Earth remains—one whose inhabitants do not remember the existence of the multiverse. Heroes and villains have died, but many have survived, including two alternate-universe versions of Superman—the Golden Age Superman of Earth-2, and the Superboy from Earth-Prime (the "real" Earth that you and I live on), who'd been introduced just months earlier. Writer Wolfman couldn't quite bring himself to snuff out their candles, so he did the next best thing—he introduced a deus ex machina, in the form of an alternate, heroic version of Lex Luthor capable of creating a "paradise dimension," where Superboy-Prime and the Superman and Lois Lane of Earth-2 can live happily ever after. At least, until 2005—but we'll get to that.

The *Crisis* was over, but the debut of John Byrne's six-issue miniseries relaunching the Man of Steel from scratch was still six months away. The creative teams of Superman's two main titles—*Action* and *Superman*—filled the time with one-off adventures in which the Man of Steel flew to Mars; faced off against psychic teens, werewolves, dinosaurs, and vampires; and met a non-copyright-infringing version of Asterix the Gaul. Steve Gerber returned to write a sequel to his grim 1982 Phantom Zone miniseries, in the final issue of *DC Comics Presents* (#97, September 1986), in which he revealed that the Zone is actually the consciousness of a sentient alien being. Coming off the sweeping, literally world-shattering events of the *Crisis*, Superman's adventures had never seemed smaller or more mundane.

Or less commercial: Marvel's surging X-Men comics were by now outselling the Man of Steel's by a 5 to 1 ratio.

Yet on his way out the door, editor Julie Schwartz ensured that the Silver Age Superman's existence would end when it ended, not with a bang or with a whimper, but with haunting, elegiac farewell. In his autobiography, Schwartz wrote,

> I started to think, "What am I going to do with my last two issues?" and in the middle of the night it came to me: I would make believe that *my* last issues on *Superman* and *Action Comics* were *actually* going to be the last issues. Therefore it was incumbent upon me to clear up, to explain all the things that had been going on in the previous years. For example, did Lois Lane ever find out that Clark was Superman? Did they ever get married? What happened to Jimmy Olsen, to Perry White, to all the villains? I had to clear it up.

In other words, he would provide Superman with the one thing no corporate-owned piece of perpetually licensed intellectual property chained to a continuous, open-ended narrative could ever have: he would give him an ending.

The corporate-owned continuous narrative is, after all, the enemy of storytelling. In fiction, characters are shaped by events and their reactions to them; they emerge irrevocably changed. Yet a character such as Superman resists change, and that essential resistance is aided and abetted by marketing departments, style sheets, and licensing contracts. Superman *has* evolved over the years, of course—this book could not exist if he hadn't—but the nature of that evolution is a function of the culture that surrounds him, not something that grows out of his character.

This is why the Imaginary Story became such a central part of the Silver Age—the intrinsic appeal of providing an ending, any ending, to a narrative that had been engineered to go on forever. Here, Schwartz decided, was a chance to cut the narrative thread that Siegel and Shuster had begun spinning in their Cleveland bedrooms almost half a decade earlier. Siegel had done it himself, to great effect, in the 1961 story "The Death of Superman!" So why not give him another shot?

Siegel jumped at the chance to write the "last" Superman story, but "it turned out there were legal problems that, because of the schedule, we didn't have time to resolve." (Read: Siegel asked for more money than DC was willing to pay.)

The next morning Schwartz mentioned his need to find a writer to his breakfast companion, Alan Moore. "At that point [Moore] literally rose out of his chair, put his hands around my neck, and said, 'If you let anybody but me write that story, I'll kill you.'"

The story would be told in two parts—beginning with the "final" issue of *Superman* (#423, September 1986) and concluding in the "final" issue of *Action Comics* (#583, September 1986). Curt Swan would pencil the story, with the inking chores divided between George Perez and old-school Superman artist Kurt Schaffenberger.

Whatever Happened to the Man of Tomorrow?

Ten years after Superman's disappearance and presumed death, a reporter from the *Daily Planet* arrives to interview the former Lois Lane for the "Superman Memorial Edition." He speaks into his recorder: "Okay, testing. August 16, 1997. Tim Crane interviewing Lois La . . . uh . . . Lois *Elliot* for the *Daily Planet* lead feature, 'The Last Days of Superman.'"

Lois's tale is long and shot through with stirring heroism and painful loss, involving as it does the deaths of Lana, Jimmy, and Krypto, as well as those of Luthor, Brainiac, and Mxyzptlk, the last of these (inadvertently) at the hands Superman. He has taken a life, something he is sworn not to do. Superman walks into a chamber that is used to store gold kryptonite, the substance that removes a Kryptonian's powers permanently.

Later, Lois tells the reporter, when the chamber was opened, Superman was gone. A secret passageway leads out to the Arctic. He is assumed to have perished somewhere on the ice, but his body was never recovered.

The *Daily Planet* reporter thanks Lois and leaves, just as Lois's husband, Jordan—a mustachioed car mechanic with a familiar-looking jaw line—brings out their infant son, Jonathan, from his nap. As the couple canoodles ("You really love it, don't you?" Lois asks her husband. "Just going to work every day, taking out the garbage, changing Jonathan's diapers . . . all this normal stuff?"), their son squeezes a lump of coal into a diamond. The end.

Once again, Moore finds, in this silly tale of flying dogs and leprechaun-like villains, a haunting power located in the tiniest of moments between its characters. Elements of the plot recall Robert Mayer's 1977 novel *Superfolks*, not to mention the climactic battle in other Moore tales. Mostly, though, "Whatever Happened to the Man of Tomorrow?" serves as a satisfyingly emotional finale to a story forty-eight years in the telling.

After all, the entire Superman Family was about to vanish completely, leaving Superman more alone than he'd been in four decades. Moore provided a beautiful, mournful melody to play them off the stage.

10

THE NEVER-ENDING BATTLE . . . ENDS. FOR A WHILE. (1986–1993)

Milestones

1986: *The Man of Steel* reboots Superman

1987: *Superman IV: The Quest for Peace* premieres

1988: *Superboy* live-action television show premieres

1992: Superman "dies" in *Superman #75*

1993: Superman returns to life in *Superman #82*—with a mullet. He would sport this hairstyle for three long, regrettable years. *Lois and Clark: The New Adventures of Superman* live-action television series premieres.

No headbands. No shoulder hoops. No little flappy capes.

A vastly different Krypton greeted readers as they tore open the more than 200,000 copies of *Man of Steel* #1 sold in the summer of 1986. Artist-writer John Byrne's ambitious biweekly, six-issue series, which bore the doughty task of rebooting the Man of Steel from scratch, makes it clear from its opening splash page that this is no cosmetic makeover. Byrne had unceremoniously tossed out any vestige of the familiar Krypton that had first been glimpsed in a newspaper strip in 1939; this was no Disneyfied Tomorrowland of graceful minarets, vertiginous floating walkways, and towering rainbow-hued obelisks. That futurist utopia was gone. In its place, Byrne created an arid desert of green rock formations, which served as both reverse homage to, and cheeky rejection of, the vast arctic wastes of *Superman: The Movie*'s Krypton. Jor-El's home, a vast industrial tower composed of golden metal panels, is the only structure visible—Byrne's Kryptonians keep to themselves.

Even when it comes to mating. We learn that technology has rendered Kryptonian culture as sterile as its landscape. Both men and women cover themselves from head to foot and mix their genetic material together only in mechanical globes called matrices. As the story opens, an angry Lara arrives at Jor-El's home, demanding to know why he has removed the matrix holding their unborn son from the communal "gestation chambers," a thing that has not been done for centuries.

Jor-El informs her that the sickness that has seized Krypton is a result of a chain reaction within Krypton's core, which is forming a strange new radioactive metal that is poisoning the populace. What's more, he says to her, this same chain reaction will destroy Krypton within the day, perhaps within the hour. He has taken the matrix and attached a hyper-light drive to it and is preparing to send it to the distant planet Earth, "a world not unlike Krypton of millennia past." There, the child will be bathed in the radiation of a yellow star, turning his cells into "living solar batteries, making him grow ever more powerful."

Out, once and for all, with Siegel and Shuster's "super-race/lesser gravity" exegesis for superpowers. Byrne instead put all of his narrative weight behind the "ultra-solar-ray" reasoning that Otto Binder had introduced back in 1961.

Byrne's original idea was to have the still-pregnant Lara fly to Earth in the rocket ship and die in childbirth, but publisher Jennette Kahn successfully argued for a less Dickensian option. The rocket carrying the Kryptonian birth matrix arrives on Earth and opens only when the loving, childless couple Jonathan and Martha Kent approach it. Thus, in Byrne's retelling, Superman is actually "born" on Earth.

From that point on, the narrative stops at the familiar Super-origin signposts: young Clark gets trampled by a bull without suffering a scratch, lifts a truck to retrieve a ball, spots Ma Kent's purse on the kitchen table through the living room wall, and learns, unceremoniously, that he can fly.

The difference—the one that stands in sharp contrast to some thirty-seven years of pre-*Crisis* history, is that Byrne made it clear that Clark is only gradually developing these powers, that they are getting stronger as he grows to adulthood. Which is to say: goodbye, Superboy.

Not that Byrne was happy about this. He fought for Superboy to stay. Or, technically, Superteen: "When I first came aboard, my understanding was I'd be allowed to work with a Superman who was new at the job and still learning his way. Then, when the contracts were signed, DC basically pulled the rug out from under me and said, 'No, that can only be in Man of Steel. By the first issue of Superman he has to be totally up to speed.'"

Losing Superboy was a drastic change, but in the grand history of the Superman character, the Boy of Steel had been a late addition, after all. It was in his characterization of Clark Kent that Byrne really shook the character to his core, tossing out a central tenet of the Siegel and Shuster Superman—or rather, neatly inverting it.

In Byrne's telling, Clark Kent's high school self is a strikingly handsome, confident, muscular athlete—a football star, in point of fact. Seeing his son delighting in the adulation of others, Jonathan Kent shows him the rocket he arrived in and enjoins him to think bigger; a humbled Clark resolves to use his tremendous gifts to help people, not "to make myself *better* than other people—to make them feel *useless*." He leaves Smallville, resolving to do good in the world, but to do so in secret.

For seven years, he manages this effort, saving thousands of lives in incidents chalked up to freak occurrences or random luck. Yet one day, in Metropolis, he is forced to go public to save the life of *Daily Planet* reporter Lois Lane. Amid the crowd that gathers, cajoling him, clawing at him, beseeching his help for thousands of petty problems, Clark is horrified. "It was all *demands*!" he tells his parents. "Everybody had something they wanted me to do, to say, to sell. . . . I know I still have to use my powers to help people who really need me . . . but they're going to be *looking for me. Expecting me*."

He resolves to adopt a persona—and a bold, symbolic costume—that will be his public face. When not in costume, he will comb his hair back, stoop his shoulders, and don a pair of big, round eyeglasses, creating a "place where no one will ever think to look for me—a Fortress of Solitude, so to speak."

In other words, Clark Kent the Kansas farm boy is the man, while Superman the powerful hero is the pose. If it reversed the polarity of Siegel and Shuster's original concept, it made a simple, implacable sense, nonetheless—why *would* anyone assume Superman had a secret identity, anyway? If he wasn't around, wouldn't they simply imagine that he was off somewhere else, saving lives?

Byrne was also banking that by locating the heart of the character in Clark, not in Superman, no one would really miss the whole meek, stumbling milksop routine, which he felt belonged to a bygone era of Charles Atlas "Hero of the Beach" ads. There was a reason Byrne chose to outfit his Clark in eyeglass frames reminiscent of those George Reeves had worn decades earlier: he remembered how Reeves had created a no-nonsense, unfussy Clark—the kind of guy you could believe had what it takes to be a shoe-leather reporter on the Metro beat of a major city.

In *Man of Steel* #2, Byrne redefined the Clark-Lois relationship. This Lois was tougher, more independent, and could hold her own physically against a host of threats. And, in a telling departure from years of continuity that would become increasingly important during the following years, she treated Superman as a story, but Clark as a man. *Man of Steel* #3 examined the Superman-Batman relationship with a firmer psychological grounding than the decades of stories that had gone before. Over the years, writers had brought the two heroes into conflict many times, but those conflicts tended to grow out of plot contrivances. Here, Byrne showed readers two heroes who shared a selfless dedication to justice, but whose worldviews were fundamentally opposed: Superman protects, Batman punishes. There could be grudging respect between them, but that respect would always be tempered by the strong conviction that the other's outlook and methods were deeply flawed.

In *Man of Steel* #4, we meet post-*Crisis* Lex Luthor. No power suit, no purple tights, no lab coat—he's no mad scientist, though he is plenty mad, at least in the "angry at the world" sense of the term. Recast as the owner of LexCorp (introduced by Marv Wolfman as "Lexcorp" before the reboot), the new Luthor is a sinister Mike Bloomberg, an impossibly rich and powerful tech tycoon who essentially owns Metropolis. His hatred for Superman stems not from adolescent follicular shenanigans, but from a much simpler place of jealousy and seething resentment. In *Man of Steel* #5, we see how far Luthor is willing to go to defeat the Man of Steel when he creates an imperfect clone of Superman, in a story that pays homage to the pre-*Crisis* Bizarro character. In the series' conclusion, Superman returns to Smallville for a visit, only to be visited by a holographic projection of Jor-El that dumps into his brain his entire Kryptonian backstory.

On *Man of Steel* #6's final page, Superman stands resplendent on a mountain top, gazing into the middle distance, cape snapping in a wind gust, delivering Byrne's new, Earth-first mission statement: "I may have been *conceived* out there in the endless depths of space . . . but I was *born* when the rocket opened on *earth*, in *America*."

By the time it was over, the *Man of Steel* miniseries had neatly revised several conceptual elements of the Superman mythos completely: Clark as the real self, Superman as "just a fancy pair of long johns that lets me operate in public without losing my private life." His status as Last Son of Krypton, a unique being with a unique power-set, was secured.

Out: the Superboy career, the longing for his alien past. In: Ma and Pa Kent, still alive and ready to offer sage counsel, and a more equal, honest relationship with Lois Lane. Where once there was a costumed arch-nemesis who plotted world domination while rubbing his hands together, there is now a villain who attacks not with death rays and doomsday devices but with leveraged buyouts and hostile takeovers.

There was also the look. That was different, too.

From the male body in the Schwarzeneggeresque eighties, more was expected. In the seventies, one could get away with skinny, but in the era of bodybuilding and Calvin Klein models, Curt Swan's classic Superman now seemed merely fit. Buff was in, and Byrne's downright steroidal Superman—with a neck thicker than a twelve-year-old elm—was on-trend. (To explain how Clark Kent managed to fill out his tight black T-shirts as absurdly well as he did, he kept a set of Nautilus equipment in his apartment.) Byrne drew a younger, more dynamic Superman than had been seen in the comics for years, with a jaw line sharp enough to cut Pecorino. He altered the super-coiffure as well, thinning the sides but adding volume and, especially, height. (The 1980s, ladies and gentlemen.)

Even the costume became more dramatic, with an enlarged S-emblem that stretched all the way across the hero's massive torso, and a longer, more regal cape that somehow managed to billow even in a locked, airless room.

Issues 5 and 6 of the biweekly *Man of Steel* bore a December 1986 cover date and set the stage for the three new Superman titles to premiere the following month.

In November 1986, the band R.E.M. released its cover of the Clique song "(I Am) Superman." The task of lead vocal on the song fell to bass player Mike Mills when Michael Stipe begged off. The song would become a darling of college radio stations during the next year, serving as an offbeat, wholly unintentional anthem to accompany Superman's resurgence.

Also in November, residents of the town of Metropolis, Illinois, bloodied but unbowed by the previous decade's failed attempts to create a Superman theme park, pitched in to erect a seven-foot-tall fiberglass Superman statue. It would keep its lonely vigil in the town square for seven long years, until the tendency for less-than-civic-minded citizens to plug it full of holes (testing the "faster than a speeding bullet" hypothesis for themselves) required that it be replaced, in 1993, with a fifteen-foot version.

Three Titles, No Waiting

As chief architect of the character's reboot, artist-writer John Byrne was tapped to helm two of the three Superman relaunch titles. First to arrive, with a January 1987 cover date, was *Action Comics* #584 (despite the four-month hiatus in publication, the new issue picked up the old *Action Comics* numbering). Now recast as a team-up title, to fill the slot vacated by *DC Comics Presents*, each issue of *Action* saw Superman meeting up with a different hero from across the DC Universe. Written and drawn by Byrne, *Action* quickly became one of DC's top-selling titles; editors soon learned that appearing alongside Superman in *Action* could boost the sales of less popular books, and the Man of Steel's dance card filled up quickly.

Superman #1 (January 1987), also written and drawn by Byrne, premiered one week after *Action*. Byrne and editor Andy Helfer wanted it clear that *Superman* was the flagship book, featuring the adventures of the newly relaunched Man of Steel—and they wanted to take advantage of comic book collectors' Pavlovian reaction to any issue marked #1, so they pulled a bit of a shell game. The book that had gone by the title *Superman* before the *Crisis* would be retitled *Adventures of Superman*, but its numbering would continue from where *Superman* #423 had left off, leaving a space that a brand-new series called *Superman* could fill.

From the very first issue, Byrne used the *Superman* title to introduce his new, post-*Crisis* iterations of pre-*Crisis* characters and concepts; part of the appeal of the book, for longtime fans, was seeing what Byrne would do to villains such as Metallo, Toyman, Mxyzptlk, and Prankster, and how he would incorporate Kirby's New Gods in the newly rebooted continuity. In *Superman* #2, for example, he summarily dispensed with a plot device that had fueled countless Silver Age stories, by having Luthor learn Superman's secret identity.

In the simplest, yet most ingeniously satisfying, story of his Superman tenure, Luthor commands a LexCorp team to amass every available bit of data on the Man of Steel, feed it into a massive database, cross-reference it, and query his state-of-the-art computer as to the nature of the connection between Clark Kent and Superman. The computer's conclusion, delivered after an impressive series of clicks and whirrs, is that "Clark Kent is Superman."

The LexCorp technician gasps. "Oh my goodness!" she exclaims. "That would never have *occurred* to me! And yet, given the body of *evidence* . . . it's so *logical*! So *flawlessly* logical!"

"Logical?" Luthor sneers. "Is it? To a *machine*, perhaps. Yes . . . a *soulless* machine might make that deduction. But not *Lex Luthor*! I know *better*! I know that no man with the power of *Superman* would ever *pretend* to be a mere *human*! Such power is to be *constantly exploited*. Such power is to be *used*!!"

The third and final Superman relaunch title to appear was *Adventures of Superman* #424, written by Marv Wolfman and penciled by Jerry Ordway. From the outset, *Adventures of Superman* had more modest aspirations; its creative team focused not on Superman's colorful fellow heroes, diabolical villains, or cosmic adventures, but on Clark's relationships with his friends at the *Daily Planet*. As a result, *AOS* quickly became an odd beast indeed—a grounded, street-level Superman book that, intentionally or not, recalled the fifties television show. One story line, for example, turned on the identity of a nonpowered costumed vigilante named Gangbuster, who dedicated himself to ending gang violence in Metropolis.

Sales of *Adventures of Superman* lagged behind the two Byrne-driven titles. "We struggled a bit in [Byrne's] shadow," Ordway admitted years later. "He was clearly the point man."

Superman editor Andy Helfer left, replaced by Mike Carlin, whose stated aim was to draw all of the Superman titles more closely together, to tighten plots and construct story lines that threaded through the three books.

Museum Piece

The reboot was a tremendous success. Sales were up, fans were excited (many carped, but they were talking about Superman, which hadn't happened in years), retailers and the trade press were effusive, and the character's fiftieth anniversary was right around the corner.

In preparation for the occasion, an exhibit called "Superman: Many Lives, Many Worlds" opened in the Smithsonian National Museum of American History in Washington, D.C., on June 24, 1987. Thousands of visitors ogled copies of *Action Comics* #1, vintage posters, storyboards, film, TV and radio scripts—including Mario Puzo's screenplay for *Superman: The Movie*—and several Superman costumes and toys. In the fall, the Smithsonian hosted a two-day Superman symposium; later still, a version of the Smithsonian exhibit toured the country.

Superman's handlers at DC Comics were delighted; clearly, something was in the air. What's more, this word-of-mouth momentum was building at the perfect time to capitalize on what was certain to be the Man of Steel's triumphant, long-awaited return to the ranks of all-time big-screen blockbusters.

On July 24, 1987, *Superman IV: The Quest for Peace* opened in theaters.

The Nuclear Winter of Our Discontent

Stinging from the debacle that was *Supergirl*, in 1985 the Salkinds essentially sublet the rights to make films starring Superman for $5 million to the Cannon Group. Owned by a pair of Israeli cousins, Cannon had spent the previous few years schizophrenically churning out both low-budget schlock starring Chuck Norris and Charles Bronson and art-house fare directed by Robert Altman, Franco Zeffirelli, and John Cassavetes. The Salkinds kept the rights to Superboy, however, and set to work prepping a television series.

Menahem Golan and Yoram Globus, for their part, were eager to elevate their profile and felt certain that Superman was the means to do so. Managing to secure some $40 million in financing from Warner Bros., they coaxed Gene Hackman back to the role of Lex Luthor relatively easily (the assurance that the Salkinds were in no way involved helped this endeavor a great deal), and Margot Kidder agreed to return as well.

Christopher Reeve proved more difficult to convince, but once the cousins agreed to produce his pet project—a tough-minded crime drama about a pimp and an unscrupulous magazine reporter called *Street Smart*—he agreed. (Reeve was eager to direct *Superman IV* as well but acceded that such a big-budget, effects-heavy project was too daunting a task; he ended up doing extensive second-unit work on the film instead.)

Golan and Globus approached Richard Donner and Tom Mankiewicz to gauge their interest, but the director and the writer were not eager to return. "What's left to do, you know?" Mankiewicz said. "It's futile. We've done it. Let's move on."

Ignoring that wise counsel, the producers found Sidney Furie, fresh from the low-budget action film *Iron Eagle*, and hired writers Lawrence Konner and Mark Rosenthal (late of the *Romancing the Stone* sequel, *Jewel of the Nile*) for the screenplay.

Reeve, for his part, had been moved by an antinuclear documentary and felt that the film should impart a message alongside its action. He approached Mankiewicz for advice, and the screenwriter warned him that Superman tackling real-world issues constituted a narrative dead-end. Reeve was undaunted, though, and pushed for a plot line in which Superman ends the arms race. (Reeve would later find himself sued—unsuccessfully—by a pair of screenwriters who claimed he'd stolen the idea from a screenplay they'd submitted to him in 1985.)

Yet just as production on *Superman IV* was gearing up, Cannon took a $60 million bath on *Over the Top*, the 1986 Sylvester Stallone paean to the semisweet science of arm-wrestling. With the threat of bankruptcy looming, Cannon slashed *Superman IV*'s budget from

$40 million to $17 million. That meant firing the special effects team and replacing them with Golan-and-Globus cronies who'd work quick and cheap.

Test screenings were abysmal, and the 134-minute running time became a somehow-still-languorous 89 minutes. Warner Bros., who'd originally slotted the film for a prestige winter release, pushed it up to summer without much in the way of marketing support. Before the film opened, Margot Kidder gutted through a promotional appearance on *Late Night with David Letterman*, only to get teased over the shoddy-looking nature of the clip she'd brought.

Superman IV: The Quest for Peace

Even the damn *credits* are low-rent.

Where the opening credits of *Superman I* and *II*, with their majestic, crystalline letters swooshing through the stars, impart a sense of cosmic scale, the names of *Superman IV*'s cast and crew flit by, dragging behind them the orange Chroma Key trails favored by 2 a.m. cable access videographers.

The film begins with Superman rescuing a cosmonaut in Earth's orbit, a scene that employs matte footage of Superman in flight so grainy, cheap-looking, and poorly inserted, it invites unflattering comparisons to the fifties television show. Given that these same clumsy shots turn up several times throughout the film, it's safe to say that no one came out of the theater believing a man could fly.

No vestige of Donner's much-vaunted verisimilitude remains, replaced here not by the archness and the mugging of *Superman III*, but by an airless, defeated sense of narrative exhaustion. No one seems able to gin up much enthusiasm or even mere effort: not Kidder, who hits her marks with merely dutiful determination; not Hackman, whose performance lacks the snap and wit of his earlier forays: and not Reeve, whose hairpiece often seems more fully present in a scene than he does.

In one scene, Clark Kent agonizes over whether to rid the world of nuclear weapons—as one lippy thirteen-year-old has requested— and is visited at his apartment by Lois Lane. In what is intended as an homage to earlier films, Clark jumps off his balcony with a screaming Lois, turns into Superman, and takes her on a flight across the country, accompanied by the syrupy strings of "Love Theme from Superman." As is the case throughout the film, however, Furie's pacing is so leaden, the effects so poor, and the actors so beleaguered that what might have been a wistful evocation of better times becomes a pointless, joyless retread.

"I remember," Lois tells him. "I remember everything." Yet before the film can follow this idea to any one of its many and intriguing subtexual conclusions, Superman kisses her, again wiping her memory. At the end of *Superman II*, the super-kiss, though certainly presumptuous, could be seen as selfless, a means to keep Lois from torturing herself. Here, it simply reads as the act of someone manipulative, selfish, and cruel.

The addition of Jon Cryer as Luthor's ineffectual nephew given to thickheaded surfer-speak is more of a subtraction, really, and the central plot device—Luthor creating a nuclear-powered doppelganger of Superman—suffers from cheesy, ham-handed choices from the get-go. We watch the evil Nuclear Man (Mark Pillow) gestate in seconds from fetus to brawny blond manhood and emerge from his fiery space-womb inexplicably clad in sleeveless yellow spandex, set off by a codpiece of gold lamé.

In keeping with the series' propensity for invoking noncanonical superpowers, a scene at the Great Wall of China shows the Man of Steel employing blue eye-beams to repair the extensive damage wrought by Nuclear Man. (Masonry-vision? Super-spackling?)

After recovering from radioactive poisoning suffered at the hands—technically, the fingernails—of Nuclear Man, Superman meets his foe on the surface of the moon. This sequence is marred by egregiously poor effects work: visible wires, folds in the black curtain meant to represent the inky vastness of space, and the use of slow motion to evoke the lesser gravity of the lunar surface.

Ultimately, the Man of Steel triumphs and makes a speech about world peace at what would have been United Nations Plaza, had the producers not balked at the cost of filming there, and instead looks a lot more like the ballroom at a Hyatt. Credits.

Superman IV's anemic box-office take was less than $16 million, delivering the first body blow to the Cannon Group. The second came with the arrival and quick departure of *Masters of the Universe* in theaters a month later. Two years later, Golan and Globus filed for Chapter 11.

The era of Superman on the big screen had come to a merciful, albeit ignominious, end; it would take nearly two decades of forced exile on the nation's television screens to wash off the stink. It wasn't how Superman's caretakers had hoped to position the character in advance of his fiftieth anniversary, but in the comics, at least, Superman was on a roll.

Byrne-ing the Midnight Oil

Despite having moved heaven and Earth—well, Earths—to clean up its continuity with the *Crisis*, and repeated avowals from various writers and editors that there would be no looking back, DC delighted in offering readers teasing glimpses of old, pre-*Crisis* characters and story elements.

In the Superman titles, that impulse was tightly controlled—at least at first. Barely a year after the *Crisis* had concluded, stray bits of pre-*Crisis* continuity began to appear. In a story line that began in *Superman* #8 (August 1987), continued in *Action* #591 (August 1987), and concluded in *Legion of Super-Heroes*, Byrne reintroduced the pre-*Crisis* Superboy.

He did so for a very specific reason—to narratively paper over one of the many cracks in continuity the *Crisis* had left in its wake: over in the *Legion of Super-Heroes* comic, Superboy (and Supergirl) had been key members of the team—how to reconcile that fact with the rebooted, there-never-was-a-Superboy reality of the new DC Universe? By revealing that the Superboy the Legion had known and loved for so many years wasn't, and had never been, real.

In the story, the Legion learns that one of its foes, the mysterious Time Trapper, had created a "pocket universe" that resembled the real one in most details—except that in it, Clark Kent became Superboy at a young age. All this time, the villain explains, whenever the Legionnaires had believed themselves to be traveling back in time to visit their friend Superboy in the twentieth century, the Time Trapper had been diverting them into this "pocket universe." In the story's third and final chapter, Superboy sacrifices his life to save the "pocket universe" from destruction—neatly ensuring that there will be no Boy of Steel hanging around to muck up Byrne's new continuity.

During the next year, Byrne's sheer output was impressive, even when the quality wasn't. He wrote three four-issue miniseries that fleshed out the history and the characters of Krypton, Smallville, and Metropolis, respectively, as well as a prestige-format one-shot (*Superman: The Earth Stealers*, penciled by Curt Swan and inked by Jerry Ordway) that saw the Man of Steel facing down planet-pilfering aliens, all while writing and drawing monthly issues of *Action*, *Superman*, and, eventually, *Adventures of Superman*.

There were hiccups along the way. In the two most infamous issues of his Superman tenure, *Action* #592 and #593 (September and October 1987), the Man of Steel gets mind-controlled into making a pornographic movie for an alien named, inevitably enough, Sleez. (Fear not for the Super-maidenhead: in the end, the Man of Steel's "strong moral fiber" allows him to resist Sleez's power).

Byrne reintroduced the notion of the Imaginary Story (which saw Superman returning to Krypton) and, in a surprising move, also brought back Supergirl (*Superman* #21, September 1988).

In a story line called "The Supergirl Saga" (September/October 1988), we learn that the Supergirl in question is *a* Supergirl, not *the* Supergirl. In the "pocket universe," an altruistic Lex Luthor has created an artificial life form—a "protoplasmic matrix"—to carry on the work of that universe's departed Superboy. The shape-shifting being, imprinted with the memories of Luthor's dead wife, Lana Lang, assumes her form and a Super-costume and flies to our universe to inform Superman that three Phantom Zone villains have escaped and are laying waste to the "pocket Earth." Superman enters the "pocket universe," alongside its Supergirl (who refers to herself as "Matrix"), to find that the three villains, including General Zod, have slaughtered millions and are only getting started.

In the ensuing fight, Matrix is gravely injured, and the villains succeed in murdering the entire population of the "pocket Earth"—some five billion people. Superman exposes them to gold kryptonite (a Silver Age relic that, the text is quick to insist, exists only in the "pocket universe"), which takes away their powers. Then, in a move that outraged fans, Byrne has Superman reach for a lead container that houses green kryptonite.

"What I must now do is harder than anything I have ever done before," he thinks. "But as the last representative of law and justice on this world, it falls to me to act as judge, jury . . . and executioner."

He exposes the villains to the kryptonite rays and watches grimly, shedding a single tear as they die slow and agonizing deaths. He buries their bodies and returns to our universe with the gravely wounded Matrix, who is taken in by Ma and Pa Kent.

Superman's execution of three villains would have far-reaching implications for the character and his story line for years, but Byrne wouldn't be there to see him through it. After two years of churning out Superman stories and engaging in regular battles with his editor, Byrne ended his run on Superman.

Golden Anniversary

In an old *Superman* letter column, Julie Schwartz had jokingly stated, in response to a reader's question, that Superman's birthday was February 29—to help explain why he never seemed to age. The joke stuck, and when it came time for the fiftieth anniversary media push, the fact that 1988 was a leap year seemed like kismet.

DC threw a birthday party for the Man of Steel on Friday, February 26, at the Puck Building in New York City. The bash, which featured a children's choir, Superman cartoons, and a "Kryptonite Tunnel" funhouse, was attended by Mayor Ed Koch, who puzzled reporters with half-jokes: "When I was a kid, I always wanted to go to Krypton. I never even made it to Brazil!"

Kirk Alyn, Noel Neill, and Jack Larson appeared on the February 29 *CBS Morning Show* to reminisce about the old days (and to complain about typecasting for good measure). That evening, CBS broadcast a one-hour TV special, *Superman's 50th Anniversary: A Celebration of the Man of Steel*. Produced by Lorne Michaels, with a script by a cadre of writers from *Saturday Night Live*—including Rosie Shuster, a distant relative of Joe Shuster—the special offered a tongue-in-cheek approach to Superman's history. Superman's fiftieth anniversary was the *Time* magazine cover story the week of March 14, and in June, Cleveland hosted a four-day International Superman Exhibition. Although the city of Cleveland designated the week of the exhibition "Siegel and Shuster Week," and the community held what was likely the first U.S. parade devoted to a comic-book character, neither man attended the event.

To the Small Screen

The fall of 1988 saw the premiere of two Superman-related television projects. Marv Wolfman had left the *Adventures of Superman* comic soon after the reboot to devote himself to his role as story editor on a new *Superman* cartoon series produced by Ruby-Spears. With character designs by the legendary artist Gil Kane, each episode concluded with a four-minute vignette that pulled deep from the character's rich history. The show premiered on September 17, 1988. The character's caretakers at DC, confident in Wolfman's deep affinity with the character and in Kane's ability to capture the visual essence of the Super-mythos, felt certain that it couldn't miss.

Yet it did. The network aired *Superman* at 7 a.m. on Saturday mornings, a time slot generally devoted to very young children, not the tweens the show was aimed at—initial ratings were low and stayed there; the show was cancelled after thirteen episodes.

Meanwhile, the Salkinds had succeeded where Whitney Ellsworth had not, twenty-seven years earlier: they'd gotten a *Superboy* television show off the ground. This, despite the complete absence of any cross-promotion or tie-in products from DC, because as far as the comics were concerned, the character didn't exist.

To save money, *Superboy* was filmed at the just-built Disney/MGM Studios in Orlando, Florida, and was shot on video. Twenty-year-old Stacy Haiduk played redhead Lana Lang; twenty-two-year-old John Haymes Newton played Superboy. The syndicated show was set at Shuster University, with Clark and Lana enrolled in the Siegel School of Journalism. As rich, ruthless fellow student Lex Luthor, Scott Wells was more handsome than convincing, and his character contented himself with distinctly un-Luthorlike petty scams.

Initial ratings were good, but the scripts and the effects of the first thirteen episodes, which saw Superboy tangling with drug dealers and the same kind of small-time crooks George Reeves had habitually faced, were flatly terrible. The numbers fell precipitously, causing considerable consternation among affiliates. Things improved marginally in the second half of the show's first season, when producers took advantage of a Screen Writers Guild strike to invite comics writers and editors such as Denny O'Neill, Cary Bates, J. M. DeMatteis, Mike Carlin, and Andy Helfer to contribute scripts. Newton's take on the role of Superboy, however, remained puzzlingly inert. He told interviewers that he set out to downplay Kent's bumbling quality in favor of making him shy and reserved; on camera, however, the actor simply failed to register.

Superboy was picked up for a second season, but Newton—and the histrionic Wells—were not. (When Newton asked for more money, Ilya Salkind invoked a morality clause in Newton's contract, citing a DUI arrest the actor had accrued.) Producers began to look for a new Superboy and Luthor.

After-Byrners

With John Byrne, the architect of the Super-reboot/renaissance, gone, DC's Superman titles took stock. Byrne's *Superman* book was taken over by writer Roger Stern, with art by Kerry Gammill. Jerry Ordway, who'd been penciling Byrne's scripts on *Adventures of Superman*, assumed that book's writing duties. As for *Action Comics*, DC decided to change the format of the book completely, turning it into a weekly anthology title that would spotlight the company's deep-bench superheroes. (This experiment lasted only one year; in July 1989, the book reverted to a monthly title focused on Superman, initially written and drawn by George Perez.)

Editor Mike Carlin instituted what he referred to as "Super Summits"—regular retreats taken by Superman's creative team where story lines would be collectively brainstormed, plotted, and assigned. He presided over an enormous chart of each title's order of publication and issue number, to help keep track of long-term subplots as they threaded through the three different Super-titles and to coordinate with the increasingly frequent company-wide crossover "events" (bearing titles such as *Millennium* and *Invasion!*), with which the publisher had grown enamored, in the wake of the sales boost brought about by the *Crisis*.

The team decided that Superman's breaking his vow never to kill would cause the Man of Steel to do some serious soul searching. In a thirteen-part story ("Superman in Exile") that ran through the February–August 1989 *Superman* titles, Superman leaves Earth and journeys through deep space on a voyage of self-discovery. Along the way, he faces off against various aliens, hallucinates encounters with the villains he's executed, gets taken prisoner on Warworld, and encounters an ancient Kryptonian weapon called the Eradicator with the power to send him home.

On his return to Earth, the device, which is tasked with preserving Kryptonian culture, begins to emit destructive energy, so Superman buries it in the Arctic. The sentient machine sets about transforming the space around it into a vast memorial to Krypton, filled with technology and artifacts it summons through the Phantom Zone. From this post-*Crisis* Fortress of Solitude, the Eradicator begins to control the mind of Superman in a story arc called "Day of the Krypton Man" (March/April 1990), transforming him into a model post-*Crisis* Kryptonian—aloof, intellectual, and unfeeling. Yet with the help of Ma and Pa Kent, Superman manages to break the device's control. The experience inspires Clark to embrace his humanity more fully, and he resolves to pursue a romantic relationship with Lois Lane.

He hurls the Eradicator into the sun—but the device . . . would return.

Night in America

While the Superman of the comics was off on his interstellar walkabout, the Tim Burton film *Batman* had broken box-office records and touched off a fresh wave of Batmania that outpaced even the 1966 craze. The bat symbol went from being an obscure emblem of nerd pride to a ubiquitous fashion statement. The film's vision of urban life as a gothic-noir nightmare resonated with audiences in the year of the Central Park jogger and the Yusef Hawkins shooting. Where the first two *Superman* films had helped lift the national mood out of its energy-crunch malaise, by 1989 Reagan's "Morning in America" had aged into a long night haunted by fears of a looming economic recession. There was one hero ideally suited to these dark times, and he didn't wear an S.

The success of the movie had inspired a boost in sales of the Batman titles, but it hadn't extended to other DC books. Even with the Bat-bump, however, DC couldn't dislodge Marvel's angst-ridden

X-Men from atop the sales charts. And with every month that passed, as the memory of the Superman reboot receded from readers' memories, the Man of Steel sold fewer and fewer issues.

Boy, Interrupted

While the Superman comics plugged away, struggling to redefine the character for a continually shrinking number of fans, the second season of the Salkinds' *Superboy* television show roared back to life. With a new Superboy (Gerard Christopher) and Luthor (Sherman Howard), the series became more action-oriented and availed itself of a coterie of comic-book villains, such as Mr. Mxyzptlk, the Yellow Peri, Metallo, Knick Knack (a spin on the Toyman), and, most notably, Bizarro.

The show became one of the top-rated syndicated programs on television. The writers and the editors of Superman's comic-book adventures couldn't help but notice that the sweeping changes they'd instituted in order to modernize the character and chase a broader audience had met with only temporary success, while the one element of the mythos they'd tossed aside—the hokey notion of a superteenager—now defined the character for millions more people than they could ever hope to reach. People with money that they could spend on things like comics.

Reintroducing Superboy into the new DC Universe was out of the question, so the publisher launched *Superboy: The Comic Book*, based on the TV show's characters and continuity. The first issue, dated February 1990, is not subtle about its provenance, featuring a photo still of Christopher and Haiduk and the familiar "As Seen on TV" stamp prominently displayed in the upper-right corner. (Beginning with issue 9, Superman veteran Curt Swan penciled the book, supplying a distinctly old-fashioned take that did not comport with that of the in-continuity Superman.)

With the third season, the show was renamed *The Adventures of Superboy* and featured Clark and Lana taking internships at the Bureau of Extra-Normal Matters. The supervillain quotient was dialed back, but the mood of the show darkened considerably—as did the look: the influence of Burton's *Batman* was everywhere. Gone were the bright, sun-blasted Florida exteriors; they were replaced with night shoots sliced by long film-noir shadows. After two seasons of formulaic super-rescues and hero vs. villain showdowns, story lines were given more room to breathe: episodes explored alternate-reality versions of the Boy of Steel (including the Golden Age Superman), body swaps, and Superboy believing he is responsible for the death of an innocent man.

Engage!

A story arc running throughout the November and December 1990 *Superman* titles ("Krisis of the Krimson Kryptonite") reintroduces red kryptonite into the Superman mythos. The post-*Crisis* twist: it's not really red kryptonite; it's a magical artifact given to Luthor by Mxyzptlk that is capable of removing Superman's powers. At the end of the ordeal, in *Superman* #50 (December 1990), Clark Kent meets Lois for a tuna sandwich at Dooley's Bar and Grill, the newspaper-reporter watering hole on the first floor of the *Daily Planet*, and proposes to her.

Lois, taken aback, asks Clark to let her "sort some things out." Later in that same issue, she visits her mother in the hospital and sees Clark waiting for her in the parking garage.

> Clark: Lois, I don't need an answer right now.
> Lois: Shh, Clark. I've already decided. Yes. I *want* to share
> my life with you.

With the January 1991 issues, "triangle numbers" appeared on the cover of each issue in the Superman comic book line. These numbers were instituted by editor Mike Carlin to help readers navigate the now tightly interwoven story lines of the three *Superman* books. They supplied readers with the precise order in which to read the story arc's individual "chapters." This numbering system lasted for more than a decade (although the "triangle" eventually morphed into an outline of the S-shield), with the numbers resetting to 1 with each new year.

In 1990, the Superman writers and editors were particularly grateful for the numbering system, because at the most recent Super Summit they had plotted out a densely layered year's worth of stories, culminating in the Lois and Clark wedding.

Carlin had also decided to add a fourth title to the Superman line. *Superman: The Man of Steel*, written by Louise Simonson and penciled by Jon Bogdanove, would debut with a July 1990 cover date. This meant DC would now be producing a new Superman comic every week.

The triangle numbers didn't completely remove the need to have characters recap the previous chapter's contents, but it did mean writers could devote fewer precious panels to exposition and more to throwing up complications between their two lovebirds.

Yet soon after the engagement issue was published, DC president Jenette Kahn informed Carlin that a television show focusing on the Lois-Clark relationship had been sold to ABC. Conceived as a romantic comedy, the show would be aimed at women, not at fanboys, and would depict two successful professionals in a love/hate relationship: think *Moonlighting* with blue tights. Though the show wouldn't actually premiere for another two years, the mere fact of such a high-profile project on the horizon had immediate and long-lasting implications for Superman's television and comics incarnations.

The fourth season of the *Superboy* television show was nearing the end of filming (although the episodes wouldn't air for nearly a year). With the new ABC project in the works, DC and Warner Bros. suddenly became less willing to negotiate with the Salkinds' small fiefdom of the Super-mythos. The show's requests for permission to use DC characters were ignored or rebuffed, and script approval slowed to a crawl. When filming on the hundredth and final episode had wrapped, the show's distributor made airy promises about television movies that would tie up unresolved plot lines, but those promises came to naught. DC and Warner Bros. also legally blocked the *Superboy* show from living on in syndicated reruns, lest its presence dilute the value of the character during the run-up to the Clark-Lois show. The Salkinds got out of the Super-business once and for all, selling the rights back to Warner Bros.

For the writers and the editors of Superman comics, the upcoming *Lois and Clark* show was simply a headache. "DC's decision was that it would be a good idea to hold off the wedding and do it at the same time as the TV show, if it got that far," Carlin said. "And I do think that there was some resentment from [the comics' writers] that they weren't able to do what they had planned."

With a year's worth of stories that now had to be delayed, if not scuttled completely, Superman's caretakers scrambled for ideas.

One idea that had come up at the very first Super Summit became a running gag.

"Let's just kill him," Ordway said.

"Clark Kent, Now There Was a Real Gent"

The prophetic video for "Superman's Song," the dirgelike March 1991 single from Canadian indie band Crash Test Dummies, depicts the Man of Steel's funeral. While middle-age heroes file past the coffin in sagging spandex, lead singer Brad Roberts offers a paean to Superman's fundamental decency and stick-to-it-iveness in his distinctive croak-croon. R.E.M.'s 1986 cover of the Clique song "Superman" had been the first rock song to invoke the Man of Steel in years, but it was the leading edge of a strange phenomenon. In 1989, college radio darlings Robyn Hitchcock and the Egyptians name-checked Superman on their *Queen Elvis* album. The year 1991 saw no fewer than three appearances of Superman in songs that lit up FM radio: the aforementioned "Superman's Song," Alanis Morissette's "Superman," and the Spin Doctors' "Jimmy Olsen's Blues," which finds everybody's favorite bowtied ginger confessing his lust for Lois Lane. During the nineties, this trend would continue, with Superman making cameo appearances in songs by Bryan Adams, A Tribe Called Quest, Stone Temple Pilots, Gaunt, Matchbox Twenty, Our Lady Peace and the Flaming Lips, and others.

Chronicle of a Death Foretold

Having been handed marching orders to put the brakes on the Lois and Clark romance, Carlin and his writers went to work stretching out every romantic development so as to position the couple for maximum heartbreak in the run-up to the tragic event they were now planning. When Clark reveals his secret identity to Lois, she balks; the couple spends months fretting over what their marriage would look like.

As if in answer, Superman is abruptly wrenched out of the present and gets buffeted back and forth in time ("Time and Time Again" story arc, March–May 1991). When he finally returns (*Action* #665), Lois finally agrees to marry both Clark and Superman.

In the meantime, a subplot involving Luthor saw twists that can only be called soap-operatic. In 1988 (*Action* #600), Luthor learns that his signet ring, set with a polished chunk of kryptonite, has given him radiation poisoning and necessitated the amputation of his hand. By 1990 (*Action* #660), as the cancer spreads further, Luthor fakes his death and has his brain transplanted into a cloned body. In the new body, he claims to be Lex Luthor Jr. (*Action* #671, November 1991).

Doomsday Scenario

Only a few months after Joe Shuster, age seventy-eight, passed away from heart failure in his Los Angeles home on July 30, 1992, DC Comics let it be known that they were going to kill Superman. The publisher played it coy—leaking, then denying, then finally, quietly, confirming. To this day, Carlin and the writers in charge maintain that the mainstream media reaction to the news took them by surprise. The writers saw it as a way to introduce some interesting tension and to explore how the world of the DC Universe would react to the passing of its top hero, just as Jerry Siegel's beloved 1961 "Death of Superman" story and countless tales since then had done. (Carlin called Siegel to "ask permission" to kill off the Man of Steel, a gesture Siegel reportedly appreciated.) "Characters die every day in comics," Mike Carlin said years later. "This is old news to us. If it had been a new idea, I would have been worried, but this is one of our cliché stories."

It's true. In superhero comics, as in soap operas, death is not, as Shakespeare described it, "That undiscover'd country, from whose bourne no traveler returns."

It's Tijuana, and there's a shuttle.

The difference—the reason this particular announcement made national and international news—came down to timing. The issue that contained Superman's death arrived in stores on Wednesday, November 18—two weeks after the election of Bill Clinton. The national news media, which had spent six months churning out heated rhetoric and horse race political coverage, now found themselves reduced to picking over bloodless stories about the selection of cabinet officials and the color of the Oval Office carpet.

To mainstream reporters, the event was a fresh excuse to whip up a nostalgic froth of sentiment and patriotism. The story also fit into a well-established media story framework—the "That thing you dimly remember from childhood has changed!" piece ("Lincoln Logs are now made of plastic!") that producers and editors count on to spark strong reactions.

"The real newspapers started getting hold of the story and actually believing it," said Carlin. "We were stunned. I can't believe that people went for it as hard as they did."

Inside the comics industry, the notion that DC would kill off its flagship, most heavily licensed character was laughable. The trade press recognized it as a publicity stunt, but comics retailers, seeing the unprecedented level of mainstream attention that was being generated, placed a record-breaking five million advance orders.

People magazine asked, "Is This Truly the End for the Man of Steel?" The fate of Superman was featured in *Newsweek* and made the cover of *New York Newsday*. *New York Times* columnist Frank Rich conflated Superman with George Bush in "Term Limits for Superman: Yes, It's Time for Him to Go." ("Superman was a goner long before Doomsday arrived, as was the heroic ideal . . . he symbolized in American culture.")

On the *Tonight Show*, Jay Leno wore the black armband DC included with the death issue. *Saturday Night Live* parodied the event with a sketch about Superman's funeral. Encomiums and obituaries and think pieces continued to pile up (Camille Paglia's description of Superman as "'very phallic, glossy, gleamingly hard-edged, hyper-masculine" appeared in many), and TV crews interviewed those waiting in line outside comics shops to buy their copy of the death issue.

Some of these interview subjects—the more credulous among them—wept openly. Yet the eyes of most people who stood in line on November 18, 1992, held not tears but dollar signs.

The late 1980s and early 1990s were a boom time for comics shops. Eager fans had taken to showing up in shops every Wednesday—when the week's new books went on sale. What's more, they were buying multiple copies of "event" books such as *Crisis*, *Batman: The Dark Knight Returns*, *Secret Wars*, and *Watchmen*, wrapping them up and squirreling them away for safekeeping, in the hopes that they would one day fetch big prices. It didn't take long for publishers to begin pandering to this "collector" or "specula-tor" mind-set—offering variant covers to encourage customers to buy multiple copies. Hologram covers, die-cut covers, glow-in-the-dark covers—publishers eagerly sent them out by the palletful and increased print runs to the millions, confident that a gimmick cover or the first issue of a series—any series—would receive droves of comics-shop pre-orders, which guaranteed those sales to the publisher (if not always to customers).

Yet of course, the reason classic issues of comics from the Golden Age fetch such astronomical prices is that so few have survived. Most kids who had purchased *Action Comics* #1 in 1938, for example, folded it up, shoved it in their back pockets, dripped peanut butter on it, and unceremoniously threw it out. The comic-book auction industry would not exist without the generations of mothers who have tossed out their children's comic book and baseball card collections without a second thought.

In the 1990s, however, speculators wouldn't even bother to read a comic before slipping it carefully into a Mylar bag and storing it far away from damaging sunlight—and closet-cleaning mothers—for years on end. This fact essentially ensured that thousands of copies of the comic in question would be around for decades—in mint condition—making that comic, for the foreseeable future, worthless.

It was in the midst of this rabid speculation boom that *Superman* #75 appeared. Now, however, the speculators were joined by hordes of non–comics readers who were setting foot into their local comics shops for the first and last time, confident that the death issue would be a historic artifact that would secure their grandkids' college educations.

Superman #75 came in a sealed black plastic bag—a comic book body bag, as it were—adorned with a bleeding S-insignia. The actual cover resembled a tombstone. (Special editions included a poster and a black armband.) The initial print run was three million copies, but this was not enough to meet demand, and the issue went through more print runs, with a cover depicting Superman's tattered cape flapping in the wind above the rubble. In the end, more than six million copies were sold, making it the highest-selling single issue of a DC comic book in history. (Marvel's 1991 *X-Men* #1 still had it beat, however, with sales nearing eight million.)

Death of a Hero

The "Death of Superman" arc ran through the December 1992 to January 1993 issues of the Superman line. The plot was minimal, the action epic and brutal. A mindless hulking alien emerges from a vessel buried below the earth and wreaks wanton destruction. It bests the Justice League easily, earning the name Doomsday, and heads straight for Metropolis.

Superman tries repeatedly to stop the beast but realizes it has been engineered to be nothing less than a force of pure destruction, incapable of surrender; it will keep coming. Allies join the fight—including a fully healed Supergirl/Matrix, who is taken out by the beast in one punch.

In the end—in *Superman* #75—it comes down to a slugfest in front of the *Daily Planet* building. In the various issues counting down to this one, the artists upped the visual tension by reducing the numbers of panels per page—four in *Adventures of Superman* #497, three in *Action Comics* #684, and two in *Superman: The Man of Steel* #19.

Artist-writer Dan Jurgens presented the final battle in *Superman* #75 as a series of full-page panels, each titan hammering away at the other, while streets crumble and windows shatter around them.

During a break in the fighting, Superman flies to Lois's side.

Lois: Please . . . maybe you should retreat and get help!
Superman: Too late, Lois. The JLA have already fallen and there are too many people in jeopardy right now. It's up to me.
Lois: Clark . . . I . . . [*they kiss*]
Superman: Just remember . . . no matter what happens . . . I'll always love you. *Always.*

Superman dives back into the fight. His cape is torn from his shoulders; the bony protrusions on the alien's joints cut Superman's skin and rip his costume to shreds. At last, Doomsday and Superman deliver final, devastating blows to each other simultaneously.

The brute dies, and Lois rushes to the fallen Man of Steel's bloodied, battered body. She cries, "Please hang on! The paramedics will be here any second! *Please!*"

But the Man of Steel is dead.

A World without a Superman

The writers knew that killing Superman would be, to put it mildly, a controversial move among fans, but they expected that criticism would be directed at the fact of his death, not at the manner of it. Yet many longtime readers—including this writer—knew what was coming and had reconciled themselves to the notion of a Super-dirtnap, howsoever temporary. What dismayed these readers was not the story's content but its execution, which struck them as inelegant, unearned, and—most important—unworthy of the character.

Writer Dan Jurgens, in a 1993 interview with *Wizard* magazine, laid out the writers' rationale. He said the idea of Doomsday began with a vision of a trail of rubble strewn through Metropolis, leading to an image of Superman fighting an unstoppable monster. In the pitch meeting, he said, "I kept calling [Doomsday] a force of nature . . . . I was absolutely convinced that we had to do a villain who was going to give Superman a run for his money. We had done so many business-suit villains, so many lame old boring guys. We had to have something that could pound the crap out of Superman. . . . [Doomsday] is primal rage incarnate."

Certainly, the notion of a physical match for Superman was one that had inspired the creation of Mongul in 1990 and Bizarro decades before that. But for Superman to give up his life as the result of nothing more than a repetitive, visually dull slog of a fistfight—and at the hands of some random, hastily introduced killing machine that could have stepped off the pages of one of the moronic, ultraviolent, laughably self-serious comics that now clogged comics shops (in which he'd likely bear a moniker such as Bonestryke or Bludspur or Calciumblayde or Osteodeth or Ragepointy)?

That? *Rankled.*

What's more, the threat to Metropolis that Doomsday may have posed never registered hard enough on readers for the Man of Steel's sacrifice to land with the weight it deserved. Superman should die saving the universe or the world or a single human life.

He should *not* die saving public works projects.

In the end, Doomsday was little more than a gimmick, a plot device. What he most certainly was not, however, was a villain. True villains have motivations, personalities, schemes within schemes.

The mindless Doomsday's vaunted "primal rage," on the other hand, was sourceless, abstract, and narratively meaningless.

All of which is to say: it should have been Luthor.

Lame, old, boring, business-suited Luthor. Siegel knew as much, all the way back in 1961, but this was comics in the 1990s, and Luthor, Superman's age-old archenemy, was deemed insufficiently . . . *extreme*.

In the story arc that followed the death ("Funeral for a Friend," January–March 1993), the heroes of the DC Universe, along with Superman's friends, family, and enemies—and members of the general public—mourn the passing of the Man of Steel.

The funeral (attendees include President Bill Clinton and his wife, Hillary) recalls Siegel's 1961 version in many respects, as separately and together, either in words or in private thoughts, characters express their grief. Throughout the DC titles, heroes wear black armbands. In Metropolis, a gloating Lex Luthor, noting that if he couldn't kill the Man of Steel (twist the knife!), he will at least bury him, builds a Super-mausoleum in which Superman's body is interred.

With the end of the "Funeral" story arc, the four Superman titles were "canceled"—or at least, appeared to be. In fact, the titles simply went on a three-month hiatus, while editor Carlin and his writers hatched a plan to milk the unprecedented attention they had garnered. Superman's return from the grave was pushed back.

The Four Horsemen of the Supe-ocalypse

Each creative team made a different suggestion for a character to replace Superman during his dirtnap. Ultimately, Carlin decided to allow all four teams to introduce their substitute Men of Steel, each in a different title. The four characters would claim to be Superman reborn, and DC would be able to milk the mystery for all it was worth. "Superman is back," blared a promotional poster that DC sent to comics shops. "But is any of them the real Man of Steel?"

For the first time in years, the writers and the artists of the various Super-titles were ceded a few months of semiautonomy to flesh out their Super-wannabes. "It was a kind of freedom for guys who have to collaborate all the time to actually have a couple months where they could call the shots," said Carlin. In the resulting story arc ("Reign of the Supermen," June–October 1993) each of the four is inspired by a different nickname for Superman, and each represents a different aspect of the Man of Steel's character.

The Man of Steel: In the pages of *Superman: The Man of Steel* #22 (June 1993), writer Louise Simonson and artist Jon Bogdanove introduced Steel, the superheroic alter ego of John Henry Irons, an African American weapons designer. Inspired by Superman's sacrifice, Irons resolves to carry on the Man of Steel's fight, inventing a suit of high-tech armor and an even-higher-tech sledgehammer. Steel never claims to be Superman; instead, he insists that he is a man who wishes to live up to Superman's legacy. He represents Superman's heart. (One year later, Steel would earn his own comic—which would attract the attention of athlete Shaquille O'Neal, who would play a version of the character in a poorly received 1997 film.).

The Man of Tomorrow: With a look inspired by James Cameron's *Terminator 2*, writer-artist Dan Jurgens introduced a Cyborg Superman in *Superman* #78 (June 1993). Claiming to be Superman patched together with Kryptonian alloys and technology and possessed of many of Superman's memories, the Cyborg Superman saves the life of the president of the United States and earns the U.S. government's official recognition as the heir to Superman's legacy. In reality, however, the Cyborg Superman is Hank Henshaw, an insane foe of Superman's whose consciousness has melded with the "birthing matrix" in the rocket that sent Superman to Earth. He has merely duplicated Superman's genetic material and Kryptonian metals and set about using Superman's knowledge to impersonate the hero and ruin his postmortem reputation.

The Metropolis Kid: Writer Karl Kesel and artist Tom Grummett introduced a cocky, hotheaded teenage clone of Superman in *The Adventures of Superman* #501. Outfitted with a "hip" leather jacket, several extraneous belts, flip-up sunglasses, red gloves, an earring, and a fade haircut, the Boy of Steel (who initially resists the moniker Superboy) is the successful result of Cadmus Labs's attempt to create a genetic duplicate of the Man of Steel. The duplication process is not perfect, however, because Superboy possesses a different power set—"tactile telekinesis"—which can only duplicate Superman's powers of flight, strength, and invulnerability. Superboy represents Superman's courage and passion. (Years later, it is revealed that Superboy's genes contain both Kryptonian and human DNA—and that his other genetic "parent" is none other than Lex Luthor.) Superboy, like Steel, would later earn his own solo title.

The Last Son of Krypton: Writer Roger Stern and artist Jackson Guice's contender for a hero to fill Superman's boots is a laconic duplicate of the Man of Steel adorned in a variation on Superman's costume. He is, in truth, the Eradicator, which has merged its energy with Superman's lifeless body and created a quasi-organic super-body for itself. This artificial body cannot process solar energy, as Superman's did, so it must wear a yellow visor to see in the daylight—and must place Superman's body in a Kryptonian "regeneration matrix" to siphon energy from it. (Note: This will become important later.) In the process of taking superhuman form, the Eradicator becomes convinced that it *is* Superman. Lois, however, struck by its cold, aloof attitude toward her—and to humanity ("Clark is gone. There is only Superman now.")—has her doubts. Ruthless in its pursuit and punishment of criminals, the Eradicator reflects what Superman's implacable drive for justice would look like were it not tempered by compassion.

Soon, the Cyborg Superman reveals itself to be a villain allied with the alien despot Mongul, and the Cyborg annihilates the Californian metropolis of Coast City, along with its seven million residents.

Meanwhile, in Metropolis Harbor, a giant robot rises out of the water and disgorges a long-haired man in a black costume bearing a silver S-shield and silver wrist gauntlets who claims to be Superman.

The would-be Man of Steel explains that when the Eradicator placed his body in the Kryptonian regeneration matrix, the machine set to work bringing him back to life. Weak and utterly powerless, Superman loaded himself into one of the Fortress of Solitude's Kryptonian battle suits and made the long trek to Metropolis. Despite his weakened condition, he resolves to join the other "Supermen" and flies with them to the ruins of Coast City, to take on the Cyborg Superman.

In the battle that follows, Superman's creators attempt to make a not-terribly-subtle point. In one panel, for example, the nonpowered, shaggy-maned Superman adopts a Rambo pose to match his Rambo hair. His black "regeneration suit" torn open to expose his massive chest, the Man of Steel stands with an ammo pouch strapped to his leg, a bandolier over his shoulder, firing a machine gun with one hand and a revolver with the other ("*Brakka brakka brakka brakka brakka brakka*").

The pose deliberately recalls that aforementioned new breed of über-violent antiheroes who were now driving comics sales and speculation: characters such as the Punisher, Deadpool, and Cable, all of whom sported a comical number of leg straps, arm straps, chest straps, pouches, pockets, armbands, holsters, and—mostly—guns. Superman had come back to life during the ascendancy of "heroes" whose names could have been formed with a set of Angry Word Magnetic Refrigerator Poetry (Bloodstrike! Knightsabre! Ripclaw! Warblade!) or simply by naming things found in a weapons locker (Shrapnel! Claymore! Ballistic!). They were the crest of the wave of grim-and-gritty comics that *Watchmen* and *The Dark Knight Returns* had propagated back in the eighties. They were the very antithesis of what Superman stood for, and they reveled in it.

So if Superman's caretakers, who'd dispatched him to the Great Beyond at the bony hands of the most quintessentially nineties creation imaginable, wanted to spend a panel or two of his comeback issue indulging in a bit of gentle parody, that was their right.

As the battle rages on, the Cyborg Superman attempts to spray the powerless Man of Steel with kryptonite radiation. The Eradicator intervenes and deliberately takes the full brunt of the blast, absorbing it, and channeling it into Superman's body. Somehow—never mind why—this act succeeds in restoring Superman's powers. With a devastating punch, he defeats the Cyborg once and for all. (Read: Not for long.)

Later, back in Metropolis, Lois Lane hears a rapping on her apartment window. She opens her drapes to see Superman, back in the familiar blue and red costume, floating in the air—just as she remembers him, save for the shaggy shoulder-length coif. She leaps into his arms and they kiss. "Whew," she says. "Been a while. I like the hair."

Back in Business?

Even as the "Reign of the Supermen" story line was barreling through the various titles in the Superman line, and the Man of Steel was struggling to return to life, things were looking pretty good for him—outside of the comics.

On June 6, 1993, in the town of Metropolis, Illinois, the Superman Museum opened for business. Curated and owned by Jim Hambrick and containing more than twenty thousand items of memorabilia, the museum stands opposite the Metropolis town square, which was officially renamed Superman Square when an impressive fifteen-foot statue of Superman was unveiled—to replace the original, cheap-looking seven-foot fiberglass statue that local toughs routinely used for target practice.

In addition, on September 12, after two years of development, *Lois and Clark: The New Adventures of Superman* finally premiered on ABC.

For the comic-book Superman, however, things weren't quite so rosy. His death and brief absence had garnered him more attention than any single comic-book character had ever achieved, and now that he was back, the inevitable question loomed: What next? "I don't think we're ever going to top the death of Superman," Carlin said at the time.

How could Superman now prove that absent any gimmicks or manufactured hype, he still had stories to tell? That he could mean as much now that he was alive as he had when was dead? And where, amid this new, violent, nihilistic era of comic-book antiheroes, did he—could he—fit in? His publisher didn't have an answer for him. "There was rust on the Man of Steel, and we decided to scrape it off to expose the essence of his character and get back to the essential of the myth," publisher Jenette Kahn said of the grand experiment.

Yet she and her team of DC editors had already moved on, eager to take what they had learned from the "Death of Superman" experience and apply it to other heroes. In the months and years ahead, Batman would suffer a broken back and be replaced by an ultra-violent, sword-wielding madman. Green Lantern would go insane, slaughter thousands of his fellow heroes, and die. Wonder Woman would die and be replaced by a darker, more violent Amazon warrior. Green Arrow and the Flash would die, briefly.

Even in that very moment, while the newly returned Superman was wondering what lay ahead for him, DC's entire line of superhero books was caught up in yet another massive crossover event. And this one, called *Bloodlines*, was perfectly suited to the newly grim and violent comic-book zeitgeist.

In the event, the Earth is invaded by a race of alien shapeshifters (whose resemblance to the HR Giger aliens of the Scott/Cameron films seems just microns shy of legally actionable). These aliens' shtick: sucking the spinal fluid from their victims. The comic book twist: in a small percentage of victims, this sucking process triggers superpowers. Because, sure.

By the time 1993 came to an end, then, the ranks of the DC Universe's heroes had swelled in number; the Earth now teemed with ridiculous heroes with ridiculous powers who bore ridiculous, trying-too-hard, I-Love-the-90s names such as Gunfire, Sparx, Hook, Loose Cannon, Shadowstryke, Edge, Terrorsmith, and, perhaps most wincingly, Razorsharp and the Cyba-Rats.

In a benighted world where a character such as Razorsharp—a teen punk computer hacker whose arms turned into swords—could pass for a hero, whither a Big Blue Boy Scout?

11

FASTER THAN A SPEEDING MULLET (1994–2001)

Milestones

1996: *Superman: The Animated Series* debuts

1997: "Electric Superman" debuts in *Superman* #121

1998: Classic Superman powers and costume return in *Superman Forever*; *Superman for All Seasons* debuts; U.S. Post Office releases Superman stamp

1999: *Superman* video game released for Nintendo 64

Health scares have a way of shaking up a guy, of making him question himself, his priorities, his relationships, his place in the world. That's essentially what death—which, to the superhero set, represents the ultimate health scare—did to the Man of Steel.

For years after Superman returned from the dead, his creators didn't know quite what to do with him. Instead, they kept iterating and reiterating the look and the feel, even the very idea, of Superman, in an attempt to sync him to the changing times. Thus, he spends long years lost in a kind of conceptual wilderness, trying on identities. First, there is the hilariously out-of-character long hair, which several artists chose to render as that achy-breakiest

of nineties styles, the mullet. On marrying Lois, he chops it off—a
move that can't help but carry discomfiting psychosexual under-
tones of the biblical Samson. Yet no sooner has he returned to his
old-school appearance than he suddenly manifests an entirely new
set of weird electrical powers—and a much-derided costume to go
with it.

The Else of All Possible Worlds

That was just for starters. Outside of his mainstream comic book
continuity, DC began to inundate comic shops with disparate one-
shots and miniseries collectively called "Elseworlds" stories. A modern update on the classic Silver Age "Imaginary Story," the many
Elseworlds tales starring Superman featured alternate-reality versions of the Man of Steel—writers and artists placed Superman in
different times and on different worlds or tweaked the character's
most familiar elements. Ostensibly, the Elseworlds titles sought to
explore the roots of his appeal. In reality, however, once readers got
past the novelty of the high-concept-du-jour, execution left much
to be desired; most served merely to flood comics shelves and water
down Superman's brand.

In various Elseworlds books released in the ten years following
his return, alternate-reality Supermen fought in the Revolutionary
War and the Civil War, became a Knight of the Round Table, fought
crime in Fritz Lang's German Expressionist Metropolis, defeated
H. G. Wells's Martians, waged war against Nazis and Greek gods,
eked out an existence in a postapocalyptic future, became Darkseid's
son, grew into a successful athlete and tycoon, got turned into
Frankenstein's monster, ruled as King of the Jungle, and grew up in
Great Britain and in Soviet Russia, to name only a few.

For fans of Superman, it was an unsettled—and unsettling—time.

Lois and Clark: The New Adventures of
Superman

Having gone through several proposed titles (*Lois Lane's Daily
Planet*; *Metropolis*), producers had finally settled on a name for their
new, Lois-centered take on a Superman TV series. As producer
Deborah Joy LeVine saw it, *Lois and Clark: The New Adventures of*

Superman would be a show about the classic romantic triangle from the woman's perspective. This Lois would be headstrong but not helpless, and in a move that placed the show's sensibility squarely in the realm of Byrne's post-*Crisis*, rebooted continuity, she would find herself strongly attracted to Clark, as well as to the Man of Steel.

Superboy's Gerard Christopher auditioned for the role of Superman, thinking it the next logical step in his career. The casting director was impressed—until Christopher's three-year stint in the Salkinds' blue tights came to light, at which point he was unceremoniously shown the door.

In the end it came down to two actors for the role of Clark/Superman: the thirty-five-year-old Kevin Sorbo (who went on to star in the hugely successful syndicated *Hercules* series) and the twenty-seven-year-old Dean Cain. At first, producers thought Cain far too young-looking, but they were impressed by his guileless sincerity in the audition and offered him the role.

Teri Hatcher brought the qualities LeVine was looking for, creating a Lois who was tough, feminine, smart, and sexy, a career woman who didn't suffer fools but could smolder on cue. As the preening, frequently mock-turtlenecked, impeccably coiffed Lex Luthor, veteran Broadway actor John Shea made for an engaging villain. He saw Luthor as more amoral than ruthless, so Shea eschewed mustache twirling in favor of smaller, more grounded choices.

The producers knew they were making a bold step in targeting women, not fanboys, and front-loaded the romantic element in the promotional campaign to let people know it. In one series of photos, Cain and Hatcher cling to each other in various stages of undress, showing off matching Superman-S tattoos. In another, a naked Hatcher wraps herself in Superman's cape—an image that managed to hit the fanboy demo squarely in their applets, and became one of the most downloaded photos in the dawning days of the Internet.

Halfway into filming the pilot, ABC decided that it would assign *Lois and Clark* to the 8:00 p.m. Sunday time slot. Producers were conflicted: Sunday at eight was the most-watched time slot on television, but the competition would be ridiculously daunting. ABC was putting them up against NBC's new, science-fiction/adventure show aimed at kids called *seaQuest DSV*, which featured a big-name actor (Roy Scheider) and an even-bigger-name producer

(Steven Spielberg). Yet the real cause for concern was that they were also going up against the deeply entrenched three-hundred-pound gorilla that was Jessica Fletcher. CBS's *Murder, She Wrote* had ruled Sunday at 8:00 p.m. with a liver-spotted fist for almost a decade and showed no sign of abdicating anytime soon.

The eight o'clock Sunday time slot also meant that the show's *Moonlighting*-inspired erotic overtones—the ones at which the promotional campaign so unsubtly hinted—now had to be tamped down. Plans to save Superman's superheroics for the closing minutes of each episode (in order to focus on the Lois/Clark badinage and really get sparks flying) had to be altered.

The pilot features Clark arriving in Metropolis, securing a job at the *Daily Planet*, and meeting Lois Lane; the chemistry between the two actors is palpable and unforced, the banter lively (if not as rapid-fire as it would later become) and family-hour sexy. Cain's Clark Kent is not so much mild-mannered as relaxed, genial. His Superman is all wry smiles and concern, and his laid-back performance admits nuance—even the occasional flicker of self-doubt—to the Man of Steel's psyche. When the pilot was shown to DC editors, writers, and artists—who'd expressed some doubt upon learning of the show's feminist-romantic take—they were overjoyed.

When the first episode premiered on September 12, 1993, it got well and truly whomped by *Murder, She Wrote*, as everyone expected. Yet producers were dismayed to learn that they had come in a distant third after *seaQuest DSV*, which had earned twice *Lois and Clark*'s viewership.

As the weeks passed, however, *seaQuest* steadily lost viewers, while *Lois and Clark* gained them. The numbers kept climbing all season long, until even the indomitable Jessica Fletcher was forced to take notice.

As the season progressed, more and more screen time was given over to super-feats and bad-guy bashing, the nature of which was literally unspectacular. As it had on the fifties TV show, the shadow of the tight budget manifested every time Superman squared off against petty thieves, arsonists, arms dealers, and bumbling scientists who inadvertently endangered lives—including that of Lois.

At the end of the first season, it was time for a bit of housecleaning. Although it had been her idiosyncratic take on the material that had sold the show to ABC in the first place, producer LeVine was sent packing; the split was more or less amicable, because the show's increasingly action-oriented focus held little interest for her. Among the cast changes during the summer hiatus: a new Jimmy Olsen (to appeal more directly to the *Teen Beat* set) and a drastic reduction in John Shea's appearances. (Shea maintains he was tired of commuting from New York to California for shooting; the producers claim they grew concerned that Luthor was overexposed as a villain.)

NPR pop culture blogger Linda Holmes has never been especially interested in the superhero genre, but she was an ardent fan of the show during its run, a fact she believes can be explained by putting the show in its proper context. She says,

> "Lois & Clark" was less a successor to other Superman adaptations and more a successor to other television action-adventure boy-girl shows. Not just *Moonlighting*, which is the one people always remember, but all the other ones—*Remington Steele, Hart to Hart, Scarecrow & Mrs. King*, stuff like that. In fact, it premiered the same season as *The X-Files*, which was obviously much darker, but had some of the same bantering/case-solving DNA.

Yet when the second season (1994–1995) began, the show foregrounded its science fiction and comic book elements: special effects, heroic action, and supervillains. Banter between Lois and Clark remained in the mix, but it took a backseat to the likes of Bronson Pinchot camping it up as the Prankster, Peter Boyle sneering his way through his role as an Intergang mob boss, and the menace of the kryptonite-hearted Metallo. To save money, Cain spent less time hung above the soundstage on wires, while more and more flying effects were created with camera tilts and sound effects. Ratings leveled off, then began to fall, and the second half of the season once again prioritized the show's romantic elements. The numbers recovered. What's more, the show's writers and producers had taken to frequenting online message boards where fans discussed, debated, and detailed their passion for the show, to determine how plot threads were being received.

This willingness to engage with its fans in an entirely new way earns the show a special place in television history, NPR's Holmes said:

> This was the first Internet fandom that I was part of, really. Not every show had active online fans then, but this one absolutely did. They called themselves Friends of Lois & Clark, or FoLC, and late in the series run, there was a stock price ticker in one scene in the newsroom, and at one point, "FoLCs +3 7/8" went by. It was one of the earliest shout-outs to Internet fans that I can remember, and people loved it.

The second season ends on a cliffhanger, with Clark proposing. To preserve the secret, the director filmed Lois making three different responses: (1) "Clark . . ."; (2) "Yes"; and (3) "Who's asking, Clark or Superman?"

The third season of *Lois and Clark* (1995–1996) opens with Lois going with option C. The viewer learns that unlike her comic book avatar at the time, TV Lois is not stunned by the revelation of Clark's secret; she's a savvy reporter who has nurtured suspicions from the very beginning. Like her comic book counterpart, however, Lois refuses to give Clark a definitive answer right away.

Producers teased viewers with a promotional photo valentine showing Clark in a tux and Lois in a wedding dress. Yet during the five-episode story line in question, it was revealed that the real Lois Lane was suffering from amnesia in the clutches of an amorous psychiatrist; Clark had mistakenly married her frog-eating clone. Viewers were outraged, and ratings plummeted. Once again, the third season ended on a cliff-hanger ending, with Superman departing Earth to rejoin a lost colony of Kryptonians, leaving Lois behind.

In the show's fourth and final season (1996–1997), producers married Lois and Clark in an episode called "Swear to God, This Time We're Not Kidding." (Warner Bros. had more or less strong-armed DC Comics into scuttling plans to marry Lois and Clark in the comics four years earlier, knowing that the television show was headed in that direction. When it finally came time for the wedding episode, however, the show's producers neglected to give DC a heads-up far enough in advance to allow them to build to the event in story lines. Instead, the comics' writers and artists were forced to scramble to produce the one-shot comic *Superman: The Wedding Album*, released the same week the wedding episode aired.)

Lois and Clark was pulled from the ABC schedule in April 1997. Months earlier, Disney had purchased ABC, and president Michael Eisner was eager to place *The Wonderful World of Disney* in the 8:00 p.m. Sunday time slot. ABC burned off the remaining episodes of *Lois and Clark* on Saturday nights.

Meanwhile, Back in the Comics

While his ABC-TV incarnation had inched up the Nielsen charts week by week, things were a bit rockier for the Man of Steel's newly shaggy-maned comic book incarnation. For one thing, the fact that Superman now sported shoulder-length hair meant that Clark Kent had taken to rocking . . . a ponytail.

The notion that Clark Kent, mild-mannered reporter, whose very existence is predicated on blending in, now spent the general run of his days looking like a Bosnian club promoter seemed wildly incongruous with everything readers knew about the character's corn-fed, small-town sensibilities.

Cringeworthy tonsorial preferences aside, you can't say that his brief stint as a corpse had slowed the guy down. He barely had time to brush off the grave dust before he was back at work—tangling with another Bizarro duplicate created by Luthor; dealing with an alien invasion/missile attack that left most of Metropolis leveled; defeating a villain named Conduit who imperiled Superman's closest friends and family; defending himself before an alien tribunal that charged him with the death of Krypton; getting body-switched with Brainiac; acquiring an entirely different, non-Kryptonian Bottle City of Kandor; breaking up with Lois; holding a rematch with the creature Doomsday (he won); and helping to save the planet after a great and terrible alien weapon called the Sun-Eater . . . ate the sun.

In the midst of all of this, DC added a fifth Superman comic, *Superman: Man of Tomorrow*, which debuted in the summer of 1995. A quarterly title, *Man of Tomorrow* was created to ensure that there would now be a new Superman book on the stands fifty-two weeks a year—even during those months with five weeks.

Endings and Beginnings

The year 1996 began with a death and ended with a wedding.

On Sunday, January 29—Super Bowl Sunday—Jerry Siegel died of heart failure in his Los Angeles home at the age of eighty-one. The *New York Times*, in a strangely ungenerous obit, noted that he would be remembered "less as the Cleveland visionary who dreamed up the greatest superhero of all time than as the naive young man who sold the rights to a billion-dollar cultural and commercial juggernaut for $130."

Later that year, DC produced its most ambitious and accomplished tale in the Elseworlds mode yet. With the four-part series *Kingdom Come*, artist Alex Ross and writer Mark Waid offered a dark vision of the DC Universe's future, anchored by an aging Superman.

The idea for the series was Ross's, who brought to *Kingdom Come* the painted, photorealistic approach he had brought to the acclaimed miniseries *Marvels*, Kurt Busiek's street-level view of the Marvel Universe, two years earlier. Waid, a one-time DC editor who had helped create the Elseworlds line, was a prolific writer midway through a highly successful run on the Flash who happened to possess an encyclopedic knowledge of Superman lore.

For a superhero comic, *Kingdom Come* offers a surprisingly ruminative meditation on the intrinsic nature of heroism, leadership, and the question of evil. To those readers disheartened by the grim, nihilistic turn that superhero comics had taken, it offered reassurance by holding a dark mirror up to most popular comics of the day. More important, it shed light on Superman's role in the DC Universe—and by extension, our culture—by depicting what happens when the Man of Steel goes away and the superhero community loses its lynchpin.

The combination of Waid's biblical imagery (prophetic eschatological dreams figure largely in the plot) and Ross's Norman-Rockwell-in-tights design aesthetic gives the whole thing a grander, deeper, more existentially fraught feel. Loaded with metatextual references to the long history of superheroes in comics, film, and TV, *Kingdom Come* is a dense, satisfying read that offers teasing glimpses of future heroes and invites readers to guess their lineage.

Perhaps the series' most lasting effect, however, was its distillation of DC's emerging attitude toward the Man of Steel. The

"Death of Superman" story line had inspired a wave of hagiographic appreciation for the hero so profound that once he came back from the dead, his continuing adventures could seem nothing but pallid, circumscribed, and small. *Kingdom Come*, with its epic sweep, seemed like a story big enough for the first and best superhero, and its explicit critique of the "new model" characters helped remind readers why Superman mattered.

The idea that Superman was more than his actions, that he represented, to the heroes and the civilians of the DC Universe, a moral compass, an inspiration, was not new, exactly. Elements of that notion went all the way back to Elliot Maggin's propensity to cast Superman as a demigod during the seventies. Yet now it wasn't unusual—and quickly became commonplace—for other DC heroes, in the pages of their own books, to acknowledge Superman's status as the greatest of their kind.

Meanwhile, in the pages of Image Comics' *Supreme* comic, beginning with issue 41 (August 1996), writer Alan Moore took over a character created by Rob Leifeld—lusty proponent of the blades, blood, and bathos school of superheroes—and set about turning him into an epic, twenty-issue homage to the Silver Age Superman.

I Now Pronounce You Superman and Wife

Back in DC's main comic-book continuity, in a one-shot, ninety-six-page comic released the week of October 6, 1996, to coincide with the Super-nuptials episode of *Lois and Clark: The New Adventures of Superman*, the comic-book Man of Steel married the comic-book Lois Lane.

This required a bit of narrative heavy lifting, however, because Lois and Superman had broken up four months earlier, in a tale called "Love Hurts." (LOIS LEAVES! blares the cover of Superman #115, which depicts a dejected Man of Steel standing atop the *Daily Planet* globe, watching Lois's plane depart.) Metropolis's toughest Metro reporter has taken a job as a foreign correspondent. Superman editor Joey Cavalieri (who'd assumed the role when Mike Carlin was promoted) scrambled to squeeze into the first few pages of the issue a story line that had been planned to stretch over months.

And just before the ceremony, the Man of Steel cuts his hair.

The couple was happy, but the comics industry was not. The speculator boom of the late eighties and early nineties had peaked in 1992, the year of the "Death of Superman," when sales of comic books topped 1 billion. As 1996 came to a close, however, the inevitable bust was busting out all over: industry sales struggled to achieve 450 million and would continue to slide.

Yet on television, the Man of Steel—freed, this time, from the tyranny of a tight special effects budget—was once again taking off.

Re-Animated

A month after the Super-wedding, a new Superman animated television show premiered on the WB.

Superman: The Animated Series was produced by Bruce Timm and Paul Dini, the team behind the successful, Emmy-winning *Batman TAS*, which had premiered in 1992 and gone on to become one of the "WB Kids" programming block's biggest hits. Yet although that show's Tim Burton–inspired chiaroscuro was perfect for a noir-gothic character such as Batman, for a creature of the bright, science-fiction daytime like Superman, it wouldn't work.

Just what would work for Superman, producer-designer Bruce Timm wasn't sure—at least, not at first. The project had begun when he'd gone to a meeting at Warner Bros. and been informed that a new, live-action Superman film was in the works. Would he be interested in working on a Superman cartoon that could keep the character alive on TV while production of the film was under way, seeing as *Lois and Clark* had run its course?

Timm agreed but felt strongly that Superman was less interesting than Batman. Less nuanced, less emotionally damaged—in short, less cool. He discussed the issue with coproducer and series writer Paul Dini. They noticed that the old Fleischer/Famous shorts—of which both men were fans—were downright laconic. The emotion they stirred derived not from dialogue but from the music, the action, and how the characters held themselves.

Timm and Dini originally conceived the show as a period piece, contemporaneous with the Fleischer shorts—but nixed the idea when they realized they'd only be inviting comparisons that would not serve them well. Instead, they resolved to use the old shorts as an inspiration—the energy, the characterizations, and, mostly, the design. Their Metropolis was an angular, sun-soaked, Modernist wonderland where the 1990s and the 1930s dissolved into each other. They turned the *Daily Planet*, for example, into an airy Philip Johnson space where Lois and Clark tapped out their stories on gleaming Bakelite word processors.

Character design carried over from *Batman: The Animated Series* but became even more stylized. Superman was a creature of fantasy, after all, so Timm and his animators felt free to broaden his shoulders, shrink his waist, and thin out his legs: he looked like an isosceles triangle with a cape.

In drawing Superman's face, Timm decided to pay homage to both the Fleischer/Famous shorts and John Byrne's moose-jawed Man of Steel. To reduce the character to its visual essence, Timm made the chin literally square, reduced the forelock curl to a squiggle, and let the eyes dwindle to black dots. This Superman was about action; he didn't need eyes like limpid, soulful pools.

Tim Daly won the role of Superman/Clark, and the role of Lois Lane went to the actress the producers had in mind when they wrote the first script: Dana Delaney. Delaney patterned Lois's attitude and delivery after Rosalind Russell in *His Girl Friday*.

When it came time to cast the show's many villains and supporting cast, they eschewed veteran Hollywood voice actors and instead chose actors with more natural and recognizable voices from film and, especially, television——Mike Farrell, Brad Garrett, Malcolm McDowell, Gilbert Gottfried, Michael Dorn, and, most ingeniously, Ed Asner as the mad matron from Apokolips, Granny Goodness. That quest for naturalism meant the cast recorded each episode in the same room, as opposed to separately in a studio, being fed lines by a producer, as was then standard operating procedure for animated shows.

Given the unlimited effects budget—anything that could be drawn was fair game—the show was free to reproduce comic book villains with accuracy and give them a chance to shine: Metallo, Toyman (always depicted, in a creepy touch, wearing an oversize doll-head), Bizarro, Mxyzptlk, and even Titano the Super-Ape showed up for an episode. Other DC heroes stopped by: Batman, the Flash, Green Lantern, the Legion of Super-Heroes, and Aquaman, voiced by Miguel Ferrer. The series reintroduced the classic Supergirl—Kal-El's cousin from Argo City—though it updated her wardrobe with a miniskirt and a belly shirt. And it created, in Michael Ironside's impassive, coolly sinister Darkseid, the ideal villain for Superman to lock mental and physical horns with.

The show even solved the sticky problem of Brainiac—a villain who'd been continually redesigned and reinterpreted for decades in the comics—by supplying it with a backstory that fed directly into Superman's origin. As was revealed in the very first episode, which aired on September 6, 1996, Brainiac was a kind of Kryptonian HAL-9000 computer, responsible for all systems on the doomed planet. Actor Corey Burton's cool, unmodulated tones drive home the character's chilling, implacable logic.

In all, *Superman: The Animated Series* flew for a highly successful three seasons, chalking up fifty-four episodes, the last of which aired on February 12, 2000.

The series inspired a tie-in comic book aimed at kids—*Superman Adventures*—the first issue of which was written by Dini. Scott McCloud, the writer-artist of the acclaimed retro-science fiction comic *ZOT!* and the author of *Understanding Comics* and other tomes on the visual language of the comics medium, took over writing chores for a year. Eventually, Scottish writer Mark Millar assumed writing duties and stayed on the book for a similar stint. For much of the book's six-year run, a combination of factors—clever writing, a clean (albeit standardized) visual style, and the need to tell simple stories simply, freed of the narrative baggage weighing down the main Superman titles that month—allowed *Superman Adventures* to distill the Man of Steel to his essence. With its light comic touch, *Superman Adventures* quietly became the best Superman comic on the stands.

Kal-El Goes Electric

During the "Weekend Update" segment of the January 18, 1997, episode of *Saturday Night Live*, Norm MacDonald read the following news item: "Beginning in March, DC Comics will change Superman's traditional red and blue costume to a new form-fitting bodysuit."

On the screen behind MacDonald, the image switched to a promotional shot of Superman wearing the "containment suit" DC would introduce when the Man of Steel developed odd new powers in *Superman* #123 (May 1997). The blue unitard, with its white streaks of lightning running down the arms and the legs, resembles the Olympic figure-skating uniform of a nation-state that just got hydroelectricity. The suit continues up his neck to form a half-cowl that allows his blue hair to peek out the top; the effect is that of a headband. White-hot electricity crackles from Superman's eyes and, weirdly, his shoulders.

MacDonald took a beat to allow viewers to soak up the picture: Superman stands not in his classic pose (legs spread, fists on hips), but rather with shoulders back, arms at his side, one leg positioned before the other. Which is to say: pageant stance.

"The problem with the old costume?" MacDonald asked, nodding at the new outfit. "Not gay enough."

Huge laugh from the studio audience. Which kept going. And going. MacDonald couldn't resist an ad-lib: "What the hell's going on in the country?" he demanded. "That's not Superman!"

At DC Comics, they were prepared for this. Any publicity was good publicity, and they knew the big change they were making would inspire some of the outrage they'd sparked with the Superman death, with none of that event's sorrow to mitigate it. Sales were down, though, and gimmicks worked. Plus, they wanted to throw the character a curveball. Ergo: the supermakeover, which brought changes that were originally intended to be permanent—or at least to continue indefinitely.

Clark Kent returns from his honeymoon, still powerless from his run-in with the Sun-Eater. Concerned that his powers might be gone for good, he reaches out to various allies to help him get them back, going so far as to get transported into the heart of the sun. He emerges recharged. It seems to work.

Yet in *Adventures of Superman* #545 (April 1997), his body begins to transform into pure electromagnetic energy. Scientists scramble to create the containment suit/leotard (*Superman* #123, May 1997), and Superman realizes that he now possesses an entirely new power set. Flight, invulnerability, and X-ray vision are out the window, replaced by the power to phase though walls, to "see" various forms of radiation, and to move at the speed of light.

The idea was to give Superman a challenge, to increase narrative tension by forcing him to learn how to use these new powers.

During the next few months, he begins to fire energy blasts and tractor beams, create force fields, commune with computers, and more.

A Place in the Pantheon

Four months before Superman switched up his wardrobe, in January 1997, writer Grant Morrison and artist Howard Porter had taken the Justice League back to basics in *JLA* #1. Morrison dispensed with the roster of "creepy preforgotten no-hopers with names like Mystek and Bloodwynd" that had filled out the League's ranks in the early nineties. Instead, he restored the classic Justice League of America lineup of the "Big 7"—Superman, Batman, Wonder Woman, Aquaman, Green Lantern, Flash, and longtime deep-bencher the Martian Manhunter. Together, they formed what Morrison called "a pantheon of Pop Art divinities. . . . Superman was Zeus; Wonder Woman, Hera; Batman, Hades."

Under Morrison's watch, the JLA would respond only when danger threatened the entire globe—or the universe. Porter's art gave a summer blockbuster mise-en-scène to Morrison's epic Jungian riot of spandex and symbology. And Superman, who'd spent much of his career as the living avatar of overkill—the nuclear missile brought to the knife fight—seemed to relish facing off against ridiculously outsize cataclysms that tested him to, and past, his limits.

Yet just five issues in, the book's primal power took a hit when Morrison was forced to pay obeisance to the vengeful god named Continuity and use Electric Superman.

Visually, he just didn't belong. The iconography of DC's "Big Seven" is simple and thus powerful, which imparts a sense of timelessness—or, more precisely, a sense that they exist outside of, and above, time. Any superheroic battle tableau that included Electric Superman seemed leached of color and emotion—but it didn't take long for Morrison to figure out how to fit the new Superman into the narrative mix. In *JLA* #7, for example, the moon has been yanked out of orbit and begins to hurtle toward Earth. Superman uses his powers to change the electromagnetic field of the moon and give it temporary poles—as a result, the Earth and the moon begin to repel each other, and the orb resumes its rightful spot in the heavens.

Throughout Morrison's run on *JLA*, his characterization of Superman, whether Electric or Classic Coke variety, remained consistent: he was the still point at the center of the chaos, the calm voice saying everything was going to work out. The seeds of Morrison's hugely successful, twenty-first-century take on the Man of Steel are all planted here.

Superman Red and Superman Blue 2: Electric Boogaloo

Just ten months after Superman's wardrobe malfunction, in a sixty-four-page one-shot comic, the Man of . . . Spark? finds himself faced with a dilemma. The Cyborg Superman has trapped him in an "energy containment structure" that splits the hero into two identical beings, both of whom believe themselves to be the "true" Superman. The only difference—one wears a blue containment suit, and one a red containment suit.

Superman Red/Superman Blue #1 (February 1998) was an homage to the beloved 1961 Leo Dorfman/Curt Swan Imaginary Story, with a twist perfectly suited to the comics of the 1990s: the two Supermen don't like each other. Both are convinced that the other is an impostor, but the truth is more complicated. The mysterious process has split Superman's personality in two. Blue is coolly cerebral and serious. Red is impulsive and humorous. What's more, both are in love with Lois—and expect to go home with her at the end of the day. As they continue, in the months that followed, to go on separate adventures, each becomes more adamant that he doesn't want to go back to being one Superman.

Ultimately, however, at the culmination of a nine-part story line ("Millennium Giants," April–June 1998) that finds the Earth threatened by ancient beings, Superman Blue and Superman Red sacrifice themselves, expending all of their electromagnetic energy to save the planet. In their wake, the original Superman returns—just in time, conveniently enough, for the ninety-six-page special *Superman Forever* (June 1998), released on the hero's sixtieth anniversary.

If the "Electric Superman" story line, which lasted more than a year, ended up straining readers' patience, it accomplished its stated goal, which was to show that Superman was more than the boots and the cape he wore, more than the powers he employed—that the character's essence lay in his selflessness and determination, regardless of the personal cost.

At the end of the day, it doesn't matter how ridiculous the getup or how silly the powers. The thing that is eternal about Superman: he will do good, even when he's not doing well.

Back to Basics

The nineties were a long, dark night of the soul for the Man of Steel, when any clear sense of who he was and what he stood for got lost beneath a constant roil of narrative gambits and marketing ploys. If Superman was to find his way again, he—and his readers—would need to cut through this noise and get in touch with his most basic, essential self. The time for showy foil covers and endless lily-gilding was past. As the *Superman* animated series was proving every week, the Man of Steel just needed a simple story, simply told.

Writer Jeph Loeb and artist Tim Sale's four-issue miniseries *Superman: For All Seasons* (September–December 1998) was one such story. Loeb stripped the character to his essence by focusing on a just-starting-out Man of Steel as he learns to accept his limitations. It is a coming-of-age tale shot through with sadness and regret, narrated by a succession of people around Superman—Pa Kent, Lois Lane, Lex Luthor, and Lana Lang.

Sale's depictions of Smallville's huge, featureless sky and Metropolis's dense forest of concrete and glass amplify the sense of loneliness and isolation in Loeb's script. Together, artist and writer avail themselves of an emotional palette not generally associated with Superman stories—Pa Kent's fear about what his son will become, Lois's self-recrimination as Superman's existence challenges her dearly held pragmatism, Luthor's love of his city, Lana's feelings of anguish and abandonment.

Writer-artist Alan Davis's Elseworlds three-issue story "The Nail" takes precisely the opposite tack by working in the negative space around the Man of Steel—positing a world that has never known Superman. Unlike many Elseworlds tales, Davis's story is more than its triggering conceit—he builds events slowly and methodically, showing how the heroes we know so well would behave in a universe lacking Superman as a moral center.

In January 1999, DC released *Superman: Peace on Earth*, an over-size graphic novel written by Paul Dini and painted by Alex Ross. The story, which carries unintentional intimations of the plot of *Superman IV: The Quest for Peace*, finds the Man of Steel resolving to fight world hunger, only to have his efforts thwarted by humankind's suspicion, self-interest, and militarism. Ultimately, he relearns the lesson he learned in *Kingdom Come*: despite his amazing abilities, he does the most good as a symbol, inspiring humanity to work together.

Yet all of these redefinitions existed outside the main Superman story line of the comics, where the Man of Steel has fallen under the control of an ancient being called Dominus who convinces him that humanity needs to be saved from itself (January–June 1999). He builds an army of Superman robots, declares himself King of the World, and patrols the planet twenty-four hours a day, earning the enmity of mankind, until Lois finally breaks through to him.

The "Dominus Effect" story line was an engaging exploration of absolute power and its tendency to corrupt absolutely. What it was not, however, was a Superman story.

Superman Now

Meanwhile, writers Grant Morrison, Mark Millar, Tom Peyer, and Mark Waid approached DC Comics with a twenty-one-page pitch for Superman. They were dismayed by the continual decline in the Superman books, and their proposal, called *Superman Now* (or *Superman 2000*), set out to "restore our beloved Superman to his preeminent place as the world's first and best superhero."

The marriage would have to go, Morrison et al. decided, but rather than use a memory wipe or a reality reset, the writers pro-posed to have the marriage simply, gradually—realistically—dissolve. "[The] newly domesticated Superman was a somewhat diminished figure, all but sleepwalking through a sequence of increasingly con-trived 'event' story lines," Morrison wrote in his 2011 treatise, *Supergods*. "*Superman Now* was to be a reaction against this often overemotional and ineffectual Man of Steel, reuniting him with his mythic potential, his archetypal purpose."

The proposal noted that Superman had been "rebooted" regu-larly, on a roughly fifteen-year cycle. Byrne in 1986. O'Neil and Schwartz in 1971. The time was ripe.

Yet the reboot DC went with instead was a soft one: Eddie Berganza became the new editor of the Superman line, the quarterly *Superman: Man of Tomorrow* was canceled (reducing the number of regular Super-titles to four), and the "triangle numbers" were on their way out, along with the tightly interconnected plots and sub-plots they denoted.

In an interview, Berganza spoke of the unintended consequences of the tightly woven story lines of the previous decade: "[The stories] kept getting farther and farther away from Superman. The cast around Superman kept growing and growing, until it came to the point that he became almost a guest star in his own book."

What Berganza was describing—an expansive network of supporting characters, written by creators who'd been at the job for years—was, of course, exactly the set of circumstances that had produced some of the Silver Age Superman's classic tales. Yet times were different. In the era of the Internet, critics and continuity cops pored over every issue, hungry to be the first to spot contradictions and oversights. The drive for interconnectedness in the Superman books only weighed down the narrative even further. By giving the audience what it said it wanted—dense story lines in a shared universe—Superman's writers had helped create and perpetuate an increasingly demanding and fractious readership.

Writer J. M. DeMatteis took over *Adventures of Superman*, penciled by Mark Miller. DeMatteis was tasked to get *Adventures of Superman* back to its roots, offering the human angle on Superman and focusing on the citizens of Metropolis. *Superman: Man of Steel*, written by Mark Schulz (a holdover from the previous creative team) and penciled by Doug Mahnke, focused on Superman's Kryptonian side. *Action Comics*, written by Joe Kelly and penciled by Kano, would live up to its name and show Superman teaming up with other heroes for big fighty-fight action. *Superman*, written by *Superman: For All Seasons'* Jeph Loeb and penciled by Joe McGuinness, would be the main book, containing all of the classic Superman elements—the *Daily Planet*, Lois, Jimmy, Luthor, and so on.

McGuinness's Superman didn't look like anyone else's. You could take one look at his manga-influenced, hilariously muscular Man of Steel and know that the era of editors enforcing DC house style—of changing Jack Kirby's Superman faces to make them look more like Curt Swan's, for example—was over. McGuinness rejected the pseudo-photorealism that had become entrenched in superhero comics since the advent of Neal Adams and instead embraced a hyperstylized, cartoony take on drawing Superman. The character's musculature ballooned from its default, merely steroidal setting to anatomically impossible. His neck grew so thick, it threatened to consume his head—and it might have, had not McGuinness also inflated the jaw line to act as a bulwark.

Superman's eyes narrowed to slits; to make up for it, McGuinness turned the eyebrows into a pair of thick, angry em-dashes, the mouth into a flat line, a space left blank. The icon had become iconography.

Superman at the Millennium

In 1999, two years after she'd brought the case to avail herself of new copyright laws, Jerry Siegel's wife, Joanne, was awarded half of the copyright to Superman's appearance in *Action Comics* #1. It was only the first step of a legal battle that continues to drag on at this writing.

Meanwhile, Superman's image was everywhere. Canada honored Joe Shuster with a 1995 Superman postage stamp, and the United States followed suit with a series devoted to "Highlights of the 1930s," in which the Man of Steel struck the elbows-out, marionette-like pose that had introduced him to the world. He showed up with a milk mustache in an ad for the Dairy Council, four roller-coasters bore his name and likeness at amusement parks across the country, and he teamed up with Bugs Bunny in a four-issue miniseries that ran from July to October 2000.

Superman also made one of his most emotionally gripping (albeit unseen) cameo appearances of all time at the climax of the 1999 Warner Bros. animated film *The Iron Giant*, when the titular alien robot decides to sacrifice itself to save the town of Rockwell, Maine, from a nuclear missile. In that moment, the robot embodies the film's simple lesson—that "we are who we choose to be"—as, hurtling to meet his doom, he says to himself, "Su-per-man." The parallels between Giant of Iron and Man of Steel (aliens on Earth possessed of tremendous, potentially destructive power who choose to use that power to save others) imbues that moment with a strange, evocative power.

In the two decades since the very first *Superman* video game was released in 1978 for Atari, the Man of Steel had been pixelated many times, for various systems, including home computers, NES, Sega devices, Game Boy, and a stand-up arcade game. A Web-based series of short games called the *Multipath Adventures of Superman* let users pilot the Man of Steel though a virtual "Choose Your Own Adventure" story. If these games tended to be unexceptional, gamers were used to that. Video games based on licensed properties such as Superman generally disappoint; this, in gaming circles, is a truth universally acknowledged.

In 1999, however, a *Superman* game produced for the Nintendo 64 game system quickly developed a reputation as uniquely and ingeniously abysmal; to this day, it makes regular appearances on "Worst Games of All Time" lists. To explain the game's poor graphics—Metropolis looks like a grainy set of children's blocks photographed through bouillabaisse—the game's makers hastily concocted a conceit in which Luthor sends Superman to a "virtual" Metropolis that is sheathed in a "kryptonite fog." There, he is forced to conduct repetitive, pointless, frustrating tasks, such as flying through airborne rings. Controls were sluggish and the game design unforgiving, and *Superman* became one of the worst-reviewed games in the history of the medium.

"What's So Funny about Truth, Justice, and the American Way?"

In *Action Comics* #775 (March 2001), writer Joe Kelly stood up for the Man of Steel, offering readers a stirring refresher course on just what sets Superman apart and why he endures.

Kelly introduced the Elite, a team of amoral, ultraviolent antiheroes who take justice into their own hands, led by a telekinetic Brit named Manchester Black. The Elite and Black were Kelly's stand-ins for a nihilistic and hugely popular team of superheroes called the Authority, written by Warren Ellis and Mark Millar and published by Wildstorm comics.

Manchester Black is outraged by Superman's "corny" moral code against killing and grows increasingly frustrated as the Man of Steel keeps preventing Black and the Elite from meting out their swift, lethal brand of justice. During a showdown on one of Jupiter's moons, Superman kills Black's teammates, and using his heat vision as a laser scalpel, removes the "overdeveloped chunk" in Black's brain that provides his mental powers. Black's swagger and bravado are revealed to be as thin as candy coating, and he is reduced to blubbering.

That's when Superman reveals that he hasn't actually killed the Elite, just super-sped them out of harm's way; nor has he truly removed the growth in Black's brain, just temporarily suppressed his powers.

"Anger is *easy*," he tells Black. "Hate is *easy*. Vengeance and spite are easy. Lucky for you . . . and for me . . . I don't like my heroes ugly and mean. Just don't believe in it."

Black, incensed and humiliated, threatens to keep coming after Superman. Superman tells him he wouldn't have it any other way: "Dreams *save* us. They lift us up and *transform* us. I swear . . . until *my* dream of a world where *dignity*, *honor* and *justice* becomes the reality we *all* share . . . I'll never stop fighting."

Corny? Sure. Yet amid the sales success of heroes who stood for nothing except themselves, it was just what Superman fans needed to hear exactly when they needed to hear it.

Return to Krypton (Bring a Headband)

In a story line that began in April/May 2001 and concluded in September 2002, Superman and Lois travel through the Phantom Zone only to end up on a Krypton that looks nothing like John Byrne's post-*Crisis* incarnation. In fact, it's the full-blown Silver Age, headbands-and-shoulder-hoops version of Krypton, complete with Shuster's gleaming retro-future towers and rocket ships. Gradually, Superman comes to believe that everything he thought he knew about his origin was wrong. In an homage to Siegel's original 1960 "Return to Krypton" story line, Superman meets Jor-El and Lara and helps them defeat a military coup by the pre-*Crisis* version of General Zod, then returns to Earth with a Kryptonian dog named . . . Krypto.

Later, Jor-El summons Superman back to this strange "classic" Krypton, and on this second visit, Superman learns that it was all an artificial reality created by Brainiac 13 to trap him forever.

In the sprawling crossover event called *Our Worlds at War* that overran all DC books from August to October 2001, Superman leads the resistance against the galactic space-tyrant Imperiex. In the ensuing global cataclysm, Topeka, Kansas, and seven other locations throughout the world are destroyed; Ma and Pa Kent—along with Lois Lane's father and several heroes—go missing and are briefly presumed dead.

To honor the fallen dead, Superman goes into mourning—an excuse for the writers to outfit him in the somber "black S-shield" look worn by the elderly Man of Steel in Waid/Ross's 1996 *Kingdom Come* series.

That S-shield took on an eerie new resonance, however, when the September 11 terrorist attacks occurred just as the story line was ending.

"Where Was Superman?"

In a grim coincidence, *Adventures of Superman* #596 (November 2001), which appeared in comics shops the day after the attacks, featured a second-page panel depicting Metropolis's twin LexCorp Towers heavily damaged from the events of the intergalactic war, as smoke rose from them. DC informed comics shops that the books could be returned without penalty.

On October 20, 2011, at the Concert for New York City in Madison Square Garden, John Ondrasik (who records as Five for Fighting) played "Superman (It's Not Easy)," his somber salute to the Man of Steel, which he'd released a year earlier. To his audience, composed largely of first responders and the families of victims, the melancholic mood of the song offered comfort, as did one particular passage that suddenly had nothing to do with Superman: "It may sound absurd, but don't be naive/Even heroes have the right to bleed." The concert was broadcast live on VH1; "Superman (It's Not Easy)" began to climb the charts the next day.

In Marvel comics, the brace of colorful costumed heroes who make their homes in Manhattan responded to September 11 by showing up at Ground Zero to pitch in with rescue and recovery. Yet a friendly neighborhood Spider-Man was one thing, a Superman quite another. DC was keenly aware that Superman's Metropolis isn't the real Manhattan, but instead a shiny, sun-dazzled version of New York City that routinely brushes off missiles and death rays and giant apes without a second thought. DC kept Superman far away from Ground Zero.

Yet he showed up there anyway, over and over again, in images posted on the Internet by grief-stricken amateur artists: Superman standing amid the rubble of the Twin Towers, weeping or scream-ing in outrage; Superman standing atop a pile of debris, wounded but resolute, while the American flag flutters and snaps behind him; Superman cradling the body of a firefighter. Whether kitschy or bitterly sardonic (Superman sitting at home watching TV, while, outside his window, a plane hits the first tower), these images illus-trate the extent to which the notions of Superman and America had become conflated (particularly in the minds of Americans). They express, with an unsubtle and uncomfortable plaintiveness, the para-dox of an immensely powerful nation rendered helpless in the face of a nigh-unimaginable loss of life: "All those things I can do. All those powers. And I couldn't even save him."

DC published a 9/11 tribute book with the unwieldy title of *9–11: September 11, 2001 (the World's Finest Comic Book Writers and Artists Tell Stories to Remember)*. Alex Ross's painted cover, an hom-age to a Golden Age one-shot comic called *The Big All-American Comic Book*, depicts Superman and Krypto gazing up reverently at a billboard depicting firefighters, EMTs, and police officers. In a two-page story, Superman ruminates about his ability to defy gravity and breathe in space, while one thing eludes him: he cannot "break free from the fictional pages" to help save people in the real world— "A world, fortunately, protected by heroes of its own." The scene widens out to reveal that the panels we've been reading are part of a comic book belonging to a child being rescued by a firefighter.

12

SECRET ORIGIN, RE-REDUX
(2001–2005)

Milestones

2001: *Smallville* debuts

2003: *Superman: Birthright* redefines Superman's origin

2004: *It's a Bird . . .* graphic novel explores the cultural impact of Superman; *Superman: Secret Identity* imagines a real-world Superman

2005: *Krypto the Superdog* cartoon premieres; *Infinite Crisis* begins

In the days and weeks following the September 11 attacks, a benumbed American populace slowly attempted to return to their routine. As they headed to and from work and tried to distract themselves with channel-surfing, one particular ad campaign managed to slice through their foggy reverie. On buses and billboards, in magazines and on television, the disturbing image appeared: A muscular young man with unnervingly handsome features stripped to the waist and tied to a cross, hanging alone and abandoned in the middle of a cornfield at night. Painted on his chest, in what could have been blood, a scarlet letter S.

Though other, newer horrors were on everyone's minds, it was impossible not to see in that violent, arresting image deliberate intimations of Il Sodoma's beautiful *St. Sebastian*—and tasteless echoes of the killing of Matthew Shepard, the Laramie, Wyoming, youth who was tortured, tied to a fence, and left to die one year earlier. (Producers denied intending to evoke the latter.)

The campaign, disquieting though it was, worked. When *Smallville* premiered on the WB network on October 16, 2001, it was the highest-rated show in the network's brief (seven-year) history, garnering more than eight million viewers.

A Buffy-Shaped Vacancy

The *Superman* animated series had come to an end in February 2000, and wheels were chugging along to get a live-action Superman movie on big screens (an effort that would not see fruition for another six years). The Warner Bros. film division looked to the WB network for another incarnation to keep interest in the character alive in the meantime.

For its part, the WB television network was faced with a dilemma. Joss Whedon's *Buffy the Vampire Slayer* was jumping ship to the UPN network, leaving the youth-targeted network without an angsty actioner awash in hormones to anchor its broadcast schedule. WB-TV president Peter Roth liked Buffy's formula: big action set pieces plus soapy complications plus attractive teenagers talking about their feelings in lots and lots of over-the-shoulder two-shots.

Mike Tollin and Brian Robbins had developed a spec script about Batman before he became Batman. Called *Bruce Wayne*, it followed the brooding young billionaire around the world as he sought the mental and physical training he would one day use in his one-man, *Chiroptera*-themed war against crime. The treatment was met with enthusiasm but killed by bad timing—at that moment, director Darren Aronofsky was in talks to direct a big-screen Batman film whose origin story would overlap too directly with Tollin/Robbins's proposed approach.

Meanwhile, two other writers, Al Gough and Miles Millar, had been trying to get their notion of a series about Lois Lane to fly. Roth asked Gough and Millar to take a stab at a "Young Superman" script instead. The two men were leery—Superboy had been done. The business with the cape, the boots—the whole thing struck them as too cheesy, too kiddie-show. They went to work, imagining a young, pubescent, awkward Clark Kent at the heart of a teen soap.

Buffy was earning critical acclaim and a cultish fanbase by cleverly using its high school setting as a metaphor for growing up. Their *Young Clark Kent Project* would do the same thing, they resolved, with superpowers standing in for secondary sex characteristics. Clark would develop them gradually and struggle with how to control them. They would confuse and humiliate him. He would feel isolated, different, alone, and that sense of alienation—combined with the assiduous, WB-mandated application of both cheesecake and beefcake—would speak directly to the teenage viewers who'd embraced Buffy.

There would be powers, adventures, thrills, and chills, but—the writers were clear at the outset—no *way* would he wear the costume, and he would not take to the air.

Or, in the construction that became synonymous with the series during its first round of press attention: "No tights, no flights."

Somebody Saaaaave Meeeee

Apart from the costume and the flying, however, Gough and Millar could avail themselves of the whole gamut of elements from the Super-mythos to symbolically assail young Clark as he struggles to become a hero. The show, now called *Smallville*, would be a *bildungsroman of steel*.

Thus, the pilot would begin with original sin, Kryptonian-style. The rocket that delivers baby Kal-El to Earth is part of a kryptonite meteor storm that wreaks havoc on the sleepy town of Smallville, Kansas. Even as the storm gives Clark a new set of loving parents, it rips those of young Lana away from her forever. That fact, and Clark's abiding sense of guilt and shame over it, would supply the show's tent-pole romance with enough tearful gazes, moony sighs, and anguished brooding to keep it going for years. The meteors make young Lex Luthor go permanently bald and affect the town's populace in weird ways, giving them strange powers or physical mutations.

From the very beginning, the writers coded a classic, none-too-subtle inverse duality into the show's DNA; Clark's father, Jonathan, would be patient, kind, and nurturing, encouraging his son to grow into a selfless man. Lex's father, Lionel, however, would constantly goad, test, and corrupt his son, turning him into a bitter, hateful villain. Yet all of that would happen later—in the beginning, Clark and Lex would meet each other still relatively unformed, as friends. The fact that the viewers would know what was coming would add a note of poignancy to their scenes together. Or, at least, that was the idea.

Eighteen-year-old Kristin Kreuk was cast as wholesome, orphaned-by-kryptonite Lana Lang. Pillow-lipped former model Tom Welling, twenty-three, wasn't interested in the role at first, afraid the show would descend into camp. He was also—rightly—worried about typecasting, given the history of those who'd stepped into the bright red boots before him. But when his father pointed out that he wouldn't ever be seen in the costume ("no tights"), he agreed. Michael Rosenbaum, age twenty-eight, was cast as Lex Luthor; he imbued the role with a sardonic, swaggering brio that let audiences know he was smarter than the ham-handed dialogue he spoke.

Fun as Rosenbaum was, the show's true dark, charismatic heart, at least in the early seasons, was John Glover as Lionel Luthor, Lex's magnificent bastard of a father. Glover could be counted on to deliver his lines with an arch, can-you-believe-this-crap? twinkle in his eye.

The show's first season fell victim to a repetitive, formulaic structure that came to be known as "Freak of the Week" syndrome—in which Clark and company were beset by a different kryptonite-affected villain (insect guy, fire-starting coach, morphing lady, mind reader, woman-who-can-sic-bees-on-people, and so on) in every episode. This was meant to recall Buffy's ability to traffic in metaphor, but Smallville's characterizations and dialogue lacked that show's distinctive wit and playfulness and evinced a more workmanlike approach to its metaphors and—especially—its foreshadowing.

"Our friendship will become the stuff of legend," Lex might say to Clark, in exactly the way nobody has actually said anything, ever.

In season 2, producers eased back on the various krypto-freaks in favor of longer, more sustained story arcs. Gough and Millar had taken some original inspiration for the series from the Jeph Loeb/Tim Sale comic Superman: For All Seasons. Loeb wrote an episode introducing red kryptonite into the show's mythology and joined the staff as a supervising producer.

During its second season, *Smallville* became the WB's most-watched program. Christopher Reeve appeared as a wheelchair-bound scientist who informs Clark of his Kryptonian origins. In a move that found the series putting its own stamp on the established mythos, Clark is contacted by the disembodied artificial intelligence of Jor-El (voiced with imperious disdain by Terence Stamp), who would spend the rest of the series as a particularly snitty spirit guide, constantly hectoring Clark about his "destiny."

Season 3 was marked by a greater emphasis on science-fiction and mind-control stories, with cameo appearances by Perry White (Michael McKean) and several other comics characters. The writers offered viewers starved for a bit of old-school red-and-blue Superman a tantalizing glimpse of it in the episode "Hereafter," which involves a kid who can see people's deaths upon touching them. When he touches Clark, he is surprised to see not his death, but a red bolt of fabric fluttering in the night sky. It was neither a flight nor a tight, exactly, but it was enough to light up the message boards.

With the introduction of Erica Durance as Lois Lane in season 4, the show's tone lightened considerably. Clark and Lois take an instant dislike to each other, while Lana gets sidelined with a new boyfriend and a discursive witchcraft story line. The season ends with a second meteor storm hitting Smallville—disguising the arrival of the evil Brainiac.

For season 5, the WB moved *Smallville* from Wednesday to Thursday, to get it out from under the heel of the mega-hit *Lost* on ABC. Clark has moved to Metropolis and now attends college, and several more DC Comics characters enter the series' universe, including Aquaman (a beefy Alan Ritchson, whose orange-and-green ensemble was cleverly explained by establishing him as a star of the University of Miami swim team); the half-human, half-machine Cyborg; and the Kryptonian despot Zod. To mark the hundredth episode of the series, a key element occurs to prompt the growth of Clark Kent into the man he will become, when Jonathan Kent dies of a heart attack.

In season 6, the WB and UPN merged to become the CW. The *Smallville* story line saw an influx of DC Comics elements and characters—Phantom Zone villains, Jimmy Olsen, Green Arrow, and the Martian Manhunter. An episode called "Justice" features a gathering of DC heroes—and, per FCC regulations, a slow-motion shot of those same heroes walking toward the camera as something explodes behind them.

In season 7, Bizarro puts in an appearance, as does Clark's cousin Supergirl (under the name Kara Zor-El), as Clark learns more about his heritage and his destiny. Lex continues further down his dark path, picking up his pace considerably when he murders his father.

With season 8, creators Gough and Millar left the show (they would later sue Warner Bros., claiming the studio undervalued the show in its sales to foreign markets). In their absence, the "no tights, no flights" rule stayed in place, but the show focused with newly unabashed glee on its superhero mythology. That meant pivoting away from old story lines: Michael Rosenbaum's Luthor is presumed dead, and Kristin Kreuk's Lana leaves Smallville to chart her own destiny, making room for the Clark-Lois relationship to blossom as the two take jobs at the *Daily Planet*. Comic book writer Geoff Johns introduced the Legion of Super-Heroes into the mix. Clark adopts a secret identity with which to fight crime—which gets dubbed "The Red-Blue Blur," a name that, despite its evocative notes of the Doppler shift, doesn't exactly stir the blood. The season ends with Clark seeming to embrace his cold Kryptonian side.

Season 9 shrinks the regular cast but widens the canvas around them considerably, admitting Golden Age heroes such as Hawkman and Doctor Fate (in the two-part episode "Absolute Justice," written by a returning Geoff Johns), Zod, an entire platoon of Kryptonians, a secret espionage agency called Checkmate, and even a pass at the *Super Friends*' old sidekicks, Wonder Twins Zan and Jayna. Lois and Clark's romance deepens.

Smallville's tenth and final season finds Clark wallowing in his past, hesitant to embrace his destiny. A sinister force—a shadowy CGI cloud of darkness and crows(?) called Darkseid—is corrupting the minds of Earthlings, causing them to distrust Clark and his fellow heroes. Clark gets a glimpse of his super-self in the future and tangles with some of Jack Kirby's Fourth World creations, and his past comes back to haunt him: his adopted father, an alternate-universe version of Lionel Luthor, and even, inevitably, the return of the totally not-dead Lex Luthor, to exchange one last round of smoldering homoerotic stares with our hero and to deliver hilarious clunkers like, "Well that's the thing about memories, Clark. You can't forget them."

The finale ends with Clark finally ripping apart his shirt to reveal the Superman S (tights: check) and a teensy, unconvincing CGI version of Superman taking to the air (flight: check check) to save the Earth from destruction at the hands of Darkseid.

Taken as a whole, the show represents a quirk-ridden, but no less major, accomplishment in the history of Superman portrayals. At 217 episodes, it not only stands as the longest running television show—animated or live-action—to feature a superhero in general and the Man of Steel in particular, it managed to carve out its own thematic path, adding its own elements to the enduring mythology.

What's more, the show continually evolved during the course of its ten-year life span. Its journey from flatly rejecting "uncool" comic-book tropes to embracing them so tightly they lost consciousness and sank drooling to the floor wasn't without hiccups, but it was real. What began as a cheesy teen soap became a cheesy superhero soap.

That's not to dismiss its accomplishments. No other single endeavor has put more of the DC Universe's disparate elements before more people who were unfamiliar with them. Like *Lois and Clark* before it, *Smallville* found a new and eager audience by outfitting the Man of Steel and his world with stealth technology, allowing it to infiltrate a neighboring genre and win over its fans. To what extent *Smallville*'s fans generalize their interest in other aspects of Superman lore remains to be seen—there's no evidence it's driven a sizable chunk of its viewers to comics shops, and its role in the box office success of *Superman Returns* is difficult to measure.

Yet through it all—through freaks of the week, witch-tattoos, clones, body-switching, and lots and lots of long, moony looks— *Smallville* hung in there. Yes, the plots were dumb and formulaic, particularly in the early going, and the plodding, expositional dialogue never sparked—remove the words *hero* and *destiny* from the scripts of the show's last few seasons, for example, and each episode would be twenty minutes shorter. And yes, the gleefully villainous Luthors, *fils* and *pere*, outclassed and overshadowed Welling's stolid Clark, but their departure gave the actor room to make the character his own.

Welling had never really jelled with the show's original intent—he simply didn't possess the range necessary to convey an awkward, haunted superteen. (Especially in the early going, whenever the actor would assay "emotional turmoil," he'd end up somewhere in the neighborhood of "enervatingly mopey.") Yet later, as Clark grappled with his Kryptonian heritage—and later still, with (sigh) his destiny—Welling's essential squareness resonated nicely with his character's arc. He enters the history books (and the *Guinness Book*) as the actor who has portrayed the Man of Steel for the longest continual period of time, a feat that is unlikely to be matched anytime soon.

Justice League

Exactly one month after *Smallville* premiered in 2001, Warner Bros. latest super-cartoon premiered on the Cartoon Network. Produced by Bruce Timm and Paul Dini, the team behind *Superman: The Animated Series* and two successful Batman shows, *Justice League* began by adopting Grant Morrison's "Big 7" approach, anchored by Superman.

The character design of the Justice League Superman accented his role of elder statesman. His legs were skinnier, his breadbasket broader, and his face was lined with care. His power set was dialed down slightly, as well, to complement those of his fellow Leaguers.

With Tim Daly unavailable, the producers tapped George Newbern to voice the Man of Steel and began to produce a season's worth of two-part story lines that delved into each hero's backstory, while fleshing out the DC Universe imagined by Timm and Dini. (*Smallville*'s Michael Rosenbaum provided the voice for the Flash.) Though Superman was only one member of the cast, the episode "Hereafter" shone the spotlight on the Man of Steel by focusing on the aftermath of the apparent death of Superman—at the hands of two-bit crook the Toyman.

After two seasons, the name of the series was changed to *Justice League Unlimited*, and the cast list lived up to that name—episodes became tight, done in one story line, and featured heroes and villains from the deepest deep benches of the DC Universe.

Justice League Unlimited ran for an additional two seasons, finding time to pay homage to the *Super Friends*' nemesis the

Legion of Doom and offer a glimpse of the future. The series' final episode, broadcast on May 13, 2006, climaxed in a show-down between Michael Ironside's gravel-voiced Darkseid and Newbern's finally-pushed-too-far Man of Steel. The slugfest, weighted as it was with the decades of history that existed between these two characters, proved profoundly satisfying in ways that the 1992 Doomsday/Superman death-rumble-in-the-rubble reso-lutely had not.

In the comics, Frank Miller followed up his grim-and-gritty 1986 master work *Batman: The Dark Knight Returns* with *The Dark Knight Strikes Again*, or *DK2* (November 2001–July 2002), a much looser, louder, and more garish assemblage of batshit-crazy crammed into a Silver Age potato sack. Characters from all corners of the DC Universe show up for this glorious, first-thought-best-thought train wreck of clashing colors and tones. Amid it all, in one of the few scenes that has endured, an aging Superman and Wonder Woman find time for a lengthy midair *schtup*.

Transitions

With the March 2003 issue (#134), *Superman: Man of Steel* was canceled; in August of that year a new comic, *Superman/Batman*, a contemporary spin on the old team-up book *World's Finest*, debuted. Written by Jeph Loeb and penciled, initially, by Ed McGuinness, issue #8 (May 2004) of the series returned the official, old-school Supergirl—Kara Zor-El, Superman's cousin—back into continuity after eighteen years.

While reconsidering decisions made almost two decades earlier, DC decided it was once again time to revisit, and update, the Man of Steel's origin for twenty-first-century readers.

True, DC had missed the window. As Grant Morrison had spelled out in the pitch he, Millar, Peyer, and Waid made in 1999, there was historically a fifteen-year-cycle by which the Man of Steel's origin story got its regular update and reimagining. DC had passed on that proposal, however, opting for changes that had more to do with publishing logistics than story. Yet now it was time for a revamp.

In the hands of writer Mark Waid, however, what DC got was something much closer to synthesis. In the stand-alone twelve-issue series *Superman: Birthright* (August 2003–September 2004), Waid didn't throw out the 1986 reboot so much as make thoughtful adjustments to its tone, overlay its essential story beats with nuanced explorations of their real-world ramifications, and integrate key elements of previous origins to produce a deeper, more resonant exploration of the Clark/Superman dynamic.

Mostly, though, it was an argument—Waid set out to make the case that for Superman to matter, he had to *act*.

In his proposal, Waid mentioned a story featured on the November 2, 2001, episode of the Public Radio International program *This American Life*, about a man who had taken to wearing a hand-sewn Superman costume as he went about his daily life.

The reporter, tagging along with "Superman" in public, noted that he tended to be most warmly accepted by people in their thirties and forties—or, as the reporter put it, "the people who grew up with Superman."

> Oh, my God . . . to hear it put like that and know instantly that it was true was quite a wake-up call for me. There are entire generations to whom Superman is about as meaning-ful and significant as Woody Woodpecker and Marmaduke. [They] perceive the world as far more dangerous, more unfair and screwed up than we ever did . . . where capitalism always wins, where politicians always lie, where sports idols take drugs and beat their wives, where white picket fences are suspect because they hide dark things . . . and to them, that's the world Superman *represents* and the status quo he *defends*.

In post-9/11 America, Waid wrote, heroes couldn't be mere symbols who inspired others. They had to take an active stand. They had to fight for the little guy. "That's what Siegel and Shuster came to the table with, and that's what we have to put out there."

Superman: Birthright

What's most intriguing about *Superman: Birthright* is that it's only incidentally the Super-origin story readers have come to expect. Yes, we once again open on Krypton as a frustrated Jor-El fumes at the

Council for ignoring his warnings. Yet even on the opening pages, Waid was already at work iterating the tale, finding new depths to explore.

In a long-overdue concession to the twenty-first-century audience, Waid established that Jor-El and Lara are equal partners not merely in life, but in their scientific endeavors as well. Artist Leinil Francis Yu dispensed with Byrne's cold, antiseptic Krypton to make Superman's home planet once again a pulpy science-fiction utopia. The design, however, is not Shuster's retro-futurist kitsch, but something bold and new and alien. His Kryptonians wear capes and tights, and boldly colored tunics that seem more fashion-forward than Flash Gordon.

Young Kal-El is sent to Earth wrapped in the flag of Krypton—the distinctive S-shield suspended in a field of red, blue, and yellow. In his pitch, Waid argued that the S-crest works only if it represents Kal-El's lost planet. If it's simply the El family crest, to wear it would reduce his significance, making him the Last Son of the El Family, not the Last Son of Krypton. ("The central question . . . of the Superman mythos . . . is not "Am I an El or a Kent?" It's "Am I an Earthman or a Kryptonian?"") Likewise, if it's simply a stylized S that Clark came up with so that he can refer to himself as Superman, "not only does it have no resonance, it makes no sense. Why would Clark think he needs something like that on his shirt? He's a humble man."

Instead of dutifully ticking the requisite boxes of a Superman origin, Waid skipped all of the refusing-the-call Joseph Campbell rigmarole and cut from the Kents' discovery of the rocket to Clark as a young journalist in Africa, because *Birthright* is less about the particulars of Superman's powers than about his quest for identity. It's here that Waid truly inverted what Byrne's 1986 reboot had accomplished, finding nuance where very little had existed before.

Superman, the story posits, is not the pose, the "hero's mantle" that Clark adopts, as Byrne had asserted. Rather, it's who he truly is, the man the Kents raised him to be: a selfless champion who fights for what's right. Thus, donning the costume isn't play-acting, it's a relief—at last, he can be who he truly is without worrying that he will frighten those who know him. (Waid illustrated this by showing a noncostumed Clark saving lives, which engenders only fear and mistrust in people—why, they wonder, has he been hiding those powers from them? What else is he hiding?)

Like Siegel and Shuster, Waid made Clark Kent the fabrication, a role he invents (after studying books on acting by Stella Adler and Sanford Meisner) to keep himself in touch with humanity.

Waid introduced other, smaller changes: Jonathan Kent at first resents Clark's embracing his Kryptonian side, thinking it a rejection of him; Martha Kent is an avid consumer of UFO conspiracy theories; the young Lex Luthor/young Clark Kent friendship is back (a concession to the success of the show *Smallville*, as much as to the Silver Age stories), but the adult Lex is simply too self-involved to recall it, and Lex Luthor is once again a brilliant scientist.

Yet the change that garnered the most Internet outrage was Waid's contention that Superman can see "life auras" surrounding all living creatures—a fact that drives him to become a vegetarian. To longtime fans who had invested too much of their inner lives in the abiding knowledge that Clark's favorite meal—as had been established for years!—was beef burgundy with ketchup, this was a blow.

Well. A "blow."

Originally, DC asked Waid to prepare *Birthright* as a noncanonical, free-standing story that would streamline the origin and make it accessible to new readers. By the time its twelfth and final issue was published, however, the publisher made it known that *Birthright* was to be regarded as the official, in-canon origin of Superman.

And so it would stay.

For a couple of years, anyway.

A Tale of Two Supermen

In June 2004, new creative teams came on board all four remaining Superman books—*Superman*, *Adventures of Superman*, *Action Comics*, and *Superman/Batman*.

By far the one that generated the most eager advance attention from critics and fans was the team of writer Brian Azzarello and artist Jim Lee, who took over the *Superman* book for a twelve-issue story arc called "For Tomorrow" in #204–#215 (June 2004–June 2005).

Azzarello, known for the critically acclaimed noir comic series *100 Bullets*, had previously teamed with the immensely popular artist Jim Lee (a key figure of the Image Comics "extreme" creator-owned superheroes scene of the 1990s) on the Batman story arc "Hush."

Azzarello's gritty, somber, gin-soaked sensibility seems more suited to Batman than to the Man of Steel, however, and although the "For Tomorrow" story line opens with an intriguing portrait of a Superman wracked with guilt over his inability to save more people from a mysterious Rapture-like event, it soon devolves into a static slugfest among two-dimensional characters sporting armor that bears Lee's distinctive I-Love-the-90s design aesthetic.

Meanwhile, in a concurrent stint on *Adventures of Superman*, writer Greg Rucka and penciler Matthew Clark were quietly and deftly capturing the essence of the Man of Steel. Their run on the book attracted only a fraction of the attention that the Azzarello/Lee team did, because Rucka's approach was subtler, and the stories he was telling considerably smaller. Yet as early as the first page of his first issue, the writer unfussily managed to nail who Superman is.

In a crowded shopping mall, Superman returns a lost little girl to her mother.

> Mother (guiltily): Thank you so much. I'm sorry to bother
>   you. I'm sure you have more important things to do.
> Superman (pause): No, not really.

From Both Sides Now

During the next several months, Superman appeared in several projects that examined past eras from fresh perspectives. Artist-writer Darwyn Cooke's six-issue series *DC: The New Frontier* (March–December 2004) imagined the formation of an Eisenhower-era Justice League in a brightly lit world of boomerang tables and Pepsodent smiles. Meanwhile, in the controversial and bathetic miniseries *Identity Crisis* (August–December 2004), writer Brad Meltzer and penciler Rags Morales revealed that the other members of the 1970s-era Justice League had kept dark secrets from Superman, Batman, and Wonder Woman, secrets involving bodyswaps, mind-wipes, and—in a cringeworthy bid on Meltzer's part to raise the narrative stakes—rape.

In the five-issue miniseries *Lex Luthor: Man of Steel* (March 2005–September 2005), Brian Azzarello got another shot at the Super-mythos, accompanied this time by artist Lee Bermejo. This time, Azzarello's dark, brooding sensibility meshed well with his subject, because the series is told from Lex Luthor's point of view. In the series' strongest moments, Bermejo provides us with insights that Luthor's hatred blinds him to—as when Superman gazes at Luthor sadly, pityingly—and Luthor reads only disgust and disdain in the Man of Steel's expression.

Countdown to *Infinite Crisis*

In the pages of the comics, however, DC was gearing up for yet another major crossover event that would once again imperil all of creation and threaten to unmake reality itself; it must be Tuesday.

Yet for that story to work, writers had to first destroy the trust and camaraderie that existed between DC's Big Three—Superman, Batman, and Wonder Woman. In a story arc called "Sacrifice," which ran through the Superman and Wonder Woman titles in September and October 2005, an old enemy of the Justice League named Maxwell Lord seizes control of Superman's mind and sends him on a destructive path, going so far as to have him brutalize fellow hero Batman within an inch of his life. Wonder Woman, ever the pragmatic warrior, encircles Lord in her Lasso of Truth, at which point he informs her that the only way to ever free Superman is to kill the man controlling him. Without further ado, Wonder Woman snaps Lord's neck, and Superman is returned to his former self.

The act cleaves the three heroes apart: Superman is horrified that Wonder Woman took a life; Wonder Woman is annoyed that Superman is judging her for an act that theoretically saved millions of lives (Wonder Woman is a creature of myth, after all; she knows that there are monsters, and monsters must be slain). The horribly beaten Batman's anger and simmering resentment of Superman's abilities flare anew.

Crisis Management, Twenty-First-Century Style

When the six-month event called *Infinite Crisis* (December 2005– June 2006) finally got under way, we learn that from the "paradise dimension" to which they disappeared following 1986's *Crisis on Infinite Earths*, the Superman and Lois of Earth-2 and the Superboy from Earth-Prime have been watching the events of the last twenty years unfold—and they are *not* happy.

For one thing, Lois has continued to age, while the Golden Age Superman and Superboy-Prime have not. She is frail and nearing death; they remain just as they were when last we saw them, two decades earlier. Superboy-Prime grows increasingly restless as he watches the contemporary DC Universe, which seems to him a dark, violent, grim place whose innocence has been corrupted. He resolves to return it to its former glory.

At this point, it became obvious to readers that *Infinite Crisis* was meant as a bit of meta-commentary on the state of superhero comics. To writer Geoff Johns, Superboy-Prime, who would shortly become the villain of the piece, represented those readers who were given to complaining about how comics weren't like they were when they were kids.

For DC, it also offered a convenient reality-altering means to mop up some narrative spills of the post-*Crisis* era—a metafictional mulligan, as it were. Superboy begins hammering away at the "walls" of the paradise dimension, which sends shockwaves through reality. These shockwaves proceed to undo several major deaths and other events that had taken place since the original *Crisis* in 1986. Finally, the walls shatter, and Superboy-Prime, convinced that something is wrong with the Earth, sets about restoring the parallel worlds lost during the *Crisis*, while searching for the one he came from—a perfect, innocent Earth, free of the grim-and-gritty corruption he sees before him.

Yet each new universe that is created further weakens the fabric of reality, and the restored "multiverse" is in danger of total collapse.

Superman and his companion, the Golden Age Superman of Earth-2, ultimately defeat Superboy-Prime by flying him into a red sun. In the process, however, the Superman of Earth-2 dies, and Superman loses his powers. Superboy-Prime is sent to galactic prison, from which he vows to escape.

In the wake of the *Infinite Crisis*, the multiple Earths created were once again merged together—but the resulting New Earth isn't the one we know. Its history has been altered in ways large and small—ways that will only come to light in the months and the years to follow.

If the *Infinite Crisis* event had been intended by its creators to be as shattering as the original 1986 *Crisis*, the fallout from it was not readily apparent. Although Superman—and two other versions of him—played a starring role in *Infinite Crisis*, it was unclear to readers exactly how Superman's place on "New Earth" was any different from how it had been before. Apart from informing readers that Superman's "batteries" had been depleted—and it would take months for the sun's rays to "recharge" his powers—DC wasn't telling.

Mercifully, rather than spend several long, dull issues chronicling the adventures of a powerless Man of Steel, DC decided to jump the time lines of its entire line of comics ahead by twelve months. Thus, the June 2006 issues of the Superman books that immediately followed the May 2006 conclusion of *Infinite Crisis* found a "One Year Later" Clark Kent delighting in the first sign of the return of his superpowers, and the citizens of Metropolis preparing to mark the one-year anniversary since Superman had disappeared.

Just as the comics were starting up their story lines about Superman returning after a long absence, a massively expensive and ambitious film starring the Man of Steel was about to premiere in theaters.

Its name, in what was in no way a coincidence: *Superman Returns*.

13

ALL-STAR (2006–2012)

Milestones

2006: *All-Star Superman* debuts; *Superman Returns* premieres

2007: *Superman: Doomsday* direct-to-DVD animated film

2009: *Superman: Secret Origin* redefines the Super-origin, again

2010: *Action Comics* #1 sells at auction for $1.5 million

2011: DC Comics reboots its superhero titles; Superman gets a new look; *Action Comics* #1 sells at auction for $2.16 million

The months preceding the release of Superman's big-budget, big-screen return were an unsettled time for his comic-book incarnation. Shakeups were the order of the day. A new editor, Matt Idelson, took over the Superman titles with the March issues. Yet another major company-wide crossover event was ending, having rewritten the DC Universe's history (again, some more), and leaving the Man of Steel and his fans uncertain as to which parts of his origin and recent history were now considered "in-canon" and which had been whisked out of existence by a combination of reality-warping intradimensional quantum collapse—and editorial fiat.

If that weren't enough, with the April issues, the entire Superman line of comics underwent a radical—and, to fans and retailers,

confusing—contraction and reshuffling. The book that had originally been called *Superman* from the time of its launch in 1939
through the 1986 John Byrne reboot—when its name had been
changed to *Adventures of Superman*, while keeping the same numbering—became simply *Superman* once more in May, with issue
#650. To the history books, it would appear as if the title had simply
tried on a temporary alias—albeit one that had lasted twenty years,
roughly one-third of its existence.

This meant, however, that the book called *Superman* that had
first launched in the wake of the John Byrne reboot two decades
earlier was now superfluous. It came to an end in April 2006, with
issue #225.

These changes were more than simply logistical. They, in effect,
constituted the fifteen-year cycle that Morrison, Waid, Millar, and
Peyer had described in their *Superman Now* pitch, begun anew. Five
years late, perhaps, and the changes would prove subtler and more
abstract than was customary, but there was no denying a new Satya
Yuga had finally arrived to nudge the John Byrne *Superman* aside—
and take his place. Just in time for *Superman Returns*.

Suddenly, there were once again only two monthly, ongoing,
in-continuity comics starring Superman on store shelves. Both
Superman and *Action Comics* kicked off with an interconnected story
line called "Up Up and Away" that ran through their May and June
2006 issues, written by Kurt Busiek and Geoff Johns. The story set
out to establish for readers just who this New Earth, post–*Infinite
Crisis*, just-getting-his-powers-back Man of Steel was.

For one thing, he was minus one junior apprentice. The character of Superboy, aka Conner Kent, aka "Kon-El," aka the teenage
Superman clone who'd been introduced as "the Metropolis Kid" in
the aftermath of the nineties "Death of Superman" story line, had
died during the latest cosmic cataclysm. (Comics being comics, of
course, the death wouldn't take.)

During the course of this eight-part story line, Busiek and
Johns intentionally adopted several narrative beats that echoed
many elements that readers might recognize in Bryan Singer's
film: Superman appearing in Metropolis following a prolonged
absence; Luthor once again reviled by humanity; a climactic fight
between Luthor wielding a strange Kryptonian crystal (called a

"sunstone" here) and a weakened Man of Steel. At the end of the story line, Superman throws the crystal into an Arctic wasteland, where it creates a perfect match for the cinematic Fortress of Solitude.

The trap was baited, in other words, should some avid moviegoer happen to wander into a comic-book store after seeing the Singer film. There, in the two main Superman comics, they might just find a familiar Man of Steel locked into a life-or-death struggle with a sneering, Kevin Spacey–esque Lex Luthor.

If that same someone happened to pick up the other regular monthly comic that featured Superman—the team-up book *Superman/Batman*—the affinities would be harder to see. *Superman/Batman* was a quirkier, more insular title that featured long, byzantine story arcs filled with action-movie set pieces steeped in backstory and obscure characters. Its barrier to entry was considerably higher.

If, however, he or she happened to pick up an issue of Grant Morrison and Frank Quitely's *All-Star Superman*, a gleefully and defiantly out-of-continuity stand-alone twelve-chapter miniseries chronicling the last days of the Man of Steel, they would find inside it nothing that would even remotely remind them of Singer's moony, depressive cinematic Superman. That series, which began to appear in comics shops in November 2005, with subsequent issues published sporadically during the next two years, cast Superman as an ebullient, monomythic sun god, limned in a Silver Age gleam, and it represented the synthesis and apotheosis of sixty-eight years of four-color history.

All-Star Superman is literally wonderful and stubbornly weird—both at once, one inextricably bound up inside the other.

"A Vitruvian Man in a Cape"

In his 2011 book *Supergods*, Grant Morrison laid out, in his characteristic purple-metallic prose, his statement of principles in crafting *All-Star Superman* with artist Frank Quitely:

> I wondered why we've chosen to develop in our children a taste for mediated prepackaged rape, degradation, violence and "bad-ass" murdering heroes. . . . And so *All-Star*

Superman: our attempt at an antidote to all that, which . . . [positioned] Superman as the Enlightenment ideal paragon of human physical, intellectual, and moral development that Siegel and Shuster had imagined. A Vitruvian Man in a cape, our restorative Superman would attempt to distill the pure essence of pop culture's finest creation: baring the soul of an indestructible hero so strong, so noble, so clever and resourceful, he had no need to kill to make his point. There was no problem Superman could not solve or overcome. He could not lose. He would never let us down because we made him that way. He dressed like Clark Kent and took the world's abuse to remind us that underneath our shirts, waiting, there is always a familiar blaze of color, a stylized lightning bolt, a burning heart.

All-Star Superman would not, could not, live up to such platonically idealized ambitions, but in finally allowing Morrison to channel the shamanic energies he'd tapped into for the *Superman Now* proposal, it would represent the most ambitious and effective interpretation of the entire Superman mythos (and, for that matter, ethos) ever undertaken.

Morrison tended to stuff his narrative with allusive, metonymic meta-meanings by the cubic ton, and *All-Star Superman* is no different. Yet here, at least, the narrative in question—the last twelve great labors of Superman as he prepares for his death—is mercifully clear and assertive enough to stare down Morrison's trademark eschatological riot of ur-ideas and use it without being used by it.

All-Star Superman

Morrison and Quitely did not write an origin story. In fact, they dispensed with the Super-origin on the miniseries' very first page.

"Dispense with" doesn't adequately capture what writer and artist accomplished on page one. In just four panels, they provided four mnemonic signposts and invited us to fill in the rest of the origin for ourselves—knowing that we can. They *distilled* the most well-known story in comics and one of the most recognized stories in all of literature to its quintessence: "Doomed planet. Desperate scientists. Last hope. Kindly couple."

Eight words. Four images. Page one of *All-Star Superman* is about as ruthlessly iconographic as the comics medium gets.

The story: During a rescue mission on the surface of the Sun (orchestrated by Lex Luthor), Superman's body grows "super-saturated" with solar energy—so much so that his cells begin to literally explode. He develops new powers, and his preexisting powers increase threefold in strength.

But Superman is dying.

He resolves to finish certain tasks before his death. He reveals his secret identity to a disbelieving Lois Lane and takes her to his Fortress of Solitude, a place of whimsical Silver Age splendors, such as Superman robots, statues of friends, and time bubbles. The issues that follow are full of homages to the Golden, Silver, and Modern Ages of Super-stories: the Greek titan Atlas and the biblical hero Samson appear (as they had in the January 1965 *Action Comics* #320); Superman turns evil, Jimmy Olsen undergoes a strange metamorphosis into a Doomsday-like creature, Bizarro World attacks Earth, a pair of haughty Kryptonians arrive to enslave the world, and Superman chronicles it all, along with his last will and testament, in a giant diary (as in 1958's "The Key to Fort Superman").

In many ways, Morrison's bold, all-encompassing vision provides a modern-day iteration of Siegel and Shuster's original narrative impulse. Their Superman easily overmatches anything thrown at him—that, in fact, was the whole point of those early stories, watching Superman triumph without mussing his pomade. Over and over, those early stories delighted in bringing a red-and-blue ballistic missile to the knife fight.

Times have changed, and Morrison's storytelling obsessions are a good deal more abstruse and psychotropic than Siegel's ever were—but the impulse is exactly the same. Here, says Morrison, is Superman. Let's just sit back and watch him. He is the best there is. He does not give up. He does not struggle. He finds a way.

Without Frank Quitely's bright, primary-colored world making, however, *All-Star Superman* would lie inert on the page, registering as little more than a clever concoction of Morrisonian memes. Yet Quitely somehow accomplishes the nigh-impossible feat of showing us a Superman we haven't seen before.

Quitely's Superman is muscular, but not in the way readers were used to seeing him—this is no gym bunny with abs for days.

Quitely's Superman is, simply, *huge*. A mesomorphic mountain of meat built like a stevedore—which is to say: a big lug.

Quitely also eschews the tradition of drawing Superman's costume as colored flesh, deigning to depict its textures and wrinkles realistically, looking for all the world like George Reeves's old monkey suit, down to the diaperlike red trunks. It was so resolutely old school, it seemed wholly new.

Arachnophobia: The Long Road Back to the Big Screen

By the time Bryan Singer's *Superman Returns* finally opened in theaters on June 21, 2006, it represented the culmination of a thirteen-year effort to return the Man of Steel to the nation's movie houses.

Technically, Singer's movie had taken only two years from script to screen and thus represented a relatively euphonious coda to a protracted, turbulent, and dissonant string of aborted attempts to restart the Superman film franchise.

Back in 1993, the famously volatile movie producer Jon Peters (*Batman*, *Rain Man*, *Flashdance*, *Caddyshack*) had been tapped by Warner Bros. to oversee a Superman film. Though many of his colleagues found his bellicose, chest-thumping approach to conflict resolution wearying, the studio could not argue with the astonishing success of Tim Burton's *Batman* and felt certain he was the man to bring their other internationally known comic-book property back to the big screen.

Peters had little fondness for the character, however, especially for his classic incarnation, and so resolved to focus on the "Death of Superman" story line that had made international news. He gave his screenwriter, Jonathan Lemkin, two edicts: (1) The red-and-blue suit, the boots, the cape? "Too faggy." He didn't want to see it in his film. (2) The sight of a man flying through the air? "Horseshit." He didn't want to see it in his film. Thus, seven years before *Smallville*, "No tights, no flights" became a basic tenet of Super-filmmaking.

Lemkin's script, called *Superman Reborn*, leaned hard into the Christ allegory. After his fight with Doomsday, Superman psychically impregnates Lois Lane as he dies in her arms. She gives birth to a second incarnation of Superman, who grows to manhood during the course of three weeks and saves the world. Peters was enthusiastic; Warner Bros. passed.

Screenwriter Gregory Poirier was brought in for a pass at the script. His Superman was moody and introspective; one scene takes place in his psychotherapy session. Poirier has him return from the afterlife weakened and don the black-and-silver "containment suit" from the comics; he resolves to fight Doomsday without his powers. Cue martial arts training montage. Peters was enthusiastic; Warner Bros. passed.

In 1996, filmmaker Kevin Smith took a pass, after mocking the Poirier script, which he felt represented a fundamental misread of the character, in meetings with Warner Bros. executives. Years later, Smith would turn the experience of working on the Superman script—and dealing with Peters—into a comedic anecdote he'd bust out during his appearances on the college lecture circuit.

Poirier's script struck Smith as too "*Batman* TV show—very campy." By 1996, Peters had added a third edict for the script, over and above the bans on red trunks and aerial acrobatics: he wanted to see the Man of Steel fight a giant spider in the third act. ("Why a spider?" Smith asked. "Spiders are the fiercest killers in the insect kingdom," Peters replied.) Warner Bros. impressed on him, as it had on the previous two screenwriters, the need to think in terms of merchandising (read: toys) during the process of script development.

Smith's *Superman Lives!* script featured a Brainiac-Luthor team, an effeminate robot butler (a Peters request), Doomsday, polar bears ("The fiercest killers in the animal kingdom"), and the Eradicator. To enforce Peters' no-fly-zone directive, Superman would be depicted only as a flying blur of red, accompanied by a sonic boom— an approach used famously by Frank Miller in *Batman*: *The Dark Knight Returns*.

The script was sent to director Tim Burton and to Nicolas Cage, who had expressed strong interest in portraying the Man of Steel. Burton, however, wanted to go in the proverbial "other direction" taken by so many Hollywood projects—in this case, that direction was straight into Burton's recognizably weird wheelhouse. Smith was out; Burton asked screenwriter Wesley Strick to play up the gloomy isolation and moody outsider status that was and remains Burton's métier. Cage's Superman would be tortured, outcast, misunderstood: Edward Superhands.

Predictably, the production design took a turn for the grotesque. A black super-suit festooned with wires that somehow exposed Superman's internal organs to public view was devised. Big-name Hollywood actors were considered: Jim Carrey for Brainiac. Tim Allen for Luthor.

As the budget increased, and the months sped by, screenwriter Dan Gilroy was brought in for more changes—though with Burton driving the ship, the no-tights, no-flights rules were suspended. Gilroy added a jetpack to appeal to Warner Bros. merchandising division, and Burton reached out to different actors: Kevin Spacey as Luthor. Chris Rock as Jimmy Olsen.

By now, with a projected budget topping $200 million, Warner Bros. considered the project unwieldy and shelved it. Gilroy tried to trim the more expensive effects and generated some renewed interest, but Burton and Cage had moved on, spurring a fresh round of treatments. Screenwriter Alex Ford wrote a dutiful, earnest take on the character that left Peters cold. Comics writer Keith Giffen submitted a humorous script in which the Man of Steel teamed up with Lobo, DC's resident alien bounty hunter. William Wisher (the cowriter of *Terminator 2: Judgment Day*) offered a heavily *Matrix*-influenced pitch at a time when *Matrix* influences found their way into most treatments for action films. An all-CGI Superman film was proposed. Paul Attanasio (of *Quiz Show*) wrote a treatment called *Superman Destruction* that attracted the attention of . . . Tim Burton.

Finally, in 2002, Warner Bros. reached out to Joseph McGinty Nichol (who directs films under the name McG), impressed with his frenetic, color-saturated aesthetic, and hired J. J. Abrams to write the screenplay. Abrams produced a script he called *Superman I* (because it was the first of a planned trilogy), which departed from the comic-book canon in a host of nerd-baiting ways: Jor-El sends infant Kal-El to Earth to save him from a political uprising, not the planet's destruction. (Subsequent films were to locate the action on Krypton.) Lex Luthor is a spy tasked with monitoring for extraterrestrial threats, who is secretly (the third act twist!) Kryptonian himself. A leaked review of the script posted on the website Ain't It Cool News earned it the blistering acrimony of fans.

In the meantime, Warner Bros. had simultaneously sent a *Batman vs. Superman* film into preproduction, under the aegis of director

Wolfgang Petersen. Written by Andrew Kevin Walker of *Se7en*, and subsequently Akiva Goldsman, *Batman vs. Superman* got green-lit, and Matt Damon was approached to star as either principal.

In the end, however, an internal studio power struggle led to the McG/Abrams *Superman I* script winning out, and *Batman vs. Superman* getting shelved permanently—but not until the timing forced McG to give up his chance to direct it, due to his commitment to film the *Charlie's Angels* sequel. Other names were floated: Steven Soderbergh, David Fincher, Michael Mann, Bryan Singer. Brett Ratner was briefly associated with the project—and secured an agreement from Anthony Hopkins, the star of Ratner's *Red Dragon*, to play Jor-El—but then the studio entered into talks with Michael Bay and M. Night Shyamalan (whose insistence on writing the screenplay himself was a dealbreaker). Talks dragged on so long that McG finished *Charlie's Angels 2* and was once again available.

Yet more complications arose. Warner Bros. had decreed that filming would take place in Australia. McG's intense fear of flying, especially flying over water, led him to beseech the studio to relocate filming to Canada, which would cost almost $30 million more. Ultimately, the bottom line won out, and the studio offered the job to Bryan Singer.

During this interminable process, it seemed as if every actor in Hollywood had his name associated with the role of Superman, including Nicolas Cage, Josh Hartnett, Paul Walker, Jude Law, Ashton Kutcher, Matthew Bomer, Brendan Fraser, Justin Timberlake, Jake Gyllenhaal, Keanu Reeves, Shia LaBeouf, Jason Behr, Henry Cavill, and Jared Padalecki. Ultimately, twenty-five-year-old Brandon Routh won the right to the tights.

By the time Singer began preproduction work, Warner Bros. had already invested eleven years and more than $70 million in flailing attempts to get a Superman film off the ground.

"Don't Be Afraid of It"

Singer felt strongly that the studio's approach to the character was missing the mark. He came up with a fresh treatment with screenwriting partners Dan Harris and Michael Dougherty.

The origin had been done to death, he decided. Instead, he'd start with the idea of Superman missing—a hole left in the American psyche. Instead of apologizing for him or "reinventing" him or adding layers of gimmicks and irony to distract from the question of how an old-fashioned concept like Superman could fit in today's world, he would make that disconnect the subject of the piece—the question that drives the action. "If you're going to make Superman, make Superman," he said. "Don't be afraid of it."

Superman is a modern American myth, Singer believed. He's still the same hero he always was—but the world around him changed. So that's what the film would be about. Stylistically, he wanted to key off Richard Donner's 1978 approach and visited Donner to seek his blessing. He also checked in with the *Smallville* producers to make sure his planned treatment didn't introduce stark contradictions, and he did due diligence to the comic-book source material.

The image of Routh standing, fists on hips, gazing skyward, wearing the film's version of the Superman suit, hit the Internet on April 22, 2005. The costume stoked consternation among hardcore fans, who critiqued the minutiae of the suit's design like tetchy *Project Runway* guest judges: The reds were too muted, a rich burgundy that evoked blood, the blue of the tunic and tights too electric. They sniffed at the iconography—why on Earth did he have a miniature Superman S on his belt buckle? Why was the chest insignia so tiny and embossed? And what was up with that leathery cape? Non-nerds didn't concern themselves with such details—the suit was blue, it had an S, it was Superman. Instead, mainstream pop culture critics and gossip magazines contented themselves with bawdy jokes about the tightness and tininess of the Speedo-like red shorts and the status of the Super-package housed within them.

Filming began in February 2005, with a projected budget of $204 million. Both Noel Neill and Jack Larson made cameo appearances—Neill as a dying dowager and Larson as a friendly bartender. Singer availed himself of a promotional technique that had been used to great effect by Peter Jackson during the making of the *Lord of the Rings* films: he released video production journals during the shoot to generate hype and keep the fans slavering.

In July 2005, Singer flew from the Superman set to San Diego for an appearance at Comic-Con before thousands of eager fans. It was a nerve-wracking experience—the director, jet-lagged and visibly nervous, dutifully established his bona fides as fans peppered him with questions: Was Superman Clark Kent, or was Clark

Kent Superman? Singer's low-key, vaguely dyspeptic temperament didn't exactly whip up the crowd, but he made it out alive, making only one nervous flub, referring to Superman as "Jor-El" instead of "Kal-El"—the teeming crowd gasped in mock horror.

Superman Returns

The film functions as a kind of *Superman V*, for better or worse, opening with John Williams's majestic score and the voice of Jor-El—Marlon Brando—committing his son to the stars.

We see the adult Clark as he returns from a five-year space odyssey, crash-landing on the Kent farm. He collapses in his mother's arms; Singer lingers over this super-pieta, which is only the first of the film's many evocations of Christian imagery. He tells his mother (Eva Marie Saint) that he found nothing of what he sought in space—just meteors ("That place was a graveyard. I'm all that's left.") where Krypton used to be.

He returns to the *Daily Planet* to find that Lois Lane (Kate Bosworth) has moved on—she's won a Pulitzer Prize for an editorial called "Why the World Doesn't Need Superman," gotten engaged, and had a son.

Superman, still pining for Lois, flies by her house and uses his X-ray vision and superhearing to eavesdrop on her conversations with her husband. Chastened by what he learns—Lois professes not to love the Man of Steel—he flies off, heartbroken, and sets off on a series of super-feats and rescues.

Eventually, Lois and her son, Jason, are taken captive aboard Luthor's yacht, where he reveals his latest diabolical real-estate-themed plan: to combine Kryptonian crystal with kryptonite, launch it into the ocean, and build an entirely new continent all his own. The resultant flooding will kill billions of people.

The landmass begins to grow, wreaking havoc in Metropolis, which Superman vainly attempts to deal with. Lois and Jason escape when Jason hurls a piano at one of Luthor's henchmen, revealing that he is in fact Superman's son.

Superman confronts Luthor on the growing continent, only to discover that the entire landmass is impregnated with kryptonite. Weakened, Superman is brutally beaten (one might say scourged) by Luthor and his henchmen. Luthor then stabs Superman's side with a shard of kryptonite ("One of the soldiers pierced his side with a spear."—John 19:34) and kicks him into the ocean far below.

Rescued by Lois, who removes the shard from his side, Superman flies above the clouds to bathe in sunlight and recharge. With Herculean effort, he manages to lift the entire crystalline continent into the air and out into space. Once the task is done, however, he plummets to earth in a Christlike pose, where his comatose body is taken to a Metropolis hospital.

Lois visits him and whispers something into his ear. Later, when a nurse arrives, she sees his bed empty and the window open. ("And they found the stone rolled away from the tomb, but when they entered, they did not find the body."—Luke 24:2–3)

Superman flies to the bedside of his sleeping son and imparts the words we heard Jor-El speak when the film began ("The son becomes the father and the father the son"). Lois begins work on an essay called "Why the World Needs Superman." Superman flies up through the atmosphere, throws the camera a Christopher Reeve smile, and disappears. Credits.

A Hugely Successful Failure

Superman Returns opened amid a flurry of hype—television specials, figures, collectibles, Burger King toys; DC produced a tie-in novelization written by Marv Wolfman and a comic adaptation written by Martin Pasko, drawn by Matt Haley. To reach the widest audience possible, marketing efforts covered the waterfront: the Red Bull Formula One Racing team wore Superman jumpsuits, while the gay-interest magazine the *Advocate* featured Routh's Superman on the cover and asked readers "How Gay Is Superman?"

The film, which cost $209 million to produce, made a record-setting amount of money (more than $84 million) in its first five days but experienced a steep drop in its second weekend, with the opening of *Pirates of the Caribbean: Dead Man's Chest* and *The Devil Wears Prada*.

Ultimately, *Superman Returns* grossed $391 million at the global box office and became the sixth highest grossing film in the United States in 2006.

The studio, however, needed such a hugely expensive film to make at least twice its budget—and had, in fact, hoped for a final take closer to $500 million. In October 2006, Singer signed a deal with Warner Bros. to direct a sequel, promising to cut the budget and provide a more action-packed story; in the press, he likened his planned follow-up to *Star Trek II: The Wrath of Khan*. Preproduction work began on a film that would feature Brainiac and the crystal continent that Superman had hurled into space—now an asteroid that had taken up an orbit between Mars and Jupiter.

After a prolonged series of delays, however, Singer left to pursue other projects, and Warner Bros. permitted Routh's option to expire, then decided to reboot the franchise from scratch.

The film's critical reaction had been generally favorable but muted. Many noted its somber, even depressive tone (Roger Ebert called it "glum"), its languorous pace, its lumpy Christian allegory. Writers who had grappled with the Man of Steel themselves were blunt: Kevin Smith referred to it as "boring" and "whiny emo Superman"; Mark Millar noted that had he written the movie, Superman wouldn't have spent the last twenty minutes of it in bed.

The film does get several things right. The space-plane sequence is literally spectacular, the super-feats dazzle, and Routh projects a kind of essential decency—and, yes, squareness—that fits the role nicely. The Lois-Superman flight scene bookends their relationship poignantly, suffused as it is with true regret and palpable sadness, and although Spacey's Luthor flirts with camp, he brings home something closer to playfulness.

Yet the scene in which Superman uses his powers to eavesdrop on the woman he loves—a woman who has embraced a new and fulfilling life without him—is at once both achingly, relatably human and creepy as all get-out. It's also true that the cinematic debt the film owes to Richard Donner is deep—so deep it becomes impossible to feel Singer's presence, making the film a murky, frequently redundant exercise. Luthor's real-estate scheme is too familiar, and what little action Parker Posey's Kitty is given simply apes the similarly nonexistent narrative arc of Valerie Perrine's Miss Teschmacher.

Yet there is a much larger and more critical problem at the core of *Superman Returns*: even before the film begins, we are asked to accept the notion that Superman—the most selfless of all selfless heroes, the living avatar of altruism—would abandon us for selfish reasons.

In other words: you will believe a man can flake.

The Man of Steel's persona and power-set have continually evolved over the decades, but at the character's heart, two tenets have not changed at all since *Action Comics* #1: First, he puts the needs of others over those of himself, and, second, he does not give up. Everything else—the suit, the hair-squiggle, the big red S—is an outward signifier, not who he is.

Spider-Man? Sure. Spider-Man would abandon Manhattan in a New York minute; over the years, he often has. Superman would not. He *could* not.

Superman Returns is interested in exploring what happens when a hero lets us down but never provides an emotionally satisfactory answer for *why* he let us down in the first place. His departure is treated as a mere story point, the means by which the film sets itself in motion and distances Superman from humanity. We don't see him making the choice to leave, so the pain—literal and emotional—he experiences in its aftermath never manages to land with the force it should. We spend two hours watching him get punished for a crime we didn't see him commit, and that crime hangs in the air, interposing itself between us and the story.

Making compelling drama out of an iconic, do-gooder character such as Superman is and always will be difficult; his weaknesses are physical and not emotional in nature—he exists as an ideal, and ideals don't have base, selfish desires and ugly secrets for writers to exploit.

Batman broods; Superman does not. In fact, the closest he can get to angst is self-recrimination; he wants always to do more, to save everybody. The most memorable Superman stories in any medium are those that examine and exploit that altruistic motivation and depict what happens when he is forced to confront his own limitations. In making *Superman Returns*, however, Singer and his screenwriters attempted to subvert that core principle and graft a selfish motivation onto the psyche of a character who fundamentally rejects it.

It didn't take.

The Donner Party

Superman Returns deliberately never left Richard Donner's long stylistic shadow, and in the December 2006 issue of *Action Comics* (#844), Donner's presence was felt even more directly, when writer

Geoff Johns (who had served as Donner's assistant, years earlier) invited him to coscript a comic book story arc, with art by Adam Kubert.

"Last Son" introduces the three Kryptonian criminals from the first two Superman films into comics continuity for the first time. (Several versions of General Zod had cropped up in the comics as far back as 1961, including a solar-powered Russian dictator, but this Zod was clearly the film version.) It also introduces a plot twist that owes a great deal to Singer's *Superman Returns*—a ten-year-old superpowered Kryptonian boy.

The boy arrives on Earth in a meteor; Superman is delighted to welcome a fellow Kryptonian but becomes concerned when the government shows interest in the boy. He takes the youth—called Lor-Zod—from their custody and asks Batman to help set him up with a secret identity: Chris Kent.

Clark, Lois, and Chris set up house, with the couple considering adopting the boy, just as his true parents—revealed to be General Zod and Ursa—arrive on Earth in similar meteor-ships, along with Zod's hulking, mute assistant Non. Zod manages to dispatch Superman to the Phantom Zone, while he and an army of Zone escapees take over the Earth. Superman escapes and secures the help of Lex Luthor to return the prisoners to the Zone. The boy—who rejects the name his cruel parents gave him and calls himself Chris Kent—is forced to return to the Zone himself, to ensure that the barrier between dimensions remains intact.

The five-issue story line was beset by delays—the final chapter didn't arrive until the July 2008 *Action Comics* annual—which led to considerable continuity problems both within and without the *Action* title. Yet Christopher Kent would become an important figure in subsequent story lines and offered writers—and readers—a glimpse of something not seen since the *Saga of the Super-Sons*, something only touched on in the final minutes of *Superman Returns*: Superman as Dad of Steel.

Caviling over Continuity

Infinite Crisis had wiped away the old comics continuity, including the Super-origin. A new title, *Superman: Confidential*, was launched in January 2007 to fill in bits of Superman's backstory. The series, by a rotating staff of writers and artists, led off with a story line by Darwyn Cooke and drawn by Tim Sale. During the course of its brief, fourteen-issue run, *Superman: Confidential* featured a young Superman still learning his powers, discovering kryptonite, and meeting other DC characters for the first time.

Such half-measures didn't appease fans who missed the tight, internecine continuity of the "triangle number" era—when a single story line extended through four and sometimes five different Superman titles; they grew increasingly restless. On message boards and websites, they picked over gnomic pronouncements from DC writers and editors, including executive editor Dan DiDio, who would often contradict one another on just what was to be considered "in-canon" in the "New Earth" continuity.

Was Waid's *Birthright* now the official Super-origin or is Byrne's *Man of Steel* still correct? "Yes. No. There have been slight changes."

If the "pocket universe" no longer exists, did Superman ever execute those three Phantom Zone criminals? "Wait and see."

Writer Kurt Busiek told fans that the post–*Infinite Crisis* DC Universe was in flux, and that all of the stories people loved—the origin, the death, every aspect of lore so prized by fans—*had* happened in some form but now existed only in the half-formed landscape of ideas. Readers would get the "official" version of past events only when some future Superman writer wrote a story about them.

Some fans accepted this proposition; others threw up their hands at what they considered a wholesale abandonment of the intricately wrought history they so prized and bemoaned DC's increasing reliance on one-shot stories, gimmicks, and bloated crossover events.

Speaking of which, rumors began to surface that still another "crisis" loomed on the horizon—one that threatened to wipe out even this newly established continuity, howsoever amorphous and murky it appeared.

Final (No, *Seriously*) Crisis

A sprawling, seven-issue miniseries written by Grant Morrison and illustrated by a series of different artists pitted Jack Kirby's Darkseid against humanity and the heroes who defend it. *Final Crisis* began by killing off DC's perennial second-stringer J'onn J'onzz, the Martian Manhunter. (For a couple of years, anyway.)

What began as a simple super-whodunit devolved, in the acetyl-choline chemical bath of Morrison's imagination, into a trippy, hard-to-follow riot of dream logic and meta-symbols.

Darkseid and his minions infiltrate Earth and possess the bodies of various humans to unleash the Anti-Life Equation, which destroys hope, enslaves humanity, and remakes the world according to Darkseid's will.

Part of this plot involves bombing the *Daily Planet* office, which leaves Lois Lane in critical condition. In the two-issue tie-in title *Final Crisis: Superman Beyond 3D* (which came with a gimmicky pair of 3-D glasses), Superman travels to an interdimensional realm where the fifty-two universes that arose in the wake of the *Infinite Crisis* two years earlier are bleeding together. There, amid a clot of particularly impenetrable Morrisonian metaphysical digressions and narrative tics (higher dimensions, stories as spells that "create" life, and so on) Superman meets an army of alternate-reality Supermen.

Meanwhile, in a tie-in book called *Final Crisis: Legion of 3 Worlds*, by writer Geoff Johns and artist George Perez (who drew the original *Crisis on Infinite Earths* some twenty-one years earlier), the villain Superboy-Prime returns. In the time-spanning three-issue series, three different Legions of Super-Heroes came together—the original, pre-1986 iteration, which had included Superboy as a member; the version chronicled in the years following the *Crisis*, after Byrne's reboot wiped Superboy from continuity; and a third version recently introduced by Mark Waid. Alongside Superman—and a resurrected Conner Kent, aka the clone Superboy—they fought Superboy-Prime. In the process, they learned that "Prime" was destined to become one of the Legion's classic age-old foes, the Time Trapper.

In the wake of *Infinite Crisis* and its central "Superboy-Prime batters at a dimensional barrier and alters reality" plot device, the notion had become a rueful joke among readers. When fans on message boards would ask about a particularly confusing piece of DC Universe history, some wag would invariably reply, "Because Superboy punched a wall."

Johns, in a knowing wink to this growing meme, ends *Final Crisis: Legion of 3 Worlds* by having Superboy-Prime slug his future villainous self, an act that winks both him and the Time Trapper out of existence. In fact, the punch merely sends Superboy-Prime back to Earth-Prime. In Johns' howlingly on-the-nose coda, we see Superboy-Prime in his parents' basement, surrounded by comic books (including *Legion of 3 Worlds*), and logging on to the DC Comics message boards to complain, vowing to return and destroy Conner Kent, the "impostor" Superboy. From mass-murdering villain to message-board troll—the line, in Johns' mind, was perilously thin.

In the seventh and final issue of *Final Crisis*, Superman secures a machine capable of turning thoughts into reality. There, he counters Darkseid's Anti-Life Equation. With . . . song? "The worlds of the multiverse *vibrate* together, Darkseid," he says, "and make this . . . *sound*, like an *orchestra*. *Everything's* just *vibrations*, really. And *counter-vibrations* that *cancel them out*."

Superman then sings a four-note melody that destroys Darkseid and, using the solar energy stored in his cells, powers the "Miracle Machine." With it, he summons versions of himself from across the multiverse—including a Super-bunny named Captain Carrot and a Superman whose secret identity is President Barack Obama—to defeat the true architect of Darkseid's scheme, a galactic vampire named Mandraak. Superman returns to Lois's side and helps nurture her back to health.

Super-President

The conflation of the Man of Steel with Barack Obama was more than just a throwaway gag; Morrison was picking up on something in the zeitgeist. In the run-up to the 2008 U.S. presidential election, comic-book artist Alex Ross painted a portrait he called "Time for a Change," which depicted Obama ripping open his shirt to reveal a stylized O. Within days, bootleg versions of the image began to appear on T-shirts in street vendor stalls across the country. In one of the presidential campaign's most e-mailed photos, candidate Obama struck the familiar fists-on-hips pose standing before the Superman statue in Metropolis, Illinois.

On October 16, 2008, Obama joked at the 63rd Annual Alfred E. Smith Memorial Foundation Dinner: "Contrary to the rumors that you've heard, I was not born in a manger. I was actually born on Krypton, and sent here by my father Jor-El to save the planet Earth." He was greeted with polite laughter.

Four years and still another DC Universe reboot later, Morrison would return to and further explore the Obama-as-Superman notion in *Action Comics*, although at a slant: in *Action* #9, he introduced the Superman of Earth-23, who was secretly Calvin Ellis, the first black president of that Earth's United States.

That Kan-Dor Spirit

Although the constant slate-clearing of comic-book events such as DC's endless *Crises* wearies readers, it can't be denied that the reintroduction of long-established story elements into a freshly rebooted continuity offers readers who are willing to embrace it a highly specialized thrill unique to superhero comics, a feeling akin to stepping out onto a vast field of untouched, new-fallen snow. And back in the Superman monthly titles, there was still one classic villain who hadn't yet put in his new, post–*Infinite Crisis* appearance: Brainiac. That changed in August 2008 with *Action Comics* #866, written by Geoff Johns, with art by Gary Frank. The two had previously teamed on an *Action* story arc that reintroduced the Legion of Super-Heroes to Superman continuity. In that series, as in this new story line, Frank had flatly rejected the cartoony, hypermuscular style favored by previous artists such as Ed McGuinness.

Instead, Frank returned to a photorealistic style reminiscent of Neal Adams. He went considerably further than that, in fact, and consciously based his Superman's look—everything from facial expressions to the fit of the costume—on the late Christopher Reeve. Where other artists' Supermen can seem to shimmer with a raw, muscular, otherworldly power, Frank's Superman instead radiates an utterly human warmth and compassion.

The Brainiac reintroduced in the eponymous *Action Comics* story line is a deliberate throwback to the Silver Age "living computer" iteration, and he's up to his old Weisinger-era tricks: shrinking cities and putting them into bottles to hoard their information. Johns introduced a zealous greed to the character's makeup: After this Brainiac collects a city, he destroys the planet it came from, to ensure that he and only he will retain its data.

It's this greed that motivates him to seek out and attack Superman. In the reordered, post–*Infinite Crisis* reality, we learn, Brainiac shrank the Kryptonian city of Kandor, as before—but

Superman never restored it to normal size. To this new/old Brainiac, the existence of a Kryptonian outside of the bottle he has stored on his spaceship could not be tolerated.

In the ensuing battle, the evil computer manages to shrink and bottle Metropolis. To rescue his home city, Superman boards Brainiac's ship and finds thousands of bottled cities, including Metropolis, Kandor, and Argo—the birthplace of Supergirl. He stops Brainiac and manages to return Metropolis to its crater mere seconds before it reverts to its normal size. Just as he reaches his Fortress of Solitude, the merged Kryptonian cities begin to grow, creating "New Kandor" on Earth—home to some one hundred thousand superpowered Kryptonians. Meanwhile, the remorseless villain Brainiac fires a remote-control missile at the Kent farm.

Jonathan Kent pushes his wife, Martha, out of the missile's path, but their farm is destroyed in the blast. Jonathan suffers a heart attack and dies before Superman can reach his side. (The cover of the Brainiac story line's fourth chapter [*Action* #869, November 2008] originally depicted Clark and Jonathan Kent leaning on a fence at the Kent farm and chatting, beers in hand. DC editorial decided that even in 2008, the Man of Steel should remain a tee-totaler and changed the beers to bottles of "Soda Pop" before the issue hit the stands.)

New Krypton

In the October 2008 one-shot comic *Superman: New Krypton Special* #1, the Man of Steel's joy at finding fellow Kryptonians gets swiftly tempered by hard realities: Earth's governments are worried about the potential threat posed by one hundred thousand beings with the power of Superman, and the Kryptonians reject Superman's offers to help them acclimate to life on Earth and cannot understand why he prizes Earth culture over their own. In addition, many of the New Kryptonians remain loyal to the imprisoned General Zod.

In the ten-part "New Krypton" story line that snakes throughout *Action*, *Superman*, and *Supergirl*, the New Kryptonians pardon and release Zod and the rest of the Phantom Zone prisoners, Supergirl is reunited with her parents Zor-El and Alura, and Superman finds himself caught in the middle as tensions escalate between humans and Kryptonians. Lois's father, General Sam Lane, secretly engineers the assassination of New Krypton's leader—Zor-El. Alura then seizes control of New Krypton's government and, following a violent confrontation with Earth's hero community, uses Kryptonian technology to fly the city of New Kandor into space—where it settles into an orbit directly opposite that of Earth's, on the other side of the sun.

A Change of Address

The conclusion of the "New Krypton" story line was only the beginning of a grand experiment entered into by all titles in the Superman line. For more than a year, Superman as we knew him would not appear in any of the Superman books.

It was a stunt, yes—only the latest attempt by DC writers and editors to demonstrate the value of their flagship character by denying readers the familiar pleasure of his company for an extended period of time. This time out, however, instead of dying as the result of a hastily devised threat or having his appearance and power-set radically altered for mysterious and narratively opaque reasons, the Superman writers and editors worked to ground the Man of Steel's departure firmly in ongoing story lines.

In the twelve-issue miniseries *World of New Krypton* (March 2009–March 2010), Superman decides to accept Alura's offer to live on New Krypton among his people and renounce Earth altogether. On the surface, of course, the decision to abandon Earth is the very same one the character makes in Bryan Singer's *Superman Returns*, but where the film left it to us to guess at Superman's motivations (which flatly contradict the character's essential selflessness), *World of New Krypton* writers Greg Rucka and James Robinson are careful to demonstrate that it's altruism that drives Superman's decision to leave. Alura has freed the tyrant General Zod from the Phantom Zone and placed him in charge of New Krypton's military. Fearing what havoc Zod might unleash against Earth, not to mention against his own people, Superman relocates to New Krypton and joins the military to keep a close eye on a man he has learned is too dangerous to trust. During the course of the series, Superman (who goes by Kal on New Krypton) and Zod work together to uncover a conspiracy to pit Earth and New Krypton against each other.

Meanwhile, in the pages of *Action Comics* and *Superman*, the "World without Superman" story line (May 2009–March 2010) lived up to its name. *Superman* followed the adventures of Mon-El, the superpowered hero from planet Daxam whom Superman had tasked with protecting Metropolis in his absence. In *Action Comics*, two Kryptonians, Chris Kent (now grown to young manhood) and Thara Ak-Var, scoured the Earth looking for Zod's Kryptonian sleeper agents.

The disparate story lines finally come together with the three-issue miniseries *Last Stand of New Krypton* (March–April 2010), which finds Brainiac attempting to shrink and bottle the space colony. After more than a year of wearing only a Kryptonian military uniform, Superman once again dons the familiar red-and-blue super-suit and joins forces with Zod to defeat Brainiac. Once the living computer's threat is ended, however, Zod and his army attack Earth (*War of the Supermen*, June–July 2010) in a five-issue series written by James Robinson and Sterling Gates, filled with high stakes and summer-blockbuster set pieces: New Krypton is destroyed by a living atomic bomb; seventy-three thousand New Kryptonians die violently in space as Lex Luthor turns the sun red, robbing them of their powers; hundreds of Earth cities are wiped out by the seven thousand New Kryptonians who remain. Finally, Superman succeeds in sending Zod and the rest of the remaining New Kryptonians back to the Phantom Zone for good (Chris Kent once again sacrifices his own freedom to ensure that his biological father remains imprisoned, alongside Mon-El).

As before, only Superman, Supergirl, and Krypto are all that remain of Krypton on Earth (plus, Superman's Earth-made clone, Superboy).

The sprawling New Krypton story lines were a concerted attempt to shake up the Superman status quo by removing the character from his superhero trappings and ensconcing him, however briefly, in the realm of pure science fiction. Asking readers to engage with the sudden influx of new characters who were necessary to tell these stories was risky, and plot lines became murkier and more overwrought as the year progressed (*Action Comics'* "Nightwing and Flamebird" arc, for example, combined its star-crossed love story with a nearly lethal dose of mystical Kryptonian hokum), but it was a bold move in a genre not known for it, and its genesis and execution remained firmly rooted in storytelling, not mere gimmickry.

And even if, during Superman's extended time off Earth and out of the tights, readers pined for Superman Classic, a six-issue miniseries that premiered in November 2009 was serving him up in spades.

Origin, All Over Again

There was no question about it: the cycle was speeding up.

Seventeen years had passed between John Byrne's *Man of Steel* and Mark Waid's *Superman: Birthright*. Yet now, just six years after *Birthright*, Superman's handlers decided it was once again time to reinterpret Superman's origin "for the twenty-first century" (the fact that *Superman: Birthright* had been published in 2003 made that choice of words particularly unfortunate).

The twin reality-shattering *Crises* of the previous three years— that is, the nagging tendency of the DC Universe to hit its own reset button with increasing frequency—had forced their hand. Readers who fretted over which parts of Superman's origin were still canonical were told that the erstwhile *Action Comics* team of Geoff Johns and Gary Frank had been tapped to create the definitive, no-seriously, this-time-we-mean-it, origin.

What they produced was anything but a radical revision of existing Super-lore—they simply hit many of the familiar story beats that writers had been duly hitting since 1938. What set *Secret Origin* apart, however, was its perspective. As the *Smallville* television series had done, Johns and Frank place the reader inside young Clark's head; he learns his history alongside the reader. That means no establishing shots of Krypton—no "I tell you Krypton is *doomed*!" speechifying, no rocket-ship flight to Earth, no amazing orphanage super-feats. Instead, *Secret Origin* opens with a Kansas boy trying to make sense of the fact that his best friend broke his arm when attempting to tackle him in a pickup game of football.

By pushing the Krypton aspects of the origin to the background in favor of a story that focuses on Clark's dawning sense of horror at what his powers can do, *Secret Origin* quickly becomes a Superman story with a beating, secular humanist heart.

In the series' first issue, Johns creates a young Superman who is something that was once anathema to DC Comics—a reluctant hero. Young Clark desperately wishes to belong but must make excuses not to join his friends in roughhousing. When kissed by Lana Lang, his heat vision suddenly manifests (heh) and nearly burns down the school.

Yet for all of the panels showing a despondent, moody Clark Kent—when his adopted parents first show him the spaceship in which he arrived on Earth, for example, he violently rejects the pre-recorded holographic greeting of his Kryptonian parents—this is no "whiny, emo Superman." Johns is careful to show that what's behind Clark's moping is that which is most essential about him: his concern for others. And when Clark rescues Lana from a tornado by flying her out of its path, Johns and Frank show us, for the first time, real joy in his features. Here is a young man discovering that he loves helping people, that he has the *means* to help people—and that he needs to do it more.

Tellingly, it's Martha Kent who comes up with the idea for a costume (made, in classic form, from his baby blankets), based on the rocket's holographic visions of lost Krypton.

> Martha: We don't know much about where you come from,
>   but I want us to embrace your *heritage* together.
> Clark (worried): But what if it's a bad place?
> Jonathan: If it gave us you, Clark, it can't be that bad.

The approach inverts Waid's *Birthright*, which had taken pains to show that the Kryptonian side to Clark Kent was central to the character. Yet *Birthright* had inverted Byrne's *Man of Steel*, which posited that Superman was just a public "pose." And *that* series had famously reversed the original Siegel conception of Clark Kent as a mere disguise.

Subsequent issues clarified a notion that had been part of the Superman mythos even before the John Byrne reboot: the Clark/Superman dichotomy was not and had never been as clear-cut as it seemed on the surface. The truth was slightly more nuanced. There was Superman (the hero), *Daily Planet* Clark (the pose), and a third persona—Smallville Clark, the "true," self: Clark when no one is looking.

Readers learned that Lex and Clark had known each other in Smallville, but (much like *Birthright*'s Lex) the villain was too self-absorbed to remember. Lex's motivation—jealousy over the public's fawning admiration of the alien Superman—remains intact. Clark meets the Legion of Super-Heroes and comes to feel part of a community of individuals like himself, meets Lois Lane and finds himself strongly attracted to her, and encounters the Parasite and Metallo for the first time.

Superman: Secret Origin didn't change the game, but it clarified some of its rules, while leaving large stretches of Superman's backstory open for future investigation.

Grounded

The issue of *Superman* cover-dated August 2010 was the comic's 700th. The team behind the "New Krypton" story line wrapped it up with a romantic reunion between Superman and Lois Lane, complete with a "Can You Read My Mind?"–inspired flight over nighttime Metropolis. In the same issue, noted writer J. Michael Straczynski and penciler Eddy Barrows offered a prologue to their planned twelve-issue story line called "Grounded," which would proceed to take the Man of Steel on a ham-fisted and cringeworthy walkabout across the United States.

Exiting a congressional committee where he has been questioned about his loyalties in the wake of the New Krypton episode, Superman is confronted with a phalanx of reporters who bluntly exposit that Superman has "lost touch" with humanity. Suddenly, he is struck across the face by a tearful woman who lost her husband to an inoperable brain tumor while Superman was off saving the planet. "You could have *seen* it with your X-ray vision," she says. "*You* could have *killed* the tumor with your heat vision without harming the surrounding tissue. But you weren't there."

Straczynski is arguably onto something here—it's certainly conceivable that Superman would feel guilt over not being able to save a single human life, and that guilt would inspire a bout of soul-searching. Yet the notion that he would embark on a year-long cross-country trek to find "the real America" and that such an uncharacteristically self-indulgent vision quest could be sparked, even in part, by an unhinged woman demanding to know why he wasted time saving the entire population of the planet from destruction when he should instead hang out a shingle and practice freelance super-oncology is laughable.

What follows is a series of nobly intentioned but clumsily exe-cuted one-off tales in which Superman visits a different American city and confronts some social issue or another. In issue 705's (January 2011) encounter with a victim of child abuse, for example, Straczynski wallows in a particularly manipulative form of bathos. Stories improved once Straczynski abruptly left the book, forcing DC to hire writer Chris Robinson to see the woefully wrong-headed premise through to its merciful end.

"Hipster Superman?"

On Monday, October 25, 2010, the comic-book Superman found his way back into the mainstream news cycle for the first time in years. The *New York Post* ran an item about a standalone graphic novel called *Superman: Earth One*, about a twenty-year-old Clark Kent sporting a hoodie, low-cut jeans, and a Justin Bieber bob. Outlet after outlet took the "They're Changing Superman into a Hipster!" bait. Many seized the opportunity to make hacky hipster jokes, such as "Will the Fortress of Solitude become a Williamsburg co-op?"

What got lost in the hype is what always gets lost when main-stream media outlets deign to tackle superhero comics: context. Few of the resulting stories bothered to note that the graphic novel—by J. Michael Straczynski and artist Shane Davis—was not meant to become part of the much-fretted-over "canon."

That said, *Superman: Earth One* was a solid boy-becomes-a-man (of steel) story. If its flashbacks featuring Jonathan Kent imparting fatherly wisdom felt hokey and homespun, well, they were supposed to. As for the sundry visual elements (hoodie, haircut) that had touched off the media fury, they were the contributions of Davis, whose line work is furiously detailed in a way that opens the page up instead of weighing it down, and who knows how to deliver a Super-pose that seems fresh and iconic when the situation calls for it.

Ultimately, all of the media hand-wringing about a "Hipster-of-Steel" was unfair. Because, after all, it could have been a lot worse than a hoodie. They could have had him sporting a porkpie hat. Or, shudder to think, a quirky mustache.

Meanwhile, in *Action Comics*, writer Paul Cornell and penciler Pete Woods were taking advantage of Superman's peripatetic inter-state therapy session to unleash a humorous and highly entertaining story arc focusing on Lex Luthor, his trusty Lois Lane robot, and a quest for power that takes Superman's greatest foe to the farthest villainous corners of the DC Universe. That story line wrapped up in *Action Comics* #900 (June 2011), which included a nine-page short story that propelled the Man of Steel back into the mainstream news cycle—but this time in a highly charged, politicized manner.

The Un-American Way

The story, called "The Incident," by *The Dark Knight* co-screenwriter David S. Goyer and artist Miguel Sepulveda, features Superman discussing his recent activity with the U.S. national security adviser at Camp David. The official demands that Superman explain why he flew into Tehran and stood in solidarity with thousands of Iranians protesting their government.

Goyer gives the Man of Steel dialogue that could have been lifted from Straczynski's good-hearted but clumsy "Grounded" story line:

> As a *Super-Hero*, as Metropolis' *protector*, I've fought just about every threat *imaginable*: Alien invaders, time-traveling despots, rogues with every kind of *costume* and *gimmick* you can think of. I'm *good* when it comes to fighting apocalyptic threats. But the everyday *degradations* that humans suffer? Dying of *thirst*? *Hunger*? People being denied their basic *human rights*? I've never been very *effective* at stopping things like that. And I *want* to be. So I showed up in *solidarity*. . . . It was an act of *civil disobedience*. *Nonviolent resistance*.

Informed that his actions have created an international incident, Superman tells the official that he intends to speak before the UN and renounce his U.S. citizenship.

> I'm tired of having my *actions* construed as instruments of *US policy*. "Truth, Justice and the *American* Way"—it's not *enough* anymore. The world's too *small*. Too *connected*. When I *look* at you, I see you in *every spectrum*. I can see the microscopic *demodex mites* that live in your *eyelashes*. The precancerous *mole* on your left cheek that you probably think is *just* a mole. The halo of *electromagnetic radiation* leaking from your *smart-phone*. I'm an *alien*. . . . Born on *another world*. I can't help but see the *big picture*.

The website ComicsAlliance broke the story of Superman's announcement, careful to note that the position represented at most a pivot away from the long-established notion that Superman was a citizen of the world, having been granted citizenship in every country in the United Nations.

Nevertheless, the "news" was picked up by mainstream media such as the *New York Times* and *Time* magazine, as well as conservative outlets like the *Drudge Report* and the *O'Reilly Factor*, which devoted a segment to the question of Superman's loyalties. Notably, these reports failed to mention that Clark Kent would remain a U.S. citizen, or that Superman's decision wasn't intended as a refutation of American policies or the country's direction (the Marvel character Captain America had given up his patriotic role for those reasons, in the 1970s). Then presidential candidate Mike Huckabee publicly lamented Superman's decision, tying it to what he saw as a regrettable trend of Americans apologizing for being Americans.

Eventually, the media outrage died down, as it must, and the Superman of the comics finally made his long-overdue return to classic superhero adventuring. In *Action Comics*, it was Old Home Week, as a story line called "Reign of the Doomsdays" brought back the hulking beast—several versions of him, in fact—and the Eradicator for a pitched battle involving Superboy, Steel, and the Cyborg Superman.

It was a fitting farewell gathering of characters who'd first appeared in the "Death of Superman" story line nineteen years earlier. Fitting, because *Action Comics* ended publication with its October 2011 issue (#904), and *Superman* was canceled the same month, with issue #714.

In fact, every DC title was canceled. Fifty-two different comics—including *Action Comics* and *Superman*—would begin again the following month, with new creative teams, new numbering (starting from scratch with fifty-two simultaneous #1s), and an entirely new DC Universe to chronicle.

That's right. With the November 2011 issues, the entire DC Universe underwent—still yet again—another profound, from-the-ground-up reality-altering reboot. Everything that had been established in 1986 and again in 2006 and again in 2008 was wiped out; they were starting over.

DC called it "The New 52." They had the decency, at least, not to call it a *Crisis*.

Flashpoint

The old DC Universe went out just the way it had come in: with a multi-issue crossover event that spawned tie-in stories by the cubic ton. The net result: the company's three lines of comics—the main DC superhero books, the line of mature-audience Vertigo comics, and a line of creator-owned books with its own separate continuity called Wildstorm—merged together, and the DC Universe was changed.

This was no organic narrative evolution, this was a coolly corporate decision rooted in branding meetings and discussions of new audiences and cross-platform synergy. Once again, DC Comics decided that it knew why its heroes weren't appealing to readers outside the increasingly shrinking audience of hard-core fans: they weren't accessible.

All of that history, all of those stories, were much too confusing, they decided. What was needed was a bold attempt to secure new readers by completely clearing the superhero slate and starting anew. At the same time, DC set out to diversify its offerings, rounding out the capes-and-cowls comics with horror comics, war comics, Western comics, and so on. While DC executives were at it, they made minor tweaks to their standing roster of pale male heroes to make it look a bit less like a Harold Bloom syllabus.

In hyping the reboot, DC executives took to the airwaves to remind potential readers that their goal was to "remove the barriers" that kept people from reading—or even sampling—their superhero comics. They had their talking points prepared:

- You say you can't make sense out of decades of complicated continuity? We're starting from square one.
- You say you're unfamiliar with these characters? Herewith, fifty-two different jumping-on points.
- You say you'd prefer to read about three-dimensional women and people of color? Meet Batwoman! She's a lesbian! And Mr. Terrific! A black dude!

In a press release, DC described the rebooted Justice League—the first of the "New 52" comics to launch, which would feature

Superman, Batman, Wonder Woman, and others meeting one another for the first time—as "younger, angrier, more brash, and more modern."

DC proudly noted that the Superman who would be appearing in November 2011's *Action Comics* #1 would be a "younger, more brooding" version. As if this weren't enough to stoke existential dread among the change-averse hard-core Superman fanbase, the first image of the New 52 Superman appeared online.

They took his trunks. Dear God in heaven, *they took the guy's red swim trunks.*

A Hot Dog—an Armored Hot Dog

The new Superman costume—created by DC Comics copublisher Jim Lee and very much in keeping with the design aesthetic that drew him fame in the 1990s—is, essentially, metallic-blue armor. The chest plate is topped by a high, priestlike collar; a new network of seams, or possibly piping, describes puzzling arcs across the torso, around the shoulders, and over the thighs. His boots remain red but seem heavier and overdesigned; his chest emblem is embossed, recalling that of Brandon Routh's *Superman Returns* outfit, and he wears a red, stylized, chunky belt—for no readily discernible reason, because there are no red trunks to hold up. A more basic question— why an invulnerable Kryptonian would wear armor in the first place—went unaddressed. (Eventually—in issue 7 of the relaunched *Action Comics*—readers learn the origin of the New 52 Super-armor: it's thought-sensitive Kryptonian formalwear that Superman liberates from Brainiac's collection.)

DC announced that the two main titles in its "New 52" Superman line would follow different time lines. *Superman*, with George Perez providing story and art, would be set in the present day, five years after Superman first went public in the DC Universe. *Action Comics*, written by Grant Morrison, with art by Rags Morales, would be set in the past, shortly after Superman's first appearance in Metropolis. (Superman would also make sporadic appearances in two other books, *Supergirl* and *Superboy*.)

To date, the relaunched *Superman* title has proved an odd, curiously downbeat book. Although Perez drew the title (issues 1–4, November 2011–February 2012), his characteristic everything-but-the-kitchen-sink dynamic style resulted in pages that seem merely cluttered, which he weighed down further with dense thickets of dialogue and exposition. Even after he handed the writing chores off to Dan Jurgens and Keith Giffen (Jurgens eventually assumed the art duties as well), the book remains remarkably morose in tone.

The *Daily Planet* has merged with the Galaxy Broadcasting System to become the Planet Global Network. Lois Lane now heads the PGN television and digital division, has a new boyfriend (the Lois and Clark marriage a casualty of the reboot), and harangues *Planet* reporter Clark Kent that "print is dying" and to get with the times.

Both Martha and Jonathan Kent are dead, in the New 52 DC Universe, and the *Superman* series seems interested in positioning the Man of Steel as an outcast, a loner. The people of Metropolis readily turn on him, and Clark Kent's unexplained absences are no longer jokingly dismissed by his closest friends, but instead engender in them feelings of resentment, isolating him from them even further.

Over in the relaunched *Action Comics*, however, Grant Morrison has dialed back his distinctive hyper-Jungian logorrhea to offer readers a remarkably clear glimpse of a young Superman as a Man of Still-Untempered Steel.

Action returns Superman to his literal and figurative beginnings. He has just arrived in Metropolis and taken up heroing. When the series begins, he wears only a blue T-shirt emblazoned with his S-emblem, a short red cape that looks to all the world like a bath towel, patched jeans, and workboots. Morales imbues this He-Man of Steel with a confidence—and an unapologetic, muscular sexuality—that carries notes of John Byrne, Joe Shuster—and Tom of Finland.

In Morrison's hands, this Superman is back to his Siegel-and-Shuster-era populism—he is a bully to bullies, a defender of the little guy. His first words, on page 1 of the first post-relaunch issue, after bursting into a meeting of crooked, wealthy businessmen: "Rats. Rats with money. And rats with guns. I'm your worst nightmare." And just before making his exit, chased by Metropolis cops: "You know the *deal*, Metropolis. Treat people *right* or expect a visit from *me*."

Morrison and Morales also recapture the rakish glint in the eye—the laughing-in-the-face-of-danger ebullience of the Siegel-and-Shuster era. This Superman is a smart-aleck with a bit of a swagger, armed only with the powers he had in his earliest adventures—able to leap an eighth of a mile.

As he did in *All-Star Superman*, Morrison engineers a frenetic mashup of every Superman era and incarnation. In *All-Star*, however, the shape of a closed narrative resulted in what felt like a synthesis of forms, a meta-Superman. Yet in *Action Comics'* ongoing, open-ended format, these constant, layered evocations of Superman Past seem merely clever (he hefts a crook over his head in an homage to Siegel, causing that crook to deliver a spoken-word rendition of the *Smallville* theme's chorus "Somebody! Save me!").

Yet clever, as employed here, *works*. His Luthor is a pudgy, snarky, energy-drink-quaffing super-scientist whose hatred of Superman is enriched by a tincture of very relatable body-conscious jealousy; over and above his distrust of aliens, Lex secretly wishes he had Superman's square jaw and abs of steel.

Morales provided an intriguing believability to the Superman/Clark distinction, having Clark completely alter his appearance by mussing his hair, wearing oversize clothes to hide his muscles, and sporting round Harry Potter, coke-bottle glasses that distort his features.

As the series progressed, Morrison reintroduced the expected elements—Metallo, Brainiac, Kandor, Metropolis, Jor-El, and Lara. In so doing, he carefully reinforced the character's essential touch points (issue 7, May 2012: "All of these people are under my protection, you got that? *Every living thing!*"; issue 8, June 2012: "I don't *stop*! *I don't give up!*"), while unceremoniously—but definitively—swatting others away:

When asked, "So, are you Clark pretending to be Superman, or is it the other way around?" Clark simply changes the subject.

EPILOGUE

MAN OF TOMORROW
(2013 AND BEYOND)

In 2008, Warner Bros., determined to restart the Superman film franchise from scratch, once again accepted pitches from a bevy of comic-book writers and screenwriters. Grant Morrison pitched an idea similar to his *All-Star Superman*. Mark Waid suggested a *Birthright*-inspired film. Director Matthew Vaughn worked with Mark Millar to plan an epic trilogy. Geoff Johns pitched an idea that keyed off *Secret Origin*; Brad Meltzer submitted an idea as well.

Ultimately, Warner Bros. decided to green-light a treatment from *Dark Knight* screenwriter David S. Goyer, produced by Christopher Nolan. Several directors, including Robert Zemeckis, Guillermo del Toro, Darren Aronofsky, and Tony Scott, were approached to helm the film, which would be called *Superman: Man of Steel*. In October 2010, the studio announced that Zack Snyder, the director of *300*, *Watchmen*, and *Sucker Punch*, would helm the film, which carried a projected budget of $175 million.

The decision signaled to both casual and hard-core fans of the character that *Man of Steel* would be no moody, languidly paced, Singerian take on the Superman legend. Snyder is a director of heavily stylized action, given to operatic, set-piece combat sequences that involve both slow- and accelerated-motion cinematography. Although many fans of the *Watchmen* graphic novel found Snyder's

2009 film adaptation a faithful interpretation of Alan Moore and Dave Gibbons' gimlet-eyed deconstruction of superhero tropes, the film was criticized for being so beholden to its source material as to seem lifeless and redundant. By the time the poorly received *Sucker Punch* arrived in theaters in 2011, the director had developed a reputation for creating visually dazzling but emotionally inert films that critics dismissed as big-screen video games.

Nevertheless, as casting news and production details began to leak out, anticipation mingled with dread in fans' hearts. Henry Cavill—an (gasp) Englishman!—won the role of Superman over Matthew Bomer. Amy Adams—a (horror!) redhead!—was tapped to play Lois Lane. Michael Shannon as General Zod; Russell Crowe as Jor-El; Kevin Costner and Diane Lane as Clark's foster parents; Laurence Fishburne as Perry White.

The first image of Cavill in costume as Superman hit the Internet on August 4, 2011, and unleashed the by now predictable, even inevitable round of cyber-*agita*. The nubbly neoprene one-piece bodysuit—sans belt, sans trunks—had its vocal critics, but few protested that the über-muscular Cavill didn't fill it out admirably.

One week before principal photography began (on August 1, 2011), Warner Bros. announced that the film, unofficially scheduled to open in December 2012, would be pushed back to 2013. Rumors blamed the usual too-many-cooks script problems for the delay, but spokespeople spun it as an attempt to release the film to coincide with the celebration of the character's seventy-fifth anniversary.

At this writing, the film is scheduled to open on June 14, 2013.

Superman at Seventy-Five

Snyder's film will succeed, or it will fail, or—most likely, like Singer's *Superman Returns* before it—it will manage to accomplish a bit of both. It doesn't matter; Superman will endure.

In the comics, writers and artists will continue to put the Man of Steel through his paces, constantly iterating and reiterating the same story beats and characters for an ever-shrinking audience of fans as the DC Universe will continue to undergo faster and faster cycles of eternal return. He will die and come back again—he started the vogue for it, after all. It doesn't matter; Superman will endure.

He will be pilloried and parodied, declared hokey and outdated, dismissed as adolescent tripe and a fascist wish dream. It doesn't matter; Superman will endure.

Superman will endure because that is what he does. It is what he is for. In his seventy-five years of fictive life, he has grown larger than the movies, the comics, the television programs, the radio shows, the novels, the video games, the action figures, the song lyrics, the Krypto-Ray guns, the Underoos, the Halloween costumes, the porn parodies, and the academic papers.

What will endure about him has nothing to do with his powers—they will change, waxing and waning as any given story requires.

His costume is not what is essential about him; it will change and change again. The red trunks? They'll be back. Ditto the cape and the forelock. The chest emblem will continue to evolve, dutifully reflecting the design aesthetic of the age.

Superman's persona is perhaps the single most fluid thing about him: in the hands of different writers, he will be paternalistic or fraternal, quippy or self-serious, empathetic or cold, as the needs of the story dictate.

What will endure about him is what he does: he helps others, and he doesn't give up.

He was the first and the best, and although one of his two creators was born in Toronto, he is powered by a uniquely American fuel mixture: part wish-fulfillment, part noble ideal, part garish hey-look-at-me spectacle.

Like us, he is a creature of immense strengths and surprising weaknesses. He's not the same guy he started out as, but who among us can say we are? He's been around for three-quarters of a century already, and, in some form, he'll be here for centuries to come, because no matter how much he changes on the outside, Superman will always speak to the most essential, the most hopeful, the most invulnerable part of us.

ACKNOWLEDGMENTS

I was flattered and surprised when Eric Nelson at Wiley tweeted me to ask if I'd be interested in writing a Superman biography for him; flattered because he said kind things about my NPR work and surprised because up to that moment I'd been using Twitter chiefly as a repository for dumb fish puns. (When the history of Twitter is written, this book should be counted as one example of a real-world project it has birthed, right up there with that Shatner sitcom.) Eric patiently helped me trim a massive and discursive manuscript into something more serviceable, and he let me keep the armored hot dog joke, so I owe him a great deal of thanks. I expect my hard-working copy editor, Lisa Burstiner, will remember the difference between "Mxyztplk" and "Mxyzptlk" for the rest of her days, poor woman. Daniel Greenberg and Monika Verma ably navigated the brackish waters of rights and percentages for me like old salts, and I am grateful.

Many people listened as I fretted endlessly over the book and its deadline; I am happy to say that their kind reassurances truly reassured. My *NPR Pop Culture Happy Hour* colleagues Trey Graham, Mike Katzif, and Jess Gitner heard more than their fair share of kvetching. It was by dropping Stephen Thompson's name that I secured an agent, so I thank him for lending it to me, just as I thank him for possessing the foresight and perspicacity to be born the son of the great and good Maggie Thompson. Maggie knows more about comics than God, and she's a lot more fun to talk to. She offered a friendly ear, a discerning eye, and sage counsel, in that order, when all three were sorely needed.

Should you ever need someone in your corner, pulling for you, assuring you that everything is going to be all right, you could do a hell of a lot worse than the ferociously funny Linda Holmes, who is freaking great at it. I only hope to return the favor one day.

Pal-for-life Chris Klimek was always up for a beer or six when I needed a break; he's a thoughtful critic who knows and loves Superman, so more than a few of his insights found their way into the book. Jack Danielson and Dawn Burton shared food, wine, and laughs throughout the process, which gave me everything I needed to keep going, and I am grateful to Laura Gardner for hosting me at her wonderful family home on Nantucket, where work on this book began. Thanks also to Maura Calsyn, Chris Calsyn, Jen Koide, and Jason Miller for periodically enticing me down from my garret with their excellent company. Nathan Englander and Chris Adrian were polite to let me whine to them about the travails of the writing life, a thing they both know a great deal more about than I do. Many writers I admire made their brains available for picking, and I thank them all (even those whose cerebella I didn't have time to access except through their work), but especially Craig Shutt, Danny Fingeroth, Tom De Haven, and Graeme McMillan. Larry Tye's exhaustive book on Superman came out the week after I'd turned in the manuscript, but I kept it by my side throughout the editing process so that it could serve as my ludicrously well-informed and voluble fact checker. It should go without saying, but I'll say it anyway, that I am profoundly indebted to the many writers, artists, editors, producers, filmmakers, and actors who have chronicled Superman's exploits over the years.

My brother and sister-in-law, Chip and Sue Weldon, offered encouragement and warm hospitality; my mother, Kay Weldon, unconditional support of the sort that makes a person feel invulnerable. The Nunez family of Miami—Faustino Sr., Maria, Addy, Maggie, and Fernando—is a source of cheer for which I am daily thankful. My late father, Don Weldon, showed me what a hero looks like. Mostly, I am deeply grateful to, and for, Faustino Nunez, who nobly suffered towering piles of books on the dining room table for a year, and who makes me a better man simply by association.

BIBLIOGRAPHY

Books

Beaty, Scott. *Superman: The Ultimate Guide to the Man of Steel*. New York: DK Publishing, 2002. A handy and attractive coffee-table guide to turn-of-the-millennium Super-lore.

Bowers, Scott. *Superman versus the Ku Klux Klan*. Washington, DC: National Geographic, 2012. An excellent history of the Klan and the *Superman* radio show's Operation: Tolerance efforts.

Cowsil, Alan, et al. *DC Comics Year by Year: A Visual Chronicle*. New York: DK Publishing, 2010. A useful, if booster-y, chronology of DC's output; great for placing developments in the Super-books in a wider context.

Daniels, Les. *Superman: The Complete History*. San Francisco: Chronicle Books, 1998. The first and still-definitive guide to the character's first sixty years. A clear-eyed, beautifully designed work.

De Haven, Tom. *It's Superman: A Novel*. New York: Ballantine Books, 2006. A great read; De Haven takes various tropes from the early years of Superman and deepens them with a novelist's attention to detail and character.

De Haven, Tom. *Our Hero: Superman on Earth*. New Haven, CT: Yale University Press, 2010. I love this book. A winning cross between personal essay and well-researched character history; De Haven's prose is funny, engaging, and wise. Reading it was like sharing a beer with a like-minded but smarter friend.

Dietrich, Brian D. *Krypton Nights: Poems*. Lincoln, NE: Zoo Press, 2002. I had to cut the reference to this book from the manuscript, but this is an intriguing and often very funny collection, worth checking out.

Dooley, Dennis, and Gary D. Engle, editors. *Superman at Fifty! The Persistence of a Legend*. Cleveland, OH: Octavia Press, 1987. I picked this book up in 1987, in the gift shop of the Superman exhibit at the Smithsonian Museum of American History. A solid collection of essays exploring various facets of the character.

Eury, Michael, editor. *The Krypton Companion*. Raleigh, NC: TwoMorrows Publishing, 2006. No better behind-the-scenes oral history of Silver and early Bronze

Age Superman comics exists; I relied heavily on Eury's interviews with various writers and artists.

Feiffer, Jules. *The Great Comic Book Heroes*. New York: Dial Press, 1965. Eight-year-old me devoured this book when I picked it up on a remainder table in 1976. The Golden Age adventures reprinted in it seemed a lot more violent and thrilling than the stuff on the stands at the time, and I delighted in Feiffer's hilariously honest, crotchety essay. That dog-eared copy lies on the table next to the laptop on which I'm typing. It's probably the single book I've returned to most often over the years.

Fingeroth, Danny. *Disguised as Clark Kent: Jews, Comics, and the Creation of the Superhero*. New York: Continuum, 2007. A great history of the comics industry, Superman, and superheroes in general and their connections to Jewish identity.

Fingeroth, Danny. *Superman on the Couch: What Superheroes Really Tell Us about Ourselves and Our Society*. New York: Continuum, 2004. A thoughtful, compelling, and well-argued treatise on the superhero's role in contemporary society that's also, not for nothing, a lot of fun to read.

Fleisher, Michael L. *The Great Superman Book*. New York: Warner Books, 1978. All hail Michael L. Fleisher, who accomplished a great deal more than simply chronicling the various villains and plot points of several decades' worth of Superman comics. I commend this book's marvelous entry on Superman to you, which contains some hard-won insights on who the character is and how he relates to the world.

Gabilliet, Jean-Paul. *Of Comics and Men: A Cultural History of American Comic Books*. Jackson: University Press of Mississippi, 2005. A more scholarly treatise, but one that's compulsively readable.

Greenberger, Robert, and Martin Pasko. *The Essential Superman Encyclopedia*. New York: Del Rey, 2010. Greenberger and Pasko take up the baton from Fleisher, bless 'em, cataloging the decades of comics lore that have come along since *The Great Superman Book* was first published.

Grossman, Gary. *Superman: Serial to Cereal*. New York: Popular Library, 1977. The first serious examination of the radio, movie serial, and television adventures of which I'm aware, and it's still definitive. I carried this thick blue paperback around with me for an entire summer at the age of nine.

Hajdu, David. *The Ten-Cent Plague: The Great Comic Book Scare and How It Changed America*. New York: Picador, 2008. If there's a better, fuller examination of the Fredric Wertham era in American popular culture, I haven't come across it.

Hayde, Michael J. *Flights of Fantasy: The Unauthorized but True Story of Radio and TV's Adventures of Superman*. Albany, NY: BearManor Media, 2009. The sections of my book that deal with the radio serial and the fifties television show are heavily indebted to this exhaustive, fact-filled history, along with Scivally's (see below).

Jacobs, Will, and Gerard Jones. *The Comic Book Heroes: From the Silver Age to the Present*. New York: Crown Publishers, 1985. An entertaining, well-written history of sixties and seventies comics, particularly good on the rise of Marvel.

Jones, Gerard. *Men of Tomorrow: Geeks, Gangsters and the Birth of the Comic Book*. New York: Basic Books, 2005. For my money, the best history of the comics industry out there. Turns out, the guys who created superheroes, our contemporary myths, are great at self-mythologizing, too, so instead of unquestioningly reporting their recollections, Jones digs deep and provides a clear-eyed 360-degree accounting of what had been a murky history. The picture of Siegel and Shuster that emerges is admirably nuanced and real.

Kakalios, James. *The Physics of Superheroes*. New York: Gotham Books, 2005. Engaging, exhaustive, and ultimately buzz-killing examination of the impossibility of super-feats in the real world.

Kashner, Sam, and Nancy Shoenberger. *Hollywood Kryptonite*. New York: St. Martin's Press, 1996. Not sure that I buy this book's account of George Reeves's last days, but it captures a time and a place vividly.

Knowles, Christopher. *Our Gods Wear Spandex: The Secret History of Comic Book Heroes*. San Francisco: Weiser Books, 2007. I wanted this book's very excitable prose to settle down a bit, because its attempts to explore the affinities between mysticism and the superhero were interesting, if ultimately not entirely convincing.

Levitz, Paul. *75 Years of DC Comics: The Art of Modern Mythmaking*. Los Angeles: Taschen, 2010. A giant tome (16 inches × 12 inches, weighing in at 16 pounds) that can't be called a coffee-table book because it's bigger than most coffee tables. A prized possession, a lively history, and a beautiful, beautiful book. Also, when the apocalypse comes, an impregnable shelter.

Lowther, George. *The Adventures of Superman*. Bedford, MA: Applewood Books, 1942. The most striking features in this first novelization of the Man of Steel are Shuster's simple, yet expressive, pen-and-ink illustrations of Superman that top each chapter.

Lupoff, Richard A., and Don Thompson. *All in Color for a Dime*. New York: Ace Books, 1970. A groundbreaking history of the Golden Age of comics, filled with facts about many creators and characters lost to history; one of the earliest and likely the most-cited work of serious comics history I've come across, and it's back in print.

Maggin, Elliot. *Superman: Last Son of Krypton*. New York: National Periodical Publications, 1978. I memorized this book as a kid, and it certainly helped crystallize Maggin's vision of Superman as a demigod with a grand destiny, at least in my mind.

Mamet, David. *Some Freaks*. New York: Penguin Books, 1989. Check out Mamet's characteristically cantankerous, yet surprisingly moving, appreciation of Superman in this collection.

McCulley, Johnston. *Zorro: The Curse of Capistrano*. Lombard, Illinois: Macmay, 2008. The only Zorro I knew growing up was *Zorro: The Gay Blade*, so it was fascinating to go back and read the original. A lot less Brenda Vaccaro, turns out. More's the pity.

Morrison, Grant. *Supergods*. New York: Spiegel & Grau, 2011. A fascinating, funny, and sometimes frustrating peek inside the mind of a man who wrote some of my favorite comic-book stories ever (Doom Patrol, guys, seriously), and whose vision of the Man of Steel is bracingly (and, it must be said, surprisingly) clear. You'll learn a lot more about his psychopharmaceutical history than you were terribly curious about, but it's a great read.

Nobleman, Marc Tyler. *Boys of Steel: The Creation of Superman*. New York: Alfred A. Knopf, 2008. A fantastic illustrated history of Siegel and Shuster for kids.

Petrou, David Michael. *The Making of Superman the Movie*. New York: Warner Books, 1978. For a kid in love with the 1978 movie, this behind-the-scenes look at its design, production, and special effects was and remains a seminal text.

Rossen, Jake. *Superman vs. Hollywood: How Fiendish Producers, Devious Directors, and Warring Writers Grounded an American Icon*. Chicago: Chicago Review Press, 2008. For the sections of this book that deal with the making of the movies, I relied heavily on Rossen, Scivally, and their sources, as well as on the various DVD extras. For what it's worth, Rossen's is the more involving, Scivally's the more exhaustive.

Rovin, Jeff. *The Encyclopedia of Superheroes*. New York: Facts on File Publications, 1985. Without this wonderful book and its follow-up on supervillains, both of which I picked up back when they were first published, I would have gone through life blithely unaware of the Flaming Carrot. For that alone, thanks are owed.

Schwartz, Julius, and Brian M. Thomsen. *Man of Two Worlds: My Life in Science Fiction and Comics*. New York: HarperCollins, 2000. Interesting stories of old-school funnybook-making from one of the medium's most beloved figures.

Scivally, Bruce. *Superman on Film, Television, Radio, and Broadway*. Jefferson, NC: McFarland, 2008. When I needed any fact about any of the Man of Steel's manifold iterations in noncomics media, Scivally was where I turned first. Noel Neill's birthday? The date *Superman III* appeared in movie theaters? That funny thing the third lead on *Smallville* said to that Australian newspaper? He's got it covered. As noted earlier, Scivally's, Rossen's, and Hayde's books became trusted friends during the long months of writing.

Simon, Joe, and Jim Simon. *The Comic Book Makers*. Lebanon, NJ: The Comic Book Makers, 2003. A straight-ahead history of the birth of the comics medium; I'm partial to the Jones book, but that's me.

Tye, Larry. *Superman: The High-Flying History of America's Most Enduring Hero*. New York: Random House, 2012. A deeper dive into the Man of Steel's history you'll not find, focusing on the behind-the-scenes legal battles, as much as on the character's place in popular culture. It came out the week after I turned in this manuscript; I used it as a rigorous and judgmental fact checker throughout the editing process.

Weinstein, Simcha. *Up, Up and Oy Vey! How Jewish History, Culture, and Values Shaped the Comic Book Superhero*. Baltimore: Leviathan Press, 2006. For the record, it was during the initial research phase for this book, as I clicked to order *Up Up and Oy Vey!* from Amazon, that I realized I wouldn't have much to add by spending a lot of time rehashing Superman's Jewish roots. This book does a great job of it, as does the Fingeroth, and really, there was no way anything I would come up with could beat that title.

Wolk, Douglas. *Reading Comics: How Graphic Novels Work and What They Mean*. Cambridge, MA: Da Capo Press, 2007. Scholarly, yet anything but stuffy. It's more like a treatise proclaiming that comics are a viable and even transgressive artistic medium (and thus, not terribly concerned with Superman), but Wolk's an tremendously engaging writer, and he knows his stuff.

Wright, Bradford W. *Comic Book Nation: The Transformation of Youth Culture in America*. Baltimore: Johns Hopkins University Press, 2001. Another early history of the medium, but it takes a broader sociocultural tack than Jones's *Men of Tomorrow*.

Wylie, Philip. *Gladiator*. New York: Manor Books, 1976. A purple-prosed hoot, but a beguiling one. Reading it today, you can still see how it would grab an imaginative kid by the frontal lobe and not let go.

Yeffeth, Glen. *The Man from Krypton: A Closer Look at Superman*. Dallas: Benbella Books, 2005. A series of essays in the *Superman at Fifty!* mode, including some very serious and thoughtful writing, as well as pieces that are considerably more glib.

Yoe, Craig. *Secret Identity: The Fetish Art of Superman's Co-Creator Joe Shuster*. New York: Abrams ComicsArts, 2008. Comics historian Yoe makes a pretty convincing case that a post-Superman Shuster supported himself by drawing saucy illustrations for saucy magazines.

Comics

All citations provided in the book's main text.

Magazines

Alter Ego. A seminal superhero fanzine in the sixties, revived as a professional magazine in 1999. A source for several interviews with creators.

Amazing Heroes. Superhero comics magazine published by Fantagraphics from 1981 to 1992; the July 1, 1986, issue contains a lengthy and enlightening John Byrne interview.

Amazing World of DC Comics. An odd creation. A pseudo-fanzine published by DC from 1974 to 1978.

Comics Buyer's Guide. Established in 1971, the longest running English-language periodical devoted to comics. Currently edited by Maggie Thompson, who, with her late husband, Don, helped establish comic-book fandom as it's known today. Regular CBG columnist Craig "Mr. Silver Age" Shutt helped me think through my approach to the Weisinger era.

The Comics Journal. A periodical devoted to comics criticism and analysis; it regularly featured some of the best comics writing around. Now exclusively online (see below).

Look. The February 27,1940, issue contains the two-page comic showing Superman ending the war; it is readable online and is deeply weird.

NEMO: The Classic Comics Library. Another Fantagraphics publication, this one published in the eighties and devoted to comic strips of the Golden Age. Issue 2 (August 1983) contains a great, fascinating interview with Siegel and Shuster.

Wizard. The glossiest (and fratty-est) comics magazine out there, which was published from 1991 to 2011. Champions of the "badass"/"extreeeeme" school of superheroes, but it featured some surprisingly good and/or clever writing.

Websites

The Beat, www.comicsbeat.com. Indispensable one-stop shop for breaking comics news and analysis.

Blue Tights Network, www.bluetights.net. Site for fans to follow the production of *Superman Returns*; shuttered in 2010, now exists as a Facebook page.

Bob Holiday's Website, www.supermanbobholiday.com. Lots of media and information by and about the star of the 1966 Broadway musical.

Comic Book Resources, www.comicbookresources.com. Superhero-focused comics news site, home of Brian Cronin's blog, *Comics Should Be Good* and its "Comic Book Legends Revealed" feature, which pointed me to sources that helped me find answers to several lingering questions.

ComicsAlliance, www.comicsalliance.com. A news site with a noticeably more engaged approach to issues of gender, race, and sexuality than the comics community is generally known for; many smart and funny writers.

Comics Chronicles, www.comichron.com. An incredibly useful chronicle of comic-book sales over the years.

Comics Journal, www.tcj.com. See "Magazines," above; the online home of the dearly departed print magazine devoted to a critical analysis of the comics medium and its many genres.

Comics Reporter, www.comicsreporter.com. Tom Spurgeon's excellent site of comics reviews, news, and interviews.

Confessions of a Superman Fan, www.supermanfan.nu. Clever, well-written Superman fansite by David Morefield.

Dial B for Blog, www.dialbforblog.com. Funny and informative site devoted to DC's Silver Age comics, run by a smart writer who goes by the pen name "Robby Reed."

Don Markstein's Toonopedia, www.toonopedia.com. Exhaustive compendium of cartoon and comics characters.

iFanboy, www.ifanboy.com. Superhero-focused site that features several very good writers.

iO9, www.io9.com. Science-fiction site that regularly features comics.

Jim Shooter, www.jimshooter.com. Personal blog of the venerable comics writer and editor.

Kryptonsite, www.kryptonsite.com. Website devoted to the TV series *Smallville*.

Mike's Amazing World of Comics, www.dcindexes.com. Exhaustive resource of DC history, stories, characters, covers, and so on.

Newsarama, www.newsarama.com. Comprehensive comics news site.

Sequential Tart, www.sequentialtart.com. Fantastic site that focuses on women in comics, characters, and creators.

The Speeding Bullet, www.thespeedingbullet.com. Devoted to the Superman comic strips.

Superman Is a Dick, www.superdickery.tumblr.com. Collection of absurd comic panels and covers illustrating Superman's Silver Age propensity for being a complete tool to his friends.

Superman Homepage, www.supermanhomepage.com. Easily the site I consulted most often while preparing this book; its archived interviews with contemporary writers, editors, and artists, along with its reviews and articles on major story lines and aspects of the character, were incredibly useful.

Superman Supersite, www.supermansupersite.com. Another exhaustive online Superman resource.

Superman through the Ages, www.supermanthrutheages.com. Associated with Confessions of a Superman Fan, a lively and content-rich site of Superman lore.

Comics Collections and Graphic Novels

Byrne, John. *Superman: The Earth Stealers*. New York: DC Comics, 1988.

Byrne, John. *Superman: The Man of Steel*. New York: DC Comics, 1991.

Davis, Alan. *The Nail*. New York: DC Comics, 1998.

Jurgens, Dan, et al. *Death of Superman*. New York: DC Comics, 1993.

Jurgens, Dan, et al. *Return of Superman*. New York: DC Comics, 1993.

Jurgens, Dan, et al. *World without a Superman*. New York: DC Comics, 1993.

Loeb, Jeph. *Superman for All Seasons*. New York: DC Comics, 1999.

Millar, Mark. *Superman: Red Son*. New York: DC Comics, 2003.

Moore, Alan. *Superman: Whatever Happened to the Man of Tomorrow?* New York: DC Comics, 2009.

O'Neil, Dennis. *Superman: Kryptonite Nevermore*. New York: DC Comics, 2009.

Waid, Mark. *Kingdom Come*. New York: DC Comics, 1997.

Waid, Mark. *Superman: Birthright*. New York: DC Comics, 2004.

Wolfman, Marv. *Crisis on Infinite Earths*. New York: DC Comics, 2000.

Reprints/Anthologies

DC's Greatest Imaginary Stories. New York: DC Comics, 2005.

The Great Superman Comic Book Collection: Time-Honored Classics. New York: DC Comics, 1981.

The Greatest Superman Stories Ever Told, volumes 1 and 2. New York: DC Comics, 2004, 2006.

Showcase Presents: Superman, volumes 1–4. New York: DC Comics, 2005, 2006, 2007, 2008.

Showcase Presents: Superman Family, volumes 1–3. New York: DC Comics, 2006, 2008, 2009.

Showcase Presents: World's Finest, volumes 1–3. New York: DC Comics, 2007, 2008, 2010.

Showcase Presents: Legion of Super-Heroes, volumes 1–4. New York: DC Comics, 2007, 2008, 2009, 2010.

The Superman Chronicles, volumes 1–8. New York: DC Comics, 2006, 2006, 2007, 2007, 2008, 2009, 2009, 2010.

Superman: From the Thirties to the Seventies. New York: National Periodical Publications, 1971.

Superman in the Forties. New York: DC Comics, 2005.

Superman in the Fifties. New York: DC Comics, 2002.

Superman in the Sixties. New York: DC Comics, 1999.

Superman in the Seventies. New York: DC Comics, 2000.

Superman in the Eighties. New York: DC Comics, 2006.

Superman: The Adventures of Nightwing and Flamebird. New York: DC Comics, 2009.

Superman: The Dailies, volumes 1–2. New York: DC Comics, 1999, 2006.

Superman: The Sunday Classics. New York: DC Comics, 1998.

INDEX